Management Science
text and applications

The Irwin Series in Quantitative Analysis for Business

Consulting Editor ROBERT B. FETTER *Yale University*

Management Science
text and applications

JOHN J. DINKEL
Associate Professor of Management Science
The Pennsylvania State University

GARY A. KOCHENBERGER
Professor of Management Science
The Pennsylvania State University

DONALD R. PLANE
Professor and Head
Division of Management Science
University of Colorado

1978

RICHARD D. IRWIN, INC. Homewood, Illinois 60430
Irwin-Dorsey Limited   Georgetown, Ontario L7G 4B3

ISBN 0-256-02037-X
Library of Congress Catalog Card No. 77–085807

Printed in the United States of America

1 2 3 4 5 6 7 8 9 0 K 5 4 3 2 1 0 9 8

to Mary, Ann, and Rosemary

Preface

THE PAST SEVERAL YEARS have seen an explosion of texts in the area of management science, operations research, or quantitative methods. For the most part these texts stress the fundamentals of the basic techniques associated with management science while including a chapter describing the difficulties of implementing management science results in a real world setting. While we do not make light of the problems of successful implementation, we feel that there have been successes and that these can be incorporated into an introductory text in such a way as not only to illustrate the techniques, but to point out some underlying concepts.

Management Science: Text and Applications takes a large view of management science—it is decision analysis and decision making in action. It involves creative modeling, solution generation, solution interpretation, and implementation. This text goes beyond other introductory books in that it presents and discusses real-world case studies illustrating the uses of management science techniques as well as presenting a readable contemporary discussion of the managerially useful models and algorithms. The book is suitable for either an MBA or an undergraduate survey course in management science, operations research, decision science, or whatever title is used at a given school. We see no useful distinction among the terms and consider them interchangeable.

The text assumes the reader is familiar with mathematics up to basic algebra. No calculus is required. Appendixes presenting the basic notions of probability theory and matrix algebra mechanics are included for students needing these topics.

Management Science: Text and Applications is divided into two major parts. Part I is a survey of management science techniques—the important models, algorithms, and decision-making approaches. Although Part I is concerned with techniques, the emphasis is on model building and decision-making uses of the techniques. This emphasis on model formulation is particularly important because it is the function of modeling to bridge the gap between the decision maker's problem and the management science techniques. While we are not so naive as to believe we can teach general model formulation, we do provide expanded coverage by providing discussions of model construction with each topic, by providing a complete chapter on formulation of linear programming models, and by extensive model descriptions with the applications. Furthermore, there is an extensive list of current references relating to the application of each of the topics.

Part II of the book further illustrates the managerial use of the material of Part I by presenting and discussing a variety of real-world case studies. These cases include fire station location, ammonia production, police patrol car scheduling, a new product decision, staff-level planning, and forecasting future service levels in fire department dispatching. The techniques used in the cases include common sense, linear programming, simulation, waiting line theory, integer programming, Markov analysis, goal programming, and decision analysis. This merger of text and application provides a way for the instructor to blend real applications into a course. A more complete description of each application, including the point in the text at which the students have sufficient background to understand that application, is included with the introductory material for Part II of the book.

Taken together, Parts I and II project management science as a useful, dynamic aid to decision making rather than a static collection of techniques. It is our hope that this view of management science will motivate readers to creatively apply a management science approach to problems encountered in the real world.

With each chapter the reader will find a contemporary set of references. These are included to lead the reader to important sources for further study as well as additional illustrative applications.

Although this is a new text, a few sections have been adapted from *Operations Research For Managerial Decisions*, by D. R. Plane and G. A. Kochenberger (Richard D. Irwin, 1972). Many people have contributed to this text; we are particularly grateful to the many students and colleagues whose comments have influenced our thinking. We are particularly grateful for the comments of Norman Chervaney, University of Minnesota, and Edward F. Stafford, Jr., University of Oklahoma. For any errors of omission or commission which remain, each of us has two coauthors to blame.

January 1978

JOHN J. DINKEL
GARY A. KOCHENBERGER
DONALD R. PLANE

Contents

PART I
Text

1

Introduction to Management Science

1.1. INTRODUCTORY COMMENTS

THE COLLECTION OF TECHNIQUES covered in this text forms part of what
is known as the discipline of Operations Research, Management Science,
or Decision Science. For the remainder of the text these terms will be
used interchangeably. They all imply the same context: analytical techniques that *aid* in the decision making process. From its very inception
in military operations to present-day industrial, service, government, and
social applications, the common thread throughout the development of
operations research has been its relevance to decision making. When
looking at the various components of Operations Research, however,
one is sure to see that each of these components has become a mini-
discipline of its own. As a result Operations Research/Management
Science/Decision Science is often viewed as a rather loosely connected
collection of theoretical techniques.

While it is certainly true that each of the techniques has developed
its own identity in terms of a body of theory and applications, their
common use is that of an aid to decision making. The aim of our text
is to uncover the underlying thread of an aid to decision making. While
this is our ultimate goal, it is necessary that the techniques be presented
individually so that the underlying principles of each can be understood. While there have been numerous successful applications of these
techniques, almost every application presents some aspects not apparent
in other applications. The decision maker who is well founded in the
basic concepts of the techniques is better able to propose, apply, and

modify the techniques to fit the problem that he faces. One must not change the problem to fit the techniques; rather, one must modify the technique to fit the problem.

Seeing some real applications of these techniques can greatly benefit the reader; therefore, we have included numerous examples. The examples take three forms: example problems and their extensions presented in the text; an extensive set of references at the end of each chapter listing readily accessible applications; and finally, a chapter that uses some cases of real applications as a teaching exercise.

1.2. MODELS AND OPERATIONS RESEARCH

The concept that is used to tie together the complex decision making environment and the OR (operations research) techniques is that of a *model. A model is some representation of a real-world phenomenon in a structure simpler than the original structure of the phenomenon.* Models are in general of two types: *physical* and *conceptual.* The idea of a physical model is well known to all of us—model airplanes, ships, and cars represent scaled-down versions of the "real thing." Physical models are often used to test the design of a component of a complex system without involving or endangering the entire system—for example, wind-tunnel tests of models of airplane wings or rockets. It is clear that if the results of testing and experimenting with physical models are to be of practical significance they must accurately represent the full-size end product.

Our concern here will be with conceptual models—abstract representations of decision making processes. We have been exposed to and have utilized this kind of models in our everyday experiences, too; for instance, the use of road maps in planning a trip.

These conceptual models are abstractions of the actual decision making situations and represent a formalized means of evaluating alternative courses of action. One of the major characteristics of modern decision making processes is the need to *evaluate a large number of alternative actions.* Another characteristic of decision making problems is their *complexity.* The environment within which the decisions are to be made or the process about which one is trying to decide may be extremely complex; a conceptual model may afford the means of capturing the essence of such a situation. If our point of view or model is too restrictive, however, the original decision making process may be completely or partially misrepresented. On the other hand, if a conceptual model is to be workable, it must not be of such complexity that we cannot deal with its computational or data requirements.

Thus we can state some—perhaps conflicting—goals of a model:

1. *The model should reflect reality.* Realizing the real decision making framework is extremely complex and not exactly representable in conceptual terms; our model must nevertheless reflect to the extent possible the real world. There are always some trade-offs to be made with this goal. In general, as the model approaches reality its complexity becomes too great for our next goal. Thus the model builder is often faced with trying to capture the essence of the model within reasonable limits.
2. *The model must be solvable in terms of existing solution and/or analysis techniques.* It does not do us any good to construct a representation so complex as to defy analysis and solution. As will be discussed later in this chapter and later in the text, the idea of solvability can mean different things. In some cases, it is interpreted as the ability to change certain inputs to the model and to be able to observe the effect of such changes on the outputs of the model. In other cases, one may want to find the optimal (best) set of inputs.
3. *The data needs of the model must be realistic.* The model must present realistic data requirements and not require either impossible amounts of data or uncollectable data. In one recently reported incident, the cost of data collection for a model of the Canadian economy would itself have had an appreciable effect on the gross national product of the country.[1] At any rate, this is a consideration that is often overlooked when constructing a model. To a large extent, a model is only as good as the data used to construct it, and if the necessary data cannot be generated the model cannot be put to use.

Thus, models represent abstractions or distillations of real-world decision making processes that we can get our hands on. Yet they represent all or most of the essential parts of the real-world process.

1.3. THE IMPORTANCE OF QUANTITATIVE TECHNIQUES

As can be seen from the references at the end of each chapter, each of the methods covered here represents a mini-discipline of its own. In view of the body of knowledge surrounding each technique, it is clear that one is not going to become an expert in any of the fields as a result of this course.

The study of these methods, however, does have some important benefits. By learning the fundamental principles of these various methods we can:

---

[1] R. E. D. Woolsey, "A Novena to St. Jude, or Four Edifying Case Studies in Mathematical Programming," *Interfaces*, vol. 4, no. 1, November 1973.

1. Better understand the limitations of each of the methods, so that they are not misused. For example—What are the implications of treating a model with integer-valued variables by ordinary linear programming?
2. Better understand and interpret the solution to the model. For example—In a waiting-line model what is the trade-off between increased service (reduced waiting time) and the cost to the system of providing such service?
3. Develop a basis for diagnosing the trouble if a technique yields no solution or a suspicious solution. For example—Is the transition matrix in a Markov process really stationary?
4. Better understand how to adapt existing models and applications to similar settings.

While all of the above benefits are important, they can be obtained only by acquiring an understanding of the underlying principles of the methods. This is particularly true with (4). As will be seen, the development of models and applications in a new setting can be extremely complex and time consuming. It is often to one's advantage to make use of any developments that have arisen in solving problems of a similar nature. Of course, for such transfers to be successful, an understanding of the effect of the assumptions is mandatory.

Finally, the advent of the new generation of computers is greatly facilitating the use of quantitative methods. The mini and micro computers provide tremendous computational capability that is certain to increase as the technology moves forward. Also the increased speed and capacity of the larger computers make possible rapid solution of problems that a few years ago were unsolvable. In order to increase the effectiveness of decision making processes, one needs to call upon this increased and increasing capability.

1.4. SUCCESSFUL APPLICATIONS

The purpose of this chapter is to motivate and excite the student about the potential for Operations Research/Management Science/Decision Science in the real-world decision making environment. One of the best motivators is a brief look at some successful applications of Operations Research to problems in business and the public sector. As will be seen in this section and in subsequent chapters, the original applications of Operations Research lay within the military and private business. Recent applications, however, have included public areas such as state and local government, health care, and conservation of resources. These new areas, along with some new applications in business, foreshadow some exciting future possibilities for Operations Research.

It is not practical for us to give complete details of the applications that follow. These examples are for expository purposes only and are not meant to be complete. Additional details are found in the references. Additional sources of applications are the journals *Operations Research, Management Science, Interfaces, Operational Research Quarterly, Omega, Decision Science, Computers and Operations Research,* and others. The reader is urged to scan these publications for applications of interest.

Linear Programming Analysis of Strip-mined Land

A recent paper describes the application of linear programming to an area of current importance—the reclamation of strip-mined land.[2] In many regions, state, local, or federal funds are available for rehabilitation of land currently being strip-mined, but large areas of previously strip-mined land lie unreclaimed for lack of funds. The purpose of the application described in the reference was to demonstrate to local and state agencies and local residents—by providing initial funding, fostering favorable legislation, and arousing interest—the economic benefits of reclaiming strip-mined land.

A linear programming model was constructed to evaluate several alternative uses of the land and to answer "What if. . . ." questions. The model indicated that cattle grazing would be the most productive use of the land. The model was then used to demonstrate the value of investment in the reclamation project.

As a result of this study the author was able to demonstrate that it would be economically feasible to reclaim 50,000 acres of strip-mined land in southeastern Kansas by utilizing the land for cattle grazing. The author constructed a linear programming model and an interactive computer program for evaluating the effect of reclaiming the land. Furthermore the author was able to persuade several landowners (who committed 1,000 acres) and the state government (which contributed $85,000) to share the cost of several demonstration projects to verify the results of the analysis. As a result of these demonstration projects a total of 5,000 acres has been reclaimed; the result has been an annual contribution of $1 million to the economy of the area.

Multiple Criteria in Decision Making

One of the major assumptions of many models is that there is a single objective (such as profit). This narrow choice of objective has caused difficulties in applications within large, complex organizations. Recent

---

[2] D. L. Been, "An Application of MS/OR in Strip Mined Land Reclamation," *Interfaces,* vol. 6, no. 1, pt. 2, November 1975, pp. 43–53.

developments, termed goal programming or multi-criteria optimization, have allowed for the inclusion of several, perhaps conflicting or incommensurable objectives. An illustrative application has to do with the allocation of resources in an academic department within a major university.[3]

The authors developed an interactive method for evaluating the trade-offs involved in allocating resources within the Graduate School of Management at UCLA. The faculty effort to be allocated must cover the three major activities of an academic department—teaching, service, and research. The *criteria* that were used to evaluate the allocation were: (1) number of graduate courses; (2) number of upper-division undergraduate courses; (3) number of lower-level undergraduate courses; (4) amount of effort devoted to service duties; and (5) amount of effort devoted to other activities including research, counselling, and so on. Given a fixed amount of resources (faculty effort), one can see that the above criteria are conflicting: one can be met only at the expense of another. Therefore, some trade-offs had to be evaluated.

As a result of the implementation of this model at the Graduate School of Management at UCLA, a shift in the allocation of resources was made away from teaching (criteria 1, 2, and 3) toward departmental duties (criterion 4). This shift reflected the need for such effort to start up a new graduate program. Also, the model has been used to study the effects of proposed course changes and program changes. In each case one is able to assess the trade-offs among criteria.

Integer Programming and Forest Management

A management problem of recurring interest deals with the management of forest resources including the construction of access roads.[4] In order to manage (harvest, plant, etc.) forest it is necessary to have access to stands of trees and to be able to transport the cut trees to processing centers. In addition, scientific forest management dictates planning over several growing cycles or "rotations"; thus the time frame, in general, encompasses decades. This research applies integer programming to the management decisions concerned with forest management and access road building.

The general problem can be suggested by Figure 1–1. The area of Figure 1–1 has been divided into various timber stands. These stands may represent different ages or species that will be harvested at the same

---

[3] A. M. Geoffrion, J. S. Dyer, and A. Feinberg, "An Interactive Approach for Multi-Criterion Optimization, with Application to the Operation of an Academic Department," *Management Science,* vol. 19, no. 4, December 1972, pp. 357–68.

[4] A. Weintraub and D. Navon, "A Forest Management Planning Model Integrating Silviculture and Transportation Activities," *Management Science,* vol. 22, no. 12, 1976, pp. 1299–1309.

time. The objective of the model is to minimize hauling cost and road costs (construction and maintenance) by choosing the best locations for the processing centers and the access roads. Also, since the time horizon may involve 60 to 200 years, one needs to take into account discounted net revenues for approximately 30 to 40 years.

The authors, using data from the western slope of the Sierra Nevada in California, carried out their analysis on several 10-year management plans. The trials resulted in 6 percent savings in road costs and 1 percent increase in revenue from timber management. The model also provides a tool for analyzing the effect of various strategies of road construction and timber management.

FIGURE 1–1

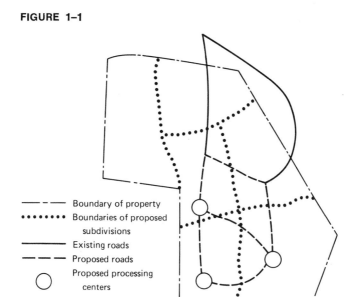

```
— — —   Boundary of property
• • • • • •   Boundaries of proposed
              subdivisions
————————   Existing roads
— — — —   Proposed roads
  ◯        Proposed processing
            centers
```

Waiting-Line Analysis of Service Time Responses

One of the major applications of waiting-line or queuing models deals with the analysis of systems in which customers call for service and then await the arrival of the service representative to repair a nonfunctioning piece of equipment. The author applied such analysis to the service strategies of Xerox Corporation for a new item of equipment—the 9200 duplicator.[5] Since the duplicator is a revenue-generating piece of equipment, delays in service not only are an inconvenience but cause a loss of revenues as well. In addition to the usual technological considerations,

---

[5] W. H. Blewel, "Management Science's Impact on Service Strategy," *Interfaces*, vol. 6, no. 1, 1975, pp. 4–12.

the author wanted to take into account certain behavioral constraints, in particular: personalized service—the service representative covers the same territory over a long term—and job satisfaction—each service representative views a territory as his own.

Within these constraints it was decided to evaluate several service strategies on the basis of the size of the service territory and the number of service representatives assigned to that territory. A waiting-line model was constructed to reflect the service strategies under various numbers of services and numbers of machines to be served. The service strategies consisted of assigning mini-teams to the service areas. As a result of the waiting-line analysis, based on response time, waiting-line length, and productivity, it was decided to deploy three-person teams. The analysis enabled Xerox to inform customers of the response time when they called for service and resulted in a 46 percent saving in total service costs.

Simulation of Scheduling of Surgical Patients

One exciting application of OR/MS techniques involves health care and its delivery. In this paper, the authors discuss the use of GPSS (General Purpose Simulation System, a computer program) as a means of evaluating the scheduling of surgical patients.[6] Because it is impractical to try out scheduling ideas on real patients, the simulation model was used to gain valuable insights into various strategies.

The subject of the study was the operating and recovery facilities of a hospital in St. Louis. Within the hospital there are five surgical suites and 12 recovery facilities that must be allocated to major and minor surgeries each day. Since the major surgeries tend to require extensive periods of time in both the operating room and recovery facilities, it is necessary to schedule uses of the facilities carefully. The purpose of the authors was to examine several strategies for scheduling patients into surgery consistent with the hospital's administrative guidelines. Strategies such as scheduling uses in the order they are requested; giving major surgeries priority over minor, serving those requiring longest surgery first, and so on, were evaluated using the simulation model. The hospital guidelines dictated that any strategy must be simple to avoid confusion and jockeying of patients at the last minute.

In the course of the simulation trials, the authors evaluated the various possible scheduling rules. The hospital administration was then able to compare the current scheduling policy with the alternative policies. In addition, as the demand on the surgical facilities increases the administration has a tool that can be used to alleviate some of the pressures. The

_____
    [6] N. K. Kwak, P. J. Kuzdrall, and H. H. Schmitz, "The GPSS Simulation of Scheduling Policies for Surgical Patients," *Management Science*, vol. 22, no. 9, pp. 982–89.

results of analyzing the simulation model did present a short-run solution to the problem of scheduling a certain class of surgical patients.

Manpower Management and Markov Chains

Operations research techniques have been effectively applied to the management of manpower. In particular, such techniques have been used to study (and predict) hiring and training requirements, the advancement of personnel through the organization, and turnover as a function of various organizational factors. In this example, the authors examined a technical department within a large corporation that exhibited a high turnover rate and faced a competitive job market.[7]

FIGURE 1–2

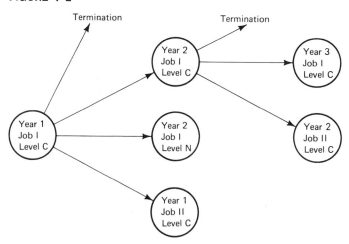

The purpose of the study was to model the hiring and promotion processes and provide a flow of relevant information for decision making regarding manpower management policies. As a result of their studies, the authors identified three job categories (I, II, III), two levels of employee competence (C, N), and a four-year time frame (1, 2, 3, 4) for movement among positions. A model of transitions among these states, including a termination state, was developed and tested against past company data. The transition diagram in part is given in Figure 1–2. The diagram depicts movement within grade with no promotion (1, I, C) to (2, I, C), movements with promotion (1, I, C) to (1, II, C), and so on, including termination initiated by either the company or the employee.

[7] G. L. Lilien and A. G. Rao, "A Model for Manpower Management," *Management Science*, vol. 21, no. 12, 1975, pp. 1447–57.

As a result of these studies, it was possible to evaluate the turnover rate in terms of the job market and the effect on the company. In addition, it was possible to test several management strategies against past data to observe the effect on the turnover rate as well as evaluate the effect on the company. That is, it is possible to assess the effect of changes in the promotion rates among job types, and to evaluate the effect of hiring at different levels.

Other cases presented in Part II show in detail the application of Operations Research/Management Science/Decision Science to such diverse topics as fire station location, a CPA firm, police patrol-car scheduling, an ammonia plant and its pollution, a state unemployment agency, and a chemical product/process decision.

1.5. OPTIMIZATION, SUBOPTIMIZATION, AND SIMULATION

As the examples of the previous section indicated, there are two methods of obtaining "solutions" to the model. The solution of models based on certain analytical results that can be used to characterize solutions in general are referred to as *optimization methods.* These methods, given a set of input data, generate the *optimal* (best) solution to the particular model. There are many well known optimization methods—the simplex method of linear programming, the general results of waiting-line models, and so on. Within these methods there are those that guarantee the optimal solution for any such model—linear programming—and some that provide optimal solutions for restrictive classes—some integer program and waiting-line models—but for the general model no optimal characterization can be given. For this latter class of models, we must rely on the computational power of modern computers to provide evaluation via *simulation methods.* In general, as the complexity of a model increases, we must rely more heavily on simulation methods for obtaining numerical results. Simulation methods essentially perform experiments on the model by changing various parameters or variables and observing how the model responds to these changes. While the results are, in general, descriptive and not optimal, they do provide a means of analyzing very complex situations.

Another distinction to be drawn with regard to optimization is the area known as *suboptimization.* Suboptimization will mean two things: in certain cases, it will mean a feasible solution that is not optimal; in other cases, it will mean the optimization of a portion of a larger system, or the optimization of a subsystem.

The first definition of suboptimization—a feasible but less than optimal solution—often applies to integer and multiple criteria programming. In these problems and some of their variants, the determination of *the optimal* solution can be extremely costly; instead, a good feasible solution will often suffice. While such a solution is not optimal, it may often provide valuable insights and/or savings when applied to the process being modeled.

The second definition of suboptimization—the optimization of a subsystem—is appropriate whenever we are dealing with large complex organizations. Typically in such situations, one cannot deal with the entire organization. Thus, while we may be optimizing the operation of one department, that optimum may be suboptimal with regard to the overall operation. Since the obvious resolution of this problem—modeling the entire organization—may not be feasible, one must be content with models of various subsystems. This question is difficult to resolve in general and awaits further research. One can argue that if the model and its results provide a better operating scheme within a subsystem, even though the scheme may be suboptimal with regard to the larger system, the entire system benefits.

1.6. IMPLEMENTATION AND LIMITATIONS OF OR

Section 4 of this chapter attempted to illustrate some of the successful implementations of Operations Research/Management Science techniques. These point to some past and future applications and areas of interest. In the literature of the area there has been some concern about the implementation of these techniques.

Two professional societies, The Operations Research Society of America (ORSA) and The Institute of Management Sciences (TIMS) have devoted a publication, *Interfaces*, to highlighting successful implementations of the techniques of Operations Research/Management Science. In addition, each year a group within The Institute of Management Sciences sponsors a competition for the best implementation of Operations Research/Management Science in either the public or private sector. As a result of these efforts more and more successful implementations are being brought to the attention of the profession.

It has been said that the theory of Operations Research/Management Science has greatly outdistanced its implementation, and that the discipline is only now beginning to catch up. There have been a number of reasons for the lack of publication and acceptance of the results of Operations Research/Management Science; among the most important are:

1. Successful implementations within a company are often maintained as confidential to avoid giving any information to competitors. As a result many publications contain only the theoretical development and give no hint as to the potential applicability. Even if there are no major problems of proprietary information in successful private-sector applications of management science, there is a real cost in-

volved in disseminating information. This cost arises from the time and effort required to prepare the results of a project in a form suitable for journal publication, and from the expense involved in disseminating results at professional meetings. For the most part, there have been no incentives for private practitioners to publish their results.

2. Firms are resistant to change. A firm has a policy or strategy that has worked in the past; so why change now? This is a particularly common attitude when the results have derogatory implications with regard to the organizational policies.

3. The model and/or its results are based on highly mathematical analyses that are not clearly explained to the user of the results. Conversely, the model may be a gross oversimplification of the real process, and the results of the model are useless with regard to the actual decision making process.

4. Additional reasons that have been pointed out include:

> The problem "solved" is not the problem facing the organization.
>
> The solution is reached after a decision has been made.
>
> The resources expended in reaching the solution are greater than the savings achieved from implementing the solution.
>
> The data used in the solution are wrong.
>
> The model builder and the manager have different goals.[8]

These statements are true for obvious reasons. From the standpoint of the practitioner of operations research or management science or the decision sciences, what steps can be taken to assist in solving the right problem with a methodology that is correct, trusted, and understood? In other words, how can the profession enhance the chances that the results of a study will be implemented?

The foremost principle of successful operations research is the *involvement of the management of the organization*. This involvement is important for all the reasons mentioned above. Further, it keeps the project focused on real problems facing the organization. Since it is the management of the organization that is responsible for addressing these problems, their involvement keeps a decision science effort focused on the right problem. Still further, this involvement helps bring understanding of the methodology to the managers. Their involvement serves to a large extent as a educational exchange for those managers who may not be familiar with decision science techniques and those analysts who are

---

[8] C. J. Grayson, Jr., "Management Science and Business Practice," *Harvard Business Review*, vol. 51, July–August 1973, pp. 41–48; A. C. Shapiro, "Incentive Systems and The Implementation of Management Science," *Interfaces*, vol. 7, no. 1, part 1, November 1976, pp. 14–17.

not familiar with the problem. Finally, the manager of an organization often has much more interest in pursuing the implementation of an analysis that represents a substantial investment of management's time and efforts. Perhaps this principle of management involvement explains what some see as a trend in which practitioners of the decision sciences function in small groups, each focusing on a part of an organization and its immediate management, rather than a large group serving as a consultant to all parts of the organization.

The aim of this book is to bridge the gap between technique and implementation. Our basic premise is that in order to succeed in, or to understand, the implementation of a technique one must first understand the basic ideas of the technique itself. On the other hand, we do not want to ignore the setting in which the technique is to be applied. As you proceed through the book you will notice many references to applications of the topics of each chapter. These references offer valuable amplification of the text material being covered.

In an attempt to draw together the quantitative techniques of the text and actual decision making processes, the second part of the book presents several detailed cases. These cases represent successful implementations of Operations Research/Management Science and should further elucidate the interaction of technique and implementation.

2

Decision Theory

2.1. INTRODUCTORY COMMENTS

DECISION MAKING must be performed in every organization. The decision is often the answer to a question. For example:

How many hours of overtime should the factory work today?

Which employee should be promoted to supervisor?

How many television commercials should be purchased for next month?

Should a hospital X-ray unit be replaced or rebuilt?

How many school buses should be purchased?

Should this new product be introduced next month?

In each of these situations two or more *courses of action*, or *acts*, are possible. A decision is made when one of these acts is selected.

2.2. ELEMENTS OF A DECISION PROBLEM

The elements of a decision problem are:

1. The *acts* or *courses of action*. The decision maker chooses one of these acts in making a decision.
2. The *events*, or things that happen. The decision maker has no control over the events.
3. The *probabilities of occurrence for each event*. These are often referred to as prior probabilities; their assessment will be discussed in Section 2.12.

4. The *payoffs of each outcome,* an outcome being a combination of one act and one event. These payoff values are often called conditional values because they are conditional upon the selection of a given act and the occurrence of a given event.

2.3. CLASSIFICATION OF DECISION PROBLEMS: CERTAINTY

In order to supply additional structure, we classify a decision problem as to whether it is made under certainty or uncertainty.

The first type of decision problem is decision making under certainty. If a decision is made under certainty, the decision maker knows what the result will be for each course of action that could be selected. At first glance decisions under certainty might appear to be trivial, since the outcome is known for any act that might be selected. Decisions under certainty are not trivial, though, because there are often so many possible courses of action that it is impossible to consider each of them individually, determine the result for each course of action, and choose the act that gives the best result. Many of the topics of operations research are specifically designed to deal with decision making under certainty. The approach in these decision problems under certainty is often to construct and manipulate a model to select the best course of action from all courses of action available to the decision maker.

2.4. UNCERTAINTY

A decision is made under uncertainty if the decision maker does not know which event will occur, and therefore does not know the outcome for each course of action. It is useful to divide uncertainty into three further categories. In the first of these categories, the decision maker has prior knowledge about the relative likelihoods or probabilities of the outcomes for each act that could be selected. The second type of decision under uncertainty occurs when the decision maker does not know these probabilities. In a later section discussing probability, it will be argued that decisions under uncertainty with known probabilities are quite prevalent in managerial decision making, while decisions under uncertainty with unknown probabilities can be recast with some estimate of the prior probabilities. The remaining decisions under uncertainty, those involving a thinking competitor, have been attacked by *game theory.* This topic is not pursued in this text; some of the references at the end of the chapter provide discussions of game theory and some application. The remainder of the discussion of decision problems under uncertainty assumes that the probabilities are known. Probability, its meaning, and its assessment are discussed in Sections 2.10 through 2.12.

2.5. AN EXAMPLE: DECISIONS UNDER UNCERTAINTY

All of the elements of a decision problem under uncertainty can easily be arrayed in a *conditional profit table*. This table takes the form of a matrix, with each column representing the payoffs (conditional profits) for one act. Each row represents the conditional profits for an event. A conditional profit table will be constructed for the following decision problem under uncertainty, faced by J. D., the owner of a successful manufacturing firm.

J. D. has just signed a contract to deliver merchandise to be sold for $400,000. J. D.'s accountant had reported to J. D. that the administrative and supervisory costs for this contract will be $140,000. Materials will cost $60,000. The other two costs that J. D. will encounter are the cost of a special-purpose machine that is useful only for this order, and the labor costs of manufacturing the merchandise. Two weeks ago J. D. and the employees' union had agreed to submit to binding arbitration the sticky question of the employee skill level for operating the machine to be used in manufacturing the merchandise for this order. If the company wins the arbitration, the cost of labor will be $8 per hour. If the union wins the arbitration, labor costs will be $12 per hour. J. D. needs to order one of two machines within the week, although it will be several weeks before the arbitrator will reach a decision.

The two machines and their characteristics are: Machine A costs $140,000, and will require 4,000 labor hours to manufacture the merchandise. Machine B costs $100,000 and will require 8,000 labor hours.

The prior probabilities for the arbitration awards have been set by J. D. at 0.7 for $8 award and 0.3 for the $12 award.

In order to set up a conditional profit table for this decision problem, *the analyst needs to make an explicit statement of the acts, the events, and the conditional profit.*

FIGURE 2–1

Conditional Profit Table for J. D.'s Decision

Events	Acts		Probabilities
	Purchase Machine A	*Purchase Machine B*	
$8 Award	$28,000	$36,000	0.7
$12 Award	$12,000	$ 4,000	0.3
EMV	$23,200	$26,400	

The *acts* are under the control of J. D., who must decide which machine to purchase.

The *events* are the things that cannot be controlled by J. D. The events are an $8 award from the arbitrator, or a $12 award from the arbitrator.

These two elements of the decision problem under uncertainty form the skeleton of the conditional profit table, shown in Figure 2–1. The four cells in this conditional profit table show the *conditional profits* for the possible outcomes, which are calculated as revenue − administrative costs − material costs − machine costs − labor costs.

$8 Award, Machine A:

$400,000 − $140,000 − $60,000 − $140,000 − 4,000 at $8 = $28,000.

$8 Award, Machine B:

$400,000 − $140,000 − $60,000 − $100,000 − 8,000 at $8 = $36,000.

$12 Award, Machine A:

$400,000 − $140,000 − $60,000 − $140,000 − 4,000 at $12 = $12,000.

$12 Award, Machine B:

$400,000 − $140,000 − $60,000 − $100,000 − 8,000 at $12 = $4,000.

2.6. EXPECTED VALUE AS A DECISION CRITERION UNDER UNCERTAINTY

Consider J. D.'s decision problem under uncertainty, for which the consequences of purchasing Machine A are receiving $28,000 with a probability of 0.7 and $12,000 with a probability of 0.3. *Expected Monetary Value* (EMV) can be used to replace this set of four numbers (two probabilities and two dollar values) with one number. The purpose of this replacement is to give one number, which J. D. may use to describe the end result of a particular course of action. For the set of consequences for Machine A, the expected value is defined to be:

EMV = ($28,000 × 0.7) + ($12,000 × 0.3) = $19,600 + $3600
$$= \$23,200;$$

for Machine B:

EMV = ($36,000 × 0.7) + ($4000 × 0.3) = $25,200 + $1200
$$= \$26,400.$$

Under the assumption that J. D. is willing to use EMV as the decision criterion under uncertainty, the analyst would recommend that Machine B be purchased by J. D., since it has the higher expected monetary value. When a conditional profit table is shown, the expected monetary value of a course of action may also be called an expected profit.

In some situations it is useful to construct a table showing the costs that will be experienced for each outcome. In this case, the *expected cost* is calculated, and the act with the lowest expected cost is selected.

In general, the expected monetary value of a set of dollar outcomes under uncertainty is found by multiplying each outcome by its probability, and adding the products. Symbolically, for a given act *j*,

$$EMV_j = \sum_i O_{ij}P_i,$$

where O_{ij} represents the dollar outcome for event *i* and act *j*, and P_i represents the probability of event *i*.

Just what is this quantity called EMV? If the decision problem is one that is repeated many times, EMV is exactly the same thing as the long-run average payoff in choosing a course of action. It is the same thing as an arithmetic mean; it is the average payoff from choosing a particular course of action when the decision problem is repeated a large number of times. As an example of the equivalence of EMV and a long-run average, assume (unrealistically) that J. D.'s decision would be repeated 100 times. If Machine A is purchased, we would expect $28,000 profit about 70 times, and $12,000 profit about 30 times, for a total profit of about

$$(\$28,000 \times 70) + (\$12,000 \times 30) = \$2,320,000,$$

which is an average profit of $23,200 for each of the 100 replications. This figure is, of course, the same as the EMV for the choice of Machine A.

If the decision problem is such that it will be repeated a large number of times regardless of the outcome of each particular repetition of the decision problem, most people would be willing to choose the act with the highest EMV. By assumption, the long-run result is going to occur in this particular situation; there is no reason not to choose the course of action that will give the best average in the long run. The difficulty with expected monetary value occurs when the long-run result might not happen because the decision problem might not be repeated a large number of times. Also in certain settings the expected value criterion does not adequately reflect the attitude of the decision maker toward the risk involved in the decision. These situations are discussed in Section 2.14, Risk Preference Analysis.

When dealing with a decision problem under uncertainty that is not repeated, an important factor in determining whether or not one is willing to use EMV as a decision criterion is the economic consequence of extreme payoffs in the decision problem. In a business setting, the consequence of a very large loss might be bankruptcy, which would preclude the occurrence of the long-run result. In this case, EMV should not be used. But if the payoffs are relatively small compared with the financial position of the organization under consideration, it is quite reasonable to accept EMV as a legitimate decision criterion even for a one-time decision. One particular "small" decision, whether it is repeated or not, does not affect the viability of the organization. Even though a particular decision is not being repeated, many other decisions will be made over time and in other parts of the organization, so that the averaging process can work. To summarize, expected monetary value appears to be a legitimate decision criterion when the problem is a relatively small one; that is, when the outcomes of any particular decision do not affect the ability of the organization to obtain the long-run averaging over many decisions.

2.7. INDIFFERENCE PROBABILITY

In J. D.'s decision, it was assumed that the probabilities for the arbitrator's award were known. For a simple problem with only two acts available to the decision maker, it may not always be necessary to assess specific probabilities for the events. We can avoid this probability assessment by finding the *indifference probabilities*, or the set of probabilities for the two events that would make J. D. indifferent between the purchase of Machine A and the purchase of Machine B.

The symbol p will be used to denote the probability of an $8 award, so that $(1 - p)$ will be the probability of the $12 award. The expected profit from the purchase of Machine A is:

$$\text{EMV(purchase Machine A)} = (28{,}000 \times p) + [12{,}000 \times (1 - p)]$$
$$= [(28{,}000 - 12{,}000) \times p] + 12{,}000$$
$$= 16{,}000p + 12{,}000,$$

and for Machine B is:

$$\text{EMV(purchase Machine B)} = (36{,}000 \times p) + [4{,}000 \times (1 - p)]$$
$$= 32{,}000p + 4{,}000.$$

If Machine A is preferred to Machine B, it must be true that:

$$\text{EMV(purchase Machine A)} > \text{EMV(purchase Machine B)}$$

or

$$16{,}000p + 12{,}000 > 32{,}000p + 4{,}000$$
$$8{,}000 > 16{,}000p$$
$$\tfrac{1}{2} > p.$$

If Machine B is preferred to Machine A, it must be true that:

$$\text{EMV(purchase Machine B)} > \text{EMV(purchase Machine A)}$$
$$32{,}000p + 4{,}000 > 16{,}000p + 12{,}000$$
$$16{,}000p > 8{,}000$$
$$p > \tfrac{1}{2}$$

If J. D. is indifferent between the two, the two expected value expressions must be equal to each other. Using the symbol $\hat{p}$ to denote the indifference probability,

$$\text{EMV(purchase Machine A)} = \text{EMV(purchase Machine B)}$$
$$16{,}000\hat{p} + 12{,}000 = 32{,}000\hat{p} + 4{,}000$$
$$16{,}000\hat{p} = 8{,}000$$
$$\hat{p} = \tfrac{1}{2}.$$

This indicates that if the probability of an $8 award is 0.5, then J. D. does not care which machine is purchased. From the expressions for the expected profit for Machines A and B, it is apparent that when p exceeds 0.5 the purchase of Machine B has a higher EMV. Hence, the analyst could have avoided the probability assessment procedure by asking J. D. one question: "Which is more likely, an $8 award or a $12 award?" If the $8 award is more likely, Machine B should be purchased; if the $12 award is more likely, Machine A should be purchased.

2.8.   DECISION TREES

The decision table or conditional profit table is a very useful model for representing some decision problems under uncertainty. Although from a technical standpoint any decision problem under uncertainty can be represented in a table, a decision table is primarily useful for a *single-stage* decision. In a single-stage decision, an act is selected and then the event occurs. In a multistage decision, there will be a succession of acts and events. To illustrate decision trees, the single-stage decision problem involving J. D.'s decision and the uncertain arbitration award will be modeled with a decision tree.

The decision tree corresponding to J. D.'s decision is shown in Figure 2–2. This tree shows the same information that was shown in Figure 2–1. The tree is constructed with squares and circles for nodes, and branches connecting the nodes. A square node is used to indicate a decision point, where an act must be selected. A circle node is used where an event occurs. In a decision tree, the time sequence of acts and events moves from left to right. As J. D. views the decision problem, an act (purchase Machine A or purchase Machine B) must first be selected at the left-most node, which is a square. If J. D. chooses to purchase Machine A, then an event occurs (an $8 award or a $12 award). The upper branch, $8 award, will be followed with a probability of 0.7 while the lower branch, $12, will be followed with a probability of 0.3. At the end of each of these branches the conditional profit, $28,000 or $12,000, is shown. Similarly, if J. D. elects to purchase Machine B, the end-point conditional profits of $36,000 and $4,000 may be reached.

Once the decision tree has been constructed, showing the sequence of

FIGURE 2–2

Decision Tree for J. D.'s Decision

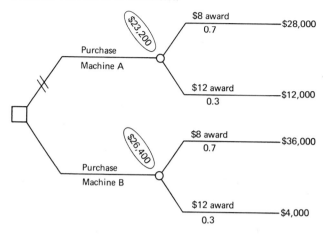

acts and events from left to right, the tree may be analyzed by *starting from the right and working to the left.* This analysis is often refered to as *pruning the tree* or *backward induction.* The reason for this backwards analysis is that when J. D. is viewing the problem from the initial act node, the consequences at the following event nodes have not yet been evaluated. Hence, before J. D. can decide which act to pursue, the right-most nodes must first be reduced. This reduction takes place by calculating the expected monetary value at each right-most event node. For the upper event node, the expected monetary value is calculated as

$$(\$28,000 \times 0.7) + (\$12,000 \times 0.3) = \$23,200.$$

For the lower event node, the expected monetary value is calculated as

$$(\$36,000 \times 0.7) + (\$4,000 \times 0.3) = \$26,400.$$

These EMV's are shown in Figure 2–2. As long as J. D. is willing to use expected monetary value as the decision criterion, J. D. is faced with a simple decision problem: Is an EMV of $23,200 or an EMV of $26,400 preferred? As has already been discussed, the higher expected profit is preferred; hence, the lower branch, purchase Machine B, has been selected. The upper branch in Figure 2–2, which has a lower EMV, has been blocked off. In general, the tree is pruned, or backward analysis is applied, by working from right to left:

1. Compute the EMV at each of the event nodes.
2. For each decision node, prune all but the maximum EMV branches.

This example can be expanded into a multi-stage or sequential problem by changing the scenario. Figure 2–3 shows the decision tree that

FIGURE 2-3

Decision Tree for J. D.'s Decision with Appeal

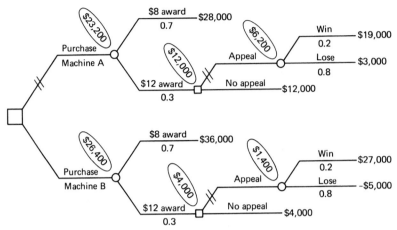

results if the following change is made in the scenario: An arbitration award can be appealed. J. D. would not appeal an award of $8, but could appeal a $12 award at a cost of $9,000. J. D. estimates that the probability of winning the appeal is 0.20. From Figure 2-3, it is apparent that J. D. should not undertake the appeal.

2.9.   A SEQUENTIAL (MULTI-STAGE) DECISION PROBLEM UNDER UNCERTAINTY: THE SUNFLAKE CORPORATION

The Sunflake Corporation has entered into a contract to supply 100 computer printer parts to a computer manufacturer. Although the printer part is not an advancement of the "state of the art" of computer technology, Sunflake has never built any of these devices before. After some investigation, Mr. Higgins, President of the Sunflake Corporation, has reached a tentative agreement with Ms. Pickering, President of the InteChip Corporation, to have InteChip make the solid-state portion of the printer part for Sunflake. However, Higgins is seriously considering setting up a production facility to make the entire printer part rather than buy a portion from InteChip.

Sunflake's contract provides for a price of $100 per printer part, or a total of $10,000 for completing the contract. The contract also provides that if Sunflake is unable to make delivery of the printer parts within six months, there will be a late-delivery penalty consisting of a reduction of the price Sunflake receives from $100 to $50. Although the current contract does not include any follow-on sales of the printer part, Higgins has learned that there is a good possibility that a second batch of 100 will be ordered. If Sunflake makes its delivery time for the first batch (either solely by its own manufacture or with purchase from InteChip) then Sunflake will be a strong contender for the second batch. However, if Sunflake does not make the delivery time, they will be out of the running for the second batch of printer parts. If Sunflake does not start the manufacturing process now, it must buy the solid-state portion from InteChip.

The tentative agreement with InteChip provides for Sunflake to purchase the solid-state portion at $40, which will permit Sunflake to complete the printer part for a total cost of $80 each. The Sunflake/InteChip agreement also provides that if the follow-on order is received by Sunflake, InteChip will reduce its price to Sunflake by $30, so that Sunflake's total cost on the follow-on will be $50 each, if the solid-state portion is purchased from InteChip.

The ability of Sunflake to manufacture the complete printer part in time to avoid the late-delivery penalty is uncertain at this time. The production process would cost $3,000 to get ready; after spending the $3,000 one time, Sunflake can make all the printer parts it needs (including the solid-state components) at a further cost of $3 each, if the manufacturing process works. If the process does not work, Sunflake cannot make any printer parts in time to meet the delivery deadline. If Sunflake takes the late-delivery penalty, however, Sunflake's production process is sure to work eventually, but at an extra set-up cost of $1,000 and a new unit cost of $20 each, which is $17 higher than the $3 cost if the process works in time. The decision of whether to abandon the production process, or to spend the additional $1,000 to make it work, must be made before the uncertainty of a follow-on contract is resolved.

When Higgins found out that the production process was not a sure thing, he called InteChip to find out how long the $40 price was effective. He found out that it would be considered to be a firm price for three weeks; after that, it would go from $40 to $60 because of other commitments that would require InteChip to do Sunflake's work on overtime. InteChip's price for the follow-on (if any) is not affected by the price on the initial batch.

Higgins was disappointed, because it would take more than three weeks to find out whether the production process at Sunflake would in fact meet the delivery deadline. What should he do? Initially, Higgins must decide either to buy from InteChip, set up the manufacturing process, or do both simultaneously.

After considerable thought, Higgins assessed the probability that the manufacturing process would be able to meet the delivery schedule was 0.4, and the probability of a follow-on contract was 0.7 if the first delivery is on time. With this information, the decision tree for the Sunflake problem can be completed. The decision tree showing all acts,

FIGURE 2–4

Sunflake's Decision Tree

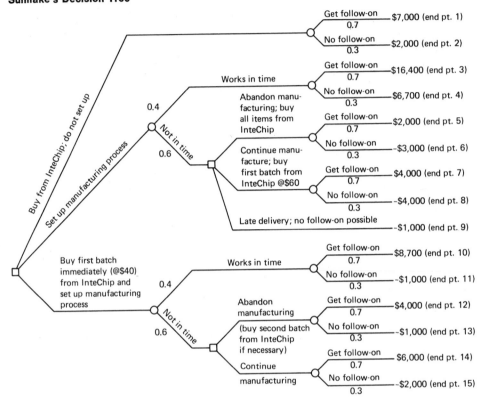

events, conditional profits, and probabilities is shown in Figure 2–4. Note the effective way in which the tree summarizes a confusing scenario! The conditional profits for Figure 2–4 have been calculated in Figure 2–5, which shows the revenues and expenses leading to each conditional profit. Each row corresponds to one numbered end point on the decision tree.

In order to use the decision tree to recommend a course of action, the analyst must start at a right-most node of the tree. If that right-most node is an event node, the expected monetary value is found at that node. If that right-most node is an act node, the course of action with the highest EMV is selected, and the remaining acts are blocked off. The value at that act node is then the EMV of the best act that has already been selected.

This process of analyzing the decision tree by working backwards is illustrated in Figure 2–6. Each right-most node in the original decision

FIGURE 2–5

Sunflake's Alternatives: Revenues, Expenses, and Conditional Profits

	Initial				Follow-On			
End-point	Revenue*	Manufacturing Set-up Costs†	Manufacturing Variable Costs‡	InteChip Costs§	Revenue	Manufacturing Variable Costs‖	InteChip Costs#	Conditional Profit**
1	$10,000			$ − 8,000	$ +10,000		$ −5,000	$ 7,000
2	10,000			− 8,000				2,000
3	10,000	$ −3,000	$ −300		+10,000	$ −300		16,400
4	10,000	−3,000	−300					6,700
5	10,000	−3,000		−10,000	+10,000		−5,000	2,000
6	10,000	−3,000		−10,000				−3,000
7	10,000	−4,000		−10,000	+10,000	−2,000		4,000
8	10,000	−4,000		−10,000				−4,000
9	5,000	−4,000	−2,000					−1,000
10	10,000	−3,000		−8,000	+10,000	−300		8,700
11	10,000	−3,000		−8,000				−1,000
12	10,000	−3,000		−8,000	+10,000		−5,000	4,000
13	10,000	−3,000		−8,000				−1,000
14	10,000	−4,000		−8,000	+10,000	−2,000		6,000
15	10,000	−4,000		−8,000				−2,000

* $10,000 if on time; $5,000 if late.
† $3,000 if process works on time or abandoned; $4,000 if late and continued.
‡ 100 at $3 if on time; 100 at $20 if late.
§ 100 at $80 if ordered now; 100 at $100 if ordered later.
‖ 100 at $3 if on time; 100 at $20 if late.
100 at $50.
** Total of other columns.

FIGURE 2–6

Sunflake's Decision Tree

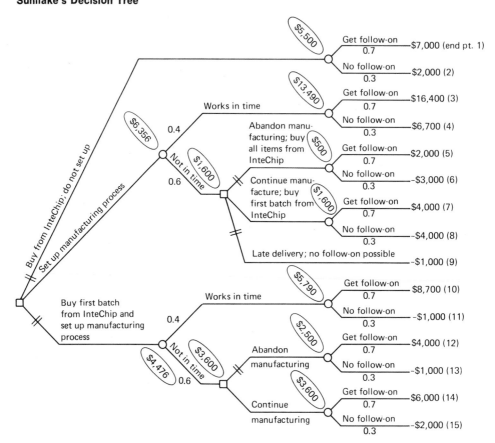

tree is an event node; at each of these right-most event nodes an EMV is noted. (In most cases these EMVs would be shown on the original decision tree. They have been shown on a separate tree for clarity.) Working from right to left in Figure 2–6, at the two act nodes (continue, abandon), it is a simple matter of choosing the act with the highest EMV. This is shown by blocking out the non-optimal act with lower EMV. The EMV for each act is written above that node. The EMV at each of the two remaining right-most nodes is calculated, and shown above the appropriate event node. The decision maker is now faced with a relatively simple choice: (1) buy all components from InteChip for an expected profit of $5,500; (2) set up the manufacturing process and not place an initial order with InteChip and have an expected monetary value of $6,356; or (3) buy the first batch from InteChip and set up the manufacturing process at the same time, yielding an expected monetary value of $4,476. The best of these is to set up the manufacturing process and not buy from InteChip, as indicated by blocking off the two non-optimal acts at the initial decision point.

The complete strategy Higgins should follow can be obtained by interpreting the decision tree. Starting at the left, the optimal act at the first decision point is to set up the manufacturing process. If the process works in time, there is no further decision. If it does not work in time, then Higgins should continue the manufacturing process but buy the first batch from InteChip.

By the use of a decision tree, Higgins has been able to reduce the rather complex sequence of acts and events into one logical diagram, which can then be analyzed piece by piece in order to define the optimal course of action.

2.10. AN OBJECTIVE DEFINITION OF PROBABILITY

Now that the probability has been used, its meaning needs a more thorough discussion. An experiment is a process or procedure that can be repeated under apparently identical conditions any number of times. An event is a particular end result of the experiment. As an example, flipping a coin is an experiment. Observing the end result as either a head or a tail is ascertaining which event has occurred.

Almost all users of probability would agree with this definition:

If an experiment is performed N times, and if event A occurs $n(A)$ times on these N repetitions, the probability of the event A is defined to be the proportion of times that A occurs, or

$$P(A) = \frac{n(A)}{N},$$

This can be written more formally as

$$P(A) = \lim_{N \to \infty} \frac{n(A)}{N}.$$

This relative frequency definition of a probability is called an objective definition because two observers should report approximately the same value for $P(A)$. This is a particularly useful definition of probabilities for many situations such as flipping coins, observing defective parts produced by a machine, rolling dice, and other procedures that can be repeated a large number of times under apparently identical conditions.

When a decision maker is studying a system that can be observed for a very large number of repetitions (or experiments), the relative frequency definition of probabilities is useful. For example, the machinery that fills milk cartons can be observed for a large number of repetitions to find out the proportion or relative frequency of cartons that contain more than 32 fluid ounces of milk. In determining the correct adjustment of the machine, this relative frequency probability would be useful.

2.11. A SUBJECTIVE DEFINITION OF PROBABILITY

The relative frequency definition of probability is not useful to answer the question, "What is the probability that this redesigned hula hoop will sell more than 50,000 units next month?" The information that it is redesigned from past hula hoops clearly indicates that a large number of repetitions of the experiment could not exist. Not only has the hula hoop changed, the economic environment in which the hula hoop will be sold has also changed. Either of these makes a large number of repetitions of an experiment of observing monthly sales impossible. Yet it would not be surprising to hear E. J., the owner of the firm making hula hoops, say, "There is a 0.40 probability that this hula hoop will sell more than 50,000 units next month." What is the meaning of such a statement? A probability can also be defined as:

A probability is a number between 0 and 1 that is used by an individual to express that individual's feelings of uncertainty about the occurrence of a particular event. A probability of 0 means the individual feels the event is impossible, while a probability of 1 means that the individual feels the event is certain to occur.

This definition is a subjective or personalistic view of probability.

There is a very strong relationship between the objective (relative frequency) definition of probability and the subjective definition of probability. When E. J., the owner of the hula hoop company, stated that the probability that more than 50,000 units would be sold is 0.40, this can be interpreted as meaning that E. J. would be *indifferent* between receiving either of the two following bargains:

Hoop Bargain: E. J. will receive $100 if sales of the hula hoop are in excess of 50,000 next month, or will receive $25 if sales of the hula hoop are not in excess of 50,000 units next month. (The values of $100 and $25 are arbitrarily chosen, but they must be used in the following bargain as well.)

Urn Bargain: One hundred balls have been placed in an urn. The balls are identical, except for color. Forty of the balls are pink, and 60 balls are brown. The balls have been stirred very well before they have been placed in the urn, so that they are very well mixed. A color-blind person, who cannot distinguish between a pink and a brown ball, will reach into the urn and select one ball. If the selected ball is pink, E. J. will receive $100. If the ball is brown, E. J. will receive $25.

The decision maker's statement "The probability of selling more than 50,000 units next month is 0.40" is a subjective probability. Different people contemplating the sales of the redesigned hula hoop would not necessarily assess the probability at the same value. On the other hand, the statement "The probability that the color-blind person will withdraw a pink ball is 0.40" is an objective probability. It is possible to conceptualize this experiment: The person withdraws a ball; observes the color of the ball withdrawn; replaces the ball and mixes well; then continues, repeating the experiment. Under these conditions, it would be anticipated that the relative frequency of 0.40 for pink ball would be reached when the number of repetitions of the experiment is very large. But if E. J., when offered a choice, is truly indifferent between the hoop bargain and the urn bargain, E. J. can see no useful distinction between these two probability numbers. If E. J. prefers one bargain to the other, this behavior is inconsistent with the stated probability for hula hoop sales.

2.12. PROBABILITY ASSESSMENT

The mechanism that a decision maker may use to assess the probability for an event has already been introduced briefly in the definition of subjective probabilities above. To be more explicit, a subjective probability is an explicit assessment made by a decision maker. The probability assessment technique, which is described in this section, is nothing more than a convenient and useful way for a decision maker to assess these subjective, personal probabilities.

The probability distribution of next month's sales of hula hoops is particularly important for decisions relating to production, cash forecasting, sizing a sales force, and so on. E. J. is the person responsible for these decisions. The discussion of subjective probabilities has considered the meaning of E. J.'s probability that sales will exceed 50,000 hoops. The purpose here is to demonstrate more explicitly the procedure that E. J. might use in assessing the probability distribution of sales. The example that follows will show how E. J. might assess the probability that sales of hula hoops in the next month will exceed 50,000.

There are many factors that E. J. would want to consider in making this probability assessment. E. J. might want to know how many hula hoops were sold in the same month last year. E. J. might also want to know specific changes that have been made in the design of the hula hoop, how other products in the firm's inventory have been selling, and what the general conditions of the economy are for this time period. But this information is not enough to reach an objective assessment of the probability that sales of hula hoops will exceed 50,000 units next month. The missing ingredient is E. J.'s expertise, knowledge, hunch, intuition, experience, judgment, and feel of the situation. To incorporate these inputs into the probability assessment, the analyst who is assisting E. J. in the probability assessment would pose a series of questions to E. J. Each question would be very simple in form: "Which do you prefer?" As long as E. J. can answer a series of these simple questions, E. J.'s probability for sales of 50,000 hula hoops next month can be assessed.

The first question the analyst might pose is which of the two bargains E. J. prefers. The first bargain is similar to the hula hoop bargain discussed above, except that E. J. is now concerned with sales exceeding 50,000 hoops next month. The bargain might be more formally stated as:

> Hoop Bargain: E. J. will receive $100 if sales of the hula hoops are in excess of 50,000 next month, but will receive $25 if sales of the hula hoop are not in excess of 50,000.

The second bargain is similar to the urn bargain described earlier, except a different mix of pink and brown balls is in the urn. This bargain could be stated as:

> Urn Bargain: A hundred balls have been placed in an urn. The balls are identical: all of them are pink, and none of the balls is brown. The balls have been stirred very well and they have been placed in the urn. A color-blind person, who cannot distinguish between a pink and a brown ball, will reach into the urn and select one ball. If the selected ball is pink, E. J. will receive $100. If the ball is brown, E. J. will receive $25.

In choosing between these two bargains, E. J. would surely choose the urn bargain because E. J. is sure to win the larger prize, $100, by choosing the urn bargain. However, if the analyst changes the urn bargain to 90 pink balls and ten brown balls, the analyst could not predict which bargain E. J. would choose. If E. J. prefers the urn bargain, E. J. believes it is more likely that a pink ball will be drawn than it is that sales of hula hoops will exceed 50,000 next month. The analyst would then change the urn bargain so that there are fewer pink balls and more brown balls in the urn for the next question. If E. J. prefers the hoop bargain, E. J. believes that it is more likely that sales will exceed 50,000 than that a pink ball would be drawn. In this case, the analyst would change the urn bargain to more pink balls and fewer brown balls.

The procedure the analyst would use is to continue adjusting the urn bargain until E. J. expresses an indifference between the two bargains. When this point of indifference has been reached, the relative frequency of pink in the urn of indifference represents E. J.'s personal, subjective probability that sales of hula hoops will exceed 50,000 next month.

This process could be repeated for other quantities of hoop sales for next month. The analyst could use a graph showing the hula hoop sales on the horizontal axis and E. J.'s probability on the vertical axis, as shown in Figure 2–7. Several points are plotted on this graph. Point A (50,000; 0.4) is the probability that was used in the previous discussion defining subjective probability. If E. J. had been indifferent between the urn and hoop bargains at the probability of 0.8 at 30,000 units, the point shown as B would be reached. Point C shows that E. J. is certain that the hula hoops sales next month will be positive, which may not be trivial if it were possible for returns of merchandise to exceed sales of merchandise. Several other points, labeled D, E, and F, could also have been obtained from the probability assessment. A curve drawn through

FIGURE 2–7

E. J.'s Probability Distribution for Hula Hoop Sales

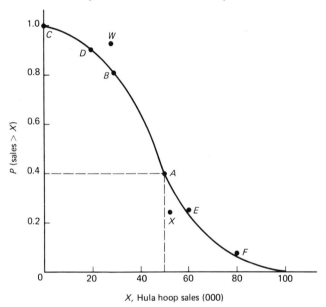

X, Hula hoop sales (000)

points such as those shown would be useful in interpolating E. J.'s probability for sales that were not explicitly used in a probability assessment. This curve, drawn freehand, is an approximation to the answers E. J. would have given to questions that were not asked. Asking more questions to obtain more points improves the approximation, but is more time-consuming and costly. The analyst should be cautious in interpreting the curve in the neighborhood of points such as W and X. The impossibility of drawing a smooth curve through the points D, B, and W, or the points A, X, and E, indicates some ambiguity in E. J.'s answers. The analyst should return to the questioning in these areas to attain more consistent probability assessments.

2.13.   OBJECTIVE VERSUS SUBJECTIVE PROBABILITIES

At this point the reader might be wondering which definition of probabilities is more useful for managerial decisions. The answer is quite straightforward: if there is enough information that a relative frequency probability can be found, it should be used. Perhaps the more usual situation is that there may be substantial amounts of information about an event, but the experiment has not been repeated under apparently identical conditions. When this occurs, the decision maker may subjectively use this past relative frequency information in probability assess-

FIGURE 2–8

A Memo to E. J. about Hula Hoop Sales

Subject: Data for Past Sales of Hula Hoops and Redesigned Products

To: E. J.

The original hula hoop has been sold for 50 months. A frequency distribution of sales for these months is:

Number of Hula Hoops Sold		Number of Months	Relative Frequency
At Least	But Less than		
0.	10,000	1	0.02
10,000.	20,000	5	0.10
20,000.	30,000	28	0.56
30,000.	40,000	10	0.20
40,000.	50,000	5	0.10
50,000.	60,000	1	0.02
		50	1.00

The history of redesigned novelty toy products is somewhat sparse. However, we have discovered five items somewhat similar to the hula hoop as far as market characteristics; these five experienced these demand changes after redesign:

Product Code	Sales after Redesign (first year), as a Percentage of Average Yearly Sales before Redesign
ZW.	132%
HP.	72
R-1.	284
V-A.	8
QQ.	175

Industry sales continue in an uncertain pattern. For the entire toy industry, the sales two quarters ago were 93 percent of the average sales for the past two years. However, last quarter the sales went up to 97 percent. The consensus of sales forecasts for the coming year, as reported in the trade publications, is "modest to guardedly optimistic."

ment, by modifying the past relative frequencies to account for other information that is relevant.

In the hula hoop example, E. J. was not acting without any information is assessing probabilities, E. J.'s staff had prepared a report, Figure 2–8, describing past sales of hula hoops and other novelty products. But there is no probability distribution in these data that E. J. could use "as is." This year is different from past years. The ways in which this year is different should be subjectively incorporated by E. J. in assessing this month's probabilities for hula hoop sales. In general, a probability assessor should use whatever past data are available and relevant. The question of relevance is subjective. But if the probability assessor is fortunate enough to encounter a situation that is substantially unchanged from the period of data collection, one would anticipate that the assessed probabilities would be very similar to the past frequency distribution.

It can be argued that there is no such thing as an objective probability that is useful for managerial decisions. By definition, an objective probability requires a large number of repetitions under apparently identical conditions. It is a subjective decision on the part of the decision maker that the next repetition of the experiment will be made under apparently identical conditions. In this interpretation, even an apparently objective probability may be viewed as a subjective probability for decision purposes.

2.14. RISK PREFERENCE ANALYSIS: WHEN EMV IS NOT A SATISFACTORY CRITERION

As mentioned in Section 2.6, there are certain settings in which the decision maker does not select that act which maximizes expected monetary value.

As a case in point, put yourself in the following setting:

You, a university student, have a cumulative grade point average of exactly 2.0 and the university requirement for graduation is a cumulative average of *at least* 2.0.

You need one credit for graduation and you are enrolled in a course for one credit. The grade you receive in this course will be entered on your record and your final grade point average will be computed. You may not repeat this course or take any additional courses.

Since this is your last term you are offered two ways in which to determine your grade.

Act 1:   You may take a grade of C with certainty (probability = 1).

Act 2:   The numbers 1–100 are put into a hat. If you draw number 100 you receive an F; if you draw any number from 90 to 99 you receive a *D;* and if you draw any number from 1 to 89 you receive an *A.*

Which act will you choose?

When this question is asked of groups, Act 1 is selected by 90 to 95 percent of the individuals. Yet if the expected grade point (EGP) for each of the choices is computed one finds for Act 1, EGP = 2; for Act 2, EGP = 0.89(4) + 0.10(1) + 0.01(0) = 3.66. Thus something other than expected grade point is the motivating factor—in this case the probability of not graduating and thus losing four years of course work. Other examples, particularly those of buying insurance or being faced with bankruptcy, can be similarly developed to show that EMV is not always a legitimate guide to action.

The analysis of such problems begins with the development of a set of numbers that replace dollar figures in the original payoff table. We will arrive at these new numbers by asking the decision maker a series of simple questions. These questions are structured in such a way that when the series of questions is answered we will have assessed (at least in part) the decision maker's attitude toward the risk involved in the original decision. The procedure being used is often given the name "modern utility theory," though the concept differs from the utility theory studied in microeconomic analysis. Hence, we shall use the term *risk preference* to describe this method of analysis.

The determination of a risk preference function and the foundations of utility theory are much more complex than indicated here. There are many difficulties one can encounter in performing this analysis and several rather technical assumptions that must be verified. The references at this end of the chapter give sources of more complete details. With those comments in mind, let us take a first look at how one would proceed with risk preference analysis.

In order to use risk preference analysis, first establish what is called a reference contract; this is a contract binding its owner to one of two outcomes. The outcome is to be selected by some chance mechanism. One of the two outcomes must be at least as good as the best outcome in the problem, and one must be at least as bad as the worst outcome in the problem. Assume that a gain of $5,000 is at least as good as the best outcome, and that a loss of $4,000 is at least as bad as the worst outcome. Then ask a series of questions of the following form: "Suppose you have the opportunity to purchase a reference contract with the probability *p* of winning $5,000 and a probability 1-*p* of losing $4,000. At what value of *p* would you be indifferent between this contract and an amount V— say $2,000—to be received for certain?" Suppose the decision maker said that the value of *p* for indifference was 0.91. Admittedly, this kind of questioning would require some soul searching on the part of the decision maker. Yet it is a relatively simple kind of decision problem that is being posed. Suppose that this question is asked for each $1,000 amount, V, between −$4,000 and +$5,000. Obviously the end points are easy to determine: the decision maker is indifferent between a certain loss of $4,000 and a $p = 0$ reference contract, in which one is also certain to lose $4,000. A similar argument holds true for the value of $p = 1$, corresponding to a value, V, of $5,000. Now that we have obtained all of the numbers such as those shown in Figure 2–9, how are these numbers used to analyze a decision problem? Consider the decision problem shown in Figure 2–10, and use risk preference analysis to recommend a course of

FIGURE 2–9

Indifference Values, V, for a Reference Contract with Probability p of Gaining $5,000 and Probability (1 − p) of Losing $4,000

V (dollars)	p
−4,000	0
−3,000	0.22
−2,000	0.43
−1,000	0.63
0	0.75
1,000	0.85
2,000	0.91
3,000	0.95
4,000	0.98
5,000	1

action to the decision maker. This recommended course of action is intended to be consistent with the choices of Figure 2–9. We are not telling the decision maker, "This is what you should do." Rather, we are saying "This is what you should do in order to be consistent with what you previously have told us about your attitudes towards various situations of risk."

Now carefully consider Part B of Figure 2–10, which we have called "risk preference payoffs." Look specifically at the entry in the upper left-hand corner, corresponding to act A_1 and event E_1, and see an entry of 0.95 in this table and an entry of $3,000 in the corresponding box of Part A, the "dollar payoff" table. Looking back at Figure 2–9, see that the decision maker revealed indifference between a certain $3,000 and a reference contract with a 0.95 probability of winning the better prize. Since the decision maker is indifferent between these two, substitute one for the other in these two payoff tables. Thus, in the risk preference payoffs we are awarding as the outcome from E_1/A_1 a reference contract with a 0.95 probability of winning $5,000 and a 0.05 probability of losing

$4,000. Looking at the rest of the A_1 column, see that the next two prizes are identical, so 0.95 is entered in the A_1 column for the E_2 and E_3 rows as well. In the E_4 row of the first act a zero is entered. This corresponds to a certain loss of $4,000. Similar substitutions are made for the remaining two acts in this payoff table.

FIGURE 2–10

Payoff Tables for Risk Preference Analysis

A. Dollar Payoffs

	A_1	A_2	A_3	Probability
E_1	$3,000	$5,000	$3,000	0.4
E_2	$3,000	−$3,000	$1,000	0.3
E_3	$3,000	$2,000	0	0.2
E_4	−$4,000	0	0	0.1

B. Risk Preference Payoffs

	A_1	A_2	A_3	Probability
E_1	0.95	1.00	0.95	0.4
E_2	0.95	0.22	0.85	0.3
E_3	0.95	0.91	0.75	0.2
E_4	0	0.75	0.75	0.1
Equivalent Reference Contract	0.855	0.723	0.860	

Sample calculations—equivalent reference contract for A_2:

$$0.4(1.00) + 0.3(0.22) + 0.2(0.91) + 0.1(0.75) = 0.723.$$

The next step in risk preference analysis is to take each of the acts and translate it into an equivalent reference contract. If we look at A_1, we see a $(0.4 + 0.3 + 0.2)$ chance of winning a reference contract which has a 0.95 chance of winning the $5,000 (and of course a 0.05 chance of losing $4,000). Thus, A_1 is equivalent to a reference contract with an overall probability of winning of

$$(0.4 \times 0.95) + (0.3 \times 0.95) + (0.2 \times 0.95) + (0.1 \times 0) = 0.855.$$

Thus, this substitution of equivalent outcomes shows that the decision maker would view A_1 as equivalent to a reference contract with a 0.855

chance of winning $5,000 and a probability of 0.145 of losing $4,000. Similarly we can reduce A_2 to an equivalent reference contract: in this case there is a 0.4 chance of receiving a reference contract with a 1.0 chance of winning, a 0.3 chance of receiving a contract with a 0.22 chance of winning, a 0.2 chance of receiving a reference contract with a 0.91 chance of winning, and a 0.1 chance of receiving a reference contract with a 0.75 chance of winning. Thus, we have an equivalent reference contract for A_2 with a probability p of

$$(0.4 \times 1.00) + (0.3 \times 0.22) + (0.2 \times 0.91) + (0.1 \times 0.75) = 0.723.$$

At this time the reader should verify that the reference contract equivalent to an act A_3 in the problem has a probability p of 0.860.

Now the recommendation to the decision maker is quite simple. There are three equivalent reference contracts, each with the same outcomes— either winning $5,000 or losing $4,000—and with different probabilities for the outcomes. Hence the decision maker certainly would prefer the reference contract with the highest probability of the gain of $5,000. Looking at the equivalent reference contract for each of the acts, see that the decision maker must prefer act A_3 in order to be consistent with his or her risk preference function as given in Figure 2–9.

What again is the reason for this substitution? As mentioned earlier, this is the way of putting into the payoff table a set of numbers so that it is legitimate to calculate expectations. Looking carefully at the manner of computing the equivalent reference contract for each act, notice that we have done nothing more than multiply the probability by a number from a payoff table and added these products for each act. *This is exactly the same way that one calculates an expectation from a dollar payoff table.* Hence, we have replaced the dollar payoffs with risk preference payoffs to construct a set of numbers for which an expected value is legitimate.

With the set of preferences revealed in Figure 2–9 one would be able to analyze in this same fashion any payoff table that was given in dollars, as long as the payoffs were in thousand-dollar amounts between −$4,000 and $5,000. At this point it should be relatively simple to use simple interpolation to find the p value for a reference contract that had a value of something other than a multiple of $1,000. One could simply plot p versus V, using V on the horizontal axis and p on the vertical axis, and draw in a smooth curve to find approximately the equivalent reference contract for any given amount under certainty, V. Thus, by asking a series of very simple questions, one has a powerful way of analyzing a complex decision problem under uncertainty.

The reader can perhaps now see some of the many difficulties that arise in determining a risk preference function. The answers given by a decision maker may not be consistent from one question to the next.

Also the responses are dependent on the decision maker's frame of mind at the time the questions are asked; the next day the responses might be quite different. In many settings decisions are made by groups rather than individuals, and the combining of individual risk preferences is an extremely complex issue. The interested reader may consult some of the references at the end of this chapter for further coverage of risk preference analysis.

There is often a confusion in students' minds between probability assessment and risk preference assessment. The confusion arises because both concepts require a similar approach of questioning to find indifferences, although the two are quite different in purpose. The purpose of subjective probability assessment is to find the decision maker's belief about the relative likelihood of various events. This is necessary for any decision problem that lacks a sufficiently stable information base for determining objective probabilities. Risk preference analysis is used when the consequences are large, so that EMV is not a suitable decision criterion. Subjective probability assessment may be needed with or without risk preference analysis; risk preference analysis may be needed with or without subjective probability assessment. Whether either (or both or neither) is necessary depends upon knowledge of probabilities and the magnitude of the consequences.

2.15. SUMMARY

A decision is made under uncertainty when the decision maker does not know with certainty the outcome that will follow every course of action. A decision analyst may assist the decision maker facing a problem under uncertainty by using a probability assessment technique for events that will occur. Although these probabilities are subjective, this procedure assists the decision maker by providing a systematic way of breaking a complex problem into its simpler components; one of these components is the probability of occurrence of each of the events. The second way in which a decision analyst may assist in a decision under uncertainty is by the use of expectation as the decision criterion. If the decision problem is "small," expected monetary value may be calculated and used as a decision criterion. If the decision problem has some large financial outcomes, then risk preference analysis may be necessary. If risk preference analysis is used, expected value is computed for these preference numbers. If not, expectation is computed for the dollar outcomes.

A decision table is a useful way for displaying elements of a single-stage problem, while a decision tree is a useful model for a sequential or multistage decision problem.

EXERCISES

2.1.   Distinguish between certainty and uncertainty.

2.2.   Discuss: "A probability value can be established by a series of questions of the form, 'Which do you prefer, A or B?' "

2.3.   Discuss: "All probabilities have some degree of subjectivity, in that a judgment must be made as to the relevance to the future of the period of data collection."

2.4.   Discuss: "After flipping a fair coin, but before the outcome is known, the probability of a head can be only zero or one."

2.5.   Calculate the expected monetary value for each course of action:

Events	Acts				Probabilities
	A_1	A_2	A_3	A_4	
E_1	$100	$60	$ 30	$ 50	0.7
E_2	$ 40	$50	$150	$200	0.3

2.6.   A small stationery store is busily planning its inventory for the Christmas season. The owner must decide the allocation of his budget between expensive Christmas cards and inexpensive Christmas cards. Once he has made a decision and placed his order, the order cannot be changed. In addition, he cannot reorder. The owner has $6 to spend for cards; he pays $1 a box for inexpensive cards, and $2 for a box of expensive cards. The retail price for a box of inexpensive cards is $2; he can sell at this price all of the inexpensive cards he stocks. The expensive cards retail for $5 a box before Christmas, or $2 a box after Christmas. The owner is willing to use the following experience-based probability distribution for before-Christmas demand for boxes of expensive cards:

x, Number of Expensive Boxes Demanded before Christmas at $5 per Box	p(x), Probability
0...................................	0.1
1...................................	0.2
2...................................	0.5
3...................................	0.2

All boxes of expensive cards that are ordered but not demanded before Christmas at $5 per box are sold after Christmas at $2 per box, as indicated previously. A customer is not displeased if no expensive cards are available when he enters the store.

a. Construct a payoff table showing the retailer's profit for his $6 outlay; consider ordering 0, 1, 2, or 3 boxes of expensive cards, and the probability distribution for demand given above.

b. Find the expected profit of each act, and indicate the act that will maximize his expected profit.

2.7. Ms. Entrep was unsure of the market acceptance (proportion of customers who order the first year) of her new line of unisex clothes. If it catches on, it will have 30 percent acceptance; if not, only 5 percent. (She was willing to ignore the in-between possibilities.) There is a 40 percent chance of catching on and 60 percent chance of not catching on. If she paces the promotion at various levels, she estimates these profits:

	Promotion Pace		
	Slow	Medium	Fast
Catches on..........	0	$4,500	$10,000
Doesn't.............	3,000	2,000	−1,000

Based on the above information, what pace should she select?

2.8. A newspaper salesperson buys papers at 8 cents, and sells them at 20 cents each. At the end of the day, unsold papers can be returned for 4 cents. The counting machine at the publishing company will set up bundles only in multiples of ten papers; the financial resources of the salesperson put an upper limit of 100 papers per day. Over the past 100 days, the demand for newspapers has been:

Number of Papers	Number of Days
20..............................	5
30..............................	15
40..............................	20
50..............................	30
60..............................	20
70..............................	5
80..............................	5

a. If the salesperson believes the period of data collection adequately resembles the anticipations for tomorrow, how many should the salesperson stock for tomorow to maximize expected profit?

b. If the salesperson believes that sales tomorrow will be "20 percent higher" than indicated during the period of data collection, how many should be stocked for tomorrow?

c. Answer Question (*a*) if newspapers have no return value.

d. Answer Question (*a*) if newspapers can be returned at 8 cents, the original cost.

2.9. Suppose the newspaper salesperson in the preceding question always made it a habit to walk away from the salesbooth whenever the supply of papers was exhausted. How would this affect the ability to gather data on demand for newspapers, as opposed to actual sales?

2.10. Suppose that a decision problem under uncertainty has two acts. If the EMV for A_1 is $200, and the EMV for A_2 is $500, explain why the difference between these two values, $300, is sometimes referred to as the *cost of irrationality* for choosing A_1.

2.11. The Vice-President, Finance, of the Acme Corporation is preparing a stock offering to present shareholders. One million shares will be offered at $4 per share, for an anticipated gross revenue of $4,000,000. However, not all shareholders will subscribe to the offering. After studying about fifteen similar offerings in the industry, the VP has concluded that the following probabilities are realistic for the number of shares subscribed to by shareholders:

Number of Shares	Probability
1,000,000	0.6
950,000	0.2
900,000	0.1
800,000	0.05
700,000	0.05

An underwriting firm has offered to stand by and purchase any shares not subscribed by shareholders. The cost of this standby underwriting is $15,000; the terms provide for a net to Acme of $3.75 per share for any sold to the underwriter. If Acme does not purchase the standby underwriting, the remaining shares will be sold (eventually) for $3.25 per share. Should the standby underwriting be used by Acme?

2.12. After test marketing, it appears that the new shadjt, just developed and tested, will sell "reasonably well." However, to get into full production of the shadjts, the firm will need to spend $200,000 for equipment. After this expenditure, the variable cost per shadjt is $5. Alternatively, the firm can use existing facilities and manufacture shadjts for $15 each. These is also uncertainty about the best price. In one city, each shadjt sold at a price of $22. In another city, a lower price of $19 was used. The advertising campaign that is appropriate for the higher price costs $25,000; for the lower price, the advertising campaign costs $15,000. At the higher price, the estimated probability distribution for demand is:

Number of Shadjts	Probability
5,000	0.1
10,000	0.2
15,000	0.3
20,000	0.2
25,000	0.1
30,000	0.1

At the lower price, the estimated probability distribution for demand is:

Number of Shadjts	Probability
10,000	0.10
15,000	0.25
20,000	0.45
25,000	0.10
30,000	0.05
35,000	0.05

What price should be used, and what production process should be used?

2.13. A used-car dealer has just purchased a year-old sports car for $10,000. The dealer can wholesale the car now for $10,500, but the wholesale value of the car will decline $200 per month as the car gets older. After quite a bit of experience with similar cars, the dealer believes that advertising the car for $12,000 will result in a sale at a price of $11,500, if the right buyer comes along. The probability that the right buyer will come along in the first month is 0.4; if it is not sold then, the probability is 0.3 for the second month. If it is not sold in the second month, the probability the right buyer will come along in the third month is 0.2. If it is not sold in the third month, the probability the right buyer will come along in the fourth month is 0.1. If it is not sold during the fourth month, it will be sold at wholesale [for $10,500 − (4 × 200) = $9,700]. Advertising costs $50 per month. What should the dealer do? Make sure that your decision rule explains what should be done at the end of each month if the car has not been sold.

2.14. The Pine Tree Corporation can buy a component for $10 each, in any quantity. It also has the opportunity to set up a production process for the component, at a fixed cost of $1,000 for the process and a variable cost of $1 per component. If the process does not work as planned, an additional expenditure of $5,000 will ensure that it does work. The probability that the production process will work without the added expenditure is 0.70. The number of components needed is 50, 100, 150, 200, or 250, with probabilities of 0.1, 0.3, 0.5, 0.05, 0.05, respectively. What strategy will minimize expected costs?

2.15. In the preceding problem, what is the indifference probability for the production process "working" that makes the decision maker indifferent between make or buy? Assume the demand probability distribution is the same as stated in the problem.

2.16. A complex piece of equipment is not working correctly. It can be repaired for $25,000 by the FIXIT Corporation or the owner of the equipment can use in-house maintenance people costing $10,000 per month. The probability that it will be fixed in the first month is 0.6. If that doesn't work, another month can be spent, leaving a 0.3 probability that the second month will do the job. If the second month doesn't fix the machine, a third month has a 0.2 chance of fixing. After three months, there is no chance that the in-house crew can do the job. At any month-end, FIXIT can be employed for $25,000. What strategy will minimize the expected cost of repair?

2.17. The decision maker for Problem 2.5 suddenly decided that EMV was not an appropriate criterion. In order to determine the DM's risk preference function, a bargain with payoff of $200 with probability p and $0 with probability $(1 - p)$ was posed to the DM. The point of indifference, for values of p and amount V to be received with certainty were:

p	V
0.0	0
0.25	20
0.35	30
0.43	40
0.50	50
0.67	75
0.72	100
0.92	150
1.00	200

   a. Recommend a course of action consistent with the decision maker's indifference points above.
   b. Would every decision maker agree with this recommended course of action?

2.18. For the data of Problem 2.17, plot p (vertical axis) against V (horizontal axis). Does it appear that a smooth curve can be fitted through the points? How might this be of use to the decision maker in other problems?

SUGGESTIONS FOR FURTHER STUDY

Brown, R. V., "Do Managers Find Decision Analysis Useful?" *Harvard Business Review*, vol. 48, 1970, pp. 78–89.

Brown, R. V., Kahr, A. S., and Peterson, C. *Decision Analysis for the Manager.* New York: Holt, Rinehart and Winston, 1974.

Davis, M. D., *Game Theory.* New York: Basic Books, Inc., 1970.

DeNeufville, R., and Keeney, R. L., "Use of Decision Analysis in Airport Development for Mexico City," in Drake, A. W., Keeney, R. L., and Morse, P. M., eds., *Analysis of Public Systems.* Cambridge, Mass.: M.I.T. Press, 1970.

Dyer, J. S., and Miles, R. F., Jr., "An Actual Application of Collective Choice Theory to the Selection of Trajectories for the Mariner Jupiter Saturn 1977 Project," *Operations Research,* vol. 24, March–April 1976, pp. 220–44.

Fishburn, P. C., *Utility Theory for Decision Making.* New York: John Wiley, 1970.

Halter, A. N., and Dean, G. W., *Decisions Under Uncertainty.* Cincinnati: South-Western Publishing Co., 1971.

Hogarth, R. W., "Cognitive Processes and the Assessment of Subjective Probability Distributions," *Journal of the American Statistical Association,* vol. 70, no. 350, June 1975, pp. 271–90.

Howard, R. A., Matheson, J. E., and North, D. W., "The Decision to Seed Hurricanes," *Science,* vol. 176, 1974, pp. 1191–1202.

Jones, J. M., *Introduction to Decision Theory.* Homewood, Ill.: Richard D. Irwin, Inc., 1977.

Luce, R. D. and Raiffa, H., *Games and Decisions.* New York: Wiley, 1958.

Newman, J. W., *Management Applications of Decision Theory.* New York: Harper & Row, 1971.

Raiffa, H., *Decision Analysis: Introductory Lectures on Choices Under Uncertainty.* Reading, Mass.: Addison-Wesley, 1970.

Schwartz, W. B., Gorry, G. A., Kassirer, J. P., and Essig, A., "Decision Analysis and Clinical Judgement," *The American Journal of Medicine,* vol. 55, 1973, pp. 459–72.

Von Neumann, J., and Morgenstern, O., *Theory of Games and Economic Behavior.* Princeton, N.J.: Princeton University Press, 1947.

Wheelwright, S. C., "Applying Decision Theory to Improve Corporate Management of Currency-Exchange Risks," *California Management Review,* vol. 17, 1975.

Winkler, R. L., *An Introduction to Bayesian Inference and Decision.* New York: Holt, Rinehart and Winston, 1972.

3

Decision Analysis with Additional Information

3.1. INTRODUCTORY COMMENTS

ONE OF THE MOST difficult and common aspects of managerial decisions is addressing one of these two questions: "When should I decide?" and "How much information should I have before I decide?" These questions are often similar to each other. One reason for deciding later is that uncertainty will be resolved over time, so that deciding later increases the amount of information available to the decision maker. The purpose of this chapter is to address the question of the value of additional information, so that rational decisions can be made about the amount of information that should be obtained before making a decision.

3.2. PERFECT INFORMATION OR CLAIRVOYANCE

Although the terms *perfect information* and *clairvoyance* may seem out of place in managerial decisions, this is not the case. Perfect information means that the decision maker is able to find out what event has occurred or will occur before the choice of an act is made. This is the same as clairvoyance: a clairvoyant is able to predict the future, as if the event has been observed before an act is selected.

To relate these concepts to managerial decisions, there often are ways that a manager can find out ahead of time what is going to happen. In some cases a telephone call will resolve an uncertainty, permitting the decision to be made with perfect information. In some cases a personal visit (and a higher expense account) will provide perfect information.

In some decision situations the information is buried in a set of filing cabinets in someone's office. In some situations building a prototype of a product will resolve uncertainties. In any of these situations, the decision maker may be able to obtain information that enables the selection of an act after the event has occurred. Of course, additional information typically costs money.

To illustrate the concept of evaluating perfect information, return to the arbitration decision problem faced by J. D. in Chapter 2. J. D.'s decision is modeled in the payoff table in Figure 3–1, which is identical to Figure 2–1. The question to be answered is: *How would J. D. behave*

FIGURE 3–1

Conditional Profit Table for J. D.'s Decision

| Events | Acts | | Probabilities |
	Purchase Machine A	Purchase Machine B	
$8 Award	$28,000	$36,000	0.7
$12 Award	$12,000	$ 4,000	0.3
	$23,200	$26,400	

knowing which award the arbitrator had made? If J. D. were able to choose the machine after an $8 award had been made, it is apparent from the table that Machine B would be selected, with a profit of $36,000. The probability of an $8 award is 0.7; hence, if J. D. is operating with perfect information, the probability of selecting Machine B and receiving the $36,000 profit is 0.7. If J. D. chooses a machine after the $12 award, Machine A will be selected, yielding a profit of $12,000. The probability of the $12 award is 0.3; hence, the probability of Machine A and $12,000 is 0.3, if J. D. is acting with perfect information. J. D.'s expected monetary value with perfect information is

$$(\$36,000 \times 0.7) + (\$12,000 \times 0.3) = \$28,800$$

To compute the benefits to J. D. of deciding after the arbitration award (if this is possible), the *expected value of perfect information* (EVPI) is the improvement in EMV when J. D. moves from the initial decision problem using prior probabilities to the decision problem with perfect information. This difference is:

$$\$28,800 - \$26,400 = \$2,400.$$
$$EVPI = \$2,400.$$

How would J. D. use this knowledge that perfect information is worth $2,400? If there is some way that the arbitrator's award can be sufficiently expedited, it would be worth anything up to $2,400 to do so. If the original time constraint for ordering the machine arises within J. D.'s organization, there might be ways of removing the requirement at a cost far less than $2,400. Perhaps the purchasing department had required lead-time for writing specifications or securing bids. If either of these procedures can be sufficiently expedited or eliminated for less than $2,400, it would be worthwhile.

To summarize the method for finding EVPI, the expected value of perfect information, several additional terms are needed. The first concept is the expected monetary value of the optimal or best act, which is usually noted EMV*. The other concept that needs formal definition is the expected monetary value of the decision when it is made with perfect information. Note that a decision that is made with perfect information is the same as a decision made under certainty; the decision maker knows at the time of decision what is going to happen. Hence, this concept is called the Expected Profit under Certainty, or EPC. If we use the symbol O_i* for the dollar profit of the best outcome when event i occurs, then

$$EPC = \sum_i O_i*P_i.$$

Then the expected value of perfect information is

$$EVPI = EPC - EMV*.$$

3.3. OPPORTUNITY LOSS

An alternative way of analyzing decision problems under uncertainty combines the selection of the optimal act and the expected value of perfect information into one computation, *expected opportunity loss*. The opportunity loss for an act/event combination is the difference between the payoff for that outcome and O^{i*}, the best payoff for that event. The opportunity loss table corresponding to Figure 3–1 is Figure 3–2.

To construct an opportunity loss table, look at all the events, one at a time. For event $8, for example, "What is the best act for this event?" Obviously it is the choice of Machine B, with a payoff of $36,000. This best act is the reference point for this event; it has zero opportunity loss.

How does the remaining act compare with this $36,000 payoff? The payoff for $8 and Machine A is $28,000, which is $8,000 less than the best one could obtain for the $8 award. In the opportunity loss table for $12 and Machine A, enter $8,000.

The $12 row is calculated in the same fashion. $12,000 is the best payoff; in the Machine A column enter zero opportunity loss. The $12/ Machine B cell yields a profit of $4,000, which is $8,000 less than the $12,000 best payoff for this event. In the opportunity loss table for $8 and Machine B, enter $8,000.

The bottom row of Figure 3–2 shows the expected opportunity loss for each of the acts. This is calculated the same way as EMV, using the opportunity loss table instead of the payoff table. Now one can observe two very important things. The selection of Machine B is suggested by choosing the act with the expected opportunity loss that is lowest, just as the selection of Machine B was suggested by the payoff table from that act with the highest EMV. This is no accident. It will always occur that the act with the best (highest) expected profit will also have the best (lowest) expected opportunity loss.

Another important result of the calculation of the expected opportunity loss is that the expected opportunity loss of the optimal act is al-

FIGURE 3–2

Opportunity Loss Table for J. D.'s Decision

| Events | Acts | | Probabilities |
	Purchase Machine A	Purchase Machine B	
$8 Award	$8,000	0	0.7
$12 Award	0	$8,000	0.3
EOL	$5,600	$2,400	

ways the same as the expected value of perfect information, EVPI. We showed above that EVPI was $2,400. We have now shown that the expected opportunity loss of Machine B, which is the optimal act, is also $2,400. Once again, this is no accident. It will always occur. In the opportunity loss table we have been able to recommend the course of action and also find the expected value of perfect information for that decision problem, all in one step.

Just what is the meaning of the opportunity loss value in each cell of Figure 3–2? Each cell simply shows how much worse off one is if that is the result, compared with the best one could have done for that event. In many decision problems, it is quite easy to construct the opportunity loss table directly, without going through the payoff table. Consider the problem faced by a Christmas tree merchant who can place only one order for Christmas trees during the entire Christmas tree selling season. Suppose that the merchant buys trees for $2 and sells them for $6, for a $4 profit on each tree sold and a $2 loss on each tree unsold, assuming that trees have no salvage value. Suppose that it is known that either one, two, or three trees will be sold, each with a probability of ⅓. We can easily construct the payoff table in terms of opportunity loss directly for this problem. Figure 3–3 is the opportunity loss table for the Christmas tree problem.

Starting with the first event, the best thing to do if demand is one tree is to stock one tree. Hence there is zero opportunity loss in the upper left-hand corner of the opportunity loss table. If two trees are stocked and demand is only one tree, the merchant is $2 worse off; the $2 represents

FIGURE 3–3

Opportunity Loss Table (Christmas tree problem)

Events	Acts		
	Stock 1	*Stock 2*	*Stock 3*
Demand is 1 Tree	0	2	4
Demand is 2 Trees	4	0	2
Demand is 3 Trees	8	4	0

the loss from stocking a tree that could not be sold. If three trees are stocked and only one tree is demanded, the merchant is $4 worse off than with the best act for this demand.

If the demand is two trees, the optimal act is to stock two trees, again with zero opportunity loss. If the demand is two and one is stocked, the merchant turns out to be $4 worse off because of the $4 profit that could have been made on the second tree if it had been stocked. If three trees are stocked when demand is two, there is an opportunity loss of $2.

If the demand is three trees, the best course of action is to stock three, hence the zero opportunity loss in the lower right-hand corner of the opportunity loss table. If the merchant stocks one when demand is three, the result is $8 less than for the best act—a loss of $4 in forgone profit on each of two trees. If two trees had been stocked when demand is three, the merchant is $4 worse off—the lost profit on the one tree that could have been sold but was not in stock.

Figure 3–4 shows the payoff table in terms of dollars for this merchant. Going through the reasoning for this table is left as an exercise for the reader. It should be obvious at this point that the opportunity loss table (Figure 3–3) is consistent with the payoff table (Figure 3–4).

FIGURE 3–4

Payoff Table (Christmas tree problem)

Events	Acts		
	Stock 1	Stock 2	Stock 3
Demand is 1 Tree	4	2	0
Demand is 2 Trees	4	8	6
Demand is 3 Trees	4	8	12

3.4. IMPERFECT INFORMATION

The examples in the preceding section have assumed that additional information available to the decision maker is perfect information. Once the information has been obtained, there is no longer any uncertainty about which act will occur. The purpose of this section is to develop a framework for evaluating imperfect information. Perhaps one way of characterizing imperfect information is by saying that after a decision maker has received imperfect information, one knows more than before, but not as much as one would like to know. A decision maker using the EMV criterion would never pay more than EVPI to obtain additional information of any kind.

To illustrate imperfect information, consider the decision on the repair procedures to be used by a pump manufacturer. In any pump that comes in for repair, there are two sets of valves that may need attention. The upper valves are easily accessible, and tearing down the pump to reach these valves and making the necessary adjustments and replacements of gaskets costs only $40. To reach the lower valves, all the labor to reach the upper valves must also be performed. The total cost to dismantle the machine to reach the lower valves, make necessary adjustments, and replace necessary gaskets, is $100. If the pump is malfunctioning because of the upper valves, and the lower valves are serviced, the pump is nonetheless fixed because all necessary adjustments and gasket replacements are made on the upper valves in the process of servicing the lower valves. If only the upper valves are serviced but the problem lies in the lower valves, the initial servicing done on the upper valves is wasted, and an additional $100 must be spent to service the lower valves. From experience, it is known that the probability that only the upper valves need service is 0.6, and the probability that the lower valves need service is 0.4. This decision problem is modeled in the decision tree of Figure 3–5. From the expected monetary value calculated on this tree, it is apparent that the optimal course of action is to service the upper valves, and then service the lower valves only if they need it.

FIGURE 3–5

Decision Tree for Pump Problem

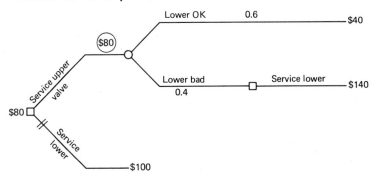

After some experimentation with pressure gauges, it was discovered that applying a pressure test at a particular port on the pump gave some additional information about the upper and lower valves. When applied to pumps with good lower valves, this pressure test yielded a high reading with probability $\frac{2}{3}$, a medium reading with probability $\frac{1}{4}$, a low reading with probability $\frac{1}{12}$. The probability that a machine with bad lower valves would yield a high pressure reading was $\frac{1}{4}$, medium $\frac{3}{8}$, and low $\frac{3}{8}$. These probabilities are shown in Figure 3–6. The pressure test

FIGURE 3–6

Probabilities for Pressure Test

If the Lower Valves Are:	The Probability for This Pressure Reading Is:		
	High	Medium	Low
OK....................	$\frac{2}{3}$	$\frac{1}{4}$	$\frac{1}{12}$
Bad...................	$\frac{1}{4}$	$\frac{3}{8}$	$\frac{3}{8}$

result is not perfect information, but it can be analyzed to see whether it can assist the decision maker in reducing the costs of fixing the pumps. It costs $5 to apply this pressure test. It is left as an exercise for the reader to show that EVPI is $16. Since the test costs less than perfect information is worth, one cannot rule out the test at this point.

The decision tree for the pump repair problem is shown in Figure 3–7, with the pressure test explicitly incorporated in the diagram. The sequence of acts and events for the use of the pressure tester is

1. The pressure gauge is read;
2. The decision about the repair procedure is made;
3. The true condition of the valves is determined.

FIGURE 3–7

Pump Repair Decision Tree

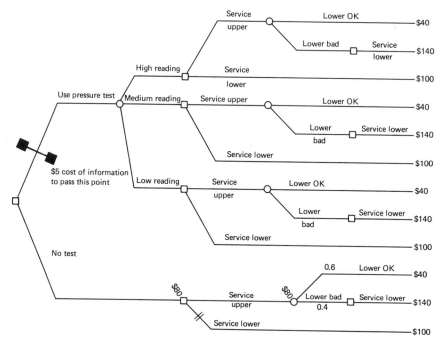

The decision tree in Figure 3–7 is complete except for probabilities. The probabilities are shown for the branch of the tree that does not use the pressure test; these are identical to the probabilities shown in Figure 3–5. There are several event nodes in Figure 3–7, however, for which the probabilities are not yet known. For example, the upper-most branch on the tree, at the right-most event node, lacks the probability that the lower valves are OK after a high reading has been observed. In Figure 3–6 the entry in the high column, OK row is tantalizingly close to the desired probability, but that probability statement says the probability that a high reading will result when the valves are OK is $\frac{2}{3}$. What is needed on the tree is the probability that the lower valves are OK when the reading has been high. *These two probability expressions are different from each other.* Similar differences occur for all of the right-most event nodes for the portion of the decision tree that uses the pressure tester. Furthermore, the decision tree also requires probabilities for high, medium, and low readings.

To find these unknown probabilities, a *probability tree* may be used. A probability tree is different from a decision tree in that only event nodes are shown. Figure 3–8 is a probability tree for the pump problem with the first event being the condition of the pump, and the subsequent events being the results of the pressure test. All probabilities for *this* tree are known from the problem statement. This statement of the problem contained

1. The probabilities for the various states of the pump, before the test.
2. The probabilities of the various pressure indications, given the information about the state of the pump.

The probability of each end point, which is the product of the probabilities on the two branches leading to that end point, is shown at each of the six end points on this probability tree. For example, the probability that the lower valves are OK and that the pressure test gives a high reading is 0.4.

FIGURE 3–8

Probability Tree for Pump Problem

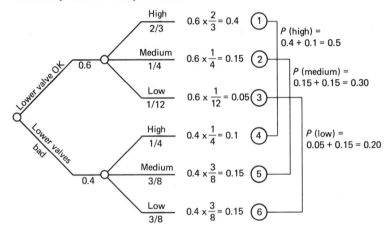

The end points in Figure 3–8 are numbered 1 through 6. End points 1 and 4 are the only end points that have a high pressure test result. Hence, the probability of a high pressure test result must be the sum of these two probabilities, or 0.5, as indicated on the diagram. End points 2 and 5 are the only two end points with a medium pressure result. The probability of obtaining the medium pressure test result is shown on the diagram to be 0.3. Similarly, the probability of a low pressure test reading is 0.2. These three numbers are three of the probabilities required for the decision tree, Figure 3–7.

Figure 3–9 is also a probability tree, but the sequence of events has been reversed so that the test result comes first, followed by the condition of the lower valves. The end point probabilities, which are identical to those shown in Figure 3–8, are also shown in this reversed probability

FIGURE 3–9

Reversed Probability Tree for Pump Problem

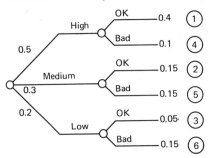

tree. The numbers of the end point nodes correspond to the same end points from Figure 3–8. In this reversed probability tree, all of the probabilities are shown except the probabilities of the right-most events. Following the upper-most branch as an example, 0.5 multiplied by the probability of following the OK branch, after a high pressure test, is equal to 0.4. Therefore, the probability of OK after high pressure is $0.4/0.5 = 0.8$, as shown in the tree of Figure 3–10. Thus, the six unknown probabilities are found by simple algebra. The complete reverse probability tree is shown in Figure 3–10.

All the probability information has now been developed for Figure 3–7. Figure 3–11 incorporates these probabilities, which were calculated in Figures 3–8, 3–9, and 3–10, into the pump repair decision tree. From the calculations shown in Figure 3–11 the expected cost of repair, if the

FIGURE 3–10

Reversed Probability Tree for Pump Problem

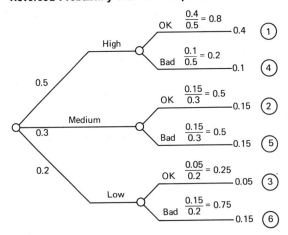

FIGURE 3–11

Pump Repair Decision Tree

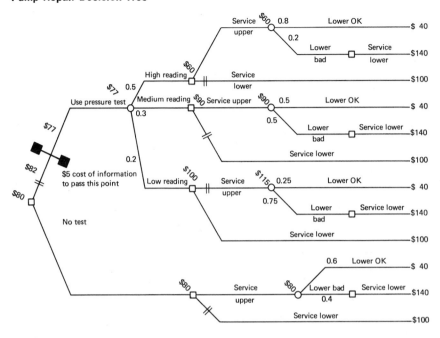

pressure tester is used, is $82, or $77 plus $5 for the test. The expected cost without the pressure tests, servicing the upper valves first, then the lower valves if needed, is $80. This analysis shows how the imperfect information available from the pressure tester can be explicitly incorporated into the decision procedure. In this particular example, it is not desirable to use the pressure tester. If the pressure test had cost only $1 (instead of $5), the expected cost of repair, using the tester, would be reduced by $4, to $78. In this case, it would be advantageous to use the pressure tester. The decision rule to be followed, which can be obtained from Figure 3–11, by following the unblocked actions, would be to service only the upper valves on either a high or a medium reading, but service both sets of valves if a low reading is obtained on the pressure test.

3.5.   EVALUATING IMPERFECT INFORMATION

The methodology that has been used above for evaluating imperfect information in the pump problem is quite general. It is sometimes helpful to state these generalizations symbolically so that their applicability is more apparent in other problems. This section states procedures for evaluating imperfect information.

One of the necessary prerequisites for this generalization is introduction of the symbolic notation for conditional probabilities. In Figure 3–6, it is stated that the probability of a high pressure reading, if the lower valves are OK, is $\frac{2}{3}$. This is stated symbolically as

$$P(\text{high}|\text{OK}) = \frac{2}{3},$$

which is read "the probability of high, given OK, is $\frac{2}{3}$." The information that appears at the right of the vertical line in the probability statement is called the "the given," or the information upon which the probability is conditioned. The information from Figure 3–6 can be shown in conditional probability notation as

$$P(\text{high}|\text{OK}) = \frac{2}{3}; \quad P(\text{medium}|\text{OK}) = \frac{1}{4}; \quad P(\text{low}|\text{OK}) = \frac{1}{12};$$
$$P(\text{high}|\text{bad}) = \frac{1}{4}; \quad P(\text{medium}|\text{bad}) = \frac{3}{8}; \quad P(\text{low}|\text{bad}) = \frac{3}{8}.$$

The probability tree shown in Figure 3–8 can be replaced by these probability statements, using the general multiplicative law of probabilities. This law of probability states

$$P(A \text{ and } B) = P(A) \times P(B|A) = P(B) \times P(A|B),$$

where A and B are any two events. Using this law the probabilities at the six end points in Figure 3–8 are calculated as

$$
\begin{array}{llll}
P(\text{OK and high}) & = P(\text{OK})P(\text{high}|\text{OK}) & = 0.6 \times \frac{2}{3} = 0.4; \\
P(\text{OK and Medium}) & = P(\text{OK})P(\text{medium}|\text{OK}) & = 0.6 \times \frac{1}{4} = 0.15; \\
P(\text{OK and low}) & = P(\text{OK})P(\text{low}|\text{OK}) & = 0.6 \times \frac{1}{12} = 0.05; \\
P(\text{bad and high}) & = P(\text{bad})P(\text{high}|\text{bad}) & = 0.4 \times \frac{1}{4} = 0.1; \\
P(\text{bad and medium}) & = P(\text{bad})P(\text{medium}|\text{bad}) & = 0.4 \times \frac{3}{8} = 0.15; \\
P(\text{bad and low}) & = P(\text{bad})P(\text{low}|\text{bad}) & = 0.4 \times \frac{3}{8} = 0.15. \\
\end{array}
$$

The probability of the test result "high" was calculated in Figure 3–5 as

$$
\begin{array}{lllll}
P(\text{high}) & = P(\text{OK and high}) & + & P(\text{bad and high}) & \\
& = \quad\quad 0.4 & + & 0.1 & = 0.5.
\end{array}
$$

A tabular format for doing these calculations is given in Figure 3–12. In general notation, using E_i to denote event i and I_k to denote information result k (pressure test result in this example), the probability of I_k is:

$$P(I_k) = \sum_i P(E_i \text{ and } I_k)$$

$$= \sum_i P(E_i) P(I_k|E_i).$$

The definition of conditional probability is

$$P(A|B) = \frac{P(A \text{ and } B)}{P(B)},$$

where A and B are any two events. This definition was used in Figure 3–7. For example,

$$P(\text{OK}|\text{high}) = \frac{P(\text{OK and high})}{P(\text{high})} = \frac{0.4}{0.5} = 0.8.$$

All of these may be combined into what is called Bayes' Theorem, for finding the conditional probability of a specific event h given an information result k:

$$P(E_h|I_k) = \frac{P(E_h \text{ and } I_k)}{P(I_k)} = \frac{P(E_h)P(I_k|E_h)}{\sum_i P(E_i)P(I_k|E_i)}.$$

The purpose of using Bayes' Theorem is to incorporate the additional information from the pressure test into the probabilities for the events.

The *prior* probabilities are the probabilities of events before additional imperfect information has been secured, $P(E_i)$. The *likelihoods* are the probabilities of the various information results, conditioned upon the events, $P(I_k|E_i)$. The information shown in Figure 3–6 could be called the likelihoods of various pressure test results, conditioned upon the events (the status of the lower valves).

The *posterior* probabilities, or the revised probabilities, are the probabilities for the events that apply after the additional information has been incorporated, $P(E_i|I_k)$. Thus, Bayes' Theorem combines the prior probabilities and the likelihoods, resulting in the revised or posterior probabilities of the events.

To evaluate imperfect information, each information result is con-

IGURE 3–12

abular Form for Computing Revised Probabilities (data from Figure 3–11)

Event E_i	$P(E_i)*$	Test Result, k	$P(I_k|E_i)$†	$P(I_k \text{ and } E_i)$‡	$P(E_i|I_k)$§
OK Bad	0.6 0.4	High	$\frac{2}{3}$ $\frac{1}{4}$	$0.6 \times \frac{2}{3} = 0.4$ $0.4 \times \frac{1}{4} = \underline{0.1}$ $0.5 = P(high)$	$0.4/0.5 = 0.8$ $0.1/0.5 = 0.2$
OK Bad	0.6 0.4	Medium	$\frac{1}{4}$ $\frac{3}{8}$	$0.6 \times \frac{1}{4} = 0.15$ $0.4 \times \frac{3}{8} = \underline{0.15}$ $0.30 = P(medium)$	$0.15/0.30 = 0.5$ $0.15/0.30 = 0.5$
OK Bad	0.6 0.4	Low	$\frac{1}{12}$ $\frac{3}{8}$	$0.6 \times \frac{1}{12} = 0.05$ $0.4 \times \frac{3}{8} = \underline{0.15}$ $0.20 = P(low)$	$0.05/0.20 = 0.25$ $0.15/0.20 = 0.75$

* Prior probability of the event.
† Likelihood, or probability of experimental result, given the event; $I_1 = High;$ $I_2 = Medium;$ $I_3 = Low.$
‡ Joint probability $= P(E_i) \times P(I_k|E_i)$.
§ Revised probability $= P(I_k \text{ and } E_i)|P(I_k)$.

sidered individually. The optimal course of action is considered for each information result, using the procedures of expectation and the revised probabilities. The best of these acts is selected. Noting the best act for information result k as $A^*|I_k$, the expected monetary value with additional information is calculated as

$$\text{EMV with additional information} = \sum_k \text{EMV}(A^*|I_k)P(I_k).$$

The difference between this value and the EMV that could be obtained without the additional information is called the *expected value of imperfect information* (EVII). This is the information cost at which the decision maker who is using EMV as a criterion is indifferent between obtaining or not obtaining the information. For any cost smaller than EVII, the decision maker would profit by obtaining the information; at a cost greater than EVII the information would not be economically justified. The result obtained by subtracting the cost of the imperfect information from EVII is called the *expected net gain from imperfect information*. If several alternative sources of imperfect information are available, the decision maker would choose that additional imperfect information that maximizes the expected net gain.

3.6. SAMPLING AS IMPERFECT INFORMATION

The evaluation of imperfect information is commonly applied in the determination of the optimal sample size in statistical problems. If the event or uncertain quantity is a population parameter, then statistical sampling theory may be used to find the likelihoods. Bayes' Theorem may be used to combine the prior probabilities and the likelihoods from sampling theory to yield a revised, or posterior, probability distribution for the events or value of the population parameter.

As an example, the unknown quantity may be the proportion of defective items in a lot of manufactured goods. A sample may be taken from that lot, and tested to find the number of defective items in the sample. Bayes' Theorem is then used to combine these two pieces of information, so that a decision can be made as to the disposition of the lot. It is important to determine the cost of imperfect information so that a rational decision on the sample size may be made. Imperfect and perfect information are related in that one would never pay more for imperfect or sample information than for perfect information. As an example, if perfect information is worth $100, and sampling costs $2 per observation, one would never buy more than 50 observations.

EXERCISES

3.1.   Construct the opportunity loss table that corresponds to this payoff table showing conditional profits:

Events	Acts			Probabilities
	A_1	A_2	A_3	
E_1.................	$300	$200	$500	0.6
E_2.................	700	900	400	0.4

3.2. Find the expected opportunity loss for each course of action in Problem 3.1, above. Compare this with the course of action that maximizes EMV for the original problem, stated in conditional profits.

3.3. Show that for each pair of acts, the difference between corresponding EOL values and EMV values is the same in absolute value, using the two preceding problems.

3.4. An entrepreneur would like to know how many sofa beds can be sold at the advertised price of $300. The sofa beds can be purchased now for $200 each; if they are not sold at the advertised price, they will be marked down and sold at $150 each. The probability distribution for demand for sofa beds indicates that 0, 1, 2, or 3 sofa beds will be sold, with probabilities of 0.4, 0.3, 0.2, and 0.1. The order for the beds must be placed before demand is known.

  a. How many should be ordered to maximize expected profits?
  b. Construct the opportunity loss table for this problem, and find the expected opportunity loss for each act.
  c. How much would it be worth to find out the number demanded before it is necessary to place the order?

3.5. Discuss: "Perfect information reverses the act/event sequence. Under uncertainty, an act is chosen, and then an event occurs. Under certainty, which is the case with perfect information, the event occurs and and then an act is selected."

3.6. Construct the opportunity loss table that corresponds to the payoff table for the Christmas Card problem, Problem 2.6. Find the expected opportunity loss for each act, and the expected value of perfect information.

3.7. Find the expected value of perfect information for the problem facing Ms. Entrep, Problem 2.7.

3.8. Find the expected value of perfect information for the newspaper salesperson, Problem 2.8(a), (c), and (d).

3.9. Find the expected value of perfect information for the Pine Tree Corporation, Problem 2.14.

3.10. A batch of flashbulbs is to be ordered for industrial use. Because of the advanced state-of-the-art of this particular type of flashbulb, a very high defect rate (bulbs that do not flash) is quite common. For several years the firm has been purchasing bulbs from Rediflash; the cost of bad flashbulbs in Rediflash's bulbs has been consistently at $2,000 for each batch. A new supplier has approached the user of flashbulbs; there is some question in the mind of the user about the defect rate for the new supplier. After checking trade references, the user believes there will be either a 10 percent defect rate or a 40 percent defect rate. The probability of the 10 percent defect rate is 0.7; the probability of the 40 percent defect rate is 0.3. If the new supplier's bulbs turn out to have a 10 percent defect rate, the cost of defects will be $1,000; if it turns out to be 40 percent, the cost of defects will be $4,000.

a. Which supplier should be used, in order to minimize cost of defective bulbs?

b. What is the value of perfect information to the user? What would constitute perfect information?

c. Suppose the new supplier offers to let the user randomly select one bulb from the batch being offered, and test the bulb to see if it is good or defective. What is the gain to the user, if this test is free?

3.11. A piece of electronic test equipment designed to test solid-state circuits is not completely reliable. Studies of the test have given these results:

When the tester is used on circuits known to be good, the test result is good with probability 0.95.

When the tester is used on circuits known to be bad, the test result is bad with probability 0.80.

The tester gives no result other than "good" or "bad"; from the probability statements above, it is obvious that a "good" test does not necessarily mean a "good" circuit.

a. If the test is being applied to circuits coming from a batch with 70 percent good circuits (and, of course, 30 percent bad circuits), what is the probability that a circuit that tests "good" is really "good"? What is the probability that a circuit that tests "bad" is really "bad"?

b. If the test is being applied to circuits coming from a batch with 95 percent good circuits (and, of course, 5 percent bad circuits), what is the probability that a circuit that tests "good" is really "good"? What is the probability that a circuit that tests "bad" is really "bad"?

c. If the test is being applied to circuits coming from a batch with 10 percent good circuits (and, of course, 90 percent bad circuits), what is the probability that a circuit that tests "good" is really "good"? What is the probability that a circuit that tests "bad" is really "bad"?

d. After observing the results from questions *a*, *b*, and *c*, above, why can the manufacturer not make a statement such as the following:

"If a test result is good, there is a _____ probability that the circuit is good"?

3.12. The test equipment described in Problem 3.11, above, is being used on a batch of circuits that is 70 percent good circuits (and, of course, 30 percent bad circuits). If a good circuit is not repaired, there is no opportunity loss. If a bad circuit is repaired, there is no opportunity loss. If a good circuit is repaired, there is an opportunity loss of $50 (the cost of the repair). If a bad circuit is not repaired, there is an opportunity loss of $200 (the subsequent costs of repairing the circuit after it has been used in a complex assembly).

    a. Without the test device, which act (repair or not repair) should be used on each circuit board? Obviously, it is impossible to look at a circuit board to determine its condition.

    b. If the test result shows "good," what should be done with a circuit board?

    c. If the test result shows "bad," what should be done with a circuit board?

    d. What is the maximum amount that the tester is worth on each circuit?

3.13. A firm is considering a final "go" decision on a new product. If the product is introduced and it is successful, the profit is $500,000. If the product is introduced and it is not successful, the loss is $300,000. There is no profit or loss if the product is not introduced. The management believes there is a 0.2 probability that the product will be successful.

    a. Based on the information above, should the product be introduced, to maximize expected profit?

    b. A consulting firm specializing in new product introduction has offered its services to the firm. Its "batting average" in similar situations is as follows:

> When advice was given on products that later proved to be successful (either by the client firm or by others in the marketplace), the firm gave "go" advice eight times out of ten.
>
> When advice was given on products that later proved to be unsuccessful (either by the client firm or by others in the marketplace), the firm gave "stop" advice 15 times out of 20.

The firm charges $5,000 to give advice. Should it be hired, in order to maximize expected profit?

3.14. A machine manufacturing struts is being set up by an inexperienced mechanic. The probability that it will be set up correctly is 0.40; the probability that it will be set up incorrectly is 0.60. When it is set up correctly, the output of the machine will have no defective struts. When it is set up incorrectly, half the time it will produce 30 percent defective, and the other half of the time it will produce 70 percent defective. Each defective part costs $100. A master mechanic can check the set-up for $2,000. A batch of 100 struts will be produced. The $2,000 for the master mechanic includes the cost of any necessary changes to assure all parts will be good.

a.   Before the batch is produced, should the set-up be checked by the master mechanic, in order to minimize expected cost?

b.   It is possible to make a pilot run of the process and produce one strut. The pilot run will have the same probabilities of a defective as the regular batch. The cost of the pilot run is $500. This cost includes the testing of the pilot strut to determine if it is defective. Should the pilot run be undertaken? Of course, the option of using the master mechanic is still available after the pilot has been produced and tested.

SUGGESTIONS FOR FURTHER STUDY

Brown, R. V., "Do Managers Find Decision Analysis Useful?" *Harvard Business Review*, vol. 48, 1970, pp. 78–79.

Brown, R. V., Kahr, A. S., and Peterson, C., *Decision Analysis for the Manager.* New York: Holt, Rinehart and Winston, 1974.

Davis, M. D., *Game Theory.* New York: Basic Books, Inc., 1970.

DeNeufville, R., and Keeney, R. L., "Use of Decision Analysis in Airport Development for Mexico City," in Drake, A. W., Keeney, R. L., and Morse, P. M., eds., *Analysis of Public Systems.* Cambridge, Mass.: M.I.T. Press, 1970.

Dyer, J. S., and Miles, R. F., Jr., "An Actual Application of Collective Choice Theory to the Selection of Trajectories for the Mariner Jupiter Saturn 1977 Project," *Operations Research*, vol. 24, March–April 1976, pp. 220–44.

Fishburn, P. C., *Utility Theory for Decision Making.* New York: John Wiley, 1970.

Halter, A. N., and Dean, G. W., *Decisions Under Uncertainty.* Cincinnati: South-Western Publishing Co., 1971.

Hogarth, R. W., "Cognitive Processes and the Assessment of Subjective Probability Distributions," *Journal of the American Statistical Association*, vol. 70, no. 350, June 1975, pp. 271–90.

Howard, R. A., Matheson, J. E., and North, D. W., "The Decision to Seed Hurricanes," *Science*, vol. 176, 1974, pp. 1191–1202.

Jones, J. M. *Introduction to Decision Theory.* Homewood, Ill.: Richard D. Irwin, Inc., 1977.

Luce, R. D., and Raiffa, H., *Games and Decisions.* New York: Wiley, 1958.

Newman, J. W., *Management Applications of Decision Theory.* New York: Harper & Row, 1971.

Raiffa, H. *Decision Analysis: Introductory Lectures on Choices Under Uncertainty.* Reading, Mass.: Addison-Wesley, 1970.

Schwartz, W. B., Gorry, G. A., Kassirer, J. P., and Essig, A., "Decision Analysis and Clinical Judgement," *The American Journal of Medicine*, vol. 55, 1973, pp. 459–72.

Von Neumann, J., and Morgenstern, O., *Theory of Games and Economic Behavior.* Princeton, N.J.: Princeton University Press, 1947.

Wheelwright, S. C., "Applying Decision Theory to Improve Corporate Management of Currency-Exchange Risks," *California Management Review*, vol. 17, 1975.

Winkler, R. L., *An Introduction to Bayesian Inference and Decision.* New York: Holt, Rinehart and Winston, 1972.

4

Linear Programming Models

4.1. INTRODUCTION

LINEAR PROGRAMMING and its special forms are probably the most widely used of all Operations Research techniques. The use of linear programming models and their solutions can be found in private industry and in the public sector dealing with a variety of problems ranging from crop selection in agriculture to the assignment of nurses to wards in a hospital to the development of fuel blending schedules in the petroleum industry. The references as well as the exercises at the end of this chapter deal with some of the above-mentioned applications and point to additional applications.

There are several reasons for the success of varied applications of linear programming:

1. The basic model is rather easily understood and dealt with by administrators and managers—that is, by people generally without a highly technical background who must make decisions.
2. The linear model is a suitable approximation for a large number of practical situations. As we noted in Chapter 1, we consider the decision making process from the point of view of a model; of course the model *must* be an accurate representation of the real-world process.
3. There are commercially available methods of solution for linear models that are economical to use. These methods will *always* find the op-

timal solution if one exists.[1] If no solution exists the methods will indicate where the model is inconsistent. The capabilities of the commercial methods include large problem size, report generation, and economy of operation. Almost any application of linear programming will require machine computation; the techniques underlying the computation methods are explained in Chapter 5.

4. The solution of the model, in addition to providing the optimal solution, provides the capability of dealing with "What if?" types of questions. That is, we can study the effect of changing resources and other aspects of the model, without having to completely re-solve the problem.

The purpose of this chapter is to introduce a variety of decision situations that can be modeled as linear programs. This introduction will also point to several models and principles that will enable you to deal with other appropriate problems that do not exactly fit the examples presented here or elsewhere. In textbook examples the data (though sometimes thinly disguised) are readily available; when you are dealing with real-world problems, knowing what data are needed is often a good part of the problem. As a result of constructing some general LP (linear programming) models in this chapter you should obtain some idea about the basic structure of LP models and the type of data required.

The term *linear programming* encompasses three notions:

1. The definition and nature of the problem and the construction of the model.
2. The solution of the model.
3. Analysis of the model and of its solution.

The additional (and perhaps the most important) aspect of LP is implementation of the model and its results. Some discussion of implementation can be found in Chapter 1 and Part II of the text. The remainder of this chapter will deal with the formulation of linear programs. The solution and analysis of the solution will be treated in subsequent chapters.

The initial aspect to be considered is the definition of the problem and construction of the LP model. While there are no clear-cut rules or formulas to be followed when constructing the model, there are some general guidelines that can aid in the modeling process. These general guidelines focus on the components of an LP model, as discussed in Section 4.2. Section 4.3 provides some general interpretations of the model's components and provides additional information about the construc-

---

[1] All of the major computer manufacturing companies provide extensive software packages that include a linear programming algorithm.

tion of a model to fit a particular situation. Section 4.4 presents a number of classical LP examples to illustrate how models have been constructed in some past situations.

While it is difficult to teach or present guidelines for proficiency in model building, the construction of the model is often half of the battle. The following sections, while not 100 percent foolproof, do provide a set of guidelines that will serve the reader well. Real proficiency in model building can come only with practice; to provide such practice, the exercises at the end of the chapter are recommended to the reader.

4.2. ELEMENTS OF A LINEAR MODEL

In general, a linear programming model is a linear representation of some decision process in which the decision maker seeks to choose, from among all possible alternatives, that one which is best according to some predetermined criterion. The set of all possible alternatives (*feasible solutions*) is determined by a set of linear relationships that describe the technology or reality of the process being modeled. The decision maker's criterion is a mathematical statement of the goals or objectives of the modeled process.

From this rather general statement we can determine the essential elements of a linear programming model:

1. *Variables.* Those quantities or aspects of the process that the decision maker is seeking to control. For the remainder of the book the decision variables will typically be denoted by lower case x with subscripts $x_1, x_2, x_3. \ldots$ Each subscript denotes a particular decision variable. The value of a variable typically answers a question, such as "How many books should I make?" or "How many tons of coal should I buy?"

2. *Objective function.* A mathematical statement of the goals or objectives of the decision maker. For the most part the examples and exercises will have as an objective either to maximize profits or to minimize costs, but other types are illustrated in the exercises. These include maximizing exposure of an advertising campaign, minimizing waste, minimizing completion time of a set of jobs and maximizing satisfaction with a set of assignments.

3. *Constraints.* These are mathematical statements that describe the technology or reality of the process being modelled and how the technology utilizes available resources. In a production setting, the constraints describe how raw materials are processed into finished products; in other settings, constraints describe resource utilization, maximum and/or minimum production levels, maximum demand, certain material balances that need to be maintained, and so on.

Associated with the above is another aspect of linear models in particular and any model in general—the problem of data collection. The data problem includes such things as what data are necessary, where they are to be found, and how accurate are the data and how accurate must other data be. These are difficult questions, and no definitive answers are now available or likely to become so in the future.[2]

In addition to the above elements, a linear programming model has associated with it a set of specific assumptions. The major assumption is that of *linearity;* that is, the mathematical relationships that express the objective function and the constraints must be *linear functions.*[3] The linearity of these functions can be expressed in terms of:

1. *Additivity property.* If a model is composed of several activities, the overall contribution to the objective function is the sum of the contributions of all the individual activities. Similarly, the utilization of each resource is the sum of utilization for each activity. That is to say, the contributions to the objective function are additive. Also, if several activities are utilizing a resource, this utilization is additive.
2. *Proportionality property.* The contribution of each variable to the objective function and to each constraint is proportional to the value of the variable. In other words, the total contribution of an activity to the objective function or a constraint is the contribution per unit multiplied by the number of units.

The second basic assumption is that we are dealing with linear functions in which the decision variables are *continuous;* that is, their values are not restricted to integers. For example, a linear programming model of a boat factory might indicate that the optimal solution is to produce 167.98 cabin cruisers; such a fractional result must have a useful interpretation if linear programming is to be used. Integer programming models (where some or all of the decision variables must be integer-valued) will be treated in Chapter 8.

The third basic assumption is that there is a *single objective function.* In some decision making settings, there may be several goals or objectives that may be conflicting. For the models and exercises of this chapter, we assume that if there is such a conflict then the decision maker can reduce the situation to a *single objective.* The case of multiple objectives will be treated in Chapter 7.

Finally, we assume the model to be *deterministic;* that is, all the data we need to construct the model are known with certainty. While this is

---

[2] R. E. D. Woolsey, *Interfaces,* vol. 5, no. 2, February 1975, has given a humorous and very appropriate discussion of some of these issues.

[3] A function f of n variables $x_1, \ldots, x_n$ is linear if and only if $f = a_1x_1 + a_2x_2 + a_3x_3 + \ldots + a_nx_n$, where $a_1, \ldots, a_n$ are arbitrary real numbers.

seldom the case with real-world problems we will, through the techniques of Chapter 6, be able to analyze the model for changes in the data.

To illustrate the above concepts consider the following example.

Example 4.1.

A butcher is mixing the day's supply of meatloaf. There are two grades of meatloaf, Grade 1 and Grade 2. The decision is to determine how many trays of each kind of meatloaf to make. There is no constraint of integrality; $3\frac{1}{3}$ trays or any fractional number of trays may be made. The profit is increased by $6 for each tray of Grade 1 that is mixed, and by $4 for each tray of Grade 2 that is mixed. If there were no constraints, the butcher would want to make a lot of both kinds of meatloaf; the profit would then be very large. The constraints that he must consider are:

Constraint 1. The butcher cannot sell more than six trays of meatloaf per day.

Constraint 2. Only nine hours of mixing time are available for the butcher and staff. It takes two hours to mix a tray of Grade 1 and one hour to mix a tray of Grade 2.

Constraint 3. The butcher has only 16 feet of shelf space for meatloaf. Each tray of grade 1 requires two feet of shelf space. Each tray of Grade 2 requires three feet of shelf space.

For this problem the elements of the linear programming model are:

Variables:

x_1 = number of trays of Grade 1 meatloaf to be mixed
x_2 = number of trays of Grade 2 meatloaf to be mixed.

Note that the variable values answer the question "How many trays should be mixed?"

Objective:

$$\text{Maximize profit:}\quad \max 6x_1 + 4x_2.$$

Constraints:

$x_1 + x_2 \leq 6$	constraint for the number of trays
$2x_1 + x_2 \leq 9$	mixing constraint
$2x_1 + 3x_2 \leq 16$	shelf constraint
$x_1, x_2 \geq 0$	negative numbers of trays have no meaning.

While this is a simplified example, it does allow one to identify the elements of an LP model. The butcher's problem can be expressed in terms of the properties of linear functions, additivity and proportionality, as follows:

Objective function: The profit *per tray* of Grade 1 meatloaf is \$6; hence, by the *proportionality property*, the *total* profit from Grade 1 is $6x_1$ where x_1 is the number of trays of Grade 1 meatloaf. Similarly the total profit for Grade 2 meatloaf is $4x_2$. The *additivity property* then says the *total profit* is $6x_1 + 4x_2$.

Constraint 1:   The additivity property states that the total number of trays is the sum of the number of trays of each type $(x_1 + x_2)$. Since the butcher cannot sell more than six trays per day the total number of trays must be less than or equal to six; *i.e.,* $(x_1 + x_2 \leq 6)$.

Constraint 2:   The proportionality property states that the total mixing time for Grade 1 is $2x_1$ and for Grade 2 is x_2. The additivity property gives the total mixing time as $(2x_1 + x_2)$, which must be less than or equal to 9; *i.e.,* $2x_1 + x_2 \leq 9$.

A similar analysis can be applied to Constraint 3.

4.3. LINEAR PROGRAMMING MODELS

One can construct the general linear programming model as:

Optimize

$$c_1x_1 + c_2x_2 + \cdots + c_nx_n$$

subject to

$$a_{11}x_1 + a_{12}x_2 + \cdots + a_{1n}x_n \left(\begin{matrix} \leq \\ = \\ \geq \end{matrix}\right) b_1$$

$$a_{21}x_1 + a_{22}x_2 + \cdots + a_{2n}x_n \left(\begin{matrix} \leq \\ = \\ \geq \end{matrix}\right) b_2$$

$$\vdots$$

$$a_{m1}x_1 + a_{m2}x_2 + \cdots + a_{mn}x_n \left(\begin{matrix} \leq \\ = \\ \geq \end{matrix}\right) b_m$$

The nature of a problem will determine which of the three relations $(\leq, =, \geq)$ appears in each constraint of a particular model.

The above model can be stated more compactly as:

Maximize or minimize

$$\sum_{j=1}^{n} c_jx_j \tag{4-1}$$

subject to

$$\sum_{j=1}^{n} a_{ij}x_j \left(\genfrac{}{}{0pt}{}{\leqq}{\genfrac{}{}{0pt}{}{=}{\geqq}}\right) b_i \quad i = 1,2, \ldots ,m \qquad (4\text{--}2)$$

$$x_j \geq 0 \qquad\qquad j = 1,2, \ldots ,n. \qquad (4\text{--}3)$$

We can identify and interpret the various components of the models as follows:

The *objective function* (Equation 4–1) will typically be either *maximize profits* (in which case each of the c_j values corresponds to the unit profit contribution of the corresponding variable) or *minimize cost* (in which case the values of the c_j correspond to the unit costs of the variables).

The *constraints* (Equation 4–2) are of three basic types:

1. *Less than or equal to* ($\leqq$): These constraints generally apply to resource utilization; the use of a resource cannot exceed the amount available. A constraint of this type could also be used to describe a maximum production or sales level. For example:

   $$a_{i1}x_1 + a_{i2}x_2 + \cdots + a_{in}x_n \leq b_i$$

   describes the technology of the process for a_{i1} is the number of units of resource i needed to produce one unit of product one (x_1) and so on. *In general, a_{ij} is the amount of resource i needed to produce one unit of product j and b_i is the amount of resource i available.* In the butcher shop example we have three constraints of this type.

2. *Equal to* ($=$): These constraints describe a set of conditions that must be met exactly. Such conditions are often specific production levels, certain proportional relationships that need to be maintained, and so on. *In this case a_{ij} has the interpretation of the contribution of one unit of product j toward the requirement of resource i.* For example in the butcher shop problem if we required *exactly* six trays of meatloaf the first constraint becomes $x_1 + x_2 = 6$ where $a_{11} = a_{12} = 1$, and the resource is number of trays.

3. *Greater than or equal to* ($\geqq$): generally used to describe minimum requirements.

   $$a_{i1}x_1 + \cdots + a_{i1}x_n \geq b_i,$$

   where b_i is the minimum level required. *The coefficient a_{ij} is interpreted as the contribution of one unit of product j to meeting the requirement on resource i.* For example, we may have required *at least* six trays, which means constraint 1 would have been

   $$x_1 + x_2 \geq 6.$$

The form and interpretation of the constraints and the input-output coefficients a_{ij} can do much to aid us in construction of models and in obtaining the data necessary for such a model. For the examples that follow we will use the previous interpretations as an aid in constructing the model.

The *nonnegativity restrictions* (Equation 4–3) are the final aspect of the general model. These require that the decision must have non-negative values. This is certainly reasonable since we need not consider producing −3 trays of meatloaf.[4]

When constructing models we will proceed in the following steps:

Step 1: Identify the variables.

Step 2: Determine the objective function—this would include the profit or cost contributions, etc.

Step 3: Formulate the constraints—

    a. Determine resource requirements and availability.

    b. Determine process technology, a_{ij}.

Example 4.2.

The **Candid** Company manufactures three grades of camera lenses—low, medium, and high. The production process involves three opera-

FIGURE 4–1

Production Data for Candid Company (minutes per lens)

Grade of Lens	Lens Formation	Inspection	Finishing
Low	2.25	3	1.5
Medium	2.50	6	2.5
High	3.0	12	5

tions: lens formation, in which the molten glass is formed into a crude lens; inspection, a complex process in which the properties of the lens are determined and the lens is classified according to grade; finishing, an automated procedure that grinds and polishes the lens.

The production time data and the cost and revenue data for the company are summarized in Figures 4–1 and 4–2.

The problem is to decide the number of each type of lens to produce on an hourly basis so that hourly profits are maximized.[5]

---

[4] If in some settings we need to consider negative variables we can express this negative variable as the difference of two positive variables. For example $x_1 < 0$ then $x_1 = x_1' - x_1''$, where $x_1'' > x_1' > 0$. (e.g., $-10 = 3 - 13$).

[5] This statement of the problem is probably a surrogate for the true production process, which is likely to be: There is a machine(s) that forms the lens; the quality of the lens is a function of the machine set-up or the material input to the machine. The number of lenses then can be directly converted to the machine requirement.

FIGURE 4–2

Cost and Revenue Data for Candid Company

Grade of Lens	Manufactur- ing Cost	Material Cost	Total Cost	Selling Price
Low......................	$18.00	$ 6.50	$24.50	$ 40.00
Medium..................	32.50	8.00	40.50	60.00
High.....................	54.00	12.50	66.50	100.00

Variables:

x_1 = number of low-grade lenses to be produced
x_2 = number of medium-grade lenses to be produced
x_3 = number of high-grade lenses to be produced.

Objective function:

Maximize profit = revenue − cost
$$= (40 - 24.50)x_1 + (60 - 40.50)x_2 + (100 - 66.50)x_3$$
$$= 15.5x_1 + 19.5x_2 + 33.50x_3.$$

Constraints:
Formulation process:

a_{11} = 2.25 minute/lens   60 minutes available
a_{12} = 2.5 minute/lens
a_{13} = 3   minute/lens;

thus

$$2.25x_1 + 2.5x_2 + 3x_3 \leq 60.$$

Inspection process:

a_{21} = 3   minute/lens 60 minutes available
a_{22} = 6   minute/lens
a_{23} = 12   minute/lens;

thus

$$3x_1 + 6x_2 + 12x_3 \leq 60.$$

Finishing process:

a_{31} = 1.5 minute/lens 60 minutes available
a_{32} = 2.5 minute/lens
a_{33} = 5   minute/lens;

thus

$$1.5x_1 + 2.5x_2 + 5x_3 \leq 60.$$

Nonnegativity restriction:

$$x_1, x_2, x_3 \geq 0.$$

4.4. SOME SPECIFIC MODELS

Resource Allocation Models

The problems within this class of models are identified by several names—resource allocation, activity analysis, product mix—and all are characterized *as problems of allocating scarce resources among competing activities in such a way to maximize profits.* The lens production example of the last section is typically called a *product-mix model*—that is, we want to determine the best mix of products. The elements of Section 3 can be identified as:

Variables: x_j = number of items of type j to produce; $j = 1, \ldots, n$.

Objective function: Maximize profit = $\displaystyle\sum_{j=1}^{n} c_j x_j$,

    where c_j = profit per unit of type j.

Constraints: Generally of the form $\displaystyle\sum_{j=1}^{n} a_{ij} x_j \leq b_i$

    b_i = amount of resource i available; $i = 1, \ldots, m$.

    a_{ij} = number of units of resource i required to produce 1 unit of product j.

Other types of constraints are: upper limit on production or sales, minimum production levels, and so on.

The following example illustrates several types of constraints.

Example 4.3.

A company manufactures wallpaper of both the unpasted or prepasted varieties and holds the rights to two exclusive designs. The manufacturing process involves three steps: printing, prepasting (which even the unpasted paper must pass through), and packaging. Because of the age of the machinery the printer can operate at most ten hours per day, the prepaster no more than 12 hours per day, and the packing machine no more than five hours per day.

From the past records of the company operation we have gathered the following information:

1. The production of 100 rolls of unpasted paper of Pattern 1 required 20 hours in the prepaster, 30 hours of printer time, and 10 hours to pack. Pattern 2 paper required 30, 50, and 10 hours, respectively.
2. The production of 100 rolls of prepasted paper of Pattern 1 required 50 hours in the prepaster, 100 hours of printer time, and 10 hours to pack. Pattern 2 paper required 70, 150, and 10 hours, respectively.

The recent trend in the market for wallpaper indicates the following profits per roll.

Type	Pattern 1	Pattern 2
Unpasted........................	$1.00	$1.25
Prepasted......................	2.25	2.75

Marketing considerations cause the company to want to have at least ten rolls of Pattern 1 and 12 rolls of Pattern 2 available. Find the production schedule to maximize profit.

The model: Let

$$x_1 = \text{number of rolls of Pattern 1, unpasted}$$
$$x_2 = \text{number of rolls of Pattern 2, unpasted}$$
$$x_3 = \text{number of rolls of Pattern 1, prepasted}$$
$$x_4 = \text{number of rolls of Pattern 2, prepasted.}$$

Assuming the company's past data is an accurate indication of the resources required per roll, we formulate the model as:

Maximize

$$x_1 + 1.25x_2 + 2.25x_3 + 2.75x_4$$

subject to

$$
\begin{aligned}
0.2x_1 + 0.3x_2 + 0.5x_3 + 0.7x_4 &\leq 12 \quad \text{(prepaster)} \\
0.3x_1 + 0.5x_2 + x_3 + 1.5x_4 &\leq 10 \quad \text{(printer)} \\
0.1x_1 + 0.1x_2 + 0.1x_3 + 0.1x_4 &\leq 5 \quad \text{(packing)} \\
x_1 + x_3 &\geq 10 \quad \text{(market} \\
& \qquad\qquad \text{requirements)} \\
x_2 + x_4 &\geq 12 \\
x_1, x_2, x_3, x_4 &\geq 0.
\end{aligned}
$$

Another resource allocation model is the so-called *Diet Problem*. The diet problem is one of the earliest applications of LP; it is still relevant today. The elements of the model can be identified as:

Variables: x_j = amount (pounds, servings, etc.) of food type j to include in the diet.

Objective function: Minimize cost = $\displaystyle\sum_{j=1}^{n} c_j x_j$;

c_j = cost per unit of food type j.

Constraints: Generally of the form $\displaystyle\sum_{j=1}^{n} a_{ij} x_j \geq b_i$

b_i = required amount of nutrient i to be present in the diet.
a_{ij} = amount of nutrient i contained in one unit of food j.

Other types of constraints could include certain food combinations for variety, certain combinations of the basic foods, and so on. For example, such constraints could be fish must be served at least once per week, each meal must include one green vegetable, eight ounces of milk must be served per day, and so on.

The following example deals with a feed mix model for animal consumption, while in Exercise 23 you will be asked to construct a diet for human consumption.

Example 4.4.

The problem is to determine the least-cost feed composition for hogs, subject to certain restrictions on the components of the feed. The ingredients and their costs are:

Ingredient	Variable	Cost per Lb.	*Proportion of Each Ingredient That Is:*				
			Protein	Fiber	Fat	Iron	Calcium
Alfalfa............	x_1	$0.041	0.19	0.17	0.023	0.016	0.0007
Corn.............	x_2	0.032	0.082	0.023	0.036	0.0006	0.0022
Barley...........	x_3	0.043	0.11	0.076	0.017	0.0057	0.0012
Fish meal........	x_4	0.084	0.048	0.09	0.072	0.048	0.027
Oats.............	x_5	0.035	0.115	0.119	0.038	0.0009	0.0011
Soybeans.........	x_6	0.064	0.48	0.028	0.005	0.0024	0.0019
Minimum requirement in total mix........			210	50	55	10	4.5
Maximum allowable in total mix........						10.5	6

If a production of at least 1,000 pounds is required, and we define the variables in terms of pounds of ingredients, the model is:

Minimize

$$0.041\ x_1 + 0.032\ x_2 + 0.043\ x_3 + 0.084x_4 + 0.035\ x_5 + 0.064\ x_6$$

subject to

$$
\begin{aligned}
x_1 + x_2 + x_3 + x_4 + x_5 + x_6 &\geq 1000 \\
0.19\ x_1 + 0.082\ x_2 + 0.11\ x_3 + 0.048x_4 + 0.115\ x_5 + 0.48\ x_6 &\geq 210 \\
0.17\ x_1 + 0.023\ x_2 + 0.076\ x_3 + 0.09\ x_4 + 0.119\ x_5 + 0.028\ x_6 &\geq 50 \\
0.023\ x_1 + 0.036\ x_2 + 0.017\ x_3 + 0.072x_4 + 0.038\ x_5 + 0.005\ x_6 &\geq 55 \\
0.016\ x_1 + 0.0006x_2 + 0.0057x_3 + 0.048x_4 + 0.0009x_5 + 0.0024x_6 &\geq 10 \\
0.016\ x_1 + 0.0006x_2 + 0.0057x_3 + 0.048x_4 + 0.0009x_5 + 0.0024x_6 &\leq 10.5 \\
0.0007x_1 + 0.0022x_2 + 0.0012x_3 + 0.027x_4 + 0.0011x_5 + 0.0019x_6 &\geq 4.5 \\
0.0007x_1 + 0.0022x_2 + 0.0012x_3 + 0.027x_4 + 0.0011x_5 + 0.0019x_6 &\leq 6 \\
x_1,\ x_2,\ x_3,\ x_4,\ x_5,\ x_6 &\geq 0.
\end{aligned}
$$

Transportation Models

A widely used special type of LP model is the *Transportation Model*. This class of problem is important for several reasons. It has a special structure that results in a computationally efficient solution procedure (to be treated in Chapter 6). It also has a wide variety of applications, and it has several modifications that further increase the range of applicability.

The transportation problem can be stated as follows: There is a set of sources (supply points, for example, factories, warehouses), which contain quantities of a single commodity *to be shipped* to a set of destina-

FIGURE 4–3

Conceptual Model of Transportation Problem

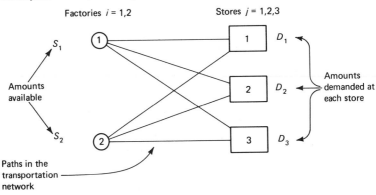

tions (demand points, for example, warehouses, stores). The shipment takes place across some transportation network—regularly scheduled airplane routes, waterways, railways, highways—and for each path in the network there is a shipping cost per unit shipped. The problem is to minimize the total shipping cost while meeting at least the demand at the demand points and not exceeding the supply at the supply points. For the present, assume that the total amount available for shipment is equal to the total amount demanded. A conceptual model is given in Figure 4–3.

The elements of the general model are:

Variables: x_{ij} amount to be shipped from factory i to store j.

Objective function: Minimize cost $= \sum_i \sum_j c_{ij} x_{ij}$,

where $c_{ij} =$ cost of shipping one unit from factory i to store j.

Constraints:

A. Amount shipped out of a supply point is equal to the amount available, for example:

$$x_{11} + x_{12} + x_{13} = S_1.$$

In general this constraint is:

$$\sum_j x_{ij} = S_i \quad \text{for each } i = 1, \ldots, m.$$

B. Amount shipped into a demand point is equal to the amount required, for example:

$$x_{11} + x_{21} = D_1.$$

In general

$$\sum_i x_{ij} = D_j \quad \text{for each } j = 1, \ldots, n.$$

C. Finally, we require that we ship only nonnegative quantities:

$$x_{ij} \geq 0.$$

The general transportation model is:

Minimize

$$\sum_i \sum_j c_{ij} x_{ij} \tag{4-4}$$

subject to

$$\sum_j x_{ij} = D_j; \quad j = 1, \ldots, n \tag{4-5}$$

$$\sum_j x_{ij} = S_i; \quad i = 1, \ldots, m \tag{4-6}$$

$$x_{ij} \geq 0, \tag{4-7}$$

where total supply equals total demand, that is:

$$\sum_j D_j = \sum_i S_i. \tag{4-8}$$

Some remarks are in order concerning the general model (4–4)–(4–8):

1. The assumptions that total supply is equal to total demand and that the constraints (4–5), (4–6) are equalities are not as restrictive as they may seem. These assumptions provide a computationally efficient method of solution (See Chapter 6).

FIGURE 4–4

Tabular Form of Transportation Problem

Origins	Destinations				Supplies
	1	2	. . .	n	
1	c_{11}	c_{12}	. . .	c_{1n}	S_1
2	c_{21}	c_{22}	. . .	c_{2n}	S_2
. . .	. . .	. . .	. . .	. . .	. . .
m	c_{m1}	c_{m2}	. . .	c_{mn}	S_m
Demands	D_1	D_2	. . .	D_n	$\Sigma D = \Sigma S$

If $\sum_j D_j < \sum_i S_i$, the condition (4–8) can be met by inserting a dummy point with demand equal to the difference $\sum_i S_i - \sum_j D_j$. For example, if $S_1 = 10$ and $S_2 = 15$, while $D_1 = D_2 = D_3 = 7$, then the dummy demand point $D_{dummy} = 4$ is created. Since this new demand point gives rise to routes $x_{1,dummy}$ and $x_{2,dummy}$ the coefficient $c_{i,dummy}$ must be properly defined so that the objective function (4–4) gives the correct value. If the coefficients are set as $c_{i,dummy} = 0$ for each i the dummy demand points will not affect the objective function. A similar situation is used to construct a dummy supply point if demand exceeds supply.[6]

Once $\sum_i S_i = \sum_j D_j$, it can be shown that supply and demand constraints of the form

$$\sum_i x_{ij} \geq D_j; \quad j = 1, \ldots, n \tag{4–9}$$

$$\sum_j x_{ij} \leq S_i; \quad i = 1, \ldots, m \tag{4–10}$$

can be converted to equalities of the form of Equations (4–5) and (4–6) without changing the meaning of the model. For those readers interested in a more thorough discussion of this matter, the references at the end of this chapter provide appropriate sources.

---

[6] After completing Chapter 5 you will recognize the dummy supply and demand points as *slack variables*.

2. As a result of the special structure of the model we can make the following remark: *If total supply equals total demand and each supply and demand is integer-valued there will be an integer optimal solution.* Here is a general class of LP problems for which we can guarantee integer solutions.

3. The general algebraic model (4-4)-(4-8) can be reduced to a *tabular model* that depicts almost graphically the nature of the problem. The tabular form is given in Figure 4-4.

4. If a particular route is not possible, this restriction can be included in the model by letting the cost associated with that route be arbitrarily large.

Example 4.5.

An oil company with three supply depots supplies four power generation stations with fuel. The capacities of the supply depots are 5,000 gallons, 10,000 gallons, and 12,000 gallons, respectively. The required amounts have been estimated at 5,000 gallons, 4,000 gallons, 7,000 gallons, 8,000 gallons. The shipping costs ($/gallon) are given in the following table.

Depot	Plant			
	1	*2*	*3*	*4*
1	0.12	0.10	0.08	0.11
2	0.09	0.11	0.11	0.13
3	0.10	0.14	0.13	0.07

In order to formulate an LP model to minimize costs we first note that

$$\Sigma S_i = 27,000 \neq \Sigma D_j = 24,000 \text{ gallons};$$

therefore we introduce a dummy demand point with demand of 3,000. The tabular representation is given in Figure 4-5.

If there is no usable route, for example, from Depot 1 to Plant 2, this fact would be modeled by changing c_{12} from 0.10 to an arbitrarily large number such as 10^9.

Within transportation models there are two special models that greatly increase the range of applicability.

Transshipment Models. The transportation model allows for shipment from *sources directly* to *destinations.* However in many real-world problems it is necessary to allow for shipments from source to source, or from source to some intermediate point and then to the destination, or from destination to destination. For example, in most production prob-

FIGURE 4–5

Tabular Model of Example 4.5

Supply Points	Demand Points					Supplies
	1	*2*	*3*	*4*	*Dummy*	
1	0.12	0.10	0.08	0.11	0	5,000
2	0.09	0.11	0.11	0.13	0	10,000
3	0.10	0.14	0.13	0.07	0	12,000
Demands	5,000	4,000	7,000	8,000	3,000	

lems the production takes place at a set of factories; the product is then shipped to regional warehouses for further distribution to the retail outlets. The shipments through the intermediate points are called *transshipments.*

Such shipments are not allowed according to general transportation model, and we might consider treating the transshipment model as any other LP model. This would fail to take advantage of the special structure of the transportation model. In order to maintain this structure and the associated efficient computational procedure, we will transform the transshipment model into the ordinary transportation problem by enlarging the model.

To illustrate the development of transshipment models consider the following description:

Example 4.6.

A company operates two quarries (Nodes 1 and 2 in Figure 4–6) to supply a particular grade of crushed limestone for three projects. Projects 1 and 2 (Nodes 5 and 6) involve the construction of highways, and the company has contracted to supply the base material for the foundations. Project 3 (Node 7) is the stockpiling of gravel for use by the state highway department during the winter months. The raw limestone is transported to two plants (Nodes 3 and 4) where it is crushed and prepared for use. Quarry 1 can supply ten loads per day; Quarry 2 can supply 15 loads per day. Plant 1 has a stockpile from which five loads per day can be taken. The demand at each project is ten loads per day. Each load is 100 tons.

In Figure 4–6, a positive number indicates a supply; a negative number indicates a demand; and a zero indicates equal supply and demand (a pure transshipment point).

Such a network can be balanced (to make total supply equal to total demand) by the addition (if necessary) of dummy supply or demand points. In this example, Nodes 1 and 2 correspond to *pure supply points* in that there is *flow only out of* these nodes. Nodes 5, 6, and 7 are *pure demand points* in that there is *flow only into* these nodes. The remaining Nodes, 3 and 4, are both supply and demand points and are referred to as *transshipment points;* there is *flow into and out of* these nodes.

FIGURE 4–6

Transshipment Model

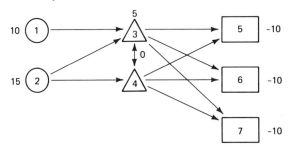

The total supply available in the entire network is $10 + 15 + 5 = 30$. (This total supply has also been called a "buffer stock.") To construct the tabular model:

Assign a *row* to each *pure supply point.*

Assign a *column* to each *pure demand point.*

Assign a *row and column* to each *transshipment point.*

For the pure supply points the supply is the original supply at that point.

For the pure demand point the demand is the original demand at that point.

For the transshipment points the supply is the buffer stock adjusted by the supply ($+$) or demand ($-$) at that point; and the demand is the buffer stock.

Since the tableau will contain routes that are not present in the original model, we adopt the following conventions:

$c_{ii} = 0$ for those i corresponding to transshipment points. These are fictitious routes added to facilitate the construction of the transportation model.

$c_{ij} = + \infty$ for route i, j not in original model. The assignment of such costs effectively eliminates those routes from consideration.

FIGURE 4–7

Transportation Tableau for Example 4.6

Supply Points	Demand Points					Supplies
	3	*4*	*5**	*6**	*7**	
1†						10
2†						15
3						30 + 5
4						30 + 0
Demands	30	30	10	10	10	

* Pure demand points.
† Pure supply points.

For Example 4.6 the buffer stock is: $10 + 15 + 5 = S_1 + S_2 + S_3$. The shaded squares indicate those routes are not allowable; for automatic computation, such a situation could be handled by giving an arbitrarily large cost to those routes. A complete description of why the above procedure is applicable would take us far afield. The reasoning for the above can be expanded as follows:

Every transshipment model is a special type of *network flow model.* A network flow model can be characterized as a set of *nodes,* a set of *arcs,* and supplies and demands. The model sets up flows over the arcs from supply to demand points. The previous model can be translated into a mathematical statement by describing the flow at each node:

Node

1	x_{13}	=	10
2	$x_{23} + x_{24}$	=	15
3	$x_{34} + x_{35} + x_{36} + x_{37} - x_{13} - x_{23} - x_{43} =$		5
4	$x_{43} + x_{45} + x_{47} - x_{34} - x_{24}$	=	0
5	$-x_{35} - x_{45}$	=	-10
6	$-x_{36} - x_{46}$	=	-10
7	$-x_{37} - x_{47}$	=	-10.

As can be seen in Figure 4–7, the above equations correspond to those rows and columns for sources (supply points) and sinks (demand points). For the transshipment points, if one subtracts the demand column from the supply row then the above equations result. The use of the buffer stock guarantees the solution to one model is feasible for the other.

Assignment Models. Another useful modification of the transportation model is the *assignment model.* The general statement of the assignment model is: There are n tasks to be performed by n persons. Each task must be done and each person can do only one task. There is a cost associated with assigning Task i to Person j; the assignment is to be made so as to minimize cost.

The general transportation model is converted to the assignment model by requiring $n = m$ and $S_i = D_j = 1$ for all i, j. This conversion results in:

Minimize

$$\sum_i \sum_j c_{ij} x_{ij} \qquad (4\text{--}11)$$

subject to

$$\sum_i x_{ij} = 1, \qquad (4\text{--}12)$$

$$\sum_j x_{ij} = 1 \qquad (4\text{--}13)$$

where $\qquad x_{ij} = \begin{cases} 1 \text{ if Person } i \text{ is assigned to Task } j \\ 0 \text{ if Person } i \text{ is } not \text{ assigned to Task } j \end{cases} \qquad (4\text{--}14)$

Earlier the value of a variable provided a quantitative answer to a question. In the assignment model the question is qualitative: "Should Person i perform Task j?" To convert this question to a quantitative form, it is rephrased: "How many times should Person i perform Task j?" By adding the requirement that the answer, x_{ij}, be either 0 or 1 the answer to either question has the same meaning. To illustrate these ideas consider the problem faced by a hospital administrator.[7]

Example 4.7.

A hospital administrator wants to study the cost of staffing the hospital. The administrator begins the study by considering the classifications head nurse (HN), assistant head nurse (AHN), staff nurse (SN), and aide and some of the possible duties to which they can be assigned. The administrator then constructs a table that delineates the cost (in dollars) of assigning various personnel to duties. These costs are given by Figure 4–8.

The administrator constructs an assingment model by defining

$$x_{ij} = \begin{cases} 1 \text{ if person } i \text{ is assigned to Job } j \\ 0 \text{ otherwise} \end{cases}$$

for which we want to:

---

[7] This example is a modification of a model presented in Wolfe and Lan, "Staffing the Nursing Unit," *Nursing Research* vol. 14, no. 4, 1965. Additional references related to such models are found among the references given at the end of this chapter.

FIGURE 4–8

Cost-Assignment Table for Example 4.7

Person	(1) Surgery Assistant	(2) Surgery Prep	(3) Technical Duty	(4) Mainte- nance	(5) Escort
HN 1	$8.52	$33.84	$9.87	$4.32	$14.10
AHN 2	7.92	31.44	9.17	3.93	13.10
SN 3	7.56	30.50	8.75	3.75	12.50
Aide 4	∞	21.12	9.24	4.17	8.40
Clerk 5	∞	43.92	∞	2.1	13.40

Minimize

$$\sum_i \sum_j c_{ij} x_{ij}$$

subject to

$$\sum_j x_{ij} = 1 \text{ (each person assigned to one task for each } i = 1, \ldots, n)$$

$$\sum_i x_{ij} = 1 \text{ (each task assigned to one person, for each } j = 1, \ldots, n),$$

where c_{ij} = cost of Person i doing Task j as given in Figure 4–8.

Comments on transportation-type models

1. The transportation models already discussed are restricted to a single product or commodity. In many real-world settings we would need to deal with multiple product problems. If there is some commonality of the products—for example, cases of food or refrigerators and stoves—one could deal with multiple products by converting the products to the common shipping unit. In such a situation an ordinary transportation model results. The more complex situation occurs when there is no such commonality or when products can require special shipment containers. Some recent research has indicated potential solution techniques. The reader should consult the references at the end of the chapter for more details.

2. The objective function for the transportation and assignment models has been stated for convenience in terms of minimizing

cost; other types of objective functions can be considered. For example, for the transportation model one could consider an objective function of maximizing profit if there is a different selling price at each destination (see Problem 11); for the assignment model one could also consider the objectives to maximize profit, or to maximize satisfaction with personnel assignment (see Problems 16 and 17).

3. The computational aspects of the transportation and assignment models differ from those of ordinary LP models. These models could be solved by the LP technique, but they have a special structure that can be exploited. The transportation algorithm is based on the dual problem, as described in Chapter 6, and takes advantage of certain structure to provide a very convenient algorithm for this class of problems. While the assignment model is a special case of the transportation model, it is not related to it computationally. In fact, as noted in the references, special algorithms can be constructed for this class of models.

Blending Models

A variation of the product-mix model is that class of problems that deal with the *blending* of raw materials into either intermediate or finished products. The best example (and perhaps the biggest user of LP techniques) is the petroleum industry, in which refined products are blended to yield various grades of gasoline. Similar models apply to the blending of other liquids, chemicals, molten materials, or even foodstuffs. The general form of the blending model is:

Variables: Let x_{ij} = amount of input i to be used in product (output) j; $i = 1, \ldots, m; j = 1, \ldots, n$.

Objective Function: Maximize profit $= \sum_i \sum_j p_{ij} x_{ij}$,

where p_{ij} is the unit profit associated with variable x_{ij}.

Constraints: In general at least two sets of constraints are associated with blending models.

A.   *Supply and demand*—as in the transportation models (4–9) and (4–6), we require

$$\sum_{j=1}^{n} x_{ij} \leq S_i, \quad i = 1, \ldots, m, \qquad (4\text{–}15)$$

which states that the input used cannot exceed the supply, and

$$\sum_{i=1}^{m} x_{ij} \geq D_j, \quad j = 1, \ldots, n, \tag{4-16}$$

which states that the product must at least meet demand.

B. *Technology Constraints:* These constraints arise from the technology of the blending process and can vary in complexity. The simplest type concerns the ratio of two inputs in a particular product.

For example

$$\frac{x_{12}}{x_{22}} \left(\begin{array}{c} \geq \\ \leq \end{array} \right) r_2 \tag{4-17}$$

states that the ratio of Input 1 to Input 2 in Product 2 must satisfy either some minimal ($\geq$) or maximal ($\leq$) value r_2.

C. More complex constraints concern the composition of the final product. For example, suppose Product 3 is composed of Inputs 1 and 2 and is required to contain a specified proportion r_3 of a certain component of the inputs. If the Inputs 1 and 2 contain proportions a_1 and a_2, respectively, of the critical component then the requirement that Product 3 contain at least r_3 can be expressed as:

$$\frac{a_1 x_{13} + a_2 x_{23}}{x_{13} + x_{23}} \geq r_3. \tag{4-18}$$

This relationship can readily be modified to deal with maximal ratios by changing the inequality to $\leq$.

Each of these constraints is non-linear as stated, but can be converted to a linear constraint by multiplying both sides of the inequality by the donominator,[8] which converts (4-17) to

$$x_{12} - r_2 x_{22} \left(\begin{array}{c} \geq \\ \leq \end{array} \right) 0 \tag{4-19}$$

and (4-18) to

$$a_1 x_{13} + a_2 x_{23} - r_3 (x_{13} + x_{23}) \geq 0. \tag{4-20}$$

The constraints given by (4-17) and (4-18) identify blending problems. Blending models arise in the petroleum industry, where in gasoline blending the critical component may be the catalytically cracked gasoline available from a particular crude oil. In other types of applications such

---

[8] While this is a common "trick" for dealing with ratio type constraints some care must be exercised when evaluating the final solution. While the variables (or their sums) that appear in the denominator are non-negative they may be driven to zero by the solution technique. While this is perfectly legitimate in (4-19) and (4-20) it yields an undefined quantity in ratio form.

constraints might be a percentage of fat in a particular grade of meat or the percentage of available iron in a particular ore. The next example gives additional interpretations of these constraints.

Example 4.8.

The I.M. NUTSY company sells mixtures of nuts. The quality of a mix is determined by the proportion of cashews to peanuts, and currently the company offers two mixes:

Mix 1 must contain at least 45 percent cashews and no more than 25 percent peanuts. The profit per pound is $0.35.

Mix 2 must contain at least 15 percent cashews and no more than 70 percent peanuts. The profit per pound is $0.30.

There is a company policy of producing at least 200 pounds of each mix, and 250 pounds of cashews and 500 pounds of peanuts are available. The company wants to determine how to blend its nuts. In order to construct a blending model we define

Variables: Let

$$x_{11} = \text{pounds of cashews in Mix 1}$$
$$x_{12} = \text{pounds of cashews in Mix 2}$$
$$x_{21} = \text{pounds of peanuts in Mix 1}$$
$$x_{22} = \text{pounds of peanuts in Mix 2.}$$

Objective function:

$$\text{Maximize profit} = 0.35(x_{11} + x_{21}) + 0.30(x_{12} + x_{22}).$$

Constraints:

$$\left.\begin{array}{c} x_{11} + x_{12} \leq 250 \\ x_{21} + x_{22} \leq 500 \end{array}\right\} \quad \text{Supply constraints}$$

$$\left.\begin{array}{c} x_{11} + x_{21} \geq 200 \\ x_{12} + x_{22} \geq 200 \end{array}\right\} \quad \text{Policy constraints}$$

$$\frac{x_{11}}{x_{11} + x_{21}} \geq 0.45 \qquad \text{Proportion of cashews in Mix 1}$$

$$\frac{x_{21}}{x_{11} + x_{21}} \leq 0.25 \qquad \text{Proportion of peanuts in Mix 1}$$

$$\frac{x_{12}}{x_{12} + x_{22}} \geq 0.15 \qquad \text{Proportion of cashews in Mix 2}$$

$$\frac{x_{22}}{x_{12} + x_{22}} \leq 0.70 \qquad \text{Proportion of peanuts in Mix 2}$$

$$x_{11}, x_{12}, x_{21}, x_{22} \geq 0.$$

The last four constraints must be converted to a linear form (Equations 4–19, 4–20) before the model can be solved using linear programming techniques.

Planning Models

To this point we have dealt with models that have a single planning period; that is, we assumed the model represented a process that started and ended with no carry-over of materials or production. If we pick a long enough planning period (horizon) this may be a valid assumption, but it is likely that the parameters of the model would change over a long time period. Hence a shorter period is desirable. When a short horizon is used, however, one must deal with the *interaction* (as explained below) of the process over time periods.

In the previous sections we described several types of general models. It is difficult to describe a general time-dependent model. The main reason is that the concept of several planning periods applies to all the models studied so far. That is, any of the models of this chapter could

FIGURE 4–9

Constraint Structure for a Planning Model

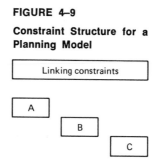

be described in terms of several time periods, several departments within a company, and so on. In order for the planning model to be realistic there must be interaction among the variables across the time periods or departments. If this were not the case, the integrated model would simply be a collection of separate models.

One distinguishing characteristic of models that include several time periods is a stair-step or block diagonal structure. The structure deals with the form of the constraints and is best illustrated by a diagram. In Figure 4–9 we present the structure of the constraints for a typical planning model.

The blocks labeled A, B, and C represent the technological constraints for each time period. As illustrated by the diagram these technologies are independent and do not interact. The long horizontal row at the top of the figure represents a constraint(s) that reflects the interaction of the process. For example, such constraints could include total resources available over each or all time periods, the effect of inventories on storage space, production requirements, and so on.

While the above structure is common when dealing with planning models, it is not the only structure possible. Another structure, particularly common when dealing with time horizon models, introduces a column of variables that serve to link together the utilization of resources by the process over the time periods. No matter what the structure is, however the point of this discussion is the presence of a certain structure that can aid in the construction of a model and its solution.

Production Scheduling and Inventory Control. LP is widely used in production scheduling because it deals effectively with problems of a recurring nature. While dealing with a production schedule problem, one may also have to deal with inventory problems. The following example of an inventory model embodies many of the aspects mentioned above. Additional examples are given in the exercises.

Example 4.9.

Consider a company that manufactures two items (Item 1, Item 2). The three-month demand for these items is:

	January	February	March
Item 1....................	1,500	3,000	4,000
Item 2....................	1,000	500	4,000

The problem is to develop a production schedule that will minimize the total costs. It is assumed for simplicity of explanation that on January 1 there are no items on hand and by March 31 all items are to be used. The total cost includes:

	Item 1	Item 2
Production cost....................	0.3	0.15
Inventory cost....................	0.2	0.10

The production costs increase by 10 percent in each month. The production process in each month requires two machines with the following time requirements:

	Item 1	Item 2	Time available
Machine 1....................	0.1	0.05	400
Machine 2....................	0.09	0.075	600

The amount of time available decreases by 5 percent in each month; the storage capacity is 3,500 square feet; each unit requires 1.5 square feet. Let,

$$x_{ij} = \text{production of product } i \text{ in month } j$$
$$s_{ij} = \text{inventory of product } i \text{ at end of month } j.$$

The objective function is to minimize total cost, which is production plus inventory cost:

Minimize $0.3x_{11} + 0.15x_{21} + 0.33x_{12} + 0.165x_{22} + 0.363x_{13} + 0.1815x_{23}$
$$+ 0.2s_{11} + 0.1s_{21} + 0.2s_{12} + 0.1s_{22}$$

The inventory balance equation

$$\begin{pmatrix} \text{Ending} \\ \text{Inventory} \\ \text{of previous} \\ \text{month} \end{pmatrix} + \begin{pmatrix} \text{Production} \\ \text{this month} \end{pmatrix} - \begin{pmatrix} \text{Inventory at} \\ \text{end of current} \\ \text{month} \end{pmatrix} = \begin{pmatrix} \text{Demand} \\ \text{this} \\ \text{month} \end{pmatrix}$$

provides the constraints:

$$\begin{array}{lll}
x_{11} - s_{11} & = 1{,}500 & \text{January, Item 1} \\
x_{21} - s_{21} & = 1{,}000 & \text{January, Item 2} \\
s_{11} + x_{12} - s_{12} & = 3{,}000 & \text{February, Item 1} \\
s_{21} + x_{22} - s_{22} & = 500 & \text{February, Item 2} \\
s_{12} + x_{13} & = 4{,}000 & \text{March, Item 1} \\
s_{22} + x_{23} & = 4{,}000 & \text{March, Item 2.}
\end{array}$$

The production process constraints are:

$$\begin{array}{lll}
0.1x_{11} + 0.05x_{21} & \leq 400 & \text{January, Machine 1} \\
0.1x_{12} + 0.05x_{22} & \leq 380 & \text{February, Machine 1} \\
0.1x_{13} + 0.05x_{23} & \leq 361 & \text{March, Machine 1} \\
0.09x_{11} + 0.075x_{21} & \leq 600 & \text{January, Machine 2} \\
0.09x_{12} + 0.075x_{22} & \leq 570 & \text{February, Machine 2} \\
0.09x_{13} + 0.075x_{23} & \leq 536\frac{1}{2} & \text{March, Machine 2.}
\end{array}$$

The storage capacity constraint is:

$$1.5(s_{11} + s_{21} + s_{12} + s_{22}) \leq 3{,}500.$$

The final conditions are the nonnegativity conditions:

$$x_{11}, x_{12}, x_{21}, x_{22}, x_{13}, x_{23} \geq 0$$
$$s_{11}, s_{12}, s_{21}, s_{22} \geq 0.$$

Planning models provide the decision maker with a tool for planning for long-range decisions or for considering several departments or operations within a larger organization. While these models are in general quite large and complex, they provide the necessary capability to study complex organizations. Also, as illustrated by the previous example, they provide for planning over extended time periods. Such planning averts the development of myopic policies that arise from planning only from one period to the next.

4.5. SUMMARY

The previous sections gave general and specific examples of various types of linear programming models. These models are meant as a guide to other types of applications. In real-world applications the model rarely fits textbook examples, but by studying the examples of the chapter and the exercises at the end of the chapter one can gain insights into transforming complex problems into linear programming models.

EXERCISES

4.1. A lumber company manufactures three grades of plywood. The production process consists of three operations: veneering, gluing, finishing. A sheet of Grade 1 plywood requires 0.2 hours of veneering, 0.025 hours of gluing, and 0.04 hours of finishing. A sheet of Grade 2 requires 0.05 hours of veneering, 0.05 hours of gluing, and 0.02 hours of finishing. A sheet of Grade 3 plywood requires 0.1 hour of veneering, 0.3 hours of gluing, and 0.2 hours of finishing. Totals of 90, 40, and 60 hours are available for each process. The profit contribution of a sheet of Grade 1 plywood is $1.25, for Grade 2 is $1.50, and for Grade 3 is $2.25. Formulate a linear model to determine the number of sheets of each grade of plywood to produce so as to maximize profit.

4.2. A manufacturing process utilizes two resources in the production of three products. The technology of the process is: Product 1 requires seven pounds of Resource 1 and five boxes of Resource 2; Product 2 requires four pounds of Resource 1 and three boxes of Resource 2; Product 3 requires three pounds of Resource 1 and two boxes of Resource 2. There are 100 pounds of Resource 1 and 150 boxes of Resource 2 available. Formulate an LP model to maximize profits of the product line when the profit contributions of the products are $10, $10, and $7.50 respectively.

4.3. An oil company produces two grades of gasoline, premium and regular, which are sold to dealers at 59½ cents and 56 cents per gallon respectively. The company can buy two grades of crude oil, A and B, at a cost of $0.25 and $0.20 per gallon, respectively. Processing of the crude oils leads to the following proportions of refined products:

	Percentage of Product		
	1	2	3
Crude A	75	15	10
Crude B	35	35	30

Premium gasoline must contain at least 60 percent of Product 1 and no more than 25 percent of Product 3; regular gasoline must contain at least 10 percent of Product 1, no more than 15 percent of Product 3, and at least 25 percent of Product 2. The company has available 100,000 gallons of A and 150,000 gallons of B. The expected demand is 90,000 gallons of premium and 135,000 gallons of regular. Formulate a blending model to maximize profits.

4.4.　A steel company wants to produce 20,000 pounds of steel with specifications:

Chromium..........................	15% min.
Silicon............................	1% max.
Manganese........................	1% "
Carbon............................	0.5% "

from materials with the following costs and compositions:

	Scrap Steel	High-Carbon Ferrochrome	Low-Carbon Ferrochrome
Cost, $ per lb....................	0.02	0.27	0.40
Chromium (%)...................	0	55.6	65
Manganese (%).................	1	0	0
Silicon (%).....................	0.2	2	1
Carbon (%).....................	0.6	8	0.1
Iron (%).......................	98.2	34.4	33.9

There is only 2,000 pounds of low-carbon ferrochrome available. Formulate a linear programming model to produce the required amount of steel at minimum cost.

4.5.　A lumber company has contracted to fill the orders of builders for lumber of certain sizes. A typical order for a day is:

Lumber Dimensions	Quantity
1 in. x 2 in. x 10 ft.......................	205
1 in. x 4 in. x 10 ft.......................	400
2 in. x 2 in. x 10 ft.......................	150

These orders are to be filled by cutting the standard lumber with dimensions 2 inches by 4 inches by 10 feet. Assume that no loss occurs in cutting.

The company wants to know how to cut the lumber in such a way that a day's order is filled and the total amount of standard lumber used is as small as possible. Model the above as a linear program.

4.6. A blending process combines two raw materials (resources) with a chemical to produce three products. The process has available 1,500 pounds of Resource A, 2,000 pounds of Resource B, 850 pounds of chemical, and 375 hours of labor. Product 1 requires 15 pounds of Resource A, 20 pounds of Resource B, 0.5 pounds of chemical, and 2 hours of labor to produce 1 bag; Product 2 requires 30 pounds of Resource B, 175 pounds of chemical, and 3 hours of labor to produce 1 bag; Product 3 requires 40 pounds of Resource A, 0.3 pounds of chemical, and 1.5 hours of labor to produce 1 bag. The profit contributions for each product have been estimated to be $1.20, $1.80, and $1.55 per bag. Formulate an LP model to maximize profits.

4.7. An advertising company wants to construct an LP model of an advertising campaign. Based on past experience the company has decided to utilize daytime TV, evening TV, radio, and the daily newspaper in its campaign. A one-minute daytime TV ad costs $1,100, reaches 800 potential customers, and is limited to a maximum of 15 per day. A 30-second evening TV ad costs $2,500, reaches 2,250 potential customers, and is limited to a maximum of ten per day. A ½-page ad in the local newspaper costs $300, reaches 1,000 potential customers, and is limited to a maximum of five per day. A 30-second radio ad costs $75, reaches 500 potential customers, and is limited to 30 per day. In order to assess the impact of an advertisement, the company has constructed an exposure index that relates the effect of an ad to market share of the product. The exposure index for dayime TV is 0.75, for evening TV is 1, for radio is 0.22, and for the newspaper is 0.45. The company wants to maximize the exposure of the product taking into account a $25,000 budget, at least ten TV commercials per day, and a maximum TV budget of $15,000. Finally, the campaign should reach at least 55,000 customers.

4.8. A paper company produces newsprint in standard rolls 100 inches wide. Typically the company receives orders for the standard rolls, but there is also demand for rolls of smaller widths. During the past week the following orders were received:

Width	Quantity
35 inches..................	200
40 inches..................	300
55 inches..................	450

Formulate a linear programming model to determine a cutting pattern of standard rolls to meet demand that requires the use of as few standard rolls as possible.

4.9. The manufacturer of a dishwashing detergent wants to model the production process with the objective of minimizing the costs of production. The detergent is composed of four ingredients: detergent base, skin conditioner, scent, and water, which cost $3, $27.5, $300, and $0.10 per gallon, respectively. In addition, the detergent must exhibit certain characteristics: suds formation, oiliness, odor, and density. The product rating requirements *per gallon* of product are:

	Minimum	Maximum
Suds formation................	100	140
Oiliness......................	10	100
Odor.........................	20	80
Density......................	45	65

The characteristics of the ingredients are: Water has a density of 1 and does not affect the other characteristics. The scent ingredient has a density of 30 and an odor rating of 30. The skin conditioner has a density of 50, odor rating of 5, an oiliness rating of 125, and suds formation rating of 10. The detergent base has a density of 70, an odor rating of 20, an oiliness rating of 5, and a suds formation rating of 150. Using this information construct the LP model.

4.10. A trash hauling company wants to analyze an expansion of its services using an LP model. The projected requirements for its five customers are 6, 9, 4, 9, and 10 loads per day. The company's current capacity is ten loads per day. There are three truck rental firms capable of supplying additional capacity of 10 for Firm A, 9 for Firm B, and 15 for Firm C. Using data from the rental firms and its own data the company has determined a cost-per-load table:

	Own	Trucks Leased from		
Customer	Trucks	A	B	C
1....................	8	8	10	7
2....................	6	9	5	4
3....................	3	10	9	11
4....................	7	7	5	8
5....................	5	8	9	6

Formulate the above as a transportation problem; the objective is to minimize costs.

4.11. A large department store chain faces a problem of allocating men's suits from warehouses to various retail stores in the chain. Each store has a different price for the item, and the cost for sending the suits from the warehouse to the store depends upon the particular warehouse-store combination. The overall problem is to determine the optimal allocation of men's suits from warehouses to retail stores. The data for this problem are shown in the tables below.

Store	Suits Requested	Selling Price	Retailing Costs
1......................	8	$50	$30
2......................	16	43	30
3......................	15	45	30

Warehouse	Number of Suits on Hand	Cost to Ship One Suit to		
		Store 1	Store 2	Store 3
1.................	13	$4	$7	$2
2.................	17	0	0	5

Formulate a transportation model; the objective is to *maximize profit*.

4.12. A manufacturer operates three factories (A, B, C) and four warehouses (1, 2, 3, 4). For the next planning period the factory capacities have been estimated as: 1,000, 2,500, and 5,000 units, respectively. The availability of storage at the warehouses has been estimated as 650, 2,500, 4,000, and 3,000, respectively. Construct an LP model to minimize the cost of shipping the products from the factories to the warehouses if the shipping costs per unit are:

Factory	Warehouse			
	1	2	3	4
A..................	13	15	28	21
B..................	22	25	12	14
C..................	18	17	25	20

4.13. During the processing of eggs for commercial sales, it is necessary to sort the eggs according to grade. A particular company employs three sorters whose past performance data is:

Inspector	Sorting Rate, Eggs per Hour	Percentage Mis-classified	Hourly Wage
A......................	24	2	$3.25
B......................	36	5	3.00
C......................	30	3	3.45

During an eight-hour shift the company needs to process at least 50 dozen eggs with no more than 5 percent of the eggs being misclassified. Construct a linear programming model to determine how many hours each inspector should be assigned during the shift so that costs are minimized.

4.14. A company has four people who can be assigned to the projects of any of three clients. The estimated time, in days, to complete a project for each of the individuals is given in the following table:

	Client		
Person	*1*	*2*	*3*
A......................	10	12	5
B......................	14	16	9
C......................	6	18	3
D......................	12	19	17

Construct an assignment model to minimize the total time to complete all projects.

4.15. A problem faced by a commercial airline is to assign its flight crews to appropriate flights between New York and Washington, D.C. The flight schedule between these cities is:

Flight	*Departs* *New York*	*Arrives* *Washington*	*Flight*	*Departs* *Washington*	*Arrives* *New York*
1.........	7:30 A.M.	9:00 A.M.	2.........	8:00 A.M.	9:00 A.M.
3.........	8:15 A.M.	9:45 A.M.	4.........	8:45 A.M.	9:45 A.M.
5.........	2:00 P.M.	3:30 P.M.	6.........	11:00 A.M.	12:00 *noon*
7.........	5:45 P.M.	6:15 P.M.	8.........	7:00 P.M.	8:00 P.M.
9.........	7:00 P.M.	8:30 P.M.	10........	8:30 P.M.	9:30 P.M.

The airline wants to decide how to assign crews to pairs of flights; that is, assign a crew to two flights so that the crew returns to its starting point. The airline wants to make such assignments so that total layover time is minimized, subject to the restriction that there be at least one hour between flights. Construct an assignment model to deal with this problem.

4.16. A typing pool has four typists (A, B, C, D). Currently there are four jobs awaiting typing, and each job must be assigned to only one typist. The following table gives the time necessary for each typist to complete each job. Construct an assignment model to determine who does each job so that the total time is minimized.

Typist	Job			
	1	*2*	*3*	*4*
A....................	1	2	6	4
B....................	4	4	2	3
C....................	5	2	3	6
D....................	2	5	5	3

4.17. A company produces a single product at three different locations (A, B, C). Before shipping the product to warehouses the company sometimes consolidates its inventory and then ships it to its four warehouses (1, 2, 3, 4) for storage. The cost per shipment among the factories is given by:

From	To		
	A	*B*	*C*
A..................	0	2	3
B..................	2	0	1
C..................	3	1	0

The cost per shipment from the factories to the warehouses is:

From	To			
	1	*2*	*3*	*4*
A....................	7	9	12	5
B....................	12	10	8	9
C....................	6	8	5	6

If the factory production capabilities are 30, 40, and 25 units, respectively, and the warehouse capacities are 25, 30, 20, and 40, respectively, construct a linear programming model to minimize the costs of shipping the product from the factory to the warehouses.

4.18. In the shipment of certain items—fresh vegetables, fresh fruits, and so on—a decision has to be made whether to ship the items directly or to ship them through intermediate points where they are treated to preserve freshness. In such decisions the cost of direct shipment generally exceeds the cost of intermediate shipment and treatment. Suppose there are three supply points S_1, S_2, and S_3 with 100, 120, and 110 units available. The two demand points, D_1 and D_2, have requirements 200 and 140, respectively. In addition there are two intermediate points,

I_1 and I_2, with unlimited capacity. The shipment costs per unit are given by

From	To			
	I_1	I_2	D_1	D_2
S_1...................	14	6	34	41
S_2...................		17	24	29
S_3...................	12	19	18	12
I_1...................	0	4	20	16
I_2...................	1	0	26	30

The blank space in the table indicates that no such shipment is possible. Construct a linear programming model to minimize shipping costs.

4.19. The student council of a college has completed a survey of students that rates the teaching ability of various professors in certain required courses. Currently there are four professors qualified to teach any of five courses. The college has decided to assign professors to courses based on the ratings so that each professor teaches one course. Construct a linear programming model to determine the assignments.

Professor	Course				
	1	*2*	*3*	*4*	*5*
A.................	40	60	90	70	90
B.................	50	40	60	30	70
C.................	60	20	70	70	40
D.................	30	90	40	60	60

4.20. A company has contracted to deliver its product on the following schedule: 20 units by January 31; 25 units by February 28; and 10 units by March 31. The production costs are $100 per unit for up to 15 units each month and $150 per unit for units 16–20 each month. The storage costs are $10 per unit per month. The inventory on January 1 is zero. Construct a model giving a production schedule a minimum total cost.

4.21. A company is planning its production schedule for the coming year. From past data the company has estimated the demand in each month as:

January..............	250	July.................	250
February............	200	August..............	225
March..............	425	September...........	200
April................	130	October..............	750
May................	230	November............	600
June................	240	December............	125

The company operates three production lines with the following production data:

Line	Capacity, Units per Month	Production Cost per Unit
1.	225	95
2.	190	80
3.	150	110

The storage costs ($3 per unit per month) are based on the month's average inventory.

$$\text{Average Inventory} = \frac{\text{Ending Inventory} - \text{Beginning Inventory.}}{2}$$

The inventory on January 1 is zero and the inventory on December 31 must also be zero. Construct a linear programming model that minimizes the total cost of the production process for the year.

4.22. A bank is planning its loan operations for the next year. The following table lists the loan types and their annual rates of return to the bank.

Type of Loan	Annual Return (percent)
Personal loans.	18
Automobile loans.	12
Home improvement loans.	10
First home mortgages.	9.5

Legal requirements and company policy place the following limits upon the amounts of the various types of loans. Personal loans cannot exceed 10 percent of the total amount of loans. The amount of personal and automobile loans together cannot exceed 20 percent of the total amount of loans. First mortgages must be at least 20 percent of the total loans, and at least 40 percent of the total amount of loans for homes. Home improvement loans may not exceed 25 percent of the total amount of loans.

The company wishes to maximize the revenue from loan interest, subject to the above restrictions. The firm can lend a maximum of $1.5 million.

a. Formulate the above as a linear programming problem.
b. After reading Chapter 6, return to this problem and investigate the effect of changing return rates (via changing interest rates) on the optimal solution. What would this suggest in terms of the planning horizon?

4.23. Class projects:

  a. Using current price data, use the LP technique to conduct a model to provide a nutritionally sound diet at minimum cost.
  b. For your particular city construct an LP model to schedule mail pickup and delivery at major mail depots so that total mileage is minimized.

SUGGESTIONS FOR FURTHER STUDY

Barnes, J. M., and Crisp, R. M., "Linear Programming: A Survey of General Purpose Algorithms," *AIIE Transactions,* vol. 7, September 1975.

Bazaraa, M. S., and Jarvis, J. J., *Linear Programming and Network Flows.* New York: Wiley, 1977.

Bell, E. F., "Mathematical Programming in Forestry," *Journal of Forestry,* vol. 75, June 1977.

Beltrami, E. J., *Models for Public Systems Analysis.* New York: Academic Press, 1977.

Cooper, L., and Steinberg, D., *Methods and Applications of Linear Programming.* Philadelphia: W. B. Saunders Co., 1974.

Daellenbach, H. G., and Bell, E. J., *User's Guide to Linear Programming.* Englewood Cliffs, N.J.: Prentice-Hall, 1970.

Dantzig, G. B., *Linear Programming and Extensions.* Princeton, N.J.: Princeton University Press, 1963.

Darnell, D. W., and Loflin, C., "National Airlines Fuel Management and Allocation Model," *Interfaces,* vol. 7, February 1977.

Driebeek, N. J., *Applied Linear Programming.* Reading, Mass.: Addison-Wesley, 1969.

Fabian, T., "Blast Furnace Burdening and Production Planning: A Linear Programming Example," *Management Science,* vol. 14, 1967.

Gass, S. I., *Linear Programming.* New York: McGraw-Hill, 4th ed., 1975.

Gray, P., and Cullinan-James, C., "Applied Optimization—A Survey," *Interfaces,* vol. 6, May 1976.

Holladay, J., "Some Transportation Problems and Techniques for Solving Them," *Naval Research Logistics Quarterly,* vol. 11, 1974.

International Business Machines Corporation, New York, "Atlas of Applications," (GC20–1764), March 1973.

———, "Atlas of Applications," vol. 2 (GC20–1768–0), November 1974.

———, "Farm Planning with the Aid of Linear Programming," (GE20–0334–0).

———, "Linear Programming—Feed Manufacturing," (GE20–0148–0), June 1970.

———, "Linear Programming—Electric Arc Furnace Steel Making," (GE20–0147–0).

————, "Linear Programming—Cotton Blending and Production Allocation," (GE20–0164–0).

————, "Linear Programming—Gasoline Blending," (GE20–0168–0), June 1970.

————, "Linear Programming—Ice Cream Blending," (GE20–0156–0).

Kim, C., *Introduction to Linear Programming*. New York: Holt, Rinehart and Winston, 1971.

Kohn, R. E., "Application of Linear Programming to a Controversy on Air Pollution Control," *Management Science*, vol. 17, 1971.

Kolesar, D. J., Rider, K. L., Crabill, T. B., and Walker, W. E., "A Queuing-Linear Programming Approach to Scheduling Police Patrol Cars," *Operations Research*, vol. 23, November–December 1975.

Kotak, D. B., "Application of Linear Programming to Plywood Manufacture," *Interfaces*, vol. 7, no. 1, pt. 2, November 1976.

Loucks, D. P., ReVelle, D. S., and Lynn, W. R., "Linear Programming Models for Water Pollution Control," *Management Science*, vol. 14, 1967.

Machol, R. E., "An Application of the Assignment Problem," *Operations Research*, vol. 18, 1970.

Meyer, M., "Applying Linear Programming to the Design of Ultimate Pit Limits," *Management Science*, vol. 17, 1969.

Miller, H. E., Pierskalla, W. P., and Rath, G. J., "Nurse Scheduling Using Mathematical Programming," *Operations Research*, vol. 24, September–October 1976.

Moore, J. R., "A Linear Programming Approach to Scheduling Nuclear Isotope Production," *IEEE Transactions on Engineering Management*, vol. EM-20, May 1973.

Salkin, H. M., and Saha, J., eds., *Studies in Linear Programming*. New York: American Elsevier Publishing Co., 1975.

Sharp, W. F., "A Linear Programming Algorithm for Mutual Fund Portfolio Selection," *Management Science*, vol. 13, 1967.

Thomas, J., "Linear Programming Models for Production Advertising Decisions," *Management Science*, vol. 17, 1971.

Thompson, E. F., and Haynes, R. W., "A Linear Programming Approach to Decisionmaking Under Certainty," *Forestry Science*, vol. 17, 1971.

Waespy, C. M., "Linear Programming Solutions for Orbital-Transfer Trajectories," *Operations Research*, vol. 18, 1970.

Wagner, H. M., *Principles of Operations Research*. Englewood Cliffs, N.J.: Prentice-Hall, 1969.

Warner, D. M., "Scheduling Nursing Personnel According to Nursing Preference: A Mathematical Programming Approach," *Operations Research*, vol. 24, September–October 1976.

Zionts, S., *Linear and Integer Programming*. Englewood Cliffs, N.J.: Prentice-Hall, 1975.

5

Solving Linear Programs:
The Simplex Algorithm

5.1. INTRODUCTION

IN THE LAST CHAPTER we saw that many important problems could be modeled as linear programs. In this chapter we will learn how to compute solutions from such models. Many of the important concepts related to linear programming solutions will be introduced by considering a small example with two decision variables. These concepts will be demonstrated by a graphical analysis. Then a general algebraic procedure, called the simplex algorithm, for solving linear programs will be discussed. This algorithm (with modifications needed primarily for numerical reasons) is routinely used today to solve linear programming problems with hundreds, even thousands, of variables and constraints. These large problems, of course, are solved with the aid of computers. Nonetheless, knowing the basic aspects of the simplex algorithm can make analysts betters users of linear programming in that they can better understand what the computer is giving them.

5.2. GRAPHICAL SOLUTION

Consider the two-variable model (two decision variables)

Maximize

$$x_0 = 10x_1 + 10x_2 \tag{5-1}$$

subject to

$$2x_1 + x_2 \leq 10 \tag{5-2}$$
$$x_1 + 2x_2 \leq 10 \tag{5-3}$$
$$x_1, x_2 \geq 0. \tag{5-4}$$

The constraints (5–2), (5–3), and (5–4) can be represented in a two-dimensional coordinate system as shown in Figure 5–1. Consider for the moment the "equality" part of constraint (5–2):

$$2x_1 + x_2 = 10. \tag{5-5}$$

This equation represents a straight line that can be plotted in a x_1, x_2 coordinate system by locating any two points that satisfy the equation and drawing the straight line through the points. To get one such point, we can let $x_1 = 0$ and solve for $x_2 = 10$. Then, we can let $x_2 = 0$ and solve for $x_1 = 5$ to get another point satisfying Equation (5–5). By drawing a straight line through these two points we get a graphical representation of Equation (5–5). This line, because of its association with constraint (5–2), is labeled (5–2) in Figure 5–1.

Recall, though, that constraint (5–2) is an inequality rather than an equation. It restricts us to x_1, x_2 pairs that make the left-hand side of (5–2) less than *or* equal to ten. On the graph of Figure 5–1, these are the x_1, x_2 pairs on or below the line labeled (5–2). An inequality will always imply the points on and to one side or the other of such a line. If it is not clear which side of the line is denoted in a given case, simply choose a side and test to see if points on that side satisfy the inequality. For instance, for the example above we could choose any point below the line and check whether or not the point satisfies constraint (5–2). The point $x_1 = x_2 = 0$ conveniently indicates that "below the line" was the right choice in this case.

In a like manner, the line representing the equality part of constraint (5–3) can be located in the same coordinate system. In Figure 5–1 this line is labeled (5–3). The x_1, x_2 pairs that satisfy constraint (5–3) are the points on or below this line.

The nonnegativity restrictions of constraint (5–4) are easily represented in the coordinate system of Figure 5–1 also. The x_1 and x_2 axes represent the equality parts of these restrictions. The points, then, that satisfy the nonnegativity conditions are the x_1, x_2 pairs on or to the right of the x_2 axis and the x_1, x_2 pairs on or above the x_1 axis.

So far we have considered our constraints individually. Solutions to our linear programming model, however, must satisfy *all* of our constraints. In Figure 5–1 we see that the x_1, x_2 pairs that simultaneously satisfy all of our constraints are on the boundary of, or interior to, the polygon labeled *abcd* (the shaded region in Figure 5–1). This collection of points is called the "feasible region." Note that each point (that is, each x_1, x_2 pair) in the feasible region represents a possible solution to our linear programming problem. The optimization problem we are faced

FIGURE 5–1

Graphical Analysis of a Two-Variable Linear Programming Problem

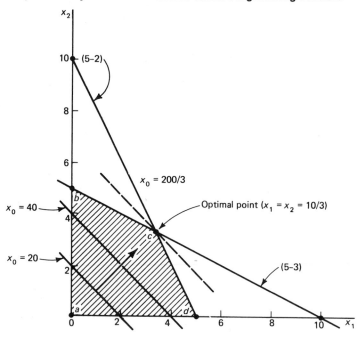

with is to search throughout the feasible region until we identify the best point; that is, until we identify the particular x_1, x_2 pair that causes the objective function to be maximized. To do this for our example problem, we have to bring the objective function into the analysis.

The objective function, expression (5–1), can be represented in Figure 5–1 by considering arbitrary values for x_0. For instance, if we choose $x_0 = 20$, we have the equation

$$10x_1 + 10x_2 = 20, \tag{5–6}$$

which can readily be plotted in Figure 5.1. Since we are interested only in feasible solutions, we can ignore the portions of the line outside the feasible region. Note, though, that there are an infinite number of points on this line within the feasible region. Thus, there are many different solutions to our example problem that would cause x_0 to equal 20.

Now let us choose another value, say 40, for x_0 and plot this line in Figure 5–1. There are two important things to notice about the relationship between the $x_0 = 20$ and the $x_0 = 40$ lines. First, these lines are parallel. Lines corresponding to different objective function values in such problems will always be parallel. This is true because their slope is uniquely determined by the coefficients of x_1 and x_2. The value of x_0

being considered does not affect the slope at all. The second relationship to note is that the $x_0 = 40$ line lies "above" the $x_0 = 20$ line.[1] This indicates that lines corresponding to "better" values of x_0 are to be found above the $x_0 = 20$ line. (If we were minimizing x_0 rather than maximizing, we would conclude that better lines lie below the $x_0 = 20$ line.)

These two observations give all the information we need to find the optimal solution to our problem. We know that if we continued to choose more attractive values for x_0 and plot the corresponding lines in Figure 5–1, these lines would be parallel to and above all previous lines. Since we want to maximize x_0, we would want to continue doing this until the lines we were considering no longer contained points within the feasible region. The last such line that touched the feasible region would correspond to the optimal value of x_0 and the optimal values for x_1 and x_2 would be given by the point where this special line touched the feasible region.

Of course, it is not necessary to explicitly draw all of these x_0 lines. All that we need to do is determine the slope of these lines by drawing one for an arbitrary case (like $x_0 = 20$) and then consider moving parallel to this line in the direction required by feasibility and optimality considerations. In this case we would move above and away from the $x_0 = 20$ line until if we moved away further we would leave the feasible region. The last feasible point we encounter is the optimal point. For this example, the optimal point is $x_1 = x_2 = 10/3$ for which $x_0 = 200/3$.

Several remarks are in order about the procedure used above. The direction of objective function improvement can always be easily assessed by drawing two different x_0 lines. However, when moving from an arbitrary x_0 line to the optimal one, we must be concerned first about feasibility and then about objective function improvement. For example, if we had initially chosen the $x_0 = 100$ line, our parallel moves would have been below—rather than above—this line because this line lies entirely above the feasible region. That is, there are no feasible points that will make the objective function as large as 100. As we move down from the $x_0 = 100$ line, the first feasible point encountered ($x_1 = x_2 = 10/3$) is the optimal point. Clearly it makes no difference whether we approach the optimal point from within or from outside the feasible region. Note, though, that the optimal point will always be on the boundary of the feasible region. This is true because the x_0 line passing through any given interior point could be improved upon by moving (in a parallel fashion) in the direction of objective function improvement to a boundary. On the boundary we might be at a corner point (the intersection of two or more constraint lines) or right on top of an entire boundary segment. The latter would occur if the slope of the objective function lines

---

[1] The use of the word "above" here is meant to imply a shift from the $x_0 = 20$ line away from the origin.

was equal to the slope of the limiting boundary segment. In such a case, every point on the boundary segment would be optimal. Thus, the end points of the boundary segment (that is, corner points) are optimal in either case. These corner points are also called "extreme" points and the terms will be used interchangeably in this chapter.

The result obtained above by an informal argument can be proved in a rigorous mathematical fashion. The interested reader is referred to any standard text on linear programming. The important concept to note here is that an optimal solution to a linear programming problem will *always* correspond to a corner point (extreme point) of the feasible region. This solution property makes large linear programming models solvable and thus makes linear programming an important real-world decision making tool. Although an infinite number of feasible solutions exist, the search for the optimal solution need be conducted only among the corner point solutions. For any linear program with a finite number of variables and constraints, there are only a finite number of extreme points. Thus, although an infinite number of feasible solutions exists for most linear programming problems, we have only to consider a finite number of them.

For problems with two variables, a graphical analysis serves us well. For problems with more than two variables, however, the graphical approach has no worthwhile application. Since we know, though, that an optimal solution will be an extreme point solution, we do not need a picture (graph) to lead us to the optimal solution. What we need is a procedure for identifying and evaluating extreme points regardless of the number of variables and constraints involved in a given problem. The *simplex algorithm* is such a procedure.

Before examining the rules of the simplex algorithm we need to review some concepts concerning basic solutions to systems of linear equations. Then we will define and illustrate the simplex algorithm for solving general linear programming problems.

5.3. BASIC SOLUTIONS

Consider a system of m linear equations in n unknowns.[2] In general, such a system can be written as

$$\sum_{j=1}^{n} a_{ij}x_j = b_i \quad i = 1, 2, \ldots, m. \tag{5-7}$$

---

[2] We will assume in this chapter that the m equations are linearly independent. Roughly, this means that each equation contains information about the relationship between the variables that is not available from the other equations—either individually or collectively.

If we have more equations than unknowns $(m > n)$ the system is over-determined and likely has no solutions.[3] If $m = n$, the system is uniquely determined and, in principle, is easily solved by any of a variety of standard linear algebra techniques.

The third possibility $(n > m)$ is more relevant to linear programming and thus our discussion here. When the number of variables is greater than the number of equations, the system has an infinite number of solutions. However, such a system has only a finite number of "basic" solutions, where a basic solution is defined as follows: Arbitrarily set $(n - m)$ variables equal to zero. Then solve the remaining m by m system for the remaining variables. The variables arbitrarily set to zero are called "nonbasic" variables and the remaining m variables are called "basic" variables. In general, there are at most $n! / [m!(n - m)!]$ basic solutions to a set of equations with $n > m$.

To illustrate this concept of a basic solution let us return to constraints (5–2) and (5–3) of our previous example.

$$2x_1 + x_2 \leq 10 \tag{5–2}$$
$$x_1 + 2x_2 \leq 10. \tag{5–3}$$

This system of inequalities can be converted to a system of equations by introducing two additional variables as follows. To the left-hand sides of (5–2) and (5–3), respectively, add non-negative variables x_3 and x_4 to yield the system

$$2x_1 + x_2 + x_3 \quad\quad = 10 \tag{5–8}$$
$$x_1 + 2x_2 \quad\quad + x_4 = 10. \tag{5–9}$$

Such variables are called "slack" variables because their numerical value is the difference (or slack) between the left- and right-hand sides of the original inequalities. These variables are required to be nonnegative in order to preserve the inequality nature of the relationships to which they were introduced.

Our system (5–8) and (5–9) now consists of $m = 2$ equations in $n = 4$ variables; there are six basic solutions. These basic solutions can be found by setting $(n - m) = 2$ variables equal to zero and solving for the remaining $m = 2$ variables. By carefully choosing which variables we want to be nonbasic, we can get one of the six possible basic solutions by inspection. Note that if we define x_1 and x_2 to be nonbasic variables (and thus equal to zero) then our system of (5–8) and (5–9) reduces to

$$x_3 \quad\quad = 10 \tag{5–10}$$
$$x_4 = 10. \tag{5–11}$$

The above system, of course, is solved by inspection. Thus, one basic solution to the system given by (5–8) and (5–9) is

---

[3] Our assumption of linear independence effectively rules out this case.

$$x_1 = 0, x_2 = 0 \quad \text{(nonbasic)} \qquad (5\text{--}12)$$
$$x_3 = 10, x_4 = 10 \quad \text{(basic)}. \qquad (5\text{--}13)$$

The system of (5–8) and (5–9) is in basic form displaying the solution of (5–12) and (5–13). Unfortunately, the other basic solutions are not quite so easy to identify from our system of equations as it now stands, but by using standard operations of linear algebra, we can change our system of equations to an equivalent system such that a different basic solution is displayed.[4] By moving from one equivalent system to another we can identify by inspection any of the basic solutions we want. We shall see later that this is precisely how linear programming solutions are found.

The movement from one system of equations to an equivalent system can be accomplished by repeated use of the following two *row operations*. An equation belonging to an equivalent system can be derived from the existing equations by either

a.   multiplying a given equation by a constant, or
b.   adding to a given equation a constant multiple of another equation.

Let us illustrate the application of these rules to the system given by (5–8) and (5–9). It will be economical to work in a tabular format with

FIGURE 5–2

Basic Form Displaying the Basic Solution
$x_1 = x_2 = 0$, $x_3 = 10$, $x_4 = 10$

	x_1	x_2	x_3	x_4	b
a^0	2	1	1	0	10
b^0	1	2	0	1	10

column headings for each variable and the right-hand-side constants as shown in Figure 5–2.

For convenience, label the first equation (first row) by the letter *a* and the second equation by the letter *b*. Moreover, give these labels superscripts to denote whether a given equation belongs to our original system, the first equivalent system, and so forth. Thus, in Figure 5–2 the first row is labeled a^0 and the second row b^0. In Figure 5–2 the elements in the basic columns (x_3 and x_4 columns) comprise an identity matrix.[5] Indeed, it is this special structure that enabled us to identify one basic solution by inspection. When moving from a given set of equations to an

---

[4] By an "equivalent" system we mean a system with the same set of solutions.
[5] An identity matrix is a square matrix with "plus-ones" on the main diagonal and zeros everywhere else.

equivalent set, we'll be guided by our desire to produce an identity matrix in those columns that we want to be basic. By doing this we will be able to identify a new basic solution by inspection.[6]

As we change one system to an equivalent system, we will at all times have m basic variables and $(n - m)$ nonbasic variables. Thus, there will always be a one-for-one exchange; one previously nonbasic variable will be made basic and one previously basic variable will be made nonbasic.

Now suppose we want the solution with x_1 and x_4 nonbasic and x_2 and x_3 basic. That is, we want to move to an equivalent system such that the x_2 and the x_3 columns have this special "identity matrix" structure. In our current system (Figure 5-2) x_3 is presently a basic variable and thus its column is already in the form desired. We need to modify the x_2 column so that it, together with the x_3 column, is in proper basic form. Specifically, we want the x_2 column to have a zero in the first row (the a^0 equation) and a +1 in the second row (the b^0 equation). These changes will be brought about by using the row operations defined earlier.

The first step involved whenever converting a nonbasic column to a basic column is to produce a +1 in the proper position in that column. This step, which generates an equation for our equivalent system, is accomplished by using the first row operation we cited. The new equation is then used to generate the other equations of the equivalent system in such a way all other elements in the column being made basic are equal to zero. This "zeroing-out" step requires repeated use of the second row operation. Once we have completely converted the column of concern, we will have generated an equivalent system of equations displaying a new basic solution.

In b^0, the coefficient of x_2 is +2. We want to derive a new equation, b^1, in which the coefficient of x_2 is +1. If we multiply b^0 by $\frac{1}{2}$ (the reciprocal of the current coefficient of x_2) we produce the desired new equation. Figure 5-3A shows the result of this first step. In the left-hand margin we have indicated that b^1 was derived by dividing b^0 by two. (As we derive other equations, we summarize in the margin the calculations involved in a similar fashion.)

To complete the transformation of x_2 from a nonbasic to a basic variable, we need to derive an equation, a^1, in which the coefficient of x_2 is equal to zero. This can be accomplished by using the second row operation. We multiply our new equation, b^1, by a constant and add the result, term by term, to a^0 to generate our new equation. By choosing the constant to be the negative of the current coefficient of x_2 (in a^0), we can be assured that the coefficient of x_2 in our new equation will be zero. The

---

[6] More precisely, we'll be producing square matrices such that each row *and* each column contains all zero elements except a single "plus one." Such columns could always be reordered so that the "ones" appear on the main diagonal.

FIGURE 5–3A

Tableau Structure Showing the Modifications to Equation b^0

	x_1	x_2	x_3	x_4	b
a^1					
$b^1 = b^0/2$	1/2	1	0	1/2	5

FIGURE 5–3B

Basic Form Displaying the Basic Solution
$x_1 = x_4 = 0$, $x_2 = 5$, $x_3 = 5$

	x_1	x_2	x_3	x_4	b
$a^1 = a^0 - 1\,(b^1)$	3/2	0	1	-1/2	5
$b^1 = b^0/2$	1/2	1	0	1/2	5

results of this step, along with the first step, are shown in Figure 5–3B. Note that if our system had involved many equations, we would have required the repeated use of this second row operation to "zero out" the new basic column.

In Figure 5–3B we have an equivalent or transformed system of equations in basic form displaying the solution

$x_1 = x_4 = 0$ (because they are nonbasic variables)
$x_3 = 5$ (by inspection from equation a^1)
$x_2 = 5$ (by inspection from equation b^1).

We could continue in this fashion to identify other basic solutions by transforming the system shown in Figure 5–3B to other equivalent systems such as those shown in Figures 5–4 and 5–5. In moving from the system of Figure 5–3B to that of Figure 5–4, x_1 was made basic and x_3 was made nonbasic. In moving from Figure 5–4 to Figure 5–5, x_4 was made basic and x_2 was made nonbasic. The reader should carefully study the calculations required to generate these basic solutions.

FIGURE 5–4

Basic Form Displaying the Basic Solution
$x_3 = x_4 = 0$, $x_1 = 10/3$, $x_2 = 10/3$

	x_1	x_2	x_3	x_4	b
$a^2 = a^1\,(2/3)$	1	0	2/3	-1/3	10/3
$b^2 = b^1 - 1/2\,(a^2)$	0	1	-1/3	2/3	10/3

FIGURE 5–5

Basic Form Displaying the Basic Solution
$x_2 = x_3 = 0$, $x_1 = 5$, $x_4 = 5$

	x_1	x_2	x_3	x_4	b
$a^3 = a^2 + 1/3\ b^3$	1	1/2	1/2	0	5
$b^3 = b^2\ (3/2)$	0	3/2	$-1/2$	1	5

The mechanics of generating equivalent systems in basic form can be summarized as follows. Assume we have m equations in basic form.

1. Identify the nonbasic variable, x_N, that is to be made basic. The corresponding column in the current tableau is called the "pivot" column.
2. Identify the basic variable, x_B, that is to be made nonbasic. The row in which this variable has the coefficient $+1$ is called the "pivot" row. The coefficient at the intersection of the pivot column and the pivot row is called the "pivot element."
3. Generate a new equation by dividing the pivot row by the pivot element. This will produce a $+1$ in the pivot element position.
4. Transform the other $(m - 1)$ equations (one at a time) by adding to them a constant multiple of the new pivot row equation, choosing the constants to be the negative of the current (corresponding) pivot column elements. These calculations will zero out the pivot column.

Having completed the transformation of all m equations, we will have a new, but equivalent, system of equations displaying a new basic solution. In moving from the previous basic solution to the new one, we say that variable x_N was put into the basis and variable x_B was taken out of the basis. Although the numerical values of the other $(m - 1)$ basic variables may be changed by the row operations used, the elements in their tableau columns will not change.

5.4. BASIC AND CORNER POINT SOLUTIONS

The previous section presented a mechanical method for identifying basic solutions of systems of linear equations. We have not yet, however, stated explicitly why we are interested in such solutions. This interest can be made clear by referring once again to the feasible region of Figure 5–1 and recalling the important result that if an optimal finite solution exists to a linear programming problem it will be a corner point solution. The corner points of the feasible region in Figure 5–1 and their corresponding values of x_1 and x_2 are presented in Figure 5–6 for ease of reference.

Now refer to the basic solution displayed in Figure 5–2. Note that in terms of x_1 and x_2 (our original decision variables) this basic solution is identical to the corner point solution at point a of our feasible region.[7] Furthermore, the basic solutions of Figures 5–3(b), 5–4, and 5–5 are identical to the corner point solutions at points b, c, and d, respectively, of our feasible region. Moreover, this correspondence is not peculiar to this particular example but is true in general. Our interest in computing basic solutions becomes apparent. Basic solutions are equivalent to corner point solutions, which, in turn, are candidates for optimal linear programming solutions. Thus, in those problems where we cannot rely on the simple graphical analysis to identify corner points, we can accomplish

FIGURE 5–6

Corner Point Solutions from Figure 5–1

Point	x_1	x_2
a...........	0	0
b...........	0	5
c...........	10/3	10/3
d...........	5	0

equivalent results by computing basic solutions to a corresponding system of equations. This is important because real-world problems have too many variables for graphical analysis.

We now know how to compute corner point solutions for any linear programming problem; but how do we know which corner point solutions to compute and how can we tell whether a given corner point solution is optimal? To answer these questions we have to bring the objective function into the analysis. Consider the following linear programming problem:

Maximize

$$x_0 = c_1 x_1 + c_2 x_2 + c_3 x_3 + c_4 x_4 \qquad (5\text{–}14)$$

subject to

$$a_{11} x_1 + a_{12} x_2 + x_3 \qquad = b_1 \qquad (5\text{–}15)$$
$$a_{21} x_1 + a_{22} x_2 \qquad + x_4 = b_2 \qquad (5\text{–}16)$$
$$x_1,\ x_2,\ x_3,\ x_4 \geq 0. \qquad (5\text{–}17)$$

Note that the Equation (5–15) and (5–16) are in basic form. Assume that b_1 and b_2 are nonnegative so that the basic solution displayed in

---

[7] The reader should not be bothered by the presence of the slack variables (x_3 and x_4) in our basic solutions. They do not detract in any way from the correspondence identified here between basic and corner point solutions.

Equations (5–15) and (5–16) also satisfies the nonnegativity conditions of (5–17). We then say that our system of equations is in "basic feasible" form since the solution displayed satisfies all of the constraints.

Our current basic solution is

$$x_1 = x_2 = 0 \qquad (5\text{–}18)$$
$$x_3 = b_1; \quad x_4 = b_2 \qquad (5\text{–}19)$$

for which the objective function has the value

$$x_O = c_3 b_1 + c_4 b_2. \qquad (5\text{–}20)$$

Since we are trying to maximize our objective function, we would like to move to some other basic solution if doing so would cause x_O to increase. If no such move is possible, the current solution is optimal, and our problem is solved. The potential attractiveness of other basic solutions can be assessed by examining our nonbasic variables, one at a time, to determine the effect (on x_O) of raising them by one unit from their current values of zero.

Let's examine x_1. Rasing x_1 from 0 to 1 would tend to increase x_O by the amount c_1. However, Equations (5–15) and (5–16) indicate that raising x_1 by one unit would cause x_3 and x_4 to be lowered by the amounts a_{11} and a_{21}, respectively. This lowering of x_3 and x_4 would decrease the objective function by the amount

$$c_3 a_{11} + c_4 a_{21}. \qquad (5\text{–}21)$$

Thus, the net increase in x_O associated with raising x_1 from its current level of 0 to a value of 1 is

$$c_1 - (c_3 a_{11} + c_4 a_{21}). \qquad (5\text{–}22)$$

If this quantity is positive, variable x_1 will be an attractive candidate for inclusion in the basis.

In a like manner, we determine that the net increase in x_O associated with raising x_2 from 0 to 1 is

$$c_2 - (c_3 a_{12} + c_4 a_{22}). \qquad (5\text{–}23)$$

If both the quantities (5–22) and (5–23) are negative, our current basic solution must be optimal. This follows because neither of the two basic solutions to which we could move is as attractive as our current solution. Otherwise, the variable with the largest associated net increase in x_O is usually chosen to be brought into the basis next.

Suppose that we decide to bring x_1 into the basis. Before we obtain a new basic solution, we have to decide which of the two basic variables (x_3 or x_4) we want to take out of the basis. This decision can be resolved as follows. We know that raising x_1 by one unit is attractive. Since the objective function is linear, it follows that raising x_1 by two units is twice as attractive, and so forth. We would like, then, to make x_1 as large as we can. Recall, though, that as we increase x_1, our basic variables decrease according to the equations

$$x_3 = b_1 - a_{11}x_1 \qquad (5\text{-}24)$$
$$x_4 = b_2 - a_{21}x_1. \qquad (5\text{-}25)$$

Since all of our variables are required to be nonnegative, we can increase x_1 only up to the point where one of these basic variables becomes equal to zero. Raising x_1 beyond this point would cause one or more basic variables to violate the nonnegativity conditions. From Equations (5–24) and (5–25) we see that x_1 will become the smaller of the ratios

$$\frac{b_1}{a_{11}}, \quad \frac{b_2}{a_{21}}. \qquad (5\text{-}26)$$

(From Equations (5–24) and (5–25) it should be clear to the reader that when comparing such ratios, we consider only those with positive denominators.)

The basic variable first driven to zero as we increase x_1 is the variable we remove from the basis. Since we now know which variable (x_1) we want to put into the basis and which variable we want to take out of the basis, we can pivot and move to the new solution.

The ideas presented above are the fundamentals of the simplex algorithm for computing the optimal solution to any linear programming problem. Before we finally get to the algorithm itself, we need to define some terminology that is useful when we are evaluating nonbasic variables. Suppose x_j is any nonbasic variable. Then, c_j is the amount by which the objective function would be increased if we raised x_j from zero to one. But such a change in x_j would affect the values of the current basic variables. Let z_j equal the amount by which the objective function is decreased by these changes in the current basic variables. Thus, z_j is the sum of the products of the elements in the jth column of our tableau and the objective function coefficients of the corresponding basic variables. For example, the quantity shown in (5–21) is z_1 and that in (5–23) is $c_2 - z_2$.

In general then, $(c_j - z_j)$ represents the net increase in the objective function that would be realized if nonbasic variable x_j was raised from zero to one. With this additional notation, we can now define the simplex algorithm.

The Simplex Algorithm (for maximization)

Step 0.   (Initialization): Convert the constraints to a set of equations in basic feasible form. (Make sure every b_i is nonnegative.) Go to Step 1.

Step 1.   (Pivot column selection): Compute $(c_j - z_j)$ for each nonbasic variable x_j. If all the $(c_j - z_j)$ values are less than or equal to zero, the solution we currently have is optimal (that is, stop!). Otherwise, identify as the pivot column the nonbasic variable column with the largest $(c_j - z_j)$ value. Go to Step 2.

Step 2. (Pivot row selection): Compute the ratio of the elements in the right-hand-side column (the b column) to the corresponding values in the pivot column. Discard ratios with nonpositive denominators. From the remaining ratios, identify the pivot row as the row yielding the smallest ratio. Go to Step 3. (If no ratios remain, stop! The problem has an unbounded solution.)

Step 3. (New solution): "Pivot" at the intersection of the pivot column and the pivot row to generate a new basic feasible solution. Go to Step 1.

With the background the reader now has, the various steps of the algorithm should be self-explanatory. However, a few comments are in order.

1. Identifying a pivot column is equivalent to assessing which nonbasic variable we want to bring into the basis. Likewise, when we identify the pivot row, we determine which basic variable we will take out of the basis.

2. When looking for a pivot column (Step 1) or a pivot row (Step 2), it is possible to encounter ties. Such ties can be arbitrarily broken.

3. The algorithm continues to move through Steps 1, 2, and 3 until it terminates in Step 1 with the optimal solution or until it indicates in Step 2 that no finite optimal solution exists. This latter case will be discussed later in this chapter.

4. Each pass through Steps 1, 2, and 3 is called an "iteration." Normally, the objective function value will improve with each iteration. Exceptions to this, caused by a condition called "degeneracy," will be discussed later.

Let's apply the algorithm to our example. The problem is:

Maximize

$$x_0 = 10x_1 + 10x_2 \tag{5-27}$$

subject to

$$2x_1 + x_2 \leq 10 \tag{5-28}$$
$$x_1 + 2x_2 \leq 10 \tag{5-29}$$
$$x_i \geq 0. \tag{5-30}$$

To satisfy Step 0, we must add (nonnegative) slack variables, x_3 and x_4, to the left-hand sides of (5-28) and (5-29), respectively. Thus, in basic feasible form, our problem becomes

Maximize

$$x_0 = 10x_1 + 10x_2 + 0x_3 + 0x_4 \tag{5-31}$$

subject to

$$2x_1 + x_2 + x_3 \qquad = 10 \qquad (5\text{--}32)$$
$$x_1 + 2x_2 \qquad + x_4 = 10. \qquad (5\text{--}33)$$

Note that the slack variables are given coefficients equal to zero in the objective function. Thus, no matter what their numerical values turn out to be, they will not affect the value of x_0. For convenience, all calculations are carried out in the tableaus shown in Figure 5–7.

In the tableau, we define a column heading for each of the n variables as well as the right-hand-side constant (the b column). In addition, a

FIGURE 5–7

Simplex Algorithm Tableaus for Example Problem

c_B	x_B	10 x_1	10 x_2	0 x_3	0 x_4	b	
0	x_3	2	1	1	0	10	Initial Tableau
0	x_4	1	2*	0	1	10	
$c_j - z_j$		10	10	0	0	0	
0	x_3	3/2*	0	1	-1/2	5	Iteration #1
10	x_2	1/2	1	0	1/2	5	
$c_j - z_j$		5	0	0	-5	50	
10	x_1	1	0	2/3	-1/3	10/3	Iteration #2 (optimal)
10	x_2	0	1	-1/3	2/3	10/3	
$c_j - z_j$		0	0	-10/3	-10/3	200/3	

* These numbers are the pivot elements.

column identifying m basic variables (labeled x_B) is defined on the left-hand side of the tableau. The objective function coefficients of these basic variables are entered in column c_B for ease of reference. The objective function coefficients of all the variables are written above the appropriate column headings.

From the coefficients of the constraint equations, (5–32) and (5–33), the main body of the initial tableau can be immediately filled in. These equations also give the initial values for the b column. Then, the x_B column is filled with x_3 and x_4, indicating that x_3 and x_4 are the basic variables of an initial tableau. The bottom row of the tableau is reserved for the $(c_j - z_j)$ calculations for the nonbasic variables as well as the current value of the objective function, which appears as the last element in the row. Note that the $(c_j - z_j)$ values for the basic variables are always equal to zero and can be immediately filled in.

The solution displayed in the initial tableau is

$$x_3 = 10$$
$$x_4 = 10$$
$$x_1 = x_2 = 0 \quad \text{by definition because they are nonbasic,}$$

for which the objective function is equal to zero.

Now for Step 1 of the algorithm. We need to compute $(c_j - z_j)$ for our nonbasic variables. The calculations are:

$$c_1 - z_1 = 10 - [2(0) + 1(0)] = 10$$
$$c_2 - z_2 = 10 - [1(0) + 2(0)] = 10.$$

Since these values are not less than or equal to zero, we know that the solution we currently have is not optimal. Thus, we should identify a pivot column. In choosing the pivot column we arbitrarily break the tie by picking x_2 as the variable to come into the basis next.

The ratios required for Step 2 of the algorithm are:

$$\text{Row 1:} \quad 10/1 = 10$$
$$\text{Row 2:} \quad 10/2 = 5.$$

Thus, Row 2 is the pivot row. We now know exactly what exchange we want to make. We want to put x_2 into the basis and take x_4 out of the basis. Step 3 tells us to bring about this change of basis by pivoting at the intersection of the pivot column and the pivot row.

Completing the pivot, we return to Step 1 with the first two rows of the tableau labeled Iteration #1. The algorithm continues in this fashion until it stops with the third tableau, where the $(c_j - z_j)$ values for the nonbasic variables are all less than zero. The optimal solution given by this final tableau is, of course, the same as the solution we identified earlier using the graphical analysis. (The reader is encouraged to verify the numbers in the second and third tableaus of Figure 5–7.)

5.5. OTHER TYPES OF CONSTRAINTS

Recall that the original constraints of our previous example, (5–28) and (5–29), were of the form

$$\sum_{j=1}^{n} a_{ij}x_j \leq b_i,$$

where
$$b_i \geq 0. \tag{5–34}$$

Thus, Step 0 of the algorithm was satisfied by simply adding a nonnegative slack variable to the left-hand side of each of our constraints. The resulting equations were automatically in basic feasible form and we were ready to proceed with Step 1 of the algorithm.

When other types of constraints are present in a problem, it is not quite so easy to satisfy Step 0. The following example illustrates the difficulty posed by (and the remedy for) "greater-than-or-equal-to" constraints.

Maximize

$$x_O = -3x_1 - 2x_2 \qquad (5\text{-}35)$$

subject to

$$x_1 + x_2 \geq 6 \qquad (5\text{-}36)$$
$$2x_1 + 5x_2 \geq 18 \qquad (5\text{-}37)$$
$$x_1, x_2 \geq 0.$$

The two inequality constraints, (5-35) and (5-36), can be converted to equations by subtracting nonnegative variables from their left-hand sides. Doing so yields the equations:

$$x_1 + x_2 - x_3 \quad\quad = 6 \qquad (5\text{-}38)$$
$$2x_1 = 5x_2 \quad\quad - x_4 = 18 \qquad (5\text{-}39)$$

These new variables, x_3 and x_4, are called "surplus" variables and are a natural counterpart to the "slack" variables we encountered earlier. Note, though, that our system of equations, (5-38) and (5-39), is not in basic feasible form since the basic solution displayed is

$$x_3 = -6$$
$$x_4 = -18$$
$$x_1 = x_2 = 0,$$

which violates the nonnegativity conditions. Thus, Step 0 of the algorithm cannot be satisfied simply by introducing surplus variables.

To circumvent this difficulty, we add an additional variable, called an "artificial" variable, to the left-hand side of each of our constraints to get

$$x_1 + x_2 - x_3 \quad\quad + x_5 \quad\quad = 6 \qquad (5\text{-}40)$$
$$2x_1 + 5x_2 \quad\quad - x_4 \quad\quad + x_6 = 18. \qquad (5\text{-}41)$$

Choosing x_5 and x_6 to be our basic variables, our system is in basic feasible form. Clearly, the system of (5-40) and (5-41) is the same as the system of (5-38) and (5-39) only if x_5 and x_6, our artificial variables, are equal to zero. On the one hand, then, we see that these variables are needed to have an initial system in basic feasible form. On the other hand, we recognize that these variables must have numerical values of zero. This apparent dilemma can be resolved in the following way. Recognizing that we are trying to maximize our objective function of (5-35), we'll give our artificial variables coefficients in the objective function that will make them unattractive (that is, penalize them) with respect to the other variables. For instance, if M is some large positive number, much larger in magnitude than any of the original objective function coefficients, then an objective function coefficient of $-M$ for our artificial variables will cause them to be made nonbasic as the iterations proceed. Once the artificial variables have been driven out of the basis, they will be equal to zero (by definition of a nonbasic variable) and, effectively, out of the problem.[8] Surplus variables, like slack variables, are legitimate variables in any problem and are given objective function coefficients equal to zero so as not to affect the value of the original objective function.

Thus, to satisfy Step 0 of the simplex algorithm, our problem should be converted to the form:

Maximize

$$x_0 = -3x_1 - 2x_2 + 0x_3 + 0x_4 - Mx_5 - Mx_6 \qquad (5\text{-}42)$$

subject to

$$x_1 + x_2 - x_3 \quad\;\; + x_5 \quad\;\; = 6 \qquad (5\text{-}43)$$
$$2x_1 + 5x_2 \quad\;\; - x_4 \quad\;\; + x_6 = 18. \qquad (5\text{-}44)$$

As long as the artificial variables end up being equal to zero, these two problems, and thus their solutions, will be equivalent. Figure 5–8 shows the simplex tableaus needed to solve this problem. For these tableaus, M was arbitrarily chosen to be $+100$.

Notice in Figure 5–8 that after two iterations both artificial variables are removed from the basis. Once an artificial variable is removed, it will never re-enter the basis (because of its penalty coefficient). Thus, as the artificial variables become nonbasic, their columns can be crossed off as no further calculations need to be made for these variables. It should be noted that only artificial variables have this behavior. Other variables (any type) may re-enter the basis several times as the iterations proceed for a given problem.

So far we have seen how to convert "less-than-or-equal-to" and "greater-than-or-equal-to" types of constraints to the form required by the simplex algorithm. The only other type of constraints that we could encounter are those that are already equations and thus need no slack or surplus variables. To facilitate finding an initial feasible basis for Step 0 of our algorithm, we usually add an artificial variable to the left-hand side of such a constraint. As before, these variables are given penalty coefficients in the objective function to insure that they end up having numerical values of zero.

Thus, we can summarize the mechanics of converting constraints to the form required by the Simplex Algorithm as follows. For each constraint:

---

[8] This procedure for penalizing artificial variables is called the "Big M" method.

FIGURE 5–8

Simplex Algorithm Tableaus for Second Example

c_B	x_B	-3 x_1	-2 x_2	0 x_3	0 x_4	-100 x_5	-100 x_6	b	
-100	x_5	1	1	-1	0	1	0	6	
-100	x_6	2	5*	0	-1	0	1	18	Initial Tableau
$c_j - z_j$		297	598	-100	-100	0	0	-2400	
-100	x_5	6/10*	0	-1	2/10	1	×	24/10	
-2	x_2	4/10	1	0	$-2/10$	0	×	36/10	
$c_j - z_j$		57.8	0	-100	-19.6	0	×	-247.2	
-3	x_1	1	0	$-5/3$	1/3*	×	×	4	
-2	x_2	0	1	2/3	$-1/3$	×	×	2	
$c_j - z_j$		0	0	$-11/3$	1/3	×	×	-16	
0	x_4	3	0	-5	1	×	×	12	
-2	x_2	1	1	-1	0	×	×	6	Optimal Tableau
$c_j - z_j$		-1	0	-2	0	×	×	-12	

Solution: $x_1 = 0$ $x_3 = 0$ $x_5 = 0$
           $x_2 = 6$ $x_4 = 12$ $x_6 = 0$
* These numbers are pivot elements.

a. Check the right-hand-side constant. If it is greater than or equal to zero, go to Step b. Otherwise, multiply the constraint by (-1) to create a nonnegative right-hand-side constant. Note that if the constraint in question is an inequality, this multiplication will change the sense of the inequality.

b. If the constraint is of the form

   (i)

$$\sum_{j=1}^{n} a_{ij}x_j \leq b_i,$$

add a nonnegative slack variable, x_s, to yield

$$\sum_{j=1}^{n} a_{ij}x_j + x_s = b_i.$$

(ii)

$$\sum_{j=1}^{n} a_{ij}x_j \geq b_i,$$

subtract a nonnegative surplus variable, x_s, and add a non-negative artificial variable, x_a, to yield

$$\sum_{j=1}^{n} a_{ij}x_j - x_s + x_a = b_i.$$

(iii)

$$\sum_{j=1}^{n} a_{ij}x_j = b_i,$$

add a nonnegative artificial variable, x_a, to yield

$$\sum_{j=1}^{n} a_{ij}x_j + x_a = b_i.$$

c. Slack and surplus variables are given coefficients equal to zero in all equations except those in which they originated. Artificial variables are given penalty coefficients in the objective function and zero co-efficients in all other equations except those in which they originate.

With these three rules, any linear programming problem can be put into the form required by the simplex algorithm. Of course, most problems will contain a mixture of the three various types of constraints. Such mixtures cause no difficulty as the constraints are converted one at a time by introducing whatever new variables are needed to do the job. For instance, consider the following example with a mixture of constraints.

Maximize

$$x_O = 2x_1 + 3x_2 \tag{5-45}$$

subject to

$$2x_1 + x_2 \leq 10 \tag{5-46}$$
$$x_1 - x_2 = 1 \tag{5-47}$$
$$x_2 \geq 2 \tag{5-48}$$
$$x_1, x_2 \geq 0.$$

Converting this for Step 0 of the algorithm, we get:

Maximize

$$x_O = 2x_1 + 3x_2 + 0x_3 - Mx_4 + 0x_5 - Mx_6 \tag{5-49}$$

subject to

$$2x_1 + x_2 + x_3 \qquad\qquad = 10 \qquad\qquad (5\text{-}50)$$
$$x_1 - x_2 \qquad + x_4 \qquad\quad = 1 \qquad\qquad (5\text{-}51)$$
$$x_2 \qquad\qquad - x_5 + x_6 = 2, \qquad\qquad (5\text{-}52)$$

where x_3 is a slack variable, x_4 is an artificial variable, x_5 is a surplus variable, and x_6 is an artificial variable.

5.6. REMARKS ON FINAL TABLEAUS

When the simplex algorithm terminates it is important to examine the final tableau to ensure that all artificial variables are equal to zero. As indicated previously, artificial variables really do not belong in a problem. They are included only to yield a convenient basic feasible solution for initializing the simplex algorithm. At termination all artificial variables must equal zero (be effectively out of the problem); otherwise, the solution displayed is not the solution to the problem we set out to solve.

Normally, the penalty coefficients we attach to artificial variables in the objective functions forces them to be nonbasic and thus equal to zero in a final tableau. However, it is permissible to have an artificial variable basic in the final tableau as long as its value is zero. If the algorithm terminates with one or more artificial variables at a nonzero value, then either the penalty coefficient M is not large enough or the constraints are inconsistent so that no feasible solutions exist for the original problem.

Besides checking for nonzero artificial variables, the final tableau should be examined for alternative optima. If when the algorithm terminates, all the $(c_j - z_j)$ values (for nonbasic variables) are strictly negative, the solution at hand is unique. That is, no other solutions exist that are as attractive as the current solution. However, if one or more $(c_j - z_j)$ values (for nonbasic variables) are equal to zero when the algorithm terminates, then other solutions exist that are equally attractive. These solutions are easily found by pivoting the appropriate columns into the basis. Geometrically, this means that the optimal objective function contour lies on an entire boundary segment rather than going through a single corner point. Every point along the boundary segment between optimal basic feasible solutions is also optimal since all such points correspond to the same objective function value. These points are not basic solutions. They are optimal solutions, however, and may be of interest for reasons that are not explicitly put into the LP model. For instance, these optimal nonbasic solutions may have more variables at a nonzero level than do the optimal basic solutions. If such a solution property is desirable, then a nonbasic optimal solution should be chosen. This may well be the case in a product-mix LP model, for example, where a nonbasic optimal solution represents a wider product line than a basic optimal solution. Marketing people may prefer the "wider" solution even though it is no more profitable than a basic optimal solution for the coming planning period.

When multiple optimal solutions exist, the nonbasic optimal solutions can be found by choosing a set of nonnegative weights that sum to unity and computing a weighted combination of optimal basic solutions.[9] Different choices for the weights will yield different, but equally attractive, solutions. For example, consider the problem

Maximize

$$x_0 = 10x_1 + 10x_2$$

subject to

$$\begin{aligned} x_1 + x_2 &\leq 14 \\ x_1 \quad\;\; &\leq 4 \\ x_1, x_2 &\geq 0. \end{aligned}$$

Applying the simplex algorithm shows that multiple optima exist. The reader should verify that the following are equally attractive basic solutions:

Solution 1: $x_1 = 0, x_2 = 14, x_0 = 140$
Solution 2: $x_1 = 4, x_2 = 10, x_0 = 140$.

Let w_1 be a nonnegative weight associated with Solution 1 and w_2 be a nonnegative weight associated with Solution 2. Furthermore, require these weights to sum to one. Then a general expression for an optimal solution to the problem is

$$\begin{aligned} x_1 &= (0)(w_1) + (4)(w_2) \\ x_2 &= (14)(w_1) + 10(w_2) \\ x_0 &= 140. \end{aligned}$$

If we arbitrarily pick $w_1 = w_2 = \frac{1}{2}$, we get the particular solution

$$\begin{aligned} x_1 &= 2 \\ x_2 &= 12, \end{aligned}$$

for which $x_0 = 140$, as expected.

5.7. MISCELLANEOUS TOPICS

This section presents a brief discussion of three additional topics associated with linear programming models and their solution. These issues are important in many application areas and help round out our discussion of LP topics.

---

[9] Such a combination is called a "convex" combination.

Unrestricted Variables

The "smallest-ratio" rule of Step 2 of the simplex algorithm insures that the basic variables can take on only nonnegative values. For most problems we want our variables to be nonnegative and thus this feature is desirable. If for some given problem we want one or more variables to be "unrestricted" in algebraic sign, then special provision must be made if the simplex algorithm is to be used for solving the problem. As we shall see in the next chapter, the need to deal with unrestricted variables often arises when we are dealing with "primal-dual" pairs of linear programs. A common way to work with unrestricted variables is as follows. Suppose we want some variable, say x_j, to be unrestricted.

Define

$$x_j = \bar{x}_j - \hat{x}_j, \tag{5-53}$$

where $\bar{x}_j$ and $\hat{x}_j$ are two new variables that are required to be nonnegative. Now, if we replace x_j everywhere it appears in the model by $(\bar{x}_j - \hat{x}_j)$, we will have our model entirely in terms of nonnegative variables. This model, in turn, can be solved by the simplex algorithm. Having optimal values for $\bar{x}_j$ and $\hat{x}_j$, we can easily compute the optimal value for x_j from equation (5-53).

Unbounded Solutions

It is possible that no finite optimal solution exists for a given LP model. That is, the objective function as well as some or all of the decision variables can be made arbitrarily large without violating feasibility considerations. This unbounded condition is readily identified by the simplex algorithm. Recall that the search for a pivot row (Step 2 of the algorithm) requires us to form the ratios of the elements in the b column to those in the pivot column. After throwing out those ratios with nonpositive denominators, the pivot row is identified as the row with the smallest ratio. If all the pivot column elements are nonpositive, then none of the basic variables are decreasing as we increase the incoming variable. Yet, all equations remain satisfied. Such problems are said to be unbounded in the direction of optimality. Ordinarily, the detection of an unbounded solution signals that an error has been made in constructing the model.

Degeneracy

A linear programming solution is said to be degenerate if one or more basic variables are equal to zero. This condition normally occurs when there are ties for the smallest ratio in Step 2 of the algorithm. However, an initial basic solution may also be degenerate.

In most cases, degenerate solutions are treated like any other solution and the simplex algorithm proceeds with no difficulty, but degeneracy can cause a certain sequence of basic solutions to be repeated and prevent the algorithm from generating successively more attractive solutions. In such cases, the algorithm presented in this chapter would not terminate naturally. Most contemporary computer codes for solving linear programming problems have special provisions for dealing with degeneracy so that this problem, called "cycling," is circumvented. Thus, real-world users of linear programming need not worry about degeneracy.

5.8. MINIMIZATION

The simplex algorithm treated in this chapter is designed to solve "maximization" problems. Since many important real-world problems are posed as minimization problems, we need to see what modifications are needed such that these problems can be readily solved also. There are two easy (and equivalent) ways we might proceed. Minimization problems can be solved by modifying Step 1 of the algorithm so that pivoting is allowed only on nonbasic variables that will cause the objective function to decrease. That is, pivot on the most negative $(c_j - z_j)$ value. When all $(c_j - z_j)$ values are nonnegative, the problem is solved. (No other change in the algorithm is needed.)

The other way to readily solve a minimization problem is to convert it to an equivalent maximization problem by multiplying the objective function through by minus one. The solution to the resulting maximization problem will be identical to the solution of the original minimization problem except for the sign of the value of the objective function. Armed with these approaches to minimization problems, we see that the simplex rules for maximization will, in principle, solve any linear programming problem (assuming that solutions exist).

This second approach to minimization problems is illustrated in the following example.

Minimize

$$x_O = 2x_1 + 4x_2 \qquad (5\text{--}54)$$

subject to

$$2x_1 + x_2 \geq 10 \qquad (5\text{--}55)$$
$$x_1 + 4x_2 \geq 16 \qquad (5\text{--}56)$$
$$x_1, x_2 \geq 0. \qquad (5\text{--}57)$$

The equivalent maximization problem is:

Maximize

$$-x_O = z = -2x_1 - 4x_2 \qquad (5\text{--}58)$$

subject to

$$2x_1 + x_2 \geq 10 \qquad (5\text{--}59)$$
$$x_1 + 4x_2 \geq 16 \qquad (5\text{--}60)$$
$$x_1, x_2 \geq 0. \qquad (5\text{--}61)$$

Notice that the constraints for these two problems are exactly the same. The problems differ only in the algebraic signs of the coefficients in the objective function. Since the problem given by (5–58) through (5–61) is a maximization problem, it can be solved by our algorithm to yield

$$z = -19.4285 \qquad (5\text{--}62)$$
$$x_1 = 3.4286 \qquad (5\text{--}63)$$
$$x_2 = 3.1428. \qquad (5\text{--}64)$$

Thus, the solution to our original minimization problem is

$$x_O = 19.4285 \qquad (5\text{--}65)$$
$$x_1 = 3.4286 \qquad (5\text{--}66)$$
$$x_2 = 3.1428. \qquad (5\text{--}67)$$

5.9. SUMMARY

This chapter has presented the basic ideas about the simplex algorithm for solving linear programming problems. Understanding how the algorithm works can make one a more effective user of linear programming. Of course, computers are used to carry out the calculations for large problems. Contemporary computer codes for linear programming are based on more sophisticated versions of the simplex algorithm than we have seen in this chapter, but the basic ideas are the same. The advanced versions deal more effectively with numerical analysis issues and often yield faster convergence than the algorithm we have presented.

Commercial LP computer packages are widely available and easy to use. They automatically incorporate slack, surplus, and artificial variables. Furthermore, their input routines make it very easy to introduce the data. For large problems, matrix-generator packages are available for inputting a problem into a commercial LP code. These are particularly useful for problems with special structures, such as multi-period planning models. The ease with which large linear programming problems can be solved makes LP an important decision aid for modern management.

EXERCISES

5.1.   Solve this LP problem graphically:

Maximize

$$x_O = 3x_1 + 2x_2$$

subject to

$$x_1 \leq 8$$
$$3x_1 + 5x_2 \leq 30$$
$$1.2x_1 + 6x_2 \leq 24$$
$$x_1, x_2 \geq 0.$$

5.2. Solve Problem 1 with the simplex method. Show that each basic feasible solution in the simplex algorithm corresponds to a corner point in the graph of Problem 1.

5.3. Solve this LP problem graphically:

Minimize

$$x_O = 4x_1 + 3x_2$$

subject to

$$4x_1 + 9x_2 \geq 18$$
$$8x_1 + 3x_2 \geq 24$$
$$x_1, x_2 \geq 0.$$

5.4. Solve Problem 3 with the simplex algorithm. Where possible, show the relationship between the basic solution in your solution and the graphical solution from the previous problem.

5.5. Find the minimum-cost blend of a breakfast cereal made from three ingredients, A, B, and C, which contain the following amounts of nutrients per pound in standard units. That is, one pound of Ingredient A contains 800 units of Nutrient 1, etc.

	Nutrient		
Ingredient	1	2	3
A............	800	0.003	1.4
B............	400	0.008	0.9
C............	900	0.020	0.7

The costs per pound are: A, $1.40; B, $1.90; C, $0.90. Each pound of blend must have no more than 750 units of Nutrient 1, no less than 0.010 units of Nutrient 2, and no less than 0.8 units of Nutrient 3.

5.6. The Narrow Gauge Company has several types of special-purpose freight cars for hauling certain cargos. Freight car type A can carry ½ ton of cargo X and ¼ ton of cargo Y. Car B can carry ½ ton of X and ½ ton of Y. Car C can carry no X, and one ton of Y. If a car is carrying less than its quota of one of the special-purpose cargos, the amount of the other cargo that can be carried is not increased because special-purpose shipping racks are permanently mounted in the cars. Five tons of X and seven tons of Y must be delivered to Santa Fe. It costs $40 for a trip with Car A, $50 for a trip with Car B, and $80 for a trip with Car C. Each car type is available in unlimited quantities. Set up and solve a linear programming problem that tells the number of trips to make with each car so as to minimize costs.

5.7.   The Narrow Gauge Company also has a small manufacturing business to absorb unneeded capacities in its maintenance shops. Two products are manufactured; Product 1 contributes $5 per unit to profit; the unit contribution of Product 2 is $7. Each of the products requires time on Machines A, B, and C. The required machine times, in hours, are:

Product	Machine (hours)		
	A	B	C
1......................	1/2	1/2	0
2......................	1/4	1/2	1
Hours available...................	40	50	80

Find the optimal product mix for this part of Narrow Gauge's operations.

5.8.   *a.*   Use the simplex algorithm to solve

Maximize

$$x_0 = 5x_1 + 8x_2 + 3x_3$$

subject to

$$2x_1 + x_2 + 4x_3 \le 10$$
$$x_1 \qquad - x_3 \le 2$$
$$x_j \ge 0; j = 1, 2, 3.$$

b.   Is the solution found in part (a) unique?

5.9.   Use the simplex algorithm to solve

Maximize

$$x_0 = 2x_1 - x_2 + 4x_3 + x_4$$

subject to

$$x_1 + 2x_2 \qquad + x_4 \le 10$$
$$x_2 \qquad \ge 1$$
$$2x_3 + x_4 \le 8$$
$$x_j \ge 0; j = 1, 2, 3, 4.$$

5.10.   Use the simplex algorithm to solve

Minimize

$$y_0 = 10y_1 + 2y_2$$

subject to

$$2y_1 + y_2 \geq 5$$
$$y_1 \qquad \geq 8$$
$$4y_1 - y_2 \geq 3$$
$$y_i \geq 0; i = 1, 2.$$

5.11. Use the simplex algorithm to solve

Minimize

$$w_O = 4w_1 + 2w_2 - 2w_3$$

subject to

$$w_1 - 2w_2 + 2w_3 \geq 10$$
$$w_2 - w_3 \leq 5$$
$$w_1, w_2 \geq 0$$
$$w_3 \text{ unrestricted.}$$

5.12. Use the simplex algorithm to solve

Maximize

$$x_O = 2x_1 + 4x_2 + 6x_3 + 3x_4$$

subject to

$$x_1 + x_2 + x_3 + x_4 = 20$$
$$2x_1 \qquad + 4x_2 + x_4 \leq 40$$
$$x_j \geq 0; j = 1, 2, 3, 4.$$

5.13. Use a locally available LP computer code to solve some of the models you developed in Chapter 4. Discuss what your results mean and how they could serve as a managerial aid.

SUGGESTIONS FOR FURTHER STUDY

Bazaraa, M. S., and Jarvis, J. J., *Linear Programming and Network Flows.* New York: Wiley, 1977.

Cooper, L., and Steinberg, D., *Methods and Applications of Linear Programming.* Philadelphia: W. B. Saunders Co., 1974.

Driebeek, N. J., *Applied Linear Programming.* Reading, Mass.: Addison-Wesley, 1969.

Gass, S. I., *Linear Programming.* 4th ed. New York: McGraw-Hill, 1975.

Hughes, A., and Grawoig, D. E., *Linear Programming: An Emphasis on Decision Making.* Reading, Mass.: Addison-Wesley, 1973.

Loomba, N. P., *Linear Programming: A Managerial Perspective.* 2d ed. New York: McGraw-Hill, 1976.

Naylor, T. H., Byrne, E. T., and Vernon, J. M., *Introduction to Linear Programming: Methods and Cases.* San Francisco: Wadsworth Publishing Co., 1971.

Salkin, H. M., and Saha, J., eds., *Studies in Linear Programming*. New York: American Elsevier Publishing Co., 1975.

Thompson, G. E., *Linear Programming*. New York: Macmillan, 1971.

Throsby, C. D., *Elementary Linear Programming*. New York: Random House, 1970.

6

Duality and Sensitivity Analysis

6.1. INTRODUCTION

IN THIS CHAPTER we will discuss some additional aspects of linear programming that are very useful for decision makers. Consider, for example, a linear programming model designed to determine the optimal allocation of scarce resources to a variety of products that a firm has the potential to make. Applying the simplex algorithm to such a model, we can easily determine the optimal product mix as well as the corresponding profitability. Suppose, though, that in addition to "the solution," we want to determine the effect on the objective function of obtaining additional units of scarce resources. Or suppose that, after solving the model, we learn that one or more of one objective function coefficients are in error by a certain amount. Is the solution at hand still optimal, given this new information about one or more parameters? These and other related issues can be readily resolved by utilizing additional information that is available (at little or no extra computational cost) from the final simplex tableau. Such post-optimality investigations come under the heading of "sensitivity analysis." In general, sensitivity analysis is designed to assess how sensitive a solution is to change in one or more parameters in the original model—without explicitly re-solving the model. We will see in this chapter that a solution's sensitivity to changes in the b vector or the objective function coefficients is very easy to assess.

Duality theory, which deals with special pairs of linear programming problems, plays an important role in sensitivity analysis. In addition, the use of duality theory leads to considerable computational savings for many problems. Special-purpose algorithms based on linear programming duality exist for certain classes of linear programming models. These special purpose algorithms are usually more efficient than the simplex algorithms for the class of models intended. One such algorithm for transportation models is presented later in this chapter.

Since duality is important in itself as well as in sensitivity analysis, we will begin the chapter with the basic ideas of duality theory. Later in the chapter some of the more important aspects of sensitivity analysis will be discussed.

6.2. DUALITY: ANOTHER WAY TO VIEW THE SAME PROBLEM

To illustrate the notion of duality consider once again the "butcher" example of Chapter 4.

$$\text{Maximize profit} = x_0 = 6x_1 + 4x_2 \tag{6-1}$$

subject to

$$
\begin{array}{lll}
x_1 + x_2 \le 6 & \text{(trays)} & \text{(6-2)} \\
2x_1 + x_2 \le 9 & \text{(mixing time)} & \text{(6-3)} \\
2x_1 + 3x_2 \le 16 & \text{(shelf space)} & \text{(6-4)} \\
x_j \ge 0; \quad j = 1, 2. & & \text{(6-5)}
\end{array}
$$

Recall that this problem deals with allocating three resources (trays, mixing time, and shelf space) to two products (different grades of meat loaf). This LP model is constructed so that we can readily determine the number of units of each product to make so that profits are maximized within the limits defined by the finite availability of the three resources. That is, the model is concerned with the optimal way to consume the three resources in the production of the two products.

Rather than viewing this problem from a resource consumption point of view, we could view it from a "resource selling" point of view. Suppose we consider selling our three resources rather than consuming them. What prices (or rent, if appropriate) should we charge for our resources? If we consume the resources, we'll realize a certain profit. We should be willing to sell the resources if doing so would yield at least the same income. Thus we want to determine the *minimum* set of prices to charge so that the total value of our resources is at least as large as the profit we could make via our production process. Certainly any prices above these minimum prices would also be acceptable.

These minimum prices can be found by linear programming. Denote the prices for our three resources by y_1, y_2, and y_3.

Since we have 6, 9, and 16 units of our three resources available—refer to (6-2), (6-3), and (6-4)—the total value of our resources is

$$y_0 = 6y_1 + 9y_2 + 16y_3.$$

We want to choose the prices (the y_i) so that this total value is minimized subject to constraints that ensure that we do at least as well by selling as we could by consuming the resources.

One unit of Product 1 contributes \$6 to profits. Such a unit consumes one, two, and two units, respectively, of resources one, two, and three. Thus the value (potential revenue) of the resources required to produce one unit of Product 1 is

$$y_1 + 2y_2 + 2y_3.$$

We want to require that this revenue from selling is at least as great as the profit we could realize from consuming rather than selling. Thus our constraint corresponding to Product 1 is

$$y_1 + 2y_2 + 2y_3 \geq 6.$$

A similar constraint (shown below) exists for Product 2. Like the above, it constrains the price levels to recognize the alternative uses of the resources.

Certainly we wouldn't want any of the resource prices to be negative. Thus, these variables will be required to be nonnegative, and we have the following linear programming problem.

Minimize

$$y_O = 6y_1 + 9y_2 + 16y_3 \tag{6-6}$$

subject to

$$y_1 + 2y_2 + 2y_3 \geq 6 \tag{6-7}$$
$$y_1 + y_2 + 3y_3 \geq 4 \tag{6-8}$$
$$y_i \geq 0. \tag{6-9}$$

The linear program (6–6) through (6–9) is the dual of the program (6–1) through (6–5). They both yield important information about the problem at hand. One looks specifically at how the resources should be consumed in the production process. The other is concerned with determining the minimum acceptable set of prices to charge for resources if they were to be sold rather than used in production. As we will see later on in the chapter, the complete solution to either problem automatically gives the complete solution to the other.

It is important to note that the dual variables have no necessary relationship with market prices. Comparisons with market prices for resources can be made in order to determine whether one should consume or sell resources. Certainly the optimal dual price associated with a given resource represents the maximum amount we would be willing to pay for an additional unit of the resource. Later in the chapter we will explore further the economic interpretation of dual variables.

It should also be emphasized that the prices computed from the dual program (6–6) through (6–9) are the minimum prices we would be willing to accept if we sold our entire inventory of resources. If only some of the resources are to be sold the prices may or may not be valid. The section on sensitivity analysis in this chapter shows how to compute a range over which these prices are valid for such cases.

The discussion in this section was intended to introduce the concept of duality by analyzing the familiar "butcher" example from a resource-selling point of view. With this "gut-feeling" under our belts, we now turn to a more general discussion of duality.

6.3. DUALITY FOR THE GENERAL LP PROBLEM

For every linear programming model there exists another and specially related linear programming model. The construction of this special pair

FIGURE 6–1

Summary of Construction Rules for Primal-Dual Pairs

	Primal	*Dual*
a.	n variables, m constraints	m variables, n constraints
b.	Right hand side constants	Objective function coefficients
c.	Objective function coefficients	Right hand side constants
d.	Columns of constraint matrix	Rows of constraint matrix*
e.	Rows of constraint matrix*	Columns of constraint matrix
f.	Inequality relationship	Nonnegative variable
g.	Nonnegative variable	Inequality relationship
h.	Equality relationship	Unrestricted variable
i.	Unrestricted variable	Equality relationship

* Row 1 corresponds to Column 1, Row 2 to Column 2, etc.

of programs ensures that if one has a finite optimal solution, so does the other. Moreover, the pair of models is related in such a way that a complete solution for one problem determines the complete solution to the other. We arbitrarily call one problem the "primal" problem and the other the "dual" problem.

The rules for constructing a dual problem from a given primal problem are presented in Figure 6–1. These rules assume that the problem in question is in one of two standard forms. If we want to construct the dual to a maximization problem, then before we use the rules of Figure 6–1, we must put our problem in the form:

Maximize

$$x_0 = \sum_{j=1}^{n} c_j x_j \tag{6-10}$$

subject to

$$\sum_{j=1}^{n} a_{ij} x_j \left(\stackrel{\leqq}{=} \right) b_i; \quad i = 1, 2, \ldots, m \tag{6-11}$$

plus any nonnegativity conditions that may be required for some or all of the variables. Note that our standard form for maximization requires that all inequality constraints (other than nonnegativity conditions) be written as "less than or equal to" constraints. Thus it may be necessary to multiply certain constraints through by minus one to produce the desired form.

The standard form for minimization problems is:

Minimize

$$y_0 = \sum_{i=1}^{m} b_i y_i \tag{6-12}$$

subject to

$$\sum_{i=1}^{m} a_{ij} y_i \left(\geqq\right) c_j; \quad j = 1, 2, \ldots, n \tag{6-13}$$

plus any nonnegativity conditions that may be required for some or all of the variables.

In constructing these primal-dual pairs, it makes no difference whether we start with a maximization problem or a minimization problem. If we start with a maximization problem, the dual problem that we construct will be a minimization problem in standard form. Likewise, if we start with a minimization problem, the dual that we construct using the rules of Figure 6-1 will be a maximization problem in standard form.

To illustrate the use of Figure 6-1, consider the following problem:

Maximize

$$x_0 = 6x_1 + 7x_2 + 5x_3 \tag{6-14}$$

subject to

$$2x_1 + 3x_2 + 4x_3 \leq 10 \tag{6-15}$$
$$2x_1 + x_2 - x_3 \leq 8 \tag{6-16}$$
$$x_j \geq 0; j = 1, 2, 3. \tag{6-17}$$

Note that this problem, which we call the primal, is already in the required form for a maximization problem. The dual will be a minimization problem in the form shown by (6-12) and (6-13). Item (*a*) of Figure 6-1 indicates that the dual problem will have $m = 2$ variables and $n = 3$ constraints. Item (*b*) indicates that the objective function coefficients for the dual are the right-hand-side values of the primal. Denoting the dual variables by y_i, we can thus write down the dual objective function

Minimize

$$y_0 = 10y_1 + 8y_2. \tag{6-18}$$

Now for the three constraints. Item (*c*) says that the right-hand-side values for our dual are the primal objective function coefficients. Item (*d*) says that the row elements (that is, constraint coefficients) of the dual problem are the column elements from the primal problem. That is, the coefficients in the first dual constraint are the coefficients (taken in natural order) from the x_1 column of the primal problem, and so forth. Item (*g*) indicates that all three dual relationships are inequalities since all three primal variables have nonnegativity conditions on them. Since the dual we are forming is a minimization problem, these inequalities must be of the "greater-than-or-equal-to" variety. Thus, the three dual constraints are:

$$2y_1 + 2y_2 \geq 6 \qquad (6\text{–}19)$$
$$3y_1 + y_2 \geq 7 \qquad (6\text{–}20)$$
$$4y_1 - y_2 \geq 5. \qquad (6\text{–}21)$$

What about nonnegativity conditions on the dual variables? Item (*f*) indicates that the dual variables are required to be nonnegative since both primal constraints are inequalities. The nonnegativity conditions together with (6–18) through (6–21) comprise the dual of the problem given by (6–14) through (6–17).

It is important to note that the variables of the dual problem are associated with constraints in the primal problem. That is, y_1 is associated with the first primal constraint (6–15) and y_2 is associated with the second primal constraint. Moreover, this association goes both ways so that x_1 is associated with the first dual constraint, and so forth. As items (*g*) and (*i*) of Figure 6–1 indicate, a given constraint in the dual problem will be either an inequality or an equality constraint depending on whether or not its associated variable (from the primal problem) is nonnegative or unrestricted. Likewise, items (*f*) and (*h*) say that a given dual variable will be nonnegative or unrestricted depending on whether or not its corresponding primal constraint is an inequality or an equation.

For example, suppose the nonnegativity conditions of (6–17) were changed to read:

$$x_1, x_3 \geq 0, \quad x_2 \text{ unrestricted.} \qquad (6\text{–}22)$$

Then in the dual program, the second constraint would have to be changed to an equation:

$$3y_1 + y_2 = 7. \qquad (6\text{–}23)$$

Furthermore, suppose that the first primal constraint, (6–15), was an equation rather than an inequality. Then the first variable of our dual problem would be unrestricted in sign.

To further illustrate the use of Figure 6–1, consider another example.

Minimize

$$x_0 = 2x_1 + 4x_2 + 5x_3 \qquad (6\text{–}24)$$

subject to

$$x_1 + 2x_2 - x_3 = 10 \tag{6-25}$$

$$x_1 \qquad\qquad \geq 4 \tag{6-26}$$

$$- x_2 + x_3 \leq 3 \tag{6-27}$$

$$x_1, x_2, x_3 \geq 0. \tag{6-28}$$

Except for the third constraint, (6-27), this problem is already in the form required for a minimization problem. Multiplying (6-27) through by minus one yields

$$x_2 - x_3 \geq -3. \tag{6-29}$$

The reader should verify that the dual of the problem given by (6-24), (6-25), (6-26), (6-29), and (6-28) is

Maximize

$$y_0 = 10y_1 + 4y_2 - 3y_3 \tag{6-30}$$

subject to

$$y_1 + y_2 \qquad \leq 2 \tag{6-31}$$

$$2y_1 \qquad + y_3 \leq 4 \tag{6-32}$$

$$-y_1 \qquad - y_3 \leq 5 \tag{6-33}$$

$$y_1 \text{ unrestricted, } y_2, y_3 \geq 0. \tag{6-34}$$

It should be noted that the standard forms discussed here are needed for constructing dual programs only and have nothing to do with the simplex algorithm. The requirements of the simplex algorithm, of course, must be satisfied when solving either primal or dual programs.

Relationships Between Solutions

The final simplex tableau displays the complete solution to the problem at hand as well as a complete solution to its dual.[1] The dual solution is obtained from the tableau as follows:

1. Optimum objective function values are equal.
2. Numerical values for the (real) dual variables are the negatives of the $(c_j - z_j)$ values (in the final tableau) associated with the slack and/or surplus variables of the primal problem.[2,3]
3. Numerical values for the slack and/or surplus variables in the dual problem are the negatives of the $(c_j - z_j)$ values associated with the real variables in the primal problem.

---

[1] If the primal problem is unbounded, the dual problem is inconsistent. The rules given here are for primal-dual pairs with finite optimal solutions.

[2] By "real" variables, we mean the original variables as opposed to slack and surplus variables.

[3] Equality constraints can be accommodated by writing them as two inequalities or by eliminating a variable and adding an inequality to insure the nonnegativity of the variable eliminated.

Note that the above relationships are between *optimal* solutions to a given primal-dual pair. Artificial variables do not enter into the relationships at all since they have nothing to do with the solution to either problem and are needed only to initialize the simplex algorithm.

Consider again the example of (6–14) through (6–17). Figure 6–2 shows the first and final simplex tableaus for this problem. The optimal primal solution is:

$$x_1 = 7/2$$
$$x_2 = 1$$
$$x_3 = x_4 = x_5 = 0$$
$$x_0 = 28.$$

The $(c_j - z_j)$ row of the final tableau contains the complete solution to the dual problem given by (6–18) through (6–21). At optimality, the

FIGURE 6–2

Initial and Final Tableaus for Example Problem

c_B	x_B	6 x_1	7 x_2	5 x_3	0 x_4	0 x_5	b	
0	x_4	2	3	4	1	0	10	Initial Tableau
0	x_5	2	1	-1	0	1	8	
$c_j - z_j$		6	7	5	0	0	0	
6	x_1	1	0	$-7/4$	$-1/4$	3/4	7/2	Optimal Tableau
7	x_2	0	1	5/2	1/2	$-1/2$	1	
$c_j - z_j$		0	0	-2	-2	-1	28	

objective function values are equal. Thus, we have immediately that $y_0 = 28$. The optimal values for the real dual variables, y_1 and y_2, are given by the negative of the $(c_j - z_j)$ values for the slack variables in the primal problem.

Thus, we have

$$y_1 = -(c_4 - z_4) = -(-2) = 2$$
$$y_2 = -(c_5 - z_5) = -(-1) = 1.$$

Finally, the optimal values for the surplus variables in the dual problem, y_3, y_4, y_5, are given by the negative of the $(c_j - z_j)$ values for the real variables in the primal problem. That is:

$$y_3 = -(c_1 - z_1) = 0$$
$$y_4 = -(c_2 - z_2) = 0$$
$$y_5 = -(c_3 - z_3) = 2,$$

which completes the solution to the dual problem. The reader should verify (either graphically or by applying the simplex algorithm) that the dual solution identified above does indeed solve the dual problem.

Thus far we have seen mechanical rules for constructing primal-dual pairs and how the solution to one problem can be readily obtained from the optimal tableau of the other problem.[4] It follows, then, that when confronted with a linear programming problem to solve, we actually have a choice—we could solve the problem at hand, or we could solve its dual and identify from the solution of the dual the solution to the original problem. This latter approach might be attractive for certain problems. The computational burden of solving a linear programming problem is more closely related to the number of rows (constraints) than to the number of variables involved. The number of rows determines the size of the basis which, in turn, determines the computational burden of pivoting in the simplex algorithm.[5] For this reason, we may want to choose to solve the dual rather than the primal in cases in which the dual has fewer rows than the primal (that is, when n is less than m).

6.4. SENSITIVITY ANALYSIS

For the sensitivity analysis that follows, it will be convenient to have the following terminology. The stopping conditions of the simplex algorithm, stating that all the $(c_j - z_j)$ values must be nonpositive for maximization problems and nonnegative for minimization problems, will be referred to as "the optimality conditions." The requirement that all the elements of the solution column must always remain nonnegative will be referred to as "the feasibility conditions." Because of the way primal-dual pairs are constructed, the optimality conditions for a primal maximization problem are the negative of the feasibility conditions for the dual minimization problem. Furthermore, the primal feasibility conditions are equivalent to the dual optimality conditions.

We will confine our analysis in this text to changes in objective function coefficients and right-hand-side values. These issues are important for decision makers and relatively easy to resolve. The ideas presented here can be extended to analyze the effect of other parameter changes on a given solution.

To conduct our sensitivity analysis, we need the following important properties of optimal solutions to primal-dual pairs of linear programming. Recall that an optimal linear programming solution is associated with an optimal basis. Suppose that we have an optimal basis and then

---

[4] The theory behind the primal-dual pairs that legitimizes the mechanics presented here can be found in any of the linear programming books listed at the end of the chapter.

[5] For problems with many rows, the effort required to carry out the pivoting operation usually exceeds the effort required to evaluate the nonbasic variables.

a. Consider changing one or more objective function coefficients.

Property 1: The basis at hand will remain optimal as long as the optimality conditions remain satisfied. This is equivalent to saying that the current basis will remain optimal as long as the dual problem, with its current solution, remains feasible.

b. Consider changing one or more of the right-hand-side values.

Property 2: The basis at hand will remain optimal as long as the feasibility conditions are satisfied. This is equivalent to saying that the current basis will remain optimal as long as the dual optimality conditions are satisfied.

To illustrate how these properties can be used to conduct sensitivity analysis, consider the following product-mix model.

Maximize

$$x_O = 5x_1 + 8x_2 + 6x_3 \qquad (6\text{-}35)$$

subject to

$$x_1 + x_2 + x_3 \leq 12 \text{ (Input 1)} \qquad (6\text{-}36)$$
$$x_1 + 2x_2 + 2x_3 \leq 20 \text{ (Input 2)} \qquad (6\text{-}37)$$
$$x_j \geq 0; \quad j = 1, 2, 3, \qquad (6\text{-}38)$$

where x_1, x_2, and x_3 represent the number of units of each product to make, and the objective function coefficients represent the unit profitability of the products. The production of each of the three products requires a certain number of units of two scarce inputs as shown in (6-36) and (6-37). Figure 6-3 shows the beginning and the optimal tableaus for this problem. Note that the optimal product-mix calls for four units of Product 1, eight units of Product 2, and none of Product 3. Moreover, note that all 12 units of Input 1 and all 20 units of Input 2 are consumed by this optimal product mix.

FIGURE 6–3

Initial and Final Tableaus for Example Problem

c_B	x_B	5 x_1	8 x_2	6 x_3	0 x_4	0 x_5	b
0	x_4	1	1	1	1	0	12
0	x_5	1	2	2	0	1	20
$c_j - z_j$		5	8	6	0	0	0
5	x_1	1	0	0	2	−1	4
8	x_2	0	1	1	−1	1	8
$c_j - z_j$		0	0	−2	−2	−3	84

Changes in Objective Function Coefficients

Suppose now that we learn that the unit profit figure for Product 1 might be in error. By how much could it differ from the current value of $5 such that the solution we have is still optimal? This can be determined by using Property 1 as follows. Denote the coefficient of x_1 in (6–35) by $5 + \Delta_1$ (instead of 5). The deviation, Δ_1, could be either positive or negative.

According to Property 1, our final tableau (Figure 6–3) will remain optimal as long as the optimality conditions remain satisfied. The procedure then is to write down the $(c_j - z_j)$ values for each nonbasic variable and then impose the optimality conditions. Doing so will yield a set of inequalities from which we can determine how far the true coefficient of x_1 could differ from 5 such that our current solution is still optimal.

The $(c_j - z_j)$ values are (working with our final tableau):

$$
\begin{aligned}
(c_3 - z_3) &= 6 - \{(5 + \Delta_1)(0) & + 8(1)\} & = -2 + 0\Delta_1 \\
(c_4 - z_4) &= 0 - \{(5 + \Delta_1)(2) & + 8(-1)\} & = -2 - 2\Delta_1 \\
(c_5 - z_5) &= 0 - \{(5 + \Delta_1)(-1) & + 8(1)\} & = -3 + \Delta_1.
\end{aligned}
$$

If our current solution is to remain optimal, each of these quantities must be nonpositive. Thus, we have the conditions:

$$
\begin{aligned}
-2 - 2\Delta_1 &\leq 0, \quad \text{or} \quad \Delta_1 \geq -1 \\
-3 + \Delta_1 &\leq 0, \quad \text{or} \quad \Delta_1 \leq 3,
\end{aligned}
$$

which together yield

$$-1 \leq \Delta_1 \leq 3. \tag{6–39}$$

This range, called the sensitivity range for c_1 about its current value, indicates that our current solution would be optimal if the profitability of Product 1 was anything from $4 per unit to $8 per unit. Outside this range some other solution would be optimal. If the error in c_1 is not likely to be more than, say, ± 20 cents, we would be quite confident that our current product-mix ($x_1 = 4$, $x_2 = 8$) is indeed the optimal mix. Of course, the objective function value of $84 will be affected by any error that might exist in c_1.

The sensitivity ranges for the other two original objective function coefficients are found in the same manner. Denote c_2 by $8 + \Delta_2$. Then the $(c_j - z_j)$ values for the nonbasic variables are:

$$
\begin{aligned}
(c_3 - z_3) &= 6 - [5(0) & + (8 + \Delta_2)(1)] & = -2 - \Delta_2 \\
(c_4 - z_4) &= 0 - [5(2) & + (8 + \Delta_2)(-1)] & = -2 + \Delta_2 \\
(c_5 - z_5) &= 0 - [5(-1) & + (8 + \Delta_2)(1)] & = -3 - \Delta_2.
\end{aligned}
$$

Applying the optimality conditions $(c_j - z_j) \leq 0$ yields:

$$-3 < -2 \leq \Delta_2 \leq 2. \tag{6–40}$$

Thus c_2 could be anything from 6 to 10 and the current product mix would still be optimal.

Since x_3 is currently a nonbasic variable, the sensitivity range for c_3 is even easier to find than the ranges were for c_1 and c_2. This is true because the objective function coefficient of a nonbasic variable appears only in its own $(c_j - z_j)$ calculation. Thus, we get a single inequality rather than a "system" of inequalities. Denoting c_3 by $6 + \Delta_3$, we have:

$$c_3 - z_3 = 6 + \Delta_3 - [5(0) + 8(1)] = -2 + \Delta_3,$$

which gives the sensitivity range of

$$-\infty \le \Delta_3 \le 2. \tag{6-41}$$

This means that as long as c_3 is less than or equal to 8, our product mix will remain optimal. A lower bound of $-\infty$ will always be present on the ranges for nonbasic variables. If an objective function coefficient of a variable is too small to cause the variable to be basic, certainly anything less than the current value could not cause the variable to become basic! (This refers, of course, to maximization problems.)

Note that in finding the ranges above, it was assumed that all other parameters remained unchanged. Using the same approach as used above, we can accommodate simultaneous change in all three objective function coefficients. Denote c_1, c_2, and c_3 by $5 + \Delta_1$, $8 + \Delta_2$, and $6 + \Delta_3$, respectively. Then the $c_j - z_j$ values and the optimality conditions are:

$$
\begin{aligned}
c_3 - z_3 &= 6 + \Delta_3 - [(5 + \Delta_1)(0) & + (8 + \Delta_2)(1)] & \le 0 \\
c_4 - z_4 &= \quad\; 0 - [(5 + \Delta_1)(2) & + (8 + \Delta_2)(-1)] & \le 0 \\
c_5 - z_5 &= \quad\; 0 - [(5 + \Delta_1)(-1) & + (8 + \Delta_2)(1)] & \le 0,
\end{aligned}
$$

which yields the set of inequalities

$$
\begin{aligned}
-\Delta_2 + \Delta_3 &\le 2 \\
-2\Delta_1 + \Delta_2 &\le 2 \\
\Delta_1 - \Delta_2 &\le 3.
\end{aligned}
\tag{6-42}
$$

As long as the changes in c_1, c_2, and c_3 satisfy the inequalities shown in (6-42), our current product-mix is still the optimal product-mix. For example, suppose we are able to determine that the maximum c_3 could be is 7, and that absolute lower bounds on c_1 and c_2 are 4.8 and 7.2, respectively. These changes imply $\Delta_1 = -0.2$, $\Delta_2 = -0.8$, $\Delta_3 = 1$, which satisfy the optimality conditions of (6-42) and, thus, our present mix would remain optimal even if these extreme changes occurred in c_1, c_2, and c_3. In such a case we would say that our current solution is not very sensitive to changes in the objective function coefficients.

Additional Columns

Suppose that after solving a linear program we want to determine whether or not our solution would remain optimal if a new column (that is, a new variable) was added to the original model. Of course, we could determine the effect of the new column by solving the enlarged model, but, Property 1 readily tells whether the new column will be basic or nonbasic in an optimal tableau for the enlarged model. If the new column is destined to be nonbasic, our current solution remains optimal and we have no need to solve the enlarged model.

The procedure is as follows. Recall that Property 1 states that a given primal basis will remain optimal as long as the dual problem remains feasible. Adding a new column to the primal problem corresponds to adding a new row (constraint) to the dual problem. Thus, if the current dual solution satisfies our new dual constraint, our current basis (and its associated solution) will remain optimal. If the new dual constraint is violated by the current dual solution, then our current solution is not optimal for the enlarged model, and the simplex algorithm will have to be applied to find the optimal solution.

Consider again the product-mix problem of (6–35) through (6–38). Suppose that before we implement the solution called for by Figure 6–3, our product development department informs us that they have developed a new product that should be considered before we go to production. We are told that the new product would have an estimated profit margin of $10 per unit. Furthermore, to make one unit of the new product requires three units of Input 1 and two units of Input 2. Note that this information about the new product corresponds to a new column in our LP model. The dual constraint corresponding to this new column (that is, this new product) is

$$3y_1 + 2y_2 \geq 10, \tag{6-43}$$

where y_1 and y_2 are the dual variables. From Figure 6–3 we see that the current optimal values for the dual variables are

$$y_1 = 2, \quad y_2 = 3,$$

which satisfy the dual constraint of (6–43). Thus, our current product-mix remains optimal, and the new product should not be made. Note that our current product-mix will remain optimal as long as the unit profit margin for the new product is less than or equal to 12. Any amount greater than 12 would cause the dual constraint to be violated by the current dual solution. In turn, this means that our primal solution could be improved by pivoting the new column into the basis.

Changes in Right-Hand-Side Values

Property 2 can be used to determine how an optimal linear programming solution would be modified if one or more b_i values were changed.

FIGURE 6-4

Initial Tableau for Product-Mix Example Allowing for a Change in b_1

c_B	x_B	x_1	x_2	x_3	x_4	x_5	b
0	x_4	1	1	1	1	0	$12 + \Delta_1$
0	x_5	1	2	2	0	1	$20 + 0\Delta_1$
$c_j - z_j$		5	8	6	0	0	0

A range can be computed for the change in a given b_i value that will leave the current optimal basis unchanged. The numerical values of the basic variables will change over this range but the basis composition will stay fixed. Such ranges are related to the important concept of a shadow price, which will be introduced later in this section.

Refer again to our product-mix model. Denote the initial availability of Input 1 by b_1 and that of Input 2 by b_2. Consider now a change in the availability of Input 1. Let $b_1 = 12 + \Delta_1$ where Δ_1 is some change from the current value of 12. The initial tableau for the simplex algorithm is shown in Figure 6-4. Note that this tableau differs from the initial tableau of Figure 6-3 only in the b columns.

Recall that slack variable x_4 is associated with Constraint 1 and the amount of Input 1 available, b_1. Furthermore, note that the elements in the x_4 column are identical to the coefficients of Δ_1 in the b column. Thus, if we were to apply the simplex algorithm to our problem, the coefficients of Δ_1 in the b column would be the same (at every iteration) as the elements in the x_4 column. If we were considering changes in b_2, the elements in the corresponding slack variable column, x_5, would be used for the coefficient of Δ_2. Thus, the final tableau for our problem can be constructed from the previous final tableau (Figure 6-3) by taking the elements in the x_4 column to be the coefficients of Δ_1 in the b column. This tableau is shown in Figure 6-5. The reader should compare Figures 6-3, 6-4, and 6-5.

FIGURE 6-5

Optimal Tableau for Product-Mix Example Showing the Basic Variables as a Function of Δ_1

c_B	x_B	x_1	x_2	x_3	x_4	x_5	b
5	x_1	1	0	0	2	-1	$4 + 2\Delta_1$
8	x_2	0	1	1	-1	1	$8 - \Delta_1$
$c_j - z_j$		0	0	-2	-2	-3	$84 + y_1\Delta_1$

Property 2 says that our tableau of Figure 6–5 will be the optimal tableau for our problem as long as the "feasibility conditions" are satisfied. That is, as long as:

$$x_1 = 4 + 2\Delta_1 \geq 0 \tag{6-44}$$
$$x_2 = 8 - \Delta_1 \geq 0. \tag{6-45}$$

The conditions of (6–44) and (6–45) yield

$$-2 \leq \Delta_1 \leq 8. \tag{6-46}$$

For any change in b_1 that satisfies (6–46), the optimal solution to our problem is given by the tableau of Figure 6–5.

Suppose, for example, that we learn that we only have 11 units of Input 1 available for use rather than the 12 units previously planned on. Rather than solving the LP model again to find the optimal product mix, we simply use the above results to show how this change ($\Delta_1 = -1$) would alter our previous optimal solution. Since $\Delta_1 = -1$ is within the allowable range of (6–46), our new optimal solution values are given by (6–44) and (6–45). That is

$$x_1 = 4 + 2(-1) = 2 \tag{6-47}$$
$$x_2 = 8 - (-1) = 9. \tag{6-48}$$

The same approach can be used to see how changes in b_2 would affect the current solution. The reader should verify that the range of allowable change in b_2 that leaves our current basis optimal is

$$-8 \leq \Delta_2 \leq 4, \tag{6-49}$$

and that for changes in the above range, the optimal solution values are given by

$$x_1 = 4 - \Delta_2 \tag{6-50}$$
$$x_2 = 8 + \Delta_2. \tag{6-51}$$

Shadow Prices

Shadow prices are defined to be the amounts by which the objective function value would be changed by unit changes in the b_i values. For resource allocation problems, the shadow prices represent the incremental worth of additional units of the various resources. Numerically, the shadow prices are simply the dual variables associated with the various constraints. This can be seen by examining the dual objective function. In general we have

$$y_0 = b_1 y_1 + b_2 y_2 + \cdots + b_m y_m. \tag{6-52}$$

Now, at optimality, the primal and dual objective function values (x_0 and y_0) are equal. Thus, if b_1 is increased by one unit, we see that both

y_0 and x_0 will be increased by y_1, and so forth. In general, y_i is the shadow price associated with the ith constraint. These shadow prices remain constant until the optimal dual solution changes. In other words, as long as the primal feasibility conditions are satisfied, the current set of shadow prices is valid.

Let's return once again to our product-mix example. We saw earlier that the optimal dual variable values are $y_1 = 2$, $y_2 = 3$. This means that an additional unit of Input 1 would increase by x_0 by 2. Moreover, we have from (6–46) that the above statement would be true for up to eight additional units of Input 1. Likewise a unit reduction in Input 1 will cause x_0 to decrease by 2 and this would be true for reductions up to 2 units of Input 1. Beyond these limits the solution would change and some other set of shadow prices would become valid. Inequality (6–49) and the shadow price $y_2 = 3$ enable us to make similar statements about the impact on x_0 of changes in Input 2. Furthermore, we could develop a set of inequalities that allow for simultaneous change in both Input 1 and Input 2. Again, the shadow prices would remain valid as long as these conditions were satisfied.

Suppose then, that we have the opportunity to obtain additional units of Input 1 for $1 per unit. Since this amount is less than the shadow price associated with Input 1, we should go ahead and obtain as many units (up to eight) as we can. Each such unit will increase profits by $(2-1) = 1$ dollar. Equations (6–44) and (6–45) would tell us how our optimal product-mix should be adjusted to reflect the change in b_1.

From the above discussion it should be clear that a shadow price represents the maximum amount you would be willing to pay for an additional unit of a resource. A shadow price of zero implies that the resource in question is currently in excess supply. Additional units would be of no value. Note that if the market price is greater than the shadow price for some resource, we should consider selling rather than buying units.

6.5. A SPECIAL ALGORITHM FOR TRANSPORTATION PROBLEMS

The above discussion of sensitivity analysis indicates how duality can be used to examine certain postoptimality issues. As mentioned previously, duality theory also yields powerful computational approaches for many special LP models. One important illustration of this role of duality is the dual-based algorithm presented below for transportation problems.

Recall that the classical transportation problem is concerned with providing the minimum cost shipping activities that will satisfy demand at the demand nodes without exceeding the supply available at the source nodes. As discussed in Chapter 4, the model is

Minimize cost

$$\sum_{i=1}^{n} \sum_{j=1}^{m} c_{ij} x_{ij} \tag{6-53}$$

subject to

$$\sum_{i=1}^{n} x_{ij} = D_j; \quad j = 1, 2 \ldots m \tag{6-54}$$

$$\sum_{j=1}^{m} x_{ij} = S_i; \quad i = 1, 2 \ldots n \tag{6-55}$$

$$x_{ij} \geq 0, \tag{6-56}$$

where

x_{ij} = amount shipped from node i to node j
c_{ij} = unit cost corresponding to x_{ij}
D_j = demand at node j
S_i = supply available at node i
n = number of supply nodes
m = number of demand nodes

and where a dummy supply or demand node has been added to the network, if necessary, so that

$$\sum_{i=1}^{n} S_i = \sum_{j=1}^{m} D_j. \tag{6-57}$$

Clearly this model is a linear program and could be solved by the simplex algorithm. However, the model has a mathematical structure that makes it even easier to solve.[6] A special purpose algorithm based on the dual to the cost minimization problem enables basic possible solutions to (6-53) through (6-55) to be readily identified and evaluated with less computational burden than required by the simplex algorithm. In fact, the calculations involved require only additions and subtractions.

The dual to our cost minimization model is

Maximize

$$\sum_{i=1}^{n} S_i v_i + \sum_{j=1}^{m} D_j \mu_j \tag{6-58}$$

subject to

$$v_i + \mu_j \leq c_{ij} \text{ for all } (i, j) \text{ pairs} \tag{6-59}$$
$$v_i, \mu_j \text{ unrestricted}, \tag{6-60}$$

---

[6] The special structure referred to is the constraint coefficient matrix which consists of only ones and zeros in such a way that the determinant of every basis matrix is equal to +1. Such a matrix is said to be "totally unimodular."

where the μ_j are dual variables associated with the demand constraints and the v_i are the dual variables for the supply constraints. Note the simple structure of the dual constraints of (6–59). The sum of each supply-demand dual variable pair must be less than or equal to the corresponding unit shipping cost.

Several comments about the above primal-dual pair are in order.

1. Because total supply equals total demand, (6–57), one of the $(m + n)$ primal constraints of (6–54) and (6–55) is redundant (and, in fact, could be thrown away). Thus the basic feasible solutions we need to examine to solve the transportation problem will each have exactly $(m + n - 1)$ basic variables. In terms of the dual, the redundant primal constraint means that any one dual variable can be given some arbitrary value. Normally we let convenience guide us in choosing a dual variable and then assign that variable a value of zero.

2. From duality theory, we know that basic variables in the primal correspond to tight constraints (that is, no slack) in the dual. Thus corresponding to each basic feasible solution in the primal we will have $(n + m - 1)$ tight dual constraints. The structure of the dual constraints makes these equations easy to solve for the dual variables.

3. Since dual feasibility is equivalent to primal optimality, we can use the dual variables to test for primal optimality by evaluating the remaining dual constraints. If the current dual solution is feasible, the corresponding primal solution is optimal. Otherwise, we must identify and test yet another basic feasible primal solution.

The above three remarks lay the foundation for the transportation algorithm that follows. It is convenient to apply the algorithm to tableaus of the form shown in Figure 6–6.

FIGURE 6–6

From	To				Supply
	1	*2*	$\cdots$	*m*	
1	c_{11}	c_{12}		c_{1m}	S_1
2	c_{21}	c_{22}		c_{2m}	S_2
$\vdots$					$\vdots$
n	c_{n1}	c_{n2}		c_{nm}	S_n
Demand	D_1	D_2	$\cdots$	D_m	$\Sigma D_j = \Sigma S_i$

In the tableau the rows correspond to supply constraints and the columns correspond to demand constraints. Each cell in the body of the tableau corresponds to one source-destination pair. This is equivalent to saying each cell corresponds to variable x_{ij} where i denotes the row the cell is in and j denotes the column. Thus we will talk about some cells being basic while others are nonbasic as if the cells were variables. The upper left hand corner of each cell is used to specify the appropriate unit shipping cost. The lower right hand portion of each cell is used to indicate the current value of the cell (variable) if the cell is basic. If the cell is nonbasic, and thus the corresponding variable is equal to zero, this portion of the cell will be left blank.

We are now ready for the algorithm. The steps of the algorithm will be listed to give an overview of the procedure. Then the details of each step will be discussed.

Step 0. *Initialization:* Obtain a basic feasible solution with $(m + n - 1)$ basic cells.

Step 1. *Test Current Solution for Optimality:* Use dual variables to test for optimality. If the current solution is optimal, stop. Otherwise, identify the most attractive nonbasic cell. Go to Step 2 and put this cell in the basis.

Step 2. *Produce New Basic Feasible Solution:* Identify a basic cell that is to leave the basis as the cell found in Step 1 enters the basis. Make the exchange and return to Step 1.

Remarks on Step 0. The algorithm can be initialized with *any* set of $(n + m - 1)$ allocations that constitute a basic feasible solution. Several procedures have been developed for finding a starting solution. The approach discussed here is often called the Northwest Corner (NWC) method.

(i) Allocate the largest amount possible to the "northwest-most" cell available in the tableau. In some cases this amount will be zero.

(ii) The allocation made in Step (i) will cause a column and/or row requirement to be exactly satisfied. Mark off the satisfied column or row and exclude its cells from consideration when future allocations are being made. If both a column and row are satisfied by the allocation made in Step (i), mark off either, but only one, of them.

(iii) Stop with a usable initial solution if $(n + m - 1)$ allocations have been made. Otherwise, return to Step (i) to make another allocation.

When this procedure stops all rows and columns except one will be marked off and all row and column equations will be satisfied.

Remarks on Step 1.

(i) The dual variables corresponding to the current basic feasible solution are found by solving the appropriate dual equations. For each *basic* cell (i,j) we have a dual equation

$$v_i + \mu_j = c_{ij}.$$

Arbitrarily set one of these dual variables to zero and solve the system of equations for the other variables. These equations can *always* be solved sequentially, so their solution is very easy. The dual variables are not unique, since a different choice for the variable set equal to zero will yield different values for the other variables. It is the relative value of the variables that is important here, however, so that one initial choice is as good as another.

(ii) Using the dual variables found in Step (i), evaluate each nonbasic cell (k,l) by computing

$$e_{kl} = c_{kl} - v_k - \mu_l.$$

Notice that this amounts to evaluating the remaining dual constraints of (6–59). (This is also equivalent to computing the $(c_j - z_j)$ values for the nonbasic variables in the simplex algorithm.)

(iii) If all the e_{kl} values are nonnegative, then the current dual solution is feasible. This means our current primal solution is optimal and thus we stop. Otherwise, select the nonbasic cell with the most negative e_{kl} value as the cell to put in the basis next.

Remarks on Step 2.

(i) Denote the cell found in Step 1 by (i,j). We would like to increase the allocation in this cell from its current amount of zero to whatever amount the equations will allow. Since the row and column equations of the tableau must hold at all times, increasing the allocation in cell (i,j) will set off a chain reaction of compensating increases and decreases in certain basic cells. These alternating adjustments appear on a closed path (called the evaluation path) in the tableau starting and ending with the cell (i,j). The path will have right-angle turns only, and the "corner" cells on the path must be basic cells. Moreover, one and only one such path exists for a given nonbasic cell. The path may skip over certain basic cells and may even cross itself. A little practice will show that an evaluation path is easy to identify.

(ii) As we increase the allocation in cell (i,j), some of the cells (every other one) on the evaluation path will have their allocations decreased. Determine the maximum amount we can allocate to cell (i,j) until the allocation in one of the "decreasing" cells goes to zero. This cell is then dropped from the basis. If more than one

cell have their allocation go to zero at the same time, drop *only
one* of the cells from the basis. Leave the others basic with
zero allocations. (For such a case we would have a degenerate
solution.)

(iii) Make the necessary adjustments around the evaluation path and
return to evaluate your new basic feasible solution. Notice that we
bring one nonbasic cell into the basis and take one basic cell out.
At all times we have $(n + m - 1)$ basic cells in the tableau.

At first the algorithm may seem tedious. The following example with
three warehouses and three retail stores will illustrate, however, how
easy it actually is. Figure 6–7 shows the basic tableau structure for the
example. Notice that total supply equals total demand. This is a requirement of the algorithm that is always easily satisfied by adding a dummy
supply or demand node to the problem if necessary. Costs associated
with any dummy node are usually assumed to be zero.

FIGURE 6–7

Initial Tableau Structure

From	To			Supply
	1	2	3	
1	2	4	4	10
2	4	5	3	14
3	3	1	4	8
Demand	8	16	8	32 / 32

Step 0. The algorithm first requires us to find an initial starting
solution with $(m + n - 1) = (3 + 3 - 1) = 5$ basic cells. Use of the
northwest corner method yields the following:

1. Allocate 8 units to Cell (1,1), mark off Column 1, and move to cell
(1,2).
2. Allocate 2 units to Cell (1,2), mark off Row 1, and move to cell
(2,2).
3. Allocate 14 units to Cell (2,2) and mark off *either* Column 2 *or* Row
2. Arbitrarily choose to mark off Column 2 and move to Cell (2,3).
4. Allocate 0 units to Cell (2,3), mark off Row 2 and move to Cell
(3,3).
5. Allocate 8 units to Cell (3,3) and mark off Column 3.

FIGURE 6–8

Tableau with Initial Solution

From	To			Supply
	1	2	3	
1	2 8	4 2	4	10
2	4	5 14	3 0	14
3	3	1	4 8	8
Demand	8	16	8	

Making these five allocations completes Step 0 and we move on to Step 1 of the algorithm to test our current (that is, initial) solution for optimality. Figure 6–8 shows our tableau with the initial solution displayed.

Step 1. Our five basic cells are $(1,1)$, $(1,2)$, $(2,2)$, $(2,3)$, and $(3,3)$. Thus our dual equations are

$$c_{11} = v_1 + \mu_1 = 2 \qquad\qquad c_{23} = v_2 + \mu_3 = 3$$
$$c_{12} = v_1 + \mu_2 = 4 \qquad\qquad c_{33} = v_3 + \mu_3 = 4.$$
$$c_{22} = v_2 + \mu_2 = 5$$

Arbitrarily setting $\mu_3 = 0$ yields $v_3 = 4$ and $v_2 = 3$. In turn, this implies $\mu_2 = 2$, $v_1 = 2$, and $\mu_1 = 0$. This set of dual variables will now be used to check the nonbasic cells.

$$e_{13} = c_{13} - v_1 - \mu_3 = 4 - 2 - 0 = +2$$
$$e_{21} = c_{21} - v_2 - \mu_1 = 4 - 3 - 0 = +1$$
$$e_{31} = c_{31} - v_3 - \mu_1 = 3 - 4 - 0 = -1$$
$$e_{32} = c_{32} - v_3 - \mu_2 = 1 - 4 - 2 = -5.$$

Since these are not all nonnegative, our current solution is not optimal. Cell $(3,2)$ is chosen to come into the basis.

Step 2. Referring again to Figure 6–8, we see that the evaluation path for Cell $(3,2)$ is[7]

$$\begin{array}{cccc} + & - & + & - \\ (3, 2) \rightarrow (2, 2) \rightarrow (2, 3) \rightarrow (3, 3) \rightarrow (3, 2). \end{array}$$

The pluses and minuses associated with the cells on the path indicate whether or not the cell allocation is increasing or decreasing. Cells $(2,2)$ and $(3,3)$ have their allocations decreasing as we allocate units to Cell $(3,2)$. Of these two, the allocation in Cell $(3,3)$ will go to zero first. Thus eight units in the maximum amount we can allocate to Cell $(3,2)$.

---

[7] It makes no difference which way the path is traversed. We could just as well use $(3,2) \rightarrow (3,3) \rightarrow (2,3) \rightarrow (2,2) \rightarrow (3,2)$.

We bring $(3,2)$ into the basis with an allocation of eight units and we remove Cell $(3,3)$ from the basis.

Making this eight-unit adjustment around the path yields the new basic feasible solution displayed in Figure 6–9. We have now completed one iteration of the transportation algorithm and are ready to return to Step 1 to test our new solution for optimality.

FIGURE 6–9

Tableau After One Iteration

From	To			Supply
	1	2	3	
1	2 8	4 2	4	10
2	4	5 6	3 8	14
3	3	1 8	4	8
Demand	8	16	8	

Step 1. The dual equations are:

$$c_{11} = v_1 + \mu_1 = 2 \qquad\qquad c_{23} = v_2 + \mu_3 = 3$$
$$c_{12} = v_1 + \mu_2 = 4 \qquad\qquad c_{32} = v_3 + \mu_2 = 1.$$
$$c_{22} = v_2 + \mu_2 = 5$$

Setting μ_2 equal to zero yields: $v_1 = 4,\ v_2 = 5,\ v_3 = 1,\ \mu_1 = -2$, and $\mu_3 = -2$. The evaluations of the nonbasic cells are

$$e_{13} = c_{13} - v_1 - \mu_3 = 4 - 4 + 2 = +2$$
$$e_{21} = c_{21} - v_2 - \mu_1 = 4 - 5 + 2 = +1$$
$$e_{31} = c_{31} - v_3 - \mu_1 = 3 - 1 + 2 = +4$$
$$e_{33} = c_{33} - v_3 - \mu_3 = 4 - 1 + 2 = +5.$$

Since these values are all positive, the algorithm stops. The solution displayed in Figure 6–9 is optimal. The minimum cost shipping schedule is:

Ship 8 units from Warehouse 1 to Retail Store 1;

Ship 2 units from Warehouse 1 to Retail Store 2;

Ship 6 units from Warehouse 2 to Retail Store 2;

Ship 8 units from Warehouse 2 to Retail Store 3;

Ship 8 units from Warehouse 3 to Retail Store 2.

The corresponding optimal cost is

$$2(8) + 4(2) + 5(6) + 3(8) + 1(8) = 86.$$

It would be instructive for the reader to rework the above example making a different choice in Step 1 for the dual variable to arbitrarily set to zero. A different choice will yield a different set of values for the dual variables. However, the relative values of the variables will adjust so that the evaluations of the nonbasic cells are the same as those we found above.

In the preceding small example the transportation algorithm found the optimal solution in one iteration. This happened because the algorithm was initialized with a good, that is, nearly optimal, starting solution. The Northwest Corner method makes no use of cost information, however, and often gives starting solutions that are far from optimal. Procedures that utilize both cost and feasibility information usually yield better starting points. The interested reader is referred to the references at the end of the chapter for a discussion of other starting point techniques.

Transportation problems often exhibit degenerate solutions as the algorithm iterates toward optimality. In principle, it is possible that such degeneracy could lead to cycling, but as with the example worked above, degeneracy causes no difficulty if we maintain $(m + n - 1)$ basic cells and take care in resolving ties when choosing a cell to remove from the basis. Computerized versions of the transportation algorithm have special provisions that ensure that degeneracy never causes cycling.

6.6. SUMMARY

In this chapter we have seen how duality theory greatly increases the power of linear programming. The dual interpretation enhances our understanding of LP models—especially resource allocation models. Moreover, duality can lead to substantial computational savings for many problems, and can be used to develop efficient special purpose algorithms for certain classes of problems.

The closely related topic of sensitivity analysis was also discussed in the chapter. Given that many parameters in our models are likely to be in error, sensitivity analysis provides a framework for assessing how likely it is that our current solutions are in fact optimal as well as other important issues.

Together, duality and sensitivity analysis greatly increase the value of LP as a decision making aid.

EXERCISES

6.1.   *a.*   Write down the duals to Problems 8, 9, 10, 11, and 12 in Chapter 5.

   b.   Solve these dual problems and compare the results with those found previously.

6.2. Consider the following product-mix problem. Production is constrained by limited availabilities of labor and two materials, A and B.

Maximize

$$x_0 = 4x_1 + 3x_2$$

subject to

$$4x_1 + 2x_2 \leq 3/10 \text{ (man-hours)}$$
$$2x_1 + 8/3x_2 \leq 8 \text{ (Material A)}$$
$$x_2 \leq 6 \text{ (Material B)}$$
$$x_j \geq 0.$$

The solution of the problem yields the following set of equations:

$$x_1 + 2/5x_3 - 3/10x_4 = 8/5$$
$$x_2 - 3/10x_3 + 3/5x_4 = 9/5$$
$$3/10x_3 - 3/5x_4 + x_5 = 21/5.$$

a. Give an interval for the objective-function coefficient of x_2 such that the above solution remains optimal.
b. Assume that the company is able to secure another two units of Material A at negligible cost. How will the optimal product mix be affected?

6.3. Consider the LP problem:

Maximize

$$x_0 = 5x_1 + 6x_2 + 4x_3$$

subject to

$$x_1 + x_2 + 2x_3 \leq 20 \text{ (Resource 1)}$$
$$2x_1 + x_2 + x_3 \leq 18 \text{ (Resource 2)}$$
$$x_j \geq 0.$$

The final simplex tableau is:

c_B	x_B	x_1	x_2	x_3	x_4	x_5	b
0	x_4	-1	0	1	1	-1	2
6	x_2	2	1	1	0	1	18
$c_j - z_j$							

a. Formulate the dual to the above linear programming problem.
b. What is the *complete* solution to the dual problem? (Explain how you got your results).
c. What is the sensitivity range for the objective function coefficient of x_1. What does this range mean?
d. What is the maximum amount you would be willing to pay for an additional unit of Resource 1? Of Resource 2?
e. Suppose c_1 and c_2 were actually 5.25 and 5.50 respectively instead of 5 and 6. Use sensitivity analysis to determine whether or not the current solution would still be the optimum solution.

6.4.   Consider the LP problem:

Maximize

$$x_0 = 4x_1 + 2x_2 + 3x_3$$

subject to

$$2x_1 + x_2 + 2x_3 \leq 20$$
$$x_1 + 3x_2 + x_3 \leq 15$$
$$x_j \geq 0.$$

Consider the *proposed* solution

$$x_1 = 10; x_2 = x_3 = x_4 = 0; x_5 = 5.$$

Use *duality* theory to see whether the proposed solution is optimal.

6.5.   Consider again the LP problem shown in Problem #4. Suppose you are now confronted with the *additional* constraint

$$x_1 + x_3 \geq 4.$$

Does the optimal solution change? If so, find the new solution.

6.6.   Consider the following product-mix problem with five products and two resource constraints.

Maximize

$$x_0 = 5x_1 + 4x_2 + 4x_3 + 6x_4 + 8x_5$$

subject to

$$2x_1 + x_3 + 2x_4 \leq 20 \text{ (Resource 1)}$$
$$2x_2 + 2x_4 + x_5 \leq 10 \text{ (Resource 2)}$$
$$x_j \geq 0.$$

a.   Compute the shadow prices for Resources 1 and 2.
b.   Compute the optimal product-mix.
c.   Suppose a sixth product (a possible addition to your product line) has a profit contribution of $10 per unit and requires (per unit) three units of Resource 1 and one unit of Resource 2. How many units of Product 6 should be produced?
d.   Suppose one additional unit of Resource 1 is available at a cost of $1.50 and one additional unit of Resource 2 is available at a cost of $2.00. Should they be purchased?

6.7.   Consider the following product-mix model where we have five products and two inputs (resources):

Maximize profits:

$$x_0 = 5x_1 + 4x_2 + 3x_3 + 8x_4 + 5x_5$$

subject to

$$2x_1 + x_2 + 4x_3 + x_4 + 2x_5 \leq 40 \text{ (Resource 1)}$$
$$x_1 + 2x_4 \leq 16 \text{ (Resource 2)}$$
$$x_i \geq 0.$$

a.   Solve the problem and develop the optimal tableau.
b.   How much would you be willing to pay for an additional unit of each resource?

c. Suppose b_1 and b_2 are both in error. Develop the conditions describing the amount of error that would leave the current final tableau optimal.

d. Suppose we are 100 percent confident that the true values of b_1 and b_2 are within ± 5 percent of the stated values. Develop the 100 percent confidence interval for the objective function value.

6.8. Consider the problem:

Maximize

$$x_0 = c_1 x_1 + 6x_2 + c_3 x_3 + 0x_4 + 0x_5$$

subject to

$$
\begin{aligned}
x_1 + x_2 + 2x_3 + x_4 &= 20 \\
2x_1 + x_2 + x_3 + x_5 &= 18 \\
x_j &\geq 0.
\end{aligned}
$$

What are the smallest values of c_1 and c_3 that will leave x_2 and x_4 in an optimal basis?

6.9. Discuss a method for determining whether a transportation problem has several optimal solutions.

6.10. Consider a transportation problem with two sources and four demand zones. Assume the following cost data:

Sources	Demand Zones			
	1	*2*	*3*	*4*
1..............	3	2	5	1
2..............	9	2	4	6

Furthermore, assume $S_1 = 100$, $S_2 = 80$, $D_1 = 40$, $D_2 = 60$, $D_3 = 40$, $D_4 = 60$.

a. Set up the appropriate transportation tableau. Note that you need to include a "dummy" source.

b. Use the NWC method to find an initial solution.

c. Find the optimal solution.

d. Discuss the meaning of your solution.

6.11. Formulate this production scheduling problem as a transportation LP problem. A firm producing one product is scheduling (allocating) its January–March production capabilities. Part of the decision involves scheduling overtime work. A unit produced on overtime costs an extra $300. Similarly, a unit made one month before it is needed incurs an inventory carrying cost of $100, two months before needed incurs an inventory carrying cost of $200/unit.
The production capacities and delivery requirements are:

	Production Capacity		Requirements
	Regular Time	*Overtime*	
January...............	100	50	80
February...............	100	40	120
March...............	100	30	150

6.12. Solve Problem 11.

6.13. A firm has items to be shipped from distribution centers to warehouses. The unit shipping costs, requirements, and supplies are:

	Distribution Center			
Warehouse	A	B	C	Needed
1..................	$14	$15	$10	9
2..................	14	16	12	12
3..................	9	7	4	11
4..................	10	7	7	14
5..................	8	5	6	8
Available............	19	26	13	

Find the least-cost shipping schedule.

6.14. Discuss: "The transportation algorithm applies only to shipping problems."

6.15. Five people are to be assigned to do five different tasks. Because of the different capabilities of the people, each requires different amounts of time for each task. The number of hours required for a given person to do a given task is:

	Task				
Person	Setup	Weld	Assemble	Inspect	Ship
Jack...............	9	2	6	4	7
Jake...............	7	4	5	4	8
John...............	10	6	7	6	5
Jorge..............	8	3	9	4	4
Jung..............	5	5	5	2	3

Find the optimal assignment of people to jobs.

SUGGESTIONS FOR FURTHER STUDY

Bazaraa, M. S., and Jarvis, J. J., *Linear Programming and Network Flows.* New York: Wiley, 1977.

Cooper, L., and Steinberg, D., *Methods and Applications of Linear Programming.* Philadelphia: W. B. Saunders Co., 1974.

Driebeek, N. J., *Applied Linear Programming.* Reading, Mass.: Addison-Wesley, 1969.

Gass, S. I., *Linear Programming.* 4th ed. New York: McGraw-Hill, 1975.

Hughes, A., and Grawoig, D. E., *Linear Programming: An Emphasis on Decision Making.* Reading, Mass.: Addison-Wesley, 1973.

Loomba, N. P., *Linear Programming: A Managerial Perspective.* 2nd ed. New York: McGraw-Hill, 1976.

Naylor, T. H., Byrne, E. T., and Vernon, J. M., *Introduction to Linear Programming: Methods and Cases.* San Francisco: Wadsworth Publishing Co., 1971.

Salkin, H. M., and Saha, J., eds., *Studies in Linear Programming*. New York: American Elsevier Publishing Co., 1975.

Thompson, G. E., *Linear Programming*. New York: Macmillan, 1971.

Throsby, C. D., *Elementary Linear Programming*. New York: Random House, 1970.

7

Multiple-Criteria Decision Making

7.1. INTRODUCTION

As NOTED in Chapter 4 one of the major components of a linear programming model is that of a single objective or goal; for example, maximize profit, minimize cost, maximize utility, and so on. The decision maker must be able to state the decision problem in terms of a single goal subject to a set of constraints. Within such a setting linear programming will find, among all solutions consistent with the constraints, the one solution that gives the optimum value of the objective function. In many decision settings, there may be more than one criterion that the decision maker would like to satisfy and perhaps optimize.[1] These decision problems are often called *multiple-criteria decision models* and may involve criteria that are incommensurate and/or conflicting. As a result such problems may not have any feasible solutions in the sense of Chapter 5. Thus we will need to redefine exactly what it means to "solve" a multicriteria problem.

The recent developments in multiple-criteria decision making have been of two types: *the goal programming model,* in which one treats multiple goals as constraints and develops a priority system for satisfying the goals; the *interactive approach,* in which one seeks to determine the trade-offs among the various goals or criteria specified by the decision maker. These different models represent different philosophical ap-

---

[1] For the results of a study to determine corporate management goals see M. Schubik, "Approaches to the Study of Decision-Making Relevant to the Firm," in the Gore and Dyson reference at the end of the chapter.

proaches to the multiple-criteria problem as well as different numerical techniques. As the chapter develops we will discuss in detail the methods and their similarities and differences.

The major differences between these approaches to multiple-criteria problems lies in the treatment of the objective function. In the goal programming model, the goals or criteria are assigned a nonpreemptive set of priorities; that is, the goals are ordered from most important to least important, and this order cannot be changed. The goal programming approach then has to satisfy the most important goal and then proceed to lower-level goals. The method terminates when it is impossible to satisfy the current goal. Since the priority assignment is nonpreemptive, if one was interested in the various trade-offs among the goals the model would have to be reformulated and re-solved in order to determine the trade-offs.

On the other hand the assignment of numerical weights can generate misleading results unless some careful analysis is performed on these weights and their effect on the optimal solution. Also the determination of the trade-offs among the criteria is the factor of major importance. The *interactive models* attempt to have the decision maker determine the tradeoffs among various criteria by relaxing and reordering the criteria. Such an algorithm requires a model of the resource utilization of the process under consideration and a set of objective functions. The interactive approach determines the amount of a particular objective the decision maker is willing to trade for the attainment of some other objective. The procedure terminates when no additional trade-offs are desirable.

These concepts can be illustrated by the following example, first introduced by Charnes and Cooper. As noted in Chapter 5 when constraints of various types ($\leq$, $\geq$, $=$) are mixed it is possible that there are no feasible solutions to the system. If in practice such a situation occurs the model may have been improperly formulated and must be reformulated in order to deal with the problem. A slightly different interpretation of such situations is possible, however. Suppose a manufacturing process has two resource constraints

$$3x_1 + 2x_2 \leq 12 \tag{7-1}$$
$$5x_1 \quad\;\; \leq 10 \tag{7-2}$$
$$x_1, x_2 \quad\; \geq \;\; 0,$$

where x_1 and x_2 represent numbers of units of Types 1 and 2, respectively. Now suppose we adjoin the additional "constraints"

$$x_1 + x_2 \geq 8 \tag{7-3}$$
$$-x_1 + x_2 \geq 4, \tag{7-4}$$

which we will interpret as "management goals." That is, constraint (7–3) is a decision that at least eight units be produced and constraint

(7–4) deals with the product mix in that it requires that the number of Type 2 produced exceed Type 1 by at least four units. If we treat these as ordinary linear constraints, Figure 7–1 presents the graphical representation.

Area I represents the feasible solutions to the resource constraints and area II represents the feasible solutions to the management goals. Since these areas do not intersect there are no feasible solutions to the problem in the usual linear programming sense. The reason for this is that there

FIGURE 7–1

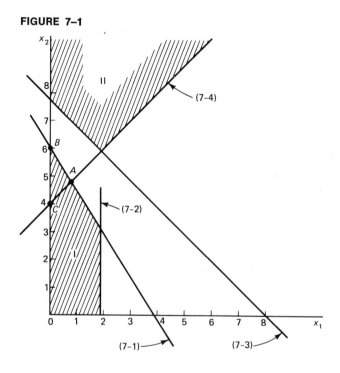

are not enough resources to meet the management-imposed production levels. Management may have known that such a situation was going to arise but set such goals anyway with the hope of coming as close as possible to attaining them. In Figure 7–1 within the triangle ABC the goal given by constraint (7–4) is satisfied within the resource limitations; also note that it is not possible to meet the goal of at least eight units of production within the resource limitations.

Since all goals cannot be met within the resource limitations, one possible measure of effectiveness of a solution is the deviation from the goals. That is, one could measure the distance of any solution from the goals, which for the remainder of the chapter will be referred to as the deviation. In this example these deviations correspond to the "constraints"

(7–3) and (7–4) and will measure by how much a solution fails to meet these inequalities. The solution will depend on precisely what types of deviations are used to measure the attainment of a goal. For example, if one interprets the problem as meeting as closely as possible both goals then the "best" solution is $x_1 = 0$, $x_2 = 6$, which is Point B in Figure 7–1.

This point corresponds to meeting goal (7–4) $(0 + 6 \geq 4)$ and underachieves goal (7–3) by two units. On the other hand, if one interprets the problem as trying to meet each goal exactly and hence minimize the absolute deviation from the goals the problem becomes:

Minimize

$$| x_1 + x_2 - 8 | + | -x_1 + x_2 - 4 |.$$

This is referred to as the *minimum absolute deviation* and results in the solution given by Point A in Figure 7–1.[2] One can see that for $x_1 = \frac{4}{5}$, $x_2 = 2\frac{4}{5}$ (Point A), the *total deviation* is $1\frac{2}{5}$ while for $x_1 = 0$, $x_2 = 6$ (Point B) the *total deviation* is 4.

Thus one must specify the criteria for evaluating the possible solutions in terms of the allowable deviations from the stated goals. Multiplecriteria optimization problems for which the attainment of the criteria is measured using the absolute deviation criterion will be referred to as *goal programming*. In other words the objective will be to minimize the deviations from the stated goals. Since goal programming is to deal with incompatible or infeasible goals *it must then be a satisficing technique rather than an optimizing technique.* That is, *goal programming seeks to come as close as possible to satisfying a set of goals rather than to optimize a single goal.*

In linear programming an objective function is to be optimized over the set of feasible solutions allowed by the constraints of the problem. In goal programming the objective function will be the deviation from the goals, which, along with any restrictions on the problem, will appear

---

[2] The vertical bars denote the absolute value function. In other words the absolute value is the value irrespective of the algebraic sign. More formally, one can define the absolute value of x as:

$$|x| = \begin{cases} x \text{ if } x \geq 0 \\ -x \text{ if } x \leq 0. \end{cases}$$

The minimum absolute deviation criterion is more frequently encountered in problems of statistical estimation where it is referred to as the MAD estimation problem. As one might suspect, just as different criteria can be applied to statistical problems, so too can they be applied to multiple-criterion problems; for example, one might very well consider the "least-squares" criterion for these problems; that is,

$$\text{Min } [(x_1 + x_2 - 8)^2 + (-x_1 + x_2 - 4)^2]^{1/2}$$

subject to (7–1) and (7–2).

More details on these issues can be found in the Cochrane and Zeleney reference at the end of the chapter.

as constraints to the problem. Thus within this framework goal programming seeks those solutions which optimize the deviations from the goals. It is important to note that in any type of mathematical programming approach those conditions that appear as constraints are more important than the objective function. That is, the programming technique first of all must find feasible solutions *and then* optimize the problem. As we shall see later in the chapter the goal programming approach will allow for the inclusion of several goals and, in addition, an ordering of the goals from least to most important.

To illustrate some of these ideas, consider the problem of an ore-smelting firm that, within its resource limitations, is seeking to maximize its profits; on the other hand, being concerned citizens, the firm wants to reduce the air pollution from the smelting process. If the firm simply maximizes profit the pollution level increases; on the other hand, one way to stop pollution is to stop smelting ore, which has an adverse effect on profit.

The smelting process reduces the ore to either 97 percent or 98 percent pure metal. The amount of each type of metal is identified as x_1 and x_2 respectively. If 300 tons of ore is available, with profit contributions of \$3.00/ton for 97 percent ore and \$3.75/ton for 98 percent ore, and air pollution production is given by $6x_1 + 7x_2$, several models can be formulated. Each of the following models depends on what is chosen as the objective.

Model 1. Objective:

Minimize pollutants = minimize $6x_1 + 7x_2$

subject to

$$x_1 + x_2 \le 300$$
$$3x_1 + 3.75x_2 = 1000 \text{ (desired profit level).}$$

For this model one can see that *without* the inclusion of a desired profit level the solution is $x_1 = x_2 = 0$; indeed with such a constraint the solution will reflect the profit level—assuming it is feasible with regard to the amount of ore available. For the above model the solution is $x_1 = 0$, $x_2 = 266\frac{2}{3}$, for which profit = 1,000 and pollutants = $1866\frac{2}{3}$.

Model 2. Objective:

Maximize profit = maximize $3x_1 + 3.75x_2$

subject to

$$x_1 + x_2 \le 300$$
$$x_1, x_2 \ge 0.$$

The solution to the above model is $x_1 = 0$, $x_2 = 300$ for which profit = 1,125 and pollutants = 2,100. If some upper limit on the amount of pollution is imposed—for example $6x_1 + 7x_2 \leq 1500$—the solution will change. With the inclusion of this constraint the solution becomes $x_1 = 0$, $x_2 = \dfrac{1500}{7} = 214.285$, for which profit $= 803.57$.

In each of these formulations the solution depends upon the form of the constraints; that is, the constraints take precedence over the objective function. The goal programming formulation sets up an objective function in terms of deviations from the goals which are treated as constraints. For example, if a profit goal of \$1,000 is introduced while maintaining a pollution level goal of 1,500 units, the goal programming formulation is:

Minimize

$$|3x_1 + 3.75x_2 - 1000| + |6x_1 + 7x_2 - 1500|$$

subject to

$$x_1 + x_2 \leq 300$$
$$x_1, x_2 \geq 0.$$

Several comments are in order regarding this formulation: first of all, the objective function will be viewed in terms of deviational units. Thus, if the profit is underachieved by \$100 and the pollution overachieved by 50 units, the value of the objective function is 150 deviational units. Secondly, the profit goal is being viewed in light of the previous discussion—exact attainment. Other types of objective functions will be discussed in Section 2. In order to convert the above model to a more convenient form we introduce the new non-negative variables $d_1{}^+$, $d_1{}^-$, $d_2{}^+$, $d_2{}^-$ with the definition that

> $d_1{}^+$ represents any *overachievement of the profit goal;* that is, if $3x_1 + 3.75x_2 > 1000$, then $d_1{}^+$ is such that $3x_1 + 3.75x_2 - d_1{}^+ = 1000$;
> $d_1{}^-$ represents any *underachievement of the profit goal;* that is, if $3x_1 + 3.75x_2 \leq 1000$, then $d_1{}^-$ is such that $3x_1 + 3.75x_2 + d_1{}^- = 1000$.

One should immediately recognize the similarity between $d_1{}^+$, $d_1{}^-$ and the surplus and slack variables of Chapters 4 and 5. Similarly for the pollution level goal

> $d_2{}^+$ represents any *overachievement of the pollution goal;* that is, if $6x_1 + 7x_2 > 1500$, then $d_2{}^+$ is such that $6x_1 + 7x_2 - d_2{}^+ = 1500$;
> $d_2{}^-$ represents any *underachievement of the pollution goal;* that is, if $6x_1 + 7x_2 < 1500$, then $d_2{}^-$ is such that $6x_1 + 7x_2 + d_2{}^- = 1500$.

The reader should note that if $d_1{}^+ > 0$, then $d_1{}^- = 0$ and vice versa; that is, only one deviation can be positive at a time. This is intuitively clear from the definitions of $d_1{}^+$, $d_1{}^-$. Similar statements hold for $d_2{}^+$, $d_2{}^-$.

The model can be restated as:[3]

Minimize

$$d_1{}^+ + d_1{}^- + d_2{}^+ + d_2{}^-$$

subject to

$$
\begin{array}{rl}
x_1 + x_2 & \leq\ 300 \\
3x_1 + 3.75x_2 + d_1{}^- - d_1{}^+ & =\ 1000 \\
6x_1 +\quad 7x_2 + d_2{}^- - d_2{}^+ & =\ 1500 \\
x_1,\ x_2,\ d_1{}^+,\ d_1{}^-,\ d_2{}^+,\ d_2{}^- & \geq\quad 0.
\end{array}
$$

Sections 2 and 3 of this chapter will be concerned with model structure and formulation; the latter half of the chapter will deal with numerical solution procedures for the goal programming model.

7.2. THE GOAL PROGRAMMING MODEL

Following the conceptual description given in the preceding section, we define the general *single priority goal programming model* as:

Minimize

$$\sum_{k=1}^{p} \{d_k{}^+ + d_k{}^-\} \tag{7-6}$$

subject to

$$\sum_{j=1}^{n} a_{ij}x_j = b_i;\ i = 1, \ldots, m \quad \begin{array}{l}\text{(technological}\\ \text{constraints)}\end{array} \tag{7-7}$$

$$\sum_{j=1}^{n} a_{ij}x_j - d_k{}^+ + d_k{}^- = g_k;\ k = 1, \ldots, p \quad \begin{array}{l}\text{(goal con-}\\ \text{straints)}\end{array} \tag{7-8}$$

$$x_j,\ d_k{}^+,\ d_k{}^- \geq 0. \tag{7-9}$$

Equation (7-7) represents the technological constraints of the ordinary linear programming type. That is, these constraints define a feasible solution space according to resource limitations. These will be viewed as true constraints with no violation allowed. Equation (7-8) represents the firm's goals (objectives) rewritten in terms of the deviations (over- and underachievements $d_k{}^+$, $d_k{}^-$) from the goals (g_k). The over- and underachievements will also be referred to as *positive and negative deviations*. That there is a single priority goal means either that there is

---

[3] The use of "deviational variables" with regard to absolute value functions is a standard transformation in linear programming. In fact, it is in common use in statistical estimation problems to convert a minimum absolute deviation problem to a standard linear programming format.

a single goal or that, if there are several goals, they are treated as all being of equal importance.[4] The case of multiple goals with different levels of importance or priorities will be treated later in the chapter.

Also, as mentioned at the end of the last section, note that d_k^+ and d_k^- *cannot* be nonzero simultaneously since they represent positive and negative deviations respectively. This is sometimes stated explicitly in the model as

$$d_k^+ \cdot d_k^- = 0. \tag{7-10}$$

In the above general statement of the single-priority model both positive *and* negative deviations have been included for each goal and the objective is to minimize *both* of these deviations. From a decision making point of view this can be interpreted as trying to *meet a goal exactly*, in other words, seeking to minimize *any* deviation (positive or negative) from the goal. In terms of the ore smelting example this corresponds to achieving a profit level of exactly $1,000. Different decision makers or different situations might specify different types of goal attainment; for example, one might specify a profit level of *at least* $1,000 or a pollution level of *at most* 1,500 units. For example, in the first example of Section 1, it is clear from Figure 7–1 that one need not be concerned with the overachievement of constraint (7–3); what we are concerned with is keeping the underachievement as small as possible. Formally, some of the most important goal structures that can be included in the objective are:

1. *Exact Achievement of a Goal:* In order to achieve a goal exactly one wants to include *both* positive and negative deviations and then *minimize the total deviation* from the goal. That is:

Minimize

$$d_k^+ + d_k^- \tag{7-11}$$

where

$$\sum_{j=1}^{n} a_{ij}x_j - d_k^+ + d_k^- = g_k \tag{7-12}$$

represents the goal for g_k equal to some stated goal level. In the smelting example the exact achievement of $1,000 in profits would be stated as:

Minimize

$$d_1^+ + d_1^-$$

---

[4] If there is a single goal that is feasible with respect to the technological constraints, then we are dealing with an ordinary linear program. That is, if the goal constraints (7–8) intersect the technological constraints (7–6) the problem has a linear programming solution. For the first example of the previous section this would be the case if one considered only constraints (7–1), (7–2), and (7–4).

subject to

$$3x_1 + 3.75x_2 - d_1{}^+ + d_1{}^- = \$1,000$$
$$x_1 + x_2 \qquad\qquad\quad \le 300$$
$$x_1, x_2, d_1{}^+, d_1{}^- \qquad\quad \ge 0.$$

2. *Avoid Underachievement of a Goal:* In this case one wants to attain *at least* the stated goal level; we *do not* care if we overachieve the goal. In order to accomplish this, minimize the underachievement (negative deviation) of the goal. That is:

Minimize

$$d_k{}^- \qquad\qquad\qquad\qquad (7\text{--}13)$$

subject to

$$\sum_{j=1}^{n} a_{ij}x_j - d_k{}^+ + d_k{}^- = g_k. \qquad\qquad (7\text{--}14)$$

Note that equation (7–14) includes the positive deviational variables $d_k{}^+$, which will be included with the understanding that they have the interpretation of surplus variables. They simply measure the overachievement of the goal. For the smelting example if a profit goal of at least $1,000 had been specified the model would be:

Minimize

$$d_1{}^-$$

subject to

$$3x_1 + 3.75x_2 - d_1{}^+ + d_1{}^- = \$1,000$$
$$x_1 + x_2 \qquad\qquad\quad \le 300$$
$$x_1, x_2, d_1{}^+, d_1{}^- \qquad\quad \ge 0.$$

3. *Avoid Overachievement of a Goal:* Such a goal is just the opposite of the previous formulation; that is:

Minimize

$$d_k{}^+ \qquad\qquad\qquad\qquad (7\text{--}15)$$

subject to

$$\sum_{j=1}^{n} a_{ij}x_j - d_k{}^+ + d_k{}^- = g_k. \qquad\qquad (7\text{--}16)$$

As in the previous formulation the minimization of $d_k{}^+$ indicates that any underachievement of the goal is allowable; and $d_k{}^-$ is included as a slack variable to measure the underachievement. For example, if in the smelting example a pollution level of *at most* 1,500 units had been specified the model would be:

Minimize

$$d_2{}^+$$

subject to

$$6x_1 + 7x_2 - d_2{}^+ + d_2{}^- = 1,500.$$
$$x_1 + x_2 \qquad\qquad\quad \leq 300$$
$$x_1, x_2, d_2{}^+, d_2{}^- \qquad \geq 0.$$

4. *Multiple Goals:* Since the previously developed structure is *linear* one can incorporate several goals in an additive way. In fact, the original statement of the smelting example included two goals: a profit goal of $1,000 and a pollution level of 1,500 units. Several structures are possible depending upon the above types of goals that are included. For example, suppose the goals are:

i.   a profit level of *at least* $1,000 and
ii. a pollution level of *at most* 1,500 units.

Then the complete model is:

Minimize

$$d_1{}^- + d_2{}^+ \qquad\qquad\qquad\qquad\qquad (7\text{--}17)$$

subject to:

$$3x_1 + 3.75x_2 + d_1{}^- - d_1{}^+ = 1,000$$
$$6x_1 + \quad 7x_2 + d_2{}^- - d_2{}^- = 1,500$$
$$x_1 + x_2 \qquad\qquad\qquad \leq 300$$
$$x_1, x_2, d_1{}^+, d_1{}^-, d_2{}^+, d_2{}^- \quad \geq 0.$$

Other possible formulations are left as an exercise for the reader.

Goals of Unequal Importance

The above model introduced the idea of multiple goals within a goal programming model in which *the goals are considered to be of equal importance.* In some cases one may want to consider situations in which some goals are more important than others; that is, the goals have been ranked from most to least important. There are several implications of trying to consider multiple goals. The need to deal effectively with multiple-goal situations was recognized very early in the development of linear programming, and the attempts to deal with such situations were made in terms of utility functions. That is, one converts the decision maker's goals into a utility measurement and then optimizes the resulting utility or dis-utility. One way to accomplish this is to assign numerical weights to the goals depending on their importance. For example, if one is trying to minimize dis-utility the assignment of large weights to the least important goals will tend to eliminate them from solution. The problem arises in the choice of the relative weights when there are several levels of importance. If one is to have a numerical solution technique based on the simplex algorithm (this is certainly reasonable since the resulting program is linear) we have seen from Chapter 5 that the solution is dependent upon the values of the coefficients of the objective function. Thus it is possible that an inappropriate choice of weights may adversely affect the solution. On the other hand the sensitivity analysis procedures of Chapter 6 could be employed to study such choices.

In order to avoid this situation we will assign to each goal a *priority factor* that will serve to order the goals but will not assign a numerical value to the goal. *The priority factors will provide an ordinal ranking of the goals;* that is priority factor one, P_1, denotes the most important goal or level of goals; priority factor two, P_2, denotes the second most important level of goals; and so on until all goals have been ordered. It is important to note that the priority factors specify a ranking that cannot be changed; in other words when P_1 signifies the most important and P_2 the second most important goal, an ordering has been established that *cannot be changed.* In *algebraic terms* this can be interpreted as: If values *were* assigned to P_1 and P_2 then $P_1 > nP_2$ for all possible choices of the number n, *no matter how large!* This property is referred to as the non-Archimedian principle of the priority factors.[5]

At this point it is worthwhile to note that the use of priority factors rather than numerical weights has avoided the problem of what specific weight to assign to a goal. On the other hand the fact that the goal priorities have the non-Archimedian property means that once the order of the goals is specified they must remain in that order. Thus one must interpret with some care the results when some goals are met and others are not met for the priority factors do not allow for any potential trade-offs. Also the solution to a goal programming model is dependent upon the order of the goals—a different ordering may yield dramatically different results. For these reasons it is advisable to use goal programming models in an interactive sense where the goals and their priorities are changed and the model re-solved. These ideas will be dealt with in more detail in Section 7 and the exercises.

The above points are illustrated by considering different versions of a rather straightforward problem. The Nuts & Bolts Company manufactures two sizes of bolts that require different amounts of two types of machinery. The LP formulation is:

---

[5] This property is also known as Archimedian law of real numbers or the Axiom of Archimedes. Formal statements and proofs can be found in most calculus or analysis texts.

Maximize profit $= 10x_1 + 12x_2$

subject to

$$x_1 + 2x_2 \leq 10 \quad \text{(Process 1)}$$
$$2x_1 + x_2 \leq 8 \quad \text{(Process 2)}$$
$$x_1, x_2 \geq 0.$$

As can be seen in Figure 7–2 the optimal LP solution is:

$$x_1 = 2; x_2 = 4$$
$$\text{Profit} = \$68.$$

Now suppose that certain management goals have been imposed on the problem; in particular:

1. (Highest priority) It has been decided to set a profit goal of exactly \$75.[6]
2. Avoid as much as possible the overutilization of the machine processes.

FIGURE 7–2

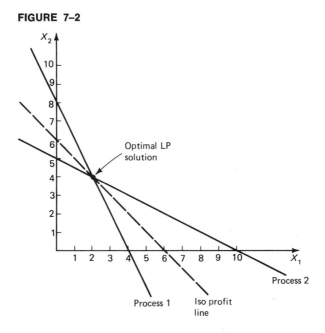

Optimal LP solution

Process 1   Iso profit line

Process 2

---

[6] From Figure 7–2 it can be seen that there is no feasible solution to this problem. That is, the optimal LP solution is the best situation—a profit of \$68—and hence, the profit goal is underachieved by \$7. If on the other hand the constraints are treated as being flexible one can obtain solutions for which the goal of \$75 is exactly met. It is important to note that such solutions depend on the validity of the assumption that the constraints are flexible.

FIGURE 7–3

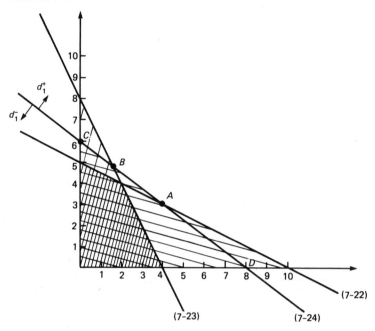

In order to model this situation we define:

d_1^+ = overachievement of the profit goal
d_1^- = underachievement of the profit goal
d_2^+ = overutilization of Machine 1 process time
d_2^- = underutilization of Machine 1 process time
d_3^+ = overutilization of Machine 2 process time
d_3^- = underutilization of Machine 2 process time.

Profit goal: In order to achieve $75 in profit it must be true that

$$10x_1 + 12x_2 = 75,$$

and to indicate any deviations from this goal write

$$10x_1 + 12x_2 - d_1^+ + d_1^- = 75. \tag{7–18}$$

Machine process time: The deviation variables are included just as slack and surplus variables would be included:

$$x_1 + 2x_2 - d_2^+ + d_2^- = 10 \text{ (Process 1)} \tag{7–19}$$
$$2x_1 + x_2 - d_3^+ + d_3^- = 8 \text{ (Process 2).} \tag{7–20}$$

Objective function: Since the highest level goal is that of avoiding *any* deviation from a profit level of $75, assign the priority factor P_1 to d_1^+ and d_1^-.

To deal with the second-level goals (avoid overutilizing of process time) assign priority factor P_2 to d_2^+ and d_3^+. The entire objective function can be written as:

Minimize

$$P_1 d_1^+ + P_1 d_1^- + P_2 d_2^+ + P_2 d_3^+ \tag{7-21}$$

subject to

$$x_1 + 2x_2 - d_2^+ + d_2^- = 10 \tag{7-22}$$
$$2x_1 + x_2 - d_3^+ + d_3^- = 8 \tag{7-23}$$
$$10x_1 + 12x_2 - d_1^+ + d_1^- = 75 \tag{7-24}$$
$$x_1,\ x_2,\ d_1^+,\ d_1^-,\ d_2^+,\ d_2^-,\ d_3^+,\ d_3^- \geq 0.$$

The problem represented above is shown graphically in Figure 7–3. As can be seen from the figure, avoiding any deviation from the profit goal restricts attention to the line described by equation (7–24); that is, any point on that line has $d_1^+ = d_1^- = 0$, which meets Goal 1. Also it can be seen that the level 2 goals cannot be satisfied; that is, the completely shaded area of Figure 7–3 satisfies these goals but not the profit goal. Thus, since the profit goal has top priority there will be some overutilization of the process time. The reader can verify that at the points *A*, *B*, *C*, and *D* the solutions are:

Point	x_1	x_2	d_2^+	d_3^+	*Total Deviation*
A	3¾	3⅛	0	2⅝	2⅝
B	1½	5	1½	0	1½
C	0	6⅕	2½	1¾	4¼
D	7½	0	2½	7	9½

Thus the optimal solution is at point *B*. We note, however, that if we were to move avoiding overutilization of Process 1 to the first priority level, the objective function would become:

Minimize

$$P_1 d_1^+ + P_1 d_1^- + P_1 d_2^+ + P_2 d_3^+,$$

and the optimal solution is now at point *A*.

This example and Figures 7–2 and 7–3 serve to point out several important aspects of goal programming models. First of all the assignment of goal priorities can alter the solution. Thus such assignments must be dealt with carefully in order to avoid distorting the model. Secondly, note that it was possible to determine the solution to this model *without* assigning numerical values to the priority factors, P_1 and P_2. Referring to Chapter 4 the reader will notice the similarity of the graphical solution method to that of linear programming. These ideas will be more fully treated in Sections 4–7. Finally, note that, just as in linear programming, the solution will lie at a corner point of the feasible region. In this example the feasible region for second-level goals is that portion of the solution space for which the first-level goals are met. Thus the need to evaluate only the points A, B, C, and D. The reader can verify that the total deviation at any other point is greater than the deviation at point B.

7.3. EXAMPLES

This section will discuss various problem formulations and applications of goal programming.

Manpower Planning

Several applications of goal programming to the problem of manpower planning have been reported (see references). In this problem, a group of personnel is to be promoted through various levels (the problem was stated originally in terms of promoting military personnel) subject to several conditions:

1. The budget for salaries after promotion is fixed (maximum budget).
2. There are a fixed number of openings in each level.
3. There is a minimum number of promotions to be given so that personnel satisfaction is maintained.

For the purposes of this example suppose the following data have been given:

Level	Salary (in thousands)	Number Currently in Level	Maximum Number in Level
1......................	$10	15	15
2......................	15	12	15
3......................	20	10	12

The minimum promotion rate is 20 percent for each level. In order to make room at the top it is assumed that the attrition rate is 10 percent at Level 3. Also the total budget is set at $700,000. It is assumed that Level 1 positions are automatically filled.

Let x_1 denote the number of new personnel hired at Level 1,
  x_2 denote the number of personnel promoted to Level 2,
  x_3 denote the number of personnel promoted to Level 3.

  Goals: Priority 1: Avoid overspending of budget.
      Priority 2: Avoid overstaffing in each level.
      Priority 3: Avoid underpromotion.

Salary: $10(15 - x_2 + x_1) + 15(12 - x_3 + x_2) + 20(10 - 0.1(10) + x_3) \leq 700$

If over- and underachievement of the budget are denoted by d_1^+ and d_1^-, then the budget constraint (stated in thousands of dollars) becomes

$$10(15 - x_2 + x_1) + 15(12 - x_3 + x_2) + 20(9 + x_3) - d_1^+ + d_1^- = 700.$$
$$(7\text{-}25)$$

Staffing Levels: With the appropriate deviational variables the staffing constraints become

$$
\begin{array}{llc}
\text{Level 1:} & 15 - x_3 + x_1 - d_2^+ + d_2^- = 15 & \\
\text{Level 2:} & 12 - x_3 + x_2 - d_3^+ + d_3^- = 15 & (7\text{-}26) \\
\text{Level 3:} & 9 + x_3 - d_4^+ + d_4^- = 12. &
\end{array}
$$

Promotion Rates:

$$
\begin{aligned}
x_2 - d_5^+ + d_5^- &= 0.2(15) \\
x_3 - d_6^+ + d_6^- &= 0.2(12).
\end{aligned}
$$
$$(7\text{-}27)$$

The *objective function* can be formulated as:

Minimize

$$\underbrace{P_1 d_1^+}_{} \qquad \underbrace{+\, P_2\,(d_2^+ + d_3^+ + d_4^+)}_{} \qquad \underbrace{+\, P_3\,(d_5^- + d_6^-)}_{},$$

Avoiding over-   Avoid *overstaffing*   Avoid *under-*
spending of   promotion.
the budget

Portfolio Selection.   The problem is to select, from some appropriate list, a subset of securities that meet some goals subject to a budget limitation. Some typical goals are growth maximization and risk minimization and risk minimization. Consider the following data:[7]

Security	Risk Factor (r_i)	Growth Factor (g_i)
Steels		
1.....................	0.2	0.5
2.....................	.2	.5
3.....................	.3	.3
4.....................	.3	.4
Chemicals		
5.....................	.4	.4
6.....................	.2	.6
7.....................	.5	.6
Oils		
8.....................	.7	.2
9.....................	.6	.1
10....................	.4	.5
11....................	.1	.3

---

[7] The generation of this type of data is dealt with in the references. A complete discussion is too far afield for this text. Certainly one way to generate such data is according to subjective assessments.

Define x_i as the proportion of the budget invested in security i and the goals of the problems as:

Priority 1:   Maximum total risk of 0.2
Priority 2:   Growth level of at least 0.55
Priority 3:   Invest entire budget.

In addition suppose the following constraints are imposed.

No more than 5 percent of the budget in any one security:

$$x_i \leq 0.05; \quad i = 1, \ldots, 11. \tag{7-28}$$

No more than 38 percent of the budget in steels:

$$x_i + x_2 + x_3 + x_4 \leq 0.38. \tag{7-29}$$

At least 15 percent of the budget in chemicals:

$$x_5 + x_6 + x_7 \geq 0.15. \tag{7-30}$$

No more than 50 percent of the budget in oils:

$$x_8 + x_9 + x_{10} + x_{11} \leq 0.5. \tag{7-31}$$

If we define

$d_1{}^+, d_1{}^-$ as deviations from the risk goal,
$d_2{}^+, d_2{}^-$ as deviations from the growth goal, and
$d_3{}^+, d_3{}^-$ as deviations from the budget limit goal,

then the goals can be expressed as:

$$\sum_{i=1}^{11} r_i x_i - d_1{}^+ + d_1{}^- = 0.2 \tag{7-32}$$

$$\sum_{i=1}^{11} g_i x_i - d_2{}^+ + d_2{}^- = 0.55 \tag{7-33}$$

$$\sum_{i=1}^{11} x_i + d_3{}^- = 1.[8] \tag{7-34}$$

The model now becomes

Minimize

$$P_1 d_1{}^- + P_2 d_2{}^+ + P_3 d_3{}^-$$

subject to

$$(7-28) \text{ to } (7-34).$$

---

[8] Since the budget limit is treated as being fixed and *cannot* be exceeded there is no need to include $d_3{}^+$.

Resource Allocation. As seen in Chapter 4, linear programming is particularly appropriate for resource allocation models. An extension of those models allows for multiple goals. For example, a firm manufactures three grades of floor covering and provides the following production data for each square yard of covering:

Type	Machine 1 Process Time (hours)	Vinyl (pounds)	Backing (square yards)	Profit Contribution
1	15	24	18	$12
2	22	21	18	15
3	42	15	24	10
Amount available	2,000	1,300	1,500	

The management has decided that its objectives for the coming production run are:

1. Maintain a production run profit of at least $900
2. Produce at least 450 square yards of Type 1 covering per production run.

To model the process define x_1, x_2, x_3 as the number of square yards of Types 1, 2, 3 respectively to be produced in the production run. The technological constraints are:[9]

$$15x_1 + 22x_2 + 40x_3 \le 2,000 \qquad (7\text{--}35)$$
$$24x_1 + 21x_2 + 15x_3 \le 1,300 \qquad (7\text{--}36)$$
$$18x_1 + 18x_2 + 24x_3 \le 1,500. \qquad (7\text{--}37)$$

The profit goal is:

$$12x_1 + 15x_2 + 10x_3 - d_1^+ + d_1^- = 900, \qquad (7\text{--}38)$$

and the production goal is

$$x_1 + d_2^- = 450. \qquad (7\text{--}39)$$

These requirements yield the objective function

Minimize

$$P_1 d_1^- + P_2 d_2^-$$

subject to

(7–35) to (7–39).

---

[9] For the example it is supposed the technological constraints are fixed and are not flexible. That is, the process must operate within the region defined by these constraints; in such cases it may be that one cannot achieve any of the goals because they are too demanding based on existing resources.

Summary

A systematic procedure such as the goal programming approach presented here can do much to extend the applicability of analytical models to decision making situations. Many applications of goal programming are listed in the references, are some different applications are given in the exercises. From these applications, goal programming seems to be particularly appropriate as a planning tool by means of which various goals, their ordering, and their cost (effect on resources) can be evaluated. It must be stressed, however, that in any application of goal programming one must be careful to distinguish technological constraints from goal constraints; that is, clearly identify those constraints that can be violated (in the sense of deviations) and those that are not flexible.

Also, in addition to the questions raised concerning LP models in Chapter 4, one needs to consider some additional questions with regard to goal programming models. Specifically one needs to be aware of the effect of a particular goal ranking.

7.4. INTRODUCTION TO NUMERICAL SOLUTIONS

This section is devoted to a study of a method for obtaining numerical solutions to goal programming models. The solution technique is based on the simplex algorithm for linear programs; as seen in the previous sections, however, the objective function of a goal program is ordinal' in nature. Thus the simplex algorithm will need to be modified so that it can deal with an objective function in which the coefficients are priority factors rather than numerical values. Our objective is to construct a linear programming type tableau without having to assign numerical values to the priority factors.

In order to facilitate the development of the algorithm for goal programs, a brief treatment of *Artificial Variables* in linear programming is given. The reader should review the appropriate sections of Chapter 5. As noted in Chapter 5, it is possible to solve, using the simplex method, problems in which the artificial variables are assigned arbitrarily large positive costs (in the case of Min cost) in the objective function.[10] The so-called *Big M Method* can be used to solve a problem without assigning a value to M. For automatic computations this means that some numerical value for M must be selected, and typically some value much larger than the original coefficients is chosen. In the goal programming model, since there may be several goal levels, several different values would need to be chosen. In order to avoid this situation a modified version of the

---

[10] For problems where the objective is to maximize, the artificial variables are assigned an arbitrarily large negative value in the objective function.

"two-phase simplex algorithm" is used as the solution method.[11] In fact, some commercially available simplex codes employ this solution method to deal with artificial variables. The two-phase simplex algorithm is the regular simplex algorithm with an additional row created for the artificial variables. In particular, the method creates a new objective function row in which the *coefficients* of the artificial variables are initially treated as 1 (for minimization problems). The algorithm first selects pivot columns from this row and attempts to find a solution that satisfies the optimality criterion. If such a solution exists it is a feasible solution to the original problem and the algorithm now attempts to find an optimal solution.[12]

In the case of only one goal level, the method to be described in the remainder of the chapter is exactly the same as the original two-phase simplex algorithm. For multiple goal levels the method will be extended to deal with such problems. This development, which incorporates an additional row for each goal level, will be given in Section 6.

7.5. THE TWO-PHASE ALGORITHM

Our discussion begins by considering the simplex algorithm with artificial variables and its relationship to the single goal level model. Consider a linear program that has been augmented to include an artificial basis:

Minimize

$$c_1x_1 + c_2x_2 + \cdots + c_nx_n + Mx_{n+1} + Mx_{n+2} + \cdots + Mx_{n+m} \quad (7\text{-}40)$$

subject to

$$
\begin{aligned}
a_{11}x_1 + \cdots + a_{1n}x_{1n} + x_{n+1} &= b_1 \\
a_{21}x_1 + \cdots + a_{2n}x_n + \qquad\qquad x_{n+2} &= b_2 \\
&\ \ \vdots \\
a_{m1}x_1 + \cdots + a_{mn}x_n + \qquad\qquad x_{n+m} &= b_m \\
x_j \geq 0; \quad j = 1, \ldots, n + m;
\end{aligned}
$$

where M is an unspecified, arbitrarily large positive number. The initial tableau for this problem is set up as in Chapter 5 except for the objective

---

[11] See the Gass reference at the end of the chapter for a general discussion of the two-phase simplex algorithm.

[12] Recall that the purpose of the artificial variables is to provide an initial solution that is feasible for the expanded problem. The simplex algorithm then attempts to drive all artificial variables out of the solution (nonbasic). If this can be done, the resulting solution is feasible for the original problem. If it is not possible to drive all artificial variables out of the solution (to a value of zero), then the original problem has no feasible solutions.

function row.[13] In place of the usual objective function row, there will be *two* objective function rows. Specifically, the first row will contain the coefficients of only the nonartificial variables and the second row will include -1 as the coefficients of each artificial variable. Thus the initial tableau is shown in Figure 7–4.

Since the entries in the objective function row for the basic variables are nonzero (M) we perform one initial iteration to remove those entries. It is important to note that it is not necessary to assign a value to the coefficient M.[14] Also note that our attention will be confined to the arti-

FIGURE 7–4

c_B	x_B	$\begin{matrix}-c_1 & -c_2 & -c_3 & \cdots & -c_n\\ x_1 & x_2 & x_3 & \cdots & x_n\end{matrix}$	$\begin{matrix}-M & -M & \cdots & -M\\ x_{n+1} & x_{n+2} & \cdots & x_{n+m}\end{matrix}$	b
$-M$	x_{n+1}	$a_{11}\, a_{12}\, a_{13} \quad\cdots\, a_{1n}$	$1 \quad 0 \quad\cdots\quad 0$	b_1
$-M$	x_{n+2}	$a_{21}\, a_{22}\, a_{23} \quad\cdots\, a_{2n}$	$0 \quad 1 \quad\cdots\quad 0$	b_2
.	.	.		.
.	.	.		.
.	.	.		.
$-M$	x_{n+m}	$a_{m1}\, a_{m2}\, a_{m3} \quad\cdots\, a_{mn}$	$0 \quad 0 \quad\cdots\quad 0$	b_m
$c_j - z_j$ for nonartificial objective function		$-c_1 \quad -c_2 \quad -c_3 \cdots -c_n$	$0 \quad 0 \quad\cdots\quad 0$	0
$c_j - z_j$ for artificial (M) objective function		$\Sigma a_{i1}\Sigma a_{i2}\Sigma a_{i3} \quad\cdots\, \Sigma a_{in}$	$0 \quad 0 \quad\cdots\quad 0$	$-\displaystyle\sum_{i=1}^{m} b_i$

ficial objective function row until a feasible solution is found. Thus the pivot column will be chosen from among the largest positive entries in the artificial row without regard to the nonartificial row. The reason for this is quite clear; up to this point it is not known whether the original model has any feasible solutions. If all the artificial variables can be made nonbasic or driven to a value of zero, then a feasible solution to the original problem is obtained. Once the feasibility of the original problem is determined the algorithm seeks to determine an optimal solution. The initial solution is then:

$$x_1 = x_2 = \cdots x_n = 0, \ x_{n+1} = b_1, \ x_{n+2} = b_2, \ \ldots, \ x_{n+m} = b_m$$

---

[13] Following the development of Chapter 5, all tableaus are stated in terms of maximization. Thus (7–40) is multiplied by (-1).

[14] This is the approach taken in Chapter 5.

with an objective function value

$$-M \sum_{i=1}^{m} b_i.$$

The ordinary simplex algorithm is now applied to the tableau; the largest positive entry of the artificial objective function is used to determine the pivot column. The procedure is continued until:

1. All the artificial variables have been eliminated from the basis, or
2. Until there are no positive elements in the artificial row.

In the first case a feasible solution for the original problem is found, and the algorithm continues using the nonartificial portion of the objective function until an optimal solution is determined. In the second case the solution has an artificial variable at a positive level, and hence there is no feasible solution to the original problem.

In terms of goal programming models the interpretation of this procedure is: Suppose in a problem with a single goal level a priority factor P_1 is assigned to all deviational variables for that goal. The resulting model is

Minimize

$$P_1 \sum_{k=1}^{p} d_k$$

subject to

$$\sum_{j=1}^{n} a_{ij}x_j = b_i \quad i = 1, \ldots, m \qquad (7\text{--}41)$$

$$\sum_{j=1}^{n} a_{ij}x_j + d_k = g_k \quad k = 1, \ldots, p$$

The priority factor corresponds to the penalty M associated with the artificial variables, and thus the tableau corresponding to Tableau 1 has only an artificial objective function. That is, there is no nonartificial portion of the objective function. The simplex algorithm will be used until:

1. The goal is satisfied, in which case

$$\sum_{k=1}^{p} d_k = 0, \text{ or}$$

2. There are no pivots possible, in which case the goal cannot be satisfied within the current structure. The solution at that point repre-

sents the best solution—in terms of minimum deviations from the stated goals.

To illustrate these ideas consider the following modification of the example of Section 2, (7–21) to (7–24):

Minimize

$$P_1(d_1{}^+ + d_1{}^-) \tag{7-42}$$

subject to

$$x_1 + 2x_2 \leq 10$$
$$2x_1 + x_2 \leq 8$$
$$10x_1 + 12x_2 - d_1{}^+ + d_1{}^- = 62.5$$
$$x_1, x_2, d_1{}^+, d_1{}^- > 0.$$

Recall that the objective is to meet the profit level of exactly 62.5 within the resource constraints. The solution for this problem via the tableau form is shown in Figure 7–5.

As can be seen the solution $x_1 = 0.625$, $x_2 = 4.6875$ meets the goal exactly. This is not surprising since the optimal LP solution is profit $= 68$, which contains the above solution. Suppose the goal is increased to a profit level of \$75. The solution to this model can be derived as shown in Figure 7–6.

Since there are no positive entries in the objective function row, the algorithm terminates with the solution $d_1{}^- = 7$. Also the objective func-

FIGURE 7–5

c_B	x_B	0 x_1	0 x_1	0 S_1	0 S_2	$-P_1$ $d_1{}^+$	$-P_1$ $d_1{}^-$	b
0	S_1	1	2	1	0	0	0	10
0	S_2	2	1	0	1	0	0	8
$-P_1$	$d_1{}^-$	10	12	0	0	-1	1	62.5
$c_j - z_j$		10	12	0	0	-2	0	-62.5
0	x_2	$\frac{1}{2}$	1	$\frac{1}{2}$	0	0	0	5
0	S_2	$\frac{3}{2}$	0	$-\frac{1}{2}$	1	0	0	3
$-P_1$	$d_1{}^-$	4	0	-6	0	-1	1	2.5
$c_j - z_j$		4	0	-6	0	-2	0	-2.5
0	x_2	0	1	$\frac{5}{4}$	0	$\frac{1}{8}$	$-\frac{1}{8}$	4.6875
0	S_2	0	0	$\frac{7}{4}$	1	$\frac{3}{8}$	$\frac{3}{8}$	2.0625
0	x_1	1	0	$-\frac{3}{2}$	0	$-\frac{1}{4}$	$\frac{1}{4}$	0.625
$c_j - z_j$		0	0	0	0	-1	-1	0

FIGURE 7–6

c_B	x_B	0 x_1	0 x_2	0 S_1	0 S_2	$-P_1$ d_1^+	$-P_1$ d_1^-	b
0	S_1	1	2	1	0	0	0	10
0	S_2	2	1	0	1	0	0	8
$-P_1$	d_1^-	10	12	0	0	-1	1	75
$c_j - z_j$		10	12	0	0	-2	0	-75
0	x_2	$\frac{1}{2}$	1	$\frac{1}{2}$	0	0	0	5
0	S_2	$\frac{3}{2}$	0	$-\frac{1}{2}$	1	0	0	3
$-P_1$	d_1^-	4	0	-6	0	-1	1	15
$c_j - z_j$		$+4$	0	-6	0	-2	0	-15
0	x_2	0	1	$\frac{2}{3}$	$-\frac{1}{3}$	0	0	4
0	x_1	1	0	$-\frac{1}{3}$	$\frac{2}{3}$	0	0	2
$-P_1$	d_1	0	0	$-1\frac{4}{3}$	$-\frac{8}{3}$	-1	1	7
$c_j - z_j$		0	0	$-1\frac{4}{3}$	$-\frac{8}{3}$	-2	0	-7

tion equals 7, which means the goal cannot be met. The "best" one can do is: $x_1 = 2$, $x_2 = 4$, for which profit $= 68$. In this case the goal programming solution corresponds to the optimal LP solution. In general, this need not occur.

7.6. TWO OR MORE GOAL LEVELS

The method described in the previous section is readily extended to include more than one goal level. In a certain sense the original two-phase simplex method is a case of two levels: at level one, one deals with the artificial variables—which must first be driven to a value of zero. Then at level two the optimal solution to the original problem is determined. For goal programs with two or more goal levels the tableaus are constructed as in the previous section with the exception *that there will be an objective function row for each goal level.* The procedure for generating the pivot column will be:

The pivot column is chosen from among the positive entries of the *highest priority level* remaining unsatisfied. When all entries in the highest goal are non-positive move to the next highest level.

The procedure terminates when either:

1. All goals are satisfied—that is, all entries in all the objective function rows are ≤ 0 and all $d_i = 0$ or

2. It is not possible to satisfy some goal level—that is, for some goal level all entries in the objective function row associated with that level are positive, yet some deviational variable has a negative value.

In either case it is important to note that lower level goals are not considered unless all higher level goals are satisfied. This statement is related to the earlier remark that stated that there is no possibility of trade-off of goal levels. This issue is treated in Section 7 on sensitivity analysis in goal programming.

The multiple goal method can be illustrated with the following modifications of the previous example.

Minimize

$$P_1 d_2^+ + P_1 d_2^- + P_2 d_1^- \tag{7-43}$$

subject to

$$2x_1 + x_2 \leq 8$$
$$x_1 + 2x_2 - d_1^+ + d_1^- = 10$$
$$10x_1 + 12x_2 - d_2^+ + d_2^- = 62.5$$
$$x_1, x_2, d_k \geq 0.$$

The solution procedure is shown in Figure 7–7. The solution satisfies both goal levels.

FIGURE 7–7

c_B	x_B	0 x_1	0 x_2	0 S_1	0 d_1^+	$-P_2$ d_1^-	$-P_1$ d_2^+	$-P_1$ d_2^-	b
0	S_1	2	1	1	0	0	0	0	8
$-P_2$	d_1^-	1	2	0	1	1	0	0	10
$-P_1$	d_2^-	10	12	0	0	0	−1	1	62.5
$c_j - z_j$ for P_1		10	12	0	0	0	−2	0	−62.5
$c_j - z_j$ for P_2		1	2	0	−1	0	0	0	−10
0	S_1	$\frac{3}{2}$	0	1	$-\frac{1}{2}$	$-\frac{1}{2}$	0	0	3
0	x_2	$\frac{1}{2}$	1	0	$-\frac{1}{2}$	$\frac{1}{2}$	0	0	5
$-P_1$	d_2^-	4	0	0	6	6	−1	1	2.5
P_1		4	0	0	6	−6	−2	0	−2.5
P_2		0	0	0	0	−1	0	0	0
0	S_1	0	0	1	$-\frac{7}{4}$	$\frac{7}{4}$	$\frac{3}{8}$	$\frac{3}{8}$	2.0625
0	x_2	0	1	0	$-\frac{5}{4}$	$\frac{5}{4}$	$\frac{1}{8}$	$-\frac{1}{8}$	4.6875
0	x_1	1	0	0	$\frac{3}{2}$	$-\frac{3}{2}$	$-\frac{1}{4}$	$\frac{1}{4}$	0.628
P_1		0	0	0	0	0	−1	−1	0
P_2		0	0	0	0	−1	0	0	0

As a second example consider the smelting process example of Section 2.

Minimize

$$P_1 d_1^- + P_2 d_2^+$$

subject to

$$x_1 + x_2 \le 300$$
$$3.75x_1 + 3x_2 - d_1^+ + d_1^- = 1{,}000 \text{ (minimum profit goal)}$$
$$7x_1 + 6x_2 - d_2^+ \quad\quad = \quad 0 \text{ (pollution goal)}.$$

The resulting linear programming tableaus are shown in Figure 7–8. The last tableau is optimal with respect to the usual optimality criterion for goal level one—the P_1 row has all nonpositive entries. The P_2 row has positive entries; however, the entry 28/15 in the d_1^- column would require alteration of the goal 1. That is, if one tries to pivot in the d_1^- column, that variable will be reintroduced into the solution and as a result violate Goal 1. Similarly, use of the 1 entry in the A_1 column as a pivot column will violate Goal 1. The solution given by the final tableau is the best solution, and it satisfies Goal 1 but not Goal 2. That

FIGURE 7–8

c_B	x_B	0 x_1	0 x_2	0 S_1	0 d_1^+	$-P_1$ d_1^-	$-P_2$ d_2^+	0 A_1	b
0	S_1	1	1	1	0	0	0	0	300
$-P_1$	d_1^-	3.75	3	0	-1	1	0	0	1,000
0	A_1	7	6	0	0	0	-1	1	0
P_1		3.75	3	0	0	0	0	0	$-1{,}000$
P_2		0	0	0	0	0	-1	0	0
0	S_1	0	$\tfrac{1}{7}$	1	0	0	$\tfrac{1}{7}$	$-\tfrac{1}{7}$	300
$-P_1$	d_1^-	0	$-\tfrac{3}{14}$	0	-1	1	$\tfrac{15}{28}$	$-\tfrac{15}{28}$	1,000
0	x_1	1	$\tfrac{6}{7}$	0	0	0	$-\tfrac{1}{7}$	$\tfrac{1}{7}$	0
P_1		0	$-\tfrac{90}{28}$	0	-1	0	$\tfrac{15}{28}$	$-\tfrac{15}{28}$	$-1{,}000$
P_2		0	0	0	0	0	1	0	0
0	S_1	0	$\tfrac{4}{70}$	1	$\tfrac{4}{15}$	$-\tfrac{4}{15}$	0	0	$500/15 = 33\tfrac{1}{3}$
$-P_2$	d_2^+	0	$-\tfrac{28}{70}$	0	$-\tfrac{28}{15}$	$\tfrac{28}{15}$	1	-1	$28{,}000/15 = 1{,}866\tfrac{2}{3}$
0	x_1	1	$\tfrac{56}{70}$	0	$-\tfrac{4}{15}$	$\tfrac{4}{15}$	0	0	$4{,}000/15 = 266\tfrac{2}{3}$
P_1		0	$-\tfrac{15}{70}$	0	0	-1	0	0	0
P_2		0	$-\tfrac{28}{70}$	0	$-\tfrac{28}{15}$	$\tfrac{28}{15}$	0	1	$2{,}800/15$

is, the solution is $x_1 = 266\frac{2}{3}$, $x_2 = 0$, which represents a zero deviation for Goal 1 ($d_1^- = 0$) and an overachievement of Goal 2 by $1,866\frac{2}{3}$ (d_2^+).

It is important to note that the modified simplex algorithm can be terminated without satisfying the usual optimality conditions of linear programming. As illustrated by the previous example, this occurs when the potential pivot column would violate a higher-level goal; that is, introducing d_1^- will violate Goal 1, which has already been satisfied. Thus, as mentioned earlier in the chapter, in addition to the usual linear programming optimality criterion, one must never pivot in such a way so as to violate a higher priority goal.

The steps of the modified simplex algorithm are summarized as:

1. Set up the initial tableau as in ordinary linear programming with an objective function row for each priority level. The negative deviation (d_1^-) provide an initial basis along with artificial variables, if necessary.

2. Choose the *pivot column* by considering the objective function row associated with the *highest nonsatisfied priority level*. That is, if goal 1 is not satisfied find the largest positive entry in the P_1 row that identifies a pivot column.

3. Determine the pivot row as in ordinary linear programming.

4. The optimality criterion for goal programming is the same as ordinary linear programming—all nonpositive entries in the objective function row—in which case *all goals are met;* or more likely, some goal is not satisfied with a positive entry in the objective function row, but there are negative entries at a higher goal level for that column.

Finally, all ties for pivot elements are broken arbitrarily.

7.7. SENSITIVITY ANALYSIS

Just as in linear programming, sensitivity analysis is a valuable aspect of goal programming. The sensitivity analysis for goal programming will take on some slightly different aspects than in linear programming.

Reordering of Goals

In the discussion of goal programming it has been carefully noted that the goals are not interchangeable within the solution procedure. The decision maker's goals may, however, vary with time, and thus it is important to study the effect of a change in the priorities. As an example consider the case of the decision maker who wants to interchange two goals. Clearly if both goals are satisfied there is no change in the solution. On the other hand, if one of the associated deviations is basic (nonzero) a change in order will clearly affect the solution. In particular, a goal that was satisfied will be replaced by a nonsatisfied goal, thus requiring an additional iteration. For example:

Minimize

$$P_1 d_1^- + P_2 d_2^- + P_2 d_3^- + P_3 d_1^+$$

subject to

$$
\begin{aligned}
x_1 + x_2 + d_1^- \qquad\qquad - d_1^+ &= 80 \\
x_1 \qquad\qquad + d_2^- \qquad\qquad &= 70 \\
x_2 \qquad\qquad + d_3^- \qquad &= 45.
\end{aligned}
$$

It is left as an exercise for the reader to verify that the final tableau is given by:

c_B	x_B	x_1	x_2	d_1^-	d_2^-	d_3^-	d_1^+	b
0	x_2	0	1	0	0	1	0	45
0	x_1	1	0	0	1	0	0	70
$-P_3$	d_1^+	0	0	-1	1	1	1	35
	P_1	0	0	-1	0	0	0	0
	P_2	0	0	0	-1	-1	0	0
	P_3	0	0	-1	1	1	0	35

The associated solution is $x_1 = 70$, $x_2 = 45$, and Goal 3 is overachieved by 35 units $(70 + 45 + (-35) = 80)$.

Now if Goals 2 and 3 are interchanged, the objective function becomes

Minimize

$$P_1 d_1^- + P_2 d_1^+ + P_3 d_2^- + P_3 d_3^-,$$

and for the previous solution Goal 1 is not satisfied; hence additional pivots are required. The final tableau for this objective function is:

c_B	x_B	x_1	x_2	d_1^-	d_2^-	d_3^-	d_1^+	b
0	x_2	0	1	0	0	1	0	45
0	x_1	1	0	0	1	0	0	70
$-P_1$	d_1^-	0	0	-1	1	1	1	35
	P_1	0	0	-1	0	0	0	0
	P_2	0	0	1	-1	-1	0	35
	P_3	0	0	0	1	1	0	0

Performing one additional pivot we obtain:

c_B	x_B	x_1	x_2	$d_1{}^-$	$d_2{}^-$	$d_3{}^-$	$d_1{}^+$	b
0	x_2	0	1	0	0	1	0	45
0	x_1	1	0	1	0	-1	-1	35
$-P_3$	$d_2{}^-$	0	0	-1	1	1	1	35
	P_1	0	0	1	0	0	0	0
	P_2	0	0	0	0	0	1	0
	P_3	0	0	1	0	0	-1	35

The new solution is $x_1 = 35$, $x_2 = 45$, for which Goal 3 is not satisfied; that is, $d_2{}^- = 35$.

By the use of this type of analysis the trade-offs necessary to interchange various goal levels can be simulated. Such analyses are related to an alternative approach to the solution of goal programs. This alternative approach is to assign numerical values rather than priority factors to the various goal levels. As shown in Chapter 6, the solution may vary considerably depending on the objective function coefficients. In the case of a single goal level the coefficient would need to be chosen large relative to the other coefficients. When there are several goal levels the relative values of the coefficients can affect the solution. Such an approach would need to include a sensitivity analysis of the choices of the coefficients. Such a study would yield information concerning the interchangeability of goal levels.

Change in the Right-Hand Sides. It is of interest to study the effect of changes in the amount of resources and/or goals on the optimal solution. The procedure for performing such analysis is much the same as for the ordinary linear programming. To illustrate this consider the previous example when the first constraint is changed to:

$$x_1 + x_2 - d_1{}^+ + d_1{}^- = 90,$$

an increase of ten units. One can readily verify that the resulting final simplex tableau is:

c_B	x_B	x_1	x_2	$d_1{}^-$	$d_2{}^-$	$d_3{}^-$	$d_1{}^+$	b
0	x_2	0	1	0	0	1	0	45
0	x_1	1	0	0	1	0	0	70
$-P_3$	$d_1{}^+$	0	0	-1	1	1	1	25
	P_1	0	0	1	0	0	0	0
	P_2	0	0	0	1	1	0	0
	P_3	0	0	1	-1	-1	0	25

which simply reduces the overachievement of Goal 3 by ten units.

As in ordinary linear programming, it is not necessary to re-solve the problem in order to determine the solution. One need merely identify the slack variables (d_i^-) for the altered constraint; multiply that column in the final simplex tableau by the amount of change; and add to the final b column to obtain the new values. Just as in Chapter 5, such analysis is *valid only as long as the new entries are positive or at least nonnegative*. Thus, in terms of the preceding example we have:

$$
(90 - 80) \times \begin{array}{c} d_1^- \\ \begin{pmatrix} 0 \\ 0 \\ -1 \end{pmatrix} \end{array} = \begin{pmatrix} 0 \\ 0 \\ -10 \end{pmatrix} \quad \begin{array}{c} b \\ 45 \\ 70 \\ 25. \end{array}
$$

Other types of sensitivity analysis are possible—they are similar to the sensitivity analysis in linear programming. The reader should consult the references for more details.

7.8. INTERACTIVE APPROACHES

The preceding development of goal programming models is based on the fact that the goals or objectives have been ordered with a set of pre-emptive priorities. As we have noted, such a set of priorities does not allow for trade-offs among the goals without redefining the priorities and re-solving the model. As an alternative to such models we now describe several interactive approaches to multiple criteria models. These approaches are characterized by the fact that we do not set up a priority system but rather attempt to get the decision maker to develop appropriate trade-offs among the objectives. The recent literature on multiple-criteria decision making contains a number of references describing interactive approaches to these models, and a number of them are given in the references at the end of the chapter. For this section we will describe two basic but different approaches to interactive multiple criteria decision making.

The basis for the approaches that follow is that the decision maker has a preference function, U, defined over the criteria or objective functions, f_i. These criteria are relative to some decision making process defined by a set of technological constraints. We do not assume, however, that the explicit form of the preference function U is specified. The main idea is to have the decision maker via man-machine interaction arrive at a set of optimal trade-offs among the criteria. The above model is very general and thus for it to be of practical value we must impose some assumptions. For our purposes here it will be assumed that:

1. All constraints are linear functions and are feasible.
2. Each criterion function, f_i, is a linear function and the overall preference function is linear as well.

Thus the objective of the interactive approaches will be to determine the decision maker's choices for the coefficients in the linear preference function U.

The first approach to multiple models is based on the STEM method described in the Benayoun *et al.* reference and is essentially *an interactive linear program*. The method requires a linear representation of the preference function and the criterion functions and seeks to determine the *best compromise* solution by sequentially exploring solutions to this problem. The method does not require an *a priori* weighting of the objectives but rather attempts to ascertain the relative importance of the various criteria.

The basic STEM model can be described as:

Maximize

$$[f_1(x), f_2(x), \ldots, f_k(x)] \tag{7-44}$$

subject to

$$Ax \le b \tag{7-45}$$
$$x_i \ge 0; \quad i = 1, \ldots, n;$$

where $f_j(x) = \sum_{i=1}^{n} c_i{}^j x_i$ represents the jth criterion or objective function, and (7-44) is to be interpreted as maximizing *each* f_j. The constraints (7-45) represent the technological constraints associated with a linear program.

The basic assumption concerning solutions to models of the form (7-44) to (7-45) is that there does not exist a feasible point (satisfying (7-45)) such that *all objective functions are maximized simultaneously*. If such a point exists, the ordinary linear programming solution will be the optimal solution. In the absence of such a point, one seeks to determine the best compromise solution. *The best compromise solution in terms of the STEM method is a feasible solution for which the decision-maker is satisfied with* all *components of the objective function*.

The basic steps of the STEM method are:

Step 1: Construct the payoff table by determining the maximum of (7-44) for each objective function treated separately. For the solution that maximizes each objective we also evaluate the other objective functions. The form of the payoff table is:

	f_1	f_2	f_3	$\cdots$	f_k
f_1	M^1	$Z_2{}^1$	$Z_3{}^1$	$\cdots$	$Z_k{}^1$
f_2	$Z_1{}^2$	M^2	$Z_3{}^2$	$\cdots$	$Z_k{}^2$
f_3	$Z_1{}^3$	$Z_2{}^3$	M^3	$\cdots$	$Z_k{}^3$
.					
.					
.					
f_k	$Z_1{}^k$	$Z_2{}^k$	$Z_3{}^k$	$\cdots$	M^k

where M^j indicates the maximum value of objective j and Z_i^j indicates the value of objective i when j is at its maximum. For the example of Figure 7–1,

Maximize

$$\{f_1 = -\mid x_1 + x_2 - 8 \mid, \quad f_2 = -\mid -x_1 + x_2 - 4 \mid\}$$

subject to

$$3x_1 + 2x_2 \le 12$$
$$5x_1 \qquad \le 10$$
$$x_1, x_2 \ge 0,$$

the payoff table is:

	f_1	f_2
f_1	-2	-2
f_2	-4	0

The M^1 entry corresponds to solving the problem:

Maximize

$$-\mid x_1 = x_2 - 8 \mid$$

subject to

$$3x_1 = 2x_2 \le 12$$
$$5x_1 \qquad \le 10$$
$$x_1, x_2 \ge 0,$$

which is equivalent to letting $d_1^+ + d_1^- = \mid x_1 + x_2 - 8 \mid$ and writing the problem as:

Maximize

$$-d_1^+ - d_1^-$$

subject to

$$x_1 + x_2 - 8 = d_1^+ - d_1^-$$
$$3x_1 + 2x_2 \le 12$$
$$5x_1 \qquad \le 10$$
$$x_1, x_2, d_1^+, d_1^- \ge 0.$$

The solution to this problem can be seen to be $x_1^* = 0$, $x_2^* = 6$. The Z_2^1 entry in (7–47) arises from evaluating $-\mid -x_1 + x_2 - 4 \mid$ at $x_1 = 0$, $x_2 = 6$. The M^2 entry of (7–47) corresponds to solving the problem:

Maximize

$$-\mid -x_1 + x_2 - 4 \mid$$

subject to

$$3x_1 + 2x_2 \le 12$$
$$5x_1 \qquad \le 10$$
$$x_1, x_2 \ge 0.$$

The optimal solution is seen to be $x_1{}^* = 0$, $x_2{}^* = 4$, which yields $M^2 = 0$. Evaluating $|x_1 + x_2 - 8|$ at this solution results in $Z_1{}^2 = -4$.

  Step 2: Compute a feasible solution that minimizes the maximum "distance" from the ideal solution to the problem. Since we are dealing with different objectives we need to construct a weighting strategy in order to deal with (7–44) as a linear program. The weights chosen in STEM will reflect the distance to the optimal solution. A weighting function that has been proposed for this method is:

$$w^j = \left(\frac{M^i - m^j}{M^j} \right) \left(\frac{1}{\sqrt{\sum_i (Z_i{}^1)^2}} \right), \tag{7–48}$$

where M^j is the maximum entry and m^j the minimum entry in column j of the payoff table.[15] The quantity $\sum_i (Z_i{}^j)^2$ is the sum of the squares of the entries in row j, including M^j.

  The w^j will be normalized as $w_j \Big/ \sum_j w_j$ before inclusion into the linear program. This set of weights corresponds to those developed by the authors of the method; other weights are possible, but we do not discuss them at this point. A feasible solution to the original problem is obtained by solving the linear program

  Minimize

$$\lambda$$

subject to

$$\lambda \ge (M^i - C^i(x))w^j; \quad j = 1, \ldots, k$$
$$x \text{ satisfying } (7\text{–}45) \text{ and } w^i \text{ defined by } (7\text{–}48). \tag{7–49}$$

In terms of the example problem the weights are

$$w^1 = \frac{-4 - (-2)}{-4} \quad \frac{1}{\sqrt{4 + 4}} = \frac{1}{2\sqrt{8}}$$

$$w_2 = \frac{-2 - (0)}{-2} \quad \frac{1}{\sqrt{16 + 0}} = \frac{1}{4}.$$

---

[15] If the maximum entry is nonpositive (≤ 0) the weighting function becomes

$$\frac{m^i - M^i}{m_j} \quad \frac{1}{\sqrt{\sum (Z_i{}^i)^2}}.$$

The normalized weights are computed as $w^1 = 0.4142$ and $w^2 = 0.5858$. The linear program associated with (7–48) is then:

Minimize

$$\lambda$$

subject to

$$\lambda \geq (-2 + |\ x_1 + x_2 - 8\ |)(0.4142)$$
$$\lambda \geq (0 + |\ -x_1 + x_2 - 4\ |)(0.5858)$$
$$3x_1 + 2x_2 \leq 12$$
$$5x_1 \qquad \leq 10$$
$$x_1, x_2,\ \lambda\ \geq 0.$$

The solution to this problem can be found to be $x_1{}^* = \frac{4}{5}$, $x_2{}^* = \frac{24}{5}$, $\lambda^* = 0.1657$, which is feasible for the original model. Although for this solution the second objective is satisfied, because $|-x_1 + x_2 - 4| = 0$, the first objective is not satisfied. The next step is to try to improve the objective that is not met by relaxing a satisfied objective.

Step 3: Decide on a trade-off between satisfactory and unsatisfactory objectives. Since the current solution is a compromise, we want to determine whether the decision maker is willing to accept some relaxation (worsening) of a satisfied objective in order to improve the unsatisfied objectives. Thus at this step the decision maker indicates which (satisfactory) objective will be relaxed and by how much. The w^j associated with the relaxed objective is set to zero, and additional constraints are adjoined to the previous linear program. These constraints have the form:

Let k denote the objective to be relaxed by some amount Δ; then,

$$f_k(x) \geq f_k(x)^* - \Delta \tag{7–50}$$
$$f_k(x) \geq f_k(x)^* \quad \text{for all other } j,$$

where x^* is the current feasible solution.

These constraints insure that the objectives "move" by the desired amount, Δ, at the very least. The algorithm continues until no further changes are desirable on the part of the decision maker.

For example, if we decide to relax objective two by 2 units; that is, we would be willing to accept up to 2 units of deviation in $|-x_1 + x_2 - 4|$ in order to reduce the deviation from $|\ x_1 + x_2 - 8\ |$; we set $w^2 = 0$ and (7–50) takes the form:

$$|-x_1 + x_2 - 4| \leq 2 \tag{7–51}$$
$$|\ x_1 + x_2 - 8| \leq 12/5,$$

where the sense of the inequality has been reversed because of the negative values of the objectives.

The new linear program to be solved is:

Minimize

$$\lambda$$

subject to

$$\lambda \geq (-2 + |x_1 + x_2 - 8|)$$
$$3x_1 + 2x_2 \qquad \leq 12$$
$$5x_1 \qquad\qquad \leq 10$$
$$|-x_1 + x_2 - 4| \leq 2$$
$$|\ \ x_1 + x_2 - 8| \leq 12/5$$
$$x_1, x_2, \qquad \lambda \geq 0.$$

The solution to this problem can be seen to be $x_1{}^* = 0$, $x_2{}^* = 6$, which is feasible and which generates functional values of 2 for each constraint in (7–51). It can be seen from Figure 7–1 that no other changes are possible and also that if the change Δ in objective two were to exceed 2 units, the current solution ($x_1 = 0$, $x_2 = 6$) would remain optimal. For changes $0 < \Delta < 2$ we would find a point on the constraint $3x_1 + 2x_2 = 12$ between the point ($\frac{4}{5}$, $2\frac{4}{5}$) and the point (0, 6).

The second approach to interactive models involves the direct determination of the decision-makers' trade-offs among the criteria. In the presentation that follows it is assumed that all criterion functions are linear and the preference function, while not known explicitly, is concave.[16] The method as implemented by Dyer involves man-computer interaction in which the decision-maker specifies trade-offs among criteria and the computer computes the best solution with regard to that set of trade-offs. The decision maker seeing the result of that set of trade-offs can then alter the trade-offs. This routine continues until the decision-maker reaches a point at which the results are satisfactory in that changing the trade-offs will not improve the results; that is, the decision-maker is unwilling to give up anything from one criterion in order to improve the results with respect to any other criterion.

We should note almost immediately that problem solving in the presence of multiple criteria is relatively new in the management science literature. As a result, at the writing of this book, the reported experience with the implementation of such models is rather limited. Thus we cannot be sure that either of the methods we present here in their present stage of development will turn out to be the most practical method. We are certain, however, that multiple criteria methods, in particular interactive methods, will become a major aid in the decision making process and deserve to be treated in a text such as this even in a rudimentary form.

The interactive approach suggested by Dyer is essentially the following:

Let the problem be written as:

---

[16] The assumption of concavity of U does rule out the use of preemptive priorities.

Maximize

$$\{f_1(x), f_2(x), \ldots, f_k(x)\}$$

subject to

$$Ax \leq b$$
$$x \geq 0,$$

where the $f_j(x)$ are the linear criterion functions.

At the current solution point supplied by the decision maker, either in terms of the decision variables x or in terms of the criterion functions f_j, the method seeks to determine the optimal direction in which to move by having the decision maker determine the weights w_i as: "With all other criteria held constant, how much of a decrease in criterion i would you accept to increase criterion 1 by the amount Δf_1." The responses to these questions Δf_i, $i = 1, \ldots, k$, are used to compute the weight $w_i = \Delta f_1 / \Delta f_i$ for each criterion, with w_1 taken to be 1 by convention. That is to say, we use an approximation for the local trade-offs:

$$\left(\frac{\partial U / \partial f_i}{\partial U / \partial f_1} \right) = \frac{\Delta f_1}{\Delta f_i} .$$

Since the preference function U is unknown, we are approximating the first derivative of each criterion with respect to a satisfactory criterion. These estimated derivatives are then used to optimize the current problem. Once this trial solution is generated, the decision maker can once again specify certain trade-offs that are acceptable and the process continues. As with the linear model the process terminates when the decision maker is unwilling to make any additional trade-offs.

These interactive approaches are relatively new in the area of multiple criteria decision making, and as a result few practical experiences have been reported. The references contain several examples of implementation of these ideas including allocation of resources within an academic department at a major university, training exercises for business men, and decision making within a steel company. While the practical experience has been limited, these methods could be extremely useful in expanding the range of application of linear and nonlinear programming models. In addition they can provide training models that can aid in the development of management skills in assessing trade-offs among various alternatives.

EXERCISES

7.1.   The manufacturer of two types (A and B) of equipment has determined the following production data:

Type A requires one hour of assembly and three hours of testing; Type B requires one hour of assembly and two hours of testing. There are a total of 40 hours of assembly and testing time available. Also the Type A equipment has a profit contribution of $100 per unit compared to $50 per unit for Type B.

The manufacturer has specified goals for the upcoming production run as:

1. Sell as many pieces of equipment as possible. The sales force has indicated a potential market of *at most* 35 units of Type A and 45 units of Type B.
2. Assuming the amount of time available is flexible, avoid any idle assembly time.
3. Avoid, as much as possible, overtime.
a. Formulate a goal programming model for this problem where Goal 1 is most important and Goal 3 is least important.
b. Using the solution techniques of Sections 5–7, solve the model.
c. What happens to the solution if Goals 1 and 3 are interchanged?
d. If Goals 1 and 2 are interchanged?

7.2. You have just inherited $100,000 (tax free) and are in the process of creating your investment portfolio. The options available are: stocks, bonds, mutual funds, and real estate. The analysis of these options is the following:

The stocks return an average total of 12 percent if left for a period of two years.
The bonds return 15 percent but require three years to mature.
The mutual fund's return has averaged 8 percent each year.
The real estate will double in six years.

Formulate a goal programming model to determine the investment to be made in each year (five-year planning horizon) when the goals are:

1. Put no more than 30 percent in any one plan.
2. Invest at least 20 percent of the inheritance in real estate.
3. Keep at least 5 percent available in cash each year.

7.3. A company operated two production lines producing a single quantity. The production capacity of Line 1 during an eight-hour shift is three units per hour and Line 2 has a capacity of two units per hour. The production manager has set the following goals:

1. A production run of 48 units.
2. A limit of at least five hours and at most 10 hours of overtime for Line 1.

a. Formulate the model as a goal program.
b. How does the solution change if the limitations of goal (2) are applied to Line 2 instead of Line 1?

7.4. An accounting firm is designing a planning model for its auditing function for the next year. The firm wants to determine the optimal number of partners, managers, senior staff, and junior staff members relative to the following set of goals. The firm wants to increase last year's billings of $2 million by 50 percent. (Based on past data, partners generate $100,000; managers $150,000; senior staff $90,000; and junior staff $85,000, in billings each year.) In addition, the firm has established limits on the number of auditing partners at two, the number of managers at five, and wants to maintain a ratio of management to staff of one to four. Formulate a goal programming model where the order of goals are:

1. Increase billing by 50 percent.
2. Maintain personnel ceiling levels.
3. Maintain the management-staff ratio.

7.5. Suppose that data for risk and growth potential for a list of stocks has been obtained. Let r_i indicate the risk index and g_i the growth index. Construct a goal programming model of the portfolio selection problem where the goals are:

a. Minimize risk;
b. Maximize growth.

Typical constraints are: a total budget available and maximum investment limits on various securities and groups of securities.

7.6. A company manufactures three products and is trying to determine a production schedule. The marketing manager has developed the following rather cryptic requirements:

There should be twice as much of Product 1 as of Product 2.
There should be as much of Product 2 as of Product 3.
There should be at least 20 units of Product 3.

If the technology of the production process is given by

$$3x_1 + 5x_2 + 4x_3 \leq 100,$$

construct a goal programming model to avoid underachievement of the above goals.

7.7. In Exercise 2 of Chapter 4, suppose the objective is to avoid the underutilization of both resources. Formulate the appropriate goal programming model.

7.8. In the bank lending model of Exercise 22 of Chapter 4, suppose that instead of maximizing revenue, management states its goals as:

1. Lend the maximum amount available.
2. Allow for home-improvement loans to be more than 25 percent of total loans, but by no more than 10 percent.
3. Allow personal loans to exceed 10 percent of the total by no more than 15 percent.

Formulate the goal programming model that reflects this goal structure.

7.9. The administration of a college has set out to determine an admission policy for the upcoming academic year. In addition to admitting (at most) 400 freshmen, there are certain goals to be met in the composition of the class. These goals, in order of decreasing priority, are:

1. Admit exactly 400 students.
2. Admit at least 40 percent women.
3. Admit no more than 25 percent out-of-state students.

The college administration has data to show that the number of applicants is distributed as:

In-state men . . . 400
In-state women . . . 100
Out-of-state men . . . 100
Out-of-state women . . . 50

Formulate the appropriate goal programming model.

Solve each of the following problems using the modified simplex algorithm of this chapter.

7.10.

Minimize

$$P_1d_3^+ + P_1d_3^- + 2P_2d_1^+ + P_2d_2^+$$

subject to

$$
\begin{aligned}
x_1 + 6x_2 - d_1^+ + d_1^- &= 60 \\
4x_1 + 2x_2 - d_2^+ + d_2^- &= 32 \\
20x_1 + 24x_2 - d_3^+ + d_3^- &= 300.
\end{aligned}
$$

7.11.

Minimize

$$P_1d_1^- + P_1d_2^-$$

subject to

$$
\begin{aligned}
3x_1 + 2x_2 &\le 12 \\
5x_1 &\le 10 \\
x_1 + x_2 - d_1^+ + d_1^- &= 8 \\
-x_1 + x_2 - d_2^+ + d_2^- &= 4.
\end{aligned}
$$

7.12.

Minimize

$$P_1d_1^+ + P_2d_2^+$$

subject to same constraints as in Problem 7.11.

7.13. For the problem of Section 7.7 analyze the result of
   a. Decreasing constraint 2 by 10 units
   b. Decreasing constraint 3 by 15 units

7.14. *a.* Solve

Minimize

$$P_1d_1^- + P_2d_3^+ + P_3d_2^+$$

subject to

$$5x_1 + 10x_2 + d_1^- - d_1^+ = 1,000$$
$$x_1 \qquad + d_2^- - d_2^+ = \quad 700$$
$$x_2 \qquad\qquad -d_3^+ = \quad 600$$

b. Solve with reordered goals $P_1(d_1^- + d_2^-) + P_2d_2^+$

SUGGESTIONS FOR FURTHER STUDY

Benayoun, R., de Montgolfier, J., Tergny, J., and Laritchev, O., "Linear Programming with Multiple Objective Functions: STEP Method (STEM)," *Mathematical Programming*, vol. 1, 1971.

Charnes, A., and Cooper, W. W., "Goal Programming and Constrained Regression," *OMEGA*, vol. 3, 1975.

Charnes, A., and Cooper, W. W., *Management Models and Industrial Applications of Linear Programming*, vol. 1. New York: Wiley, 1961.

Charnes, A., Cooper, W. W., DeVoe, J. K., Learner, D. B., and Reinecke, W., "A Goal Programming Model for Media Planning," *Management Science*, vol. 14, 1968.

Charnes, A., Cooper, W. W., DeVoe, J. K., Learner, D. B., Reinecke, W., and Snow, E. F., "Note on an Application of a Goal Programming Model for Media Planning," *Management Science*, vol. 14, 1968.

Charnes, A., Cooper, W. W., and Niehaus, R. J., "Studies in Manpower Planning," Washington, D.C.: U.S. Navy Office of Civilian Manpower Management, 1972.

Cochrane, J. L., and Zelany, M., *Multiple Criteria Decision Making*. Columbia, S.C.: University of South Carolina Press, 1973.

Contini, B., "A Stochastic Approach to Goal Programming," *Operations Research*, vol. 16, May–June 1968.

Courtney, J., Klastorian, T., and Ruesli, T., "A Goal Programming Approach to Urban-Suburban Location Preferences," *Management Science*, vol. 18, 1972.

Dane, C. W., Meador, N. C., and White, J. B., "Goal Programming in Land-Use Planning," *Journal of Forestry*, vol. 75, June 1977.

Dyer, J. S., "A Time Sharing Computer Program for the Solution of the Multiple Criteria Problem," *Management Science*, vol. 19, August 1973.

Dyer, J. S., and Miles, R. E., "An Actual Application of Collective Choice Theory to the Selection of Trajectories for the Mariner Jupiter/Saturn 1977 Project," *Operations Research*, vol. 24, March–April 1976.

Elion, S., "Goals and Constraints in Decision Making," *Operational Research Quarterly*, vol. 23, 1972.

Gass, S. I., *Linear Programming*. 4th ed. New York: McGraw-Hill, 1975.

Geoffrion, A. M., Dyer, J. S., and Feinberg, A., "An Interactive Approach for Multi-Criterion Optimization, with an Application to the Operation of an Academic Department," *Management Science*, vol. 19, December 1972.

Gore, W. J., and Dyson, J. W., eds., *The Making of Decisions*. London: The Free Press, 1964.

Ijiri, Y., *Management Goals and Accounting for Control*. Chicago: Rand McNally, 1965.

Keeney, R. L., and Raiffa, H., *Decisions with Multiple Objectives: Preferences and Value Tradeoffs*. New York: Wiley, 1976.

Krischer, J. P., "Utility Structure of a Medical Decision-Making Problem," *Operations Research*, vol. 24, September–October 1976.

Lee, S. M., *Goal Programming for Decision Analysis*. Philadelphia: Auerbach, 1972.

Lee, S. M., and Clayton, E. R., "A Goal Programming Model for Academic Resource Allocation," *Management Science*, vol. 18, 1972.

Lee, S. M., Lerro, A., and McGinnis, B., "Optimization of Tax Switching for Commercial Banks," *Journal of Money, Credit and Banking*, vol. 3, 1971.

Lee, S. M., and Moore, L. J., "Multi-Criteria School Busing Models," *Management Science*, vol. 23, March 1977.

Ruefli, T., "A Generalized Goal Decomposition Model," *Management Science*, vol. 17, 1971.

Schuler, A. T., Webster, H. H., and Meadows, J. C., "Goal Programming in Forest Management," *Journal of Forestry*, vol. 75, June 1977.

Soldofsky, R. M., "Yield-Risk Performance Measurements," *Financial Analyst Journal*, vol. 24, 1968.

Steuer, R. E., and Schuler, A. T., "An Interactive Multiple Objective Linear Programming Approach to a Problem in Forest Management," Working Paper BA2, College of Business, University of Kentucky, 1976.

Wallenius, J., "Comparative Evaluation of Some Interactive Approaches to Multiple Criterion Optimization," *Management Science*, vol. 21, no. 12, August 1975.

Zeleny, M., "MCDM Bibliography—1975," in Zeleny, M., ed., *Multiple Criteria Decision Making: Kyoto 1975*. New York: Springer-Verlag, 1976.

Zionts, S., and Wallenius, J., "An Interactive Programming Method for Solving the Multiple Criteria Problem," *Management Science*, vol. 22, February 1976.

8

Integer Programming

8.1. INTRODUCTION

RECALL THAT one of the key assumptions of linear programming is that all decision variables are *continuous*. In *integer programming* problems, some or all of the variables are required to be integer valued. The models we build for integer programming problems, then, look exactly like LP models except that we append to the models the requirement that certain (or all) variables must be integer valued. When all the variables are required to be integer valued, we say we have a "pure" integer model. Otherwise we have a "mixed" integer model.

Many important managerial problems fall into the realm of integer programming. Consider for example, a product-mix problem in which the potential products are different types of radios. The decision variables for such a problem represent the numbers of each type of radio that should be made. Because a radio cannot be meaningfully subdivided into fractional parts, these decision variables must be required to be integer valued. To build an integer programming model for this problem, we build an LP product-mix model and simply add the integer restrictions to it.

There are many other types of problems where the decision variables are inherently integer variables. For example, consider a capital budgeting problem where our objective is to optimally allocate a fixed budget to a few investments, given that we have a large number of potential investment opportunities available to us. Here, our decision variables are inherently binary. For each potential investment, we must make a "yes-no" decision. Many other important problems exist where the decision variables (or at least some of them) are binary. Several important examples will be explored later in the chapter.

In addition to arising naturally in certain problem settings as decision variables, integer (particularly binary) variables are useful in yet another sense. Many relationships (logical relationships between variables, quantity discounts, and so forth) that cannot be modeled with continuous (that is, LP) variables can be modeled by introducing integer variables. Thus, using integer variables greatly increases our ability to formulate realistic models of complex optimization problems. The following examples illustrate how binary variables can be used to model some common relationships that cannot be handled by linear programming. In each case it is implied that these relationships are to be incorporated into larger models.

8.2. INTEGER MODELING PRINCIPLES

Fixed Charge Relationships

Many activities have cost structures consisting of both fixed and variable components. That is, if x_j is the level of activity j, then the cost structure is

$$\text{Cost} = \begin{cases} F_j + c_j x_j & \text{if } x_j > 0 \\ 0 & \text{if } x_j = 0, \end{cases} \tag{8-1}$$

where

$$F_j = \text{fixed cost}$$
$$c_j = \text{unit variable cost.}$$

Such a cost structure[1] can be modeled by introducing a binary variable and an upper bound on x_j as follows:

$$y_j = \begin{cases} 1 & \text{if } x_j > 0 \\ 0 & \text{if } x_j = 0 \end{cases}$$
$$U_j = \text{upper bound on } x_j \text{ (some large number).}$$

Then, the fixed-charge cost structure can be modeled by the following cost equation and constraint:

$$\text{Cost} = F_j y_j + c_j x_j \tag{8-2}$$
$$x_j \leq U_j y_j. \tag{8-3}$$

Compare carefully the model of (8-2) and (8-3) with the original cost structure of (8-1). Note particularly the role of constraint (8-3). If $y_j = 1$, then (8-3) really does not constrain x_j (since U_j is any arbitrary upper bound). In such a case, (8-2) indicates that the fixed charge, F_j,

---

[1] Linear programming would require F_j to be zero.

as well as the appropriate variable cost, will be incurred. On the other hand, if $y_j = 0$, then (8–3) requires that $x_j = 0$ and thus the cost is equal to zero. (We are assuming $x_j \geq 0$.)

Logical Relationships among Alternatives

Often complex decision environments require that certain alternatives are allowable only if certain other events take place. Thus, choices open to the decision maker depend upon what other decisions have been or will be made. These logical relationships between alternatives can be modeled using binary variables. The following illustrate the basic idea. More complex logical relationships can be modeled by extending the ideas presented below. Assume in each case that a binary variable is associated with each available alternative, with a value of plus one implying that the alternative is selected.

1. Suppose alternatives j and k are open to us and we can choose either j or k but not both. This relationship is captured by the constraint

    $$y_j + y_k \leq 1, \qquad (8\text{--}4)$$

    where y_j and y_k are the binary variables associated with alternatives j and k respectively. Note that (8–4) would not allow both alternatives to be chosen simultaneously.

2. Suppose alternative i is to be chosen if and only if either alternative j or k is chosen. This situation is modeled by the following two constraints:

    $$y_j + y_k \leq 2y_i \qquad (8\text{--}5)$$
    $$2y_i - y_j - y_k \leq 1. \qquad (8\text{--}6)$$

    Note that if either y_j or y_k equals one, then (8–5) forces y_i to be one. Likewise, if both y_j and y_k equal zero, (8–6) forces y_i to be zero. Collectively then, (8–5) and (8–6) impose the desired condition on y_i.

3. Suppose alternative i is to be chosen if and only if alternatives j, k, and ℓ are all chosen. This can be modeled by the following two constraints

    $$y_j + y_k + y_\ell - 3y_i \leq 2 \qquad (8\text{--}7)$$
    $$3y_i - y_j - y_k - y_\ell \leq 0. \qquad (8\text{--}8)$$

    If y_j, y_k, and y_ℓ equal one, (8–7) forces y_i to be one. If one or more of the three variables, y_j, y_k, and y_ℓ, equals zero, (8–8) forces y_i to be zero.

Alternative Constraints

In many situations we want to impose certain constraints (and effectively remove others) depending on the outcome of various binary variables. For example, suppose we are considering building a productive facility whose capacity could be either 1,000 units, 2,000 units, or 3,000 units. Let x_1 be the level of production at that plant. Then depending on which size plant we choose, the capacity constraint on x_1 will be *one* of the following

$$x_1 \leq 1,000$$
$$x_1 \leq 2,000$$
$$x_1 \leq 3,000.$$

This situation can be modeled as follows:
Associate with each plant size a binary variable. Let $y_1 = 1$ if plant size 1,000 is chosen; 0 otherwise. Likewise define y_2 and y_3. Then the imposition of one of the three capacity constraints can be modeled by the following four constraints:

$$y_1 + y_2 + y_3 = 1 \qquad\qquad (8\text{--}9)$$
$$x_1 \leq 1,000y_1 + U(1-y_1) \qquad\qquad (8\text{--}10)$$
$$x_1 \leq 2,000y_2 + U(1-y_2) \qquad\qquad (8\text{--}11)$$
$$x_1 \leq 3,000y_3 + U(1-y_3) \qquad\qquad (8\text{--}12)$$

where U is sufficiently large that *any* feasible solution would satisfy $x_i \leq U$. In this example, $U = 3,000$ would work.

To illustrate how the above constraints work, consider the case for which $y_2 = 1$. Equation (8–9) requires that $y_1 = y_3 = 0$. Thus, constraints (8–10), (8–11), and (8–12) become

$$x_1 \leq U \qquad\qquad (8\text{--}10)$$
$$x_1 \leq 2,000 \qquad\qquad (8\text{--}11)$$
$$x_1 \leq U, \qquad\qquad (8\text{--}12)$$

which means that (8–10) and (8–12) are essentially removed from the problem since they have no chance of being binding. The other cases ($y_1 = 1$ and $y_3 = 1$) work in a similar fashion.

The above approach to imposing certain constraints depending on the outcome of binary decisions can be generalized as follows: Suppose we want to impose ℓ of the following m constraints:

$$\sum_{j=1}^{n} a_{ij}x_j \leq b_i; \quad i = 1,2, \ldots ,m. \qquad\qquad (8\text{--}13)$$

This can be accomplished by associating a binary variable, y_i, with each constraint of (8–13) and using the following $(m + 1)$ constraints:

$$\sum_{i=1}^{m} y_i = \ell \qquad\qquad (8\text{--}14)$$

$$\sum_{j=1}^{n} a_{ij}x_j \leq b_iy_i + U(1 - y_i); \quad i = 1, 2, \ldots ,m; \qquad\qquad (8\text{--}15)$$

where U is sufficiently large that any feasible solution to (8–13) will satisfy

$$\sum_{j=1}^{n} a_{ij}x_j \leq U; \quad i = 1, 2, \ldots, m.$$

Discrete Values Only

Sometimes we want to restrict certain decision variables to a discrete set of values. For instance, in the plant capacity example above we could think of plant capacity as a variable (denoted), say, by PC) whose only permissible values are 1,000, 2,000, and 3,000. By associating a binary variable with each possible outcome, we can model the plant capacity as follows:

$$PC = 1,000y_1 + 2,000y_2 + 3,000y_3 \tag{8–16}$$
$$y_1 + y_2 + y_3 = 1, y_i = 0, 1. \tag{8–17}$$

Equation (8–17) allows one and only one of the y_i to be +1 (all others are zero). Equation (8–16) then forces PC to be identically equal to one of the intended discrete values.

The above idea can be used to represent general integer variables by a set of binary variables.[2] Suppose we have a nonnegative integer variable x_i that must be less than or equal to 6. That is, x_i can be either 0, 1, 2, 3, 4, 5, or 6. We could introduce three binary variables and represent x_i by

$$x_i = y_1 + 2y_2 + 3y_3; \quad y_i = 0, 1; i = 1, 2, 3. \tag{8–18}$$

The various binary combinations for y_1, y_2, and y_3 will allow x_i to assume any of the values from 0 to 6. The procedure would be to replace x_i everywhere it appears in the model by the binary expansion of (8–18). Then, after the problem is solved, the value of x_i would be computed from the optimal y_i values.

The binary expansion illustrated above can be generalized as follows: If x is a nonnegative integer with an upper bound of U, then x can be replaced by

$$x = \sum_{k=0}^{p} 2^k y_{k+1} \leq U \tag{8–19}$$

where p is the smallest integer such that

$$U \leq 2^{p+1} - 1. \tag{8–20}$$

---

[2] Such a representation is often required because many computer programs for integer programming will allow only binary integer variables.

8.3. SOME CLASSICAL MODELS

The following are illustrative of some of the well known models in integer programming. Not only are they important in their own right, but understanding them (and how they were composed) will yield insights useful in modeling problems different from these but containing similar mathematical relationships.

Transportation-Plant Location Model

Consider the problem of locating productive facilities as well as determining which facilities should serve various customers. Assume that m possible plant locations, along with the relevant cost and capacity information, have been enumerated. Furthermore assume that the demand level for each of the n demand zones is known. The variable and parameter definitions needed are:

$w_i = \begin{cases} 1 \text{ if site } i \text{ is chosen for a plant} \\ 0 \text{ otherwise} \end{cases}$

$x_{ij} =$ number of units shipped from site i to demand zone j. (x_{ij} must equal zero if $w_i = 0$)

$F_i =$ fixed cost associated with site i (to be incurred only if site i is chosen)

$c_{ij} =$ unit cost associated with shipping from plant i to demand zone j

$d_j =$ demand level at zone j

$s_i =$ capacity of proposed plant i.

Given these definitions, the model is:

$$\text{Minimize cost} = \sum_{i=1}^{m} F_i w_i + \sum_{i=1}^{m} \sum_{j=1}^{n} c_{ij} x_{ij} \tag{8-21}$$

subject to

$$\sum_{j=1}^{n} x_{ij} \leq s_i w_i \quad i = 1, 2, \ldots, m \text{ (Supply)} \tag{8-22}$$

$$\sum_{i=1}^{m} x_{ij} \geq d_j \quad j = 1, 2, \ldots, n \text{ (Demand)} \tag{8-23}$$

$$x_{ij} \geq 0, \, w_i = 0, 1. \tag{8-24}$$

Several remarks are in order. Notice that this is a "mixed" integer model. The w_i are integral and the x_{ij} are, in general, continuous. Notice also that the objective function contains both fixed and variable costs. Finally, note that the supply constraints (8-22) impose the capacity restrictions and tie the two sets of variables together.

Capital-Budgeting Model

Consider the capital-budgeting problem where a budget of $\$B_j$ for each of T years is to be allocated among n different investment opportunities. Assume that all projects run for the duration of T years. Assume that the following parameters are known:

$$\$a_{ij} = \text{expenditure required for project } i \text{ in year } j$$
$$r_i = \text{expected return from investment (project) } i.$$

The problem is to determine which investments to make so that total returns will be maximized. This problem can be modeled with a binary decision variable x_i defined by

$$x_i = \begin{cases} 1 & \text{if investment opportunity } i \text{ is chosen} \\ 0 & \text{otherwise.} \end{cases}$$

Then the model is

$$\text{Maximize returns} = \sum_{i=1}^{n} r_i x_i \tag{8-25}$$

subject to

$$\sum_{i=1}^{n} a_{ij} x_i \le B_j; \quad j = 1, 2, \ldots, T. \tag{8-25}$$

Note that this is a pure 0–1 model. It may be desired to add additional constraints to the model for diversification purposes. For instance, perhaps we do not want to allow both projects 10 and 23 to be selected. We could impose this consideration simply by adding the constraint

$$x_{10} + x_{23} \le 1. \tag{8-26}$$

This constraint would allow either but not both to be selected. Other important considerations about the composition of our portfolio of investments could be included as constraints in a similar manner.

Traveling Salesman Problem

Consider a salesman who wants to visit each of n different cities and then return to the home city in such a way that total travel time is minimized. Each city is to be visited only once. This problem can be modeled as follows:

Denote the intercity times by

$$t_{ij} = \text{time to travel from city } i \text{ to city } j \ (t_{ii} = 0).$$

Define a binary decision variable

$$x_{ijk} = \begin{cases} 1 & \text{if the } k\text{th leg of the trip is from city } i \text{ to city } j \\ 0 & \text{otherwise} \end{cases}$$

Then the model becomes:

$$\text{Minimize time} = \sum_{i=1}^{n} \sum_{j=1}^{n} \sum_{k=1}^{n} t_{ij} x_{ijk} \tag{8-27}$$

subject to the constraints

$$\sum_{j=1}^{n} \sum_{k=1}^{n} x_{ijk} = 1; \qquad i = 1, 2, \dots, n \tag{8-28}$$

$$\sum_{i=1}^{n} \sum_{j=1}^{n} x_{ijk} = 1; \qquad k = 1, 2, \dots, n \tag{8-29}$$

$$\sum_{i=1}^{n} \sum_{k=1}^{n} x_{ijk} = 1; \qquad j = 1, 2, \dots, n \tag{8-30}$$

$$\sum_{i=1}^{n} x_{ijk-1} = \sum_{l=1}^{n} x_{jlk}; \quad j = 1, 2, \dots, n;$$

$$k = 2, 3, \dots, n. \tag{8-31}$$

The reader should study the constraints carefully. Equations (8–28) insure that a given city i is the immediate predecessor of only one city. Equations (8–29) impose the requirement that given leg of the complete trip can be associated with only two cities. Equations (8–30) require that a given city j can be the immediate successor of only one city. Finally, the constraints of (8–31) insure that the solution found will consist of a complete round trip tour of all the cities rather than a set of disconnected subtours. This is accomplished by requiring that if the $(k-1)$st leg of the trip ends in city j, then the kth leg of the trip must start in city j.

Assembly-Line Balancing Model

Assembly-line balancing refers to the problem of determining the minimum number of work stations required along an assembly line and the assignment of tasks to these stations. Two important considerations are that all tasks needed to produce a finished product be completed (in proper order) and that the production rate of the system be maintained. Given that these considerations are satisfied, we want to determine how many work stations we need and which tasks to schedule for each work station. In principle, any task can be accomplished at any work station. We assume that a task must be completed at one and only one station, but that a given station may have more than one task. To illustrate the problem, consider an example in which the product involved requires n tasks with completion times denoted by t_j minutes and with various precedent requirements.[3] Furthermore, assume that the system output rate is required to be a minimum of r units per hour. This means that the total time required to complete the tasks assigned to *any* station must be less than or equal to $60/r$ minutes. Since we have n tasks, we clearly do not need more than n work stations. Thus, the model will allow for a maximum of n stations. With the following decision variables,

$$w_i = \begin{cases} 1 \text{ if work station } i \text{ is opened} \\ 0 \text{ otherwise} \end{cases}$$

$$x_{ij} = \begin{cases} 1 \text{ if task } j \text{ is assigned to station } i \\ 0 \text{ otherwise} \end{cases}$$

the model becomes

Minimize

$$\sum_{i=1}^{n} w_i \tag{8-32}$$

subject to

$$\sum_{j=1}^{n} t_j x_{ij} \leq 60/r; \quad i = 1, 2, \ldots, n \tag{8-33}$$

$$\sum_{i=1}^{n} x_{ij} = 1; \quad j = 1, 2, \ldots, n \tag{8-34}$$

$$\sum_{j=1}^{n} x_{ij} \leq n w_i; \quad i = 1, 2, \ldots, n; \tag{8-35}$$

and a precedence constraint of the form

$$\sum_{j=1}^{n} (jx_{jk}) \geq \sum_{j=1}^{n} jx_{j\ell} \tag{8-36}$$

for each requirement that a given task ℓ must precede task k.

As with the previous examples, it is important that the reader understand the purpose of the above constraints. The constraints of (8–33) ensure that the total time spent at each work station is less than or equal to the time allowed by the production rate r. The equations of (8–34) require that each of the n tasks will be completed (assigned to some work station).

The conditional constraints of (8–35) tie the two sets of decision variables together. If a given station, i, is open (that is, $w_i = 1$), the constraint simply indicates that any or all tasks may be considered for assignment to Station i. However, if Station i is unused (that is, $w_i = 0$), (8–35) insures that no task can be assigned to the station.

---

[3] Assume that the precedent requirement may be satisfied at the same work station.

The precedent constraints of (8–36) require a little more thought. For illustrative purposes, assume $n = 5$ and consider the precedent relation that Task 1 must precede Task 3. For this condition, (8–36) would become

$$1x_{13} + 2x_{23} + 3x_{33} + 4x_{43} + 5x_{53}$$
$$\geq 1x_{11} + 2x_{21} + 3x_{31} + 4x_{41} + 5x_{51}. \quad (8\text{–}37)$$

Now suppose Task 1 is assigned to Station 2. Then with $x_{21} = 1$ and all other $x_{i1} = 0$, the above constraint effectively becomes

$$1x_{13} + 2x_{23} + 3x_{33} + 4x_{43} + 5x_{53} \geq 2. \quad (8\text{–}38)$$

This means that Task 3 could be assigned to any station with index greater than or equal to 2 but not to Station 1. (Recall that one and only one of the variables in (8–38) can equal plus one.) Similarly, if Task 1 were to be assigned to Station 4, (8–37) would effectively become

$$x_{13} + 2x_{23} + 3x_{33} + 4x_{43} + 5x_{53} \geq 4, \quad (8\text{–}39)$$

which would only allow either x_{43} or x_{53} to be plus 1.

8.4. SOLVING INTEGER PROGRAMMING PROBLEMS

Just as integer programming models differ from linear programming models, their solution properties also differ. In general, solutions to integer problems are not simple extreme point solutions of the kind we found in linear programming. Thus, integer models cannot be solved (in general) by simply applying the simplex algorithm.[4] To illustrate the nature of solutions to integer problems, consider the example

Maximize
$$x_0 = 4x_1 + 3x_2 \quad (8\text{–}40)$$

subject to

$$9x_1 + 6x_2 \leq 54 \quad (8\text{–}41)$$
$$7x_1 + 8x_2 \leq 56 \quad (8\text{–}42)$$
$$0 \leq x_1 \leq 5; \quad 0 \leq x_2 \leq 5 \quad (8\text{–}43)$$
$$x_1, x_2 \text{ integer.} \quad (8\text{–}44)$$

Figure 8–1 shows the feasible region for this problem. Ignoring the integer restrictions, we have just a linear programming problem with the feasible region given by the points on the boundary and interior to the polygon labeled $a \ b \ c \ d \ e \ f$ in Figure 8–1. The LP problem associated with any integer programming problem is called the LP relaxation of the integer problem. With the integer restrictions, the feasible region

---

[4] Recall that the simplex algorithm computes and evaluates extreme point solutions only.

FIGURE 8–1

Feasible Region for Integer Example

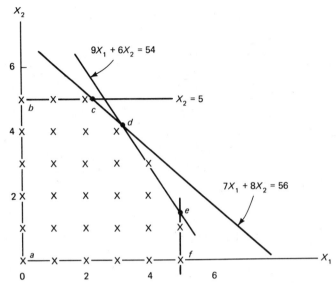

becomes the set of integer points (also called lattice points) contained in the LP feasible region. These points are marked with small crosses in Figure 8–1. Note that for this pure integer problem there are only a finite number (in this case 29) of feasible points to consider. Furthermore, the optimal integer point may or may not be an extreme point of the original LP relaxation.

Generally speaking, there are two approaches available for solving integer programming problems—optimizing techniques and heuristic techniques. Optimizing techniques are designed to compute optimal solutions. Typically, these approaches employ repeated use of linear programming to locate an optimal integer (or mixed integer) solution.[5] Thus, the computational burden of solving mixed and/or pure integer problems is usually much greater than that of solving a linear program of comparable size. Nonetheless, the benefits derived from having optimal solutions often justify the computational expense.

In this chapter, we will study a "branch-and-bound" algorithm for solving integer programming problems optimally. Branch-and-bound algorithms are widely recognized as the most successful approach to

---

[5] Many special purpose algorithms exist for solving integer problems with special structure that do not require the repeated use of linear programming. Most contemporary, commercially available computer codes for solving real-world sized problems, however, are based on so-called "branch-and-bound" algorithms, which require the solution of a sequence of linear programs.

general integer and mixed integer problems. For descriptions of other optimizing algorithms (such as cutting planes methods, decomposition, network algorithms, and "group theoretic" methods) the reader is referred to the references at the end of the chapter. These algorithms are not discussed here, primarily because they have been less successful than branch-and-bound as general purpose optimizers for integer programming problems. In addition, they tend to be considerably more difficult to understand than branch-and-bound.[6]

Heuristics

Heuristic techniques, in contrast to the optimizing techniques, are designed to give quick, usable solutions, but they guarantee nothing

FIGURE 8-2

Intercity Distances for Traveling Salesman Example

			To			
From	*1*	*2*	*3*	*4*	*5*	*6*
1	0	5	2	4	7	9
2	5	0	4	3	5	1
3	2	4	0	6	2	7
4	4	3	6	0	5	4
5	7	5	2	5	0	2
6	9	1	7	4	2	0

about the optimality of the solutions found. Heuristic approaches are often nothing more than a set of rules tailor-made for generating solutions to certain types of problems. These techniques are usually very easy to program[7] for computers and typically require only a fraction of the time that an optimizing technique would require. Their simplicity and speed often make them attractive candidates for solution techniques. To illustrate the idea of a heuristic, consider the traveling salesman problem depicted by (8–27) through (8–31). Suppose we are dealing with six cities with intercity distances given by Figure 8–2. One heuristic approach (called the "nearest neighbor" heuristic) used for finding solutions to traveling salesman problems is as follows:

---

[6] It should be noted that it is possible to represent many integer programming models as equivalent network flow models, which, in turn, can be solved by network algorithms. These network algorithms tend to be relatively fast. Thus, this approach offers considerable promise. Discussion of these network algorithms is beyond the scope of this text.

[7] In fact, many heuristics are so simple that they can be used manually without the aid of a computer.

a. Start a path with any city.
b. From among the cities not yet on the path, find the city closest to the city last added to the path. Connect these two cities. Continue until all cities have been added to the path. (Arbitrarily break any ties that might occur.)
c. Connect the first and last city to yield a completed round trip.

Applying this heuristic to the six-city problem of Figure 8–2 gives the results shown in Figure 8–3. These results indicate a complete tour from 1 to 3 to 5 to 6 to 2 to 4 and back to 1 for a total distance of 14. To find the optimal solution to the problem, we would have to solve the model given by (8–27) through (8–31) with $n = 6$ and the data of Figure 8–2. This model would have 216 binary variables and 48 constraints. Even on contemporary computers, this model would take considerable time to

FIGURE 8–3

Nearest Neighbor Solution to Traveling Salesman Problem

Last City Added to Path	Nearest Neighbor	Cumulative Distance
1	3	2
3	5	4
5	6	6
6	2	7
2	4	10
4	1	14

solve. Moreover, it would take quite some time (perhaps hours) to prepare and input the data required for the computer run. In contrast, the "nearest neighbor" solution was found manually in less than one minute.

Nearest neighbor type heuristics are commonly used to solve many real-world problems today. Other heuristics, typically made up by the problem solver involved, are likewise routinely used today to solve a wide variety of integer and mixed-integer problems that would be expensive (if not impossible) to solve optimally.

Another example of a heuristic approach to solving integer programming problems is the practice of "rounding" a linear programming solution to a "nearby" integer-valued solution. As long as the integer solution so obtained satisfies all of the constraints, this approach quickly yields usable solutions. However, it is not always obvious which way to round the LP solution values so that the integer solution generated is feasible. Moreover, if the LP solution values are fairly small in magnitude (say, less than 20), integer solutions so obtained may differ appreciably from the true optimum. Nonetheless, this approach is widely used in practice today because of its speed and simplicity.

Even though heuristics offer an attractive way to compute usable solutions to many integer problems, there are many models for which we do not want to settle for anything less than the optimal solution. The difference between a heuristically generated solution that is 90 percent optimal and the actual optimal solution might be several thousand dollars or more. Even if an optimizing technique would cost several hundred dollars of computer time, it would be worthwhile to use one. In such cases, optimal solutions are usually computed by a branch-and-bound algorithm.

In general, branch-and-bound is a problem-solving philosophy that can form a foundation for analysis useful for many different types of problems—not just integer programming problems. We first present the general framework and then specialize it for integer programming problems.

General Branch-and-Bound Approach

Suppose we have some function $x_o = f(x_1, x_2, \ldots, x_n)$ that we want to maximize where $x_1, x_2, \ldots, x_n$ are required to satisfy some well defined restrictions. Furthermore, assume that we have a *lower* bound on x_0. (Perhaps the best feasible value found so far, some user supplied value, or, in the absence of any knowledge about the problem, we could use $-\infty$ initially.) Then, a branch and bound approach is the following:

a. Partition the set of possible solutions into two or more subsets and obtain an *upper* bound on x_0 for each subset.

b. Discard any subject whose upper bound is *less* than the current lower bound on x_0.

c. Choose one of the remaining subsets for further partitioning. Obtain upper bounds for these new subsets. Again, any subset whose upper bound is less than the current lower bound on x_0 is discarded.

d. From the subsets that remain, pick any one for further partitioning, etc. As this procedure is repeated, the current lower bound on x_0 is updated as more attractive feasible solutions are encountered.

e. The optimal solution is identified when a feasible solution is found such that its objective function value is no less than the *upper bound* on any remaining subset.

When solving integer programming problems, upper bounds for each subset can be computed by solving the associated LP relaxation.[8] This follows because an integer solution to a model can never have a more

---

[8] For problems with all binary variables, upper bounds can be found without using linear programming. However, we restrict ourselves here to the more general algorithm that applies to all integer problems.

attractive objective function value than that given by the optimal continuous solution. At best they can be equally attractive. If at a given subset the LP solution also satisfies the integer requirements, the corresponding objective function value is a *lower bound* on the optimal objective function value for the original problem. Partitioning is usually accomplished by choosing some fractional-valued variable and "branching" on this variable to create two new subsets such that the current solution (but no integer solution) is excluded from further consideration. To implement a branch-and-bound algorithm for integer programming, we need to develop a list of LP problems. Each LP problem on the list will be a descendant of the original problem and will differ from other problems on the list only in the bounds that are placed on one or more integer variables.

Before specifying the details of the algorithm, we need to specify some notation and a definition. Let b be any real number. Then the greatest integer part of b, denoted by $[b]$, and the fractional part of b, denoted by f, are defined by

$$[b] + f = b \qquad (8\text{--}45)$$

when f is required to be ≥ 0. For example, if $b = 2.3$, $[b] = 2$, if $b = -3.7$, $[b] = -4$; and so forth. The "bracket" notation is used in the algorithm. Moreover, the algorithm assumes an integer problem of the form

Maximize

$$x_0 = \sum_{j=1}^{n} c_j x_j \qquad (8\text{--}46)$$

subject to

$$\sum_{j=1}^{n} a_{ij} x_j = b_i; \quad i = 1, 2, \ldots, m \qquad (8\text{--}47)$$

$$L_j \leq x_j \leq U_j \qquad (8\text{--}48)$$
$$x_j \text{ integer,} \qquad (8\text{--}49)$$

where L_j and U_j are lower and upper bounds respectively on variable x_j. A branch-and-bound algorithm for solving this problem is:

Step 0. Initialization: Put the LP problem of (8–46), (8–47), and (8–48) on the LP list. Denote by X_0 the best available lower bound on x_0.

Step 1. Node (Problem) Selection: Terminate if the list is empty. Otherwise remove (select) one LP problem from the list.

Step 2. LP Solution: Solve the LP problem at hand. If the problem has no feasible solution or if the objective function value is less than or equal to X_0, go to Step 1. Otherwise, go to Step 3.

Step 3.   Check Integer Restrictions: If the LP solution just obtained satisfies the integer restrictions, record it, update X_0, and return to Step 1. Otherwise, go to Step 4.

Step 4.   Partitioning: Select a fractional-valued variable x_k. Denote its value by b_k. Modify the problem chosen in Step 1 to create two new problems such that in one, the upper bound on x_k is replaced by $[b_k]$ and in the other, the lower bound on x_k is replaced by $[b_k] + 1$. Add these two problems to the list and return to Step 1.

Remarks

1.   When the algorithm terminates (Step 1) the solution giving the current value of X_0 is the optimal solution. If we initiate the algorithm with $X_0 = -\infty$ and find at termination X_0 is still $-\infty$, then no feasible integer solution exists for the problem.

2.   The problem selection decision in Step 1 is often made on a last in-first out (Lifo) basis where one of the most recently created problems is chosen and the other is returned to at the first opportunity.

3.   Mixed-integer problems can be handled by creating at the outset two sets of variables—one for the integer and one for the continuous variable—and by restricting our choice in Step 4 only to those variables in the integer set.

Let's apply the algorithm to the example problem given by (8–40) through (8–44). The step-by-step results are:

Step 0. $X_0 = 0$ (corresponding to $x_1 = x_2 = 0$). The list consists of the problem given by (8–40) through (8–43), which we call Problem 1.

Step 1.   Remove Problem 1 from the list.

Step 2.   Solution is: $x_1 = 1\%$, $x_2 = 2\frac{1}{5}$, $x_0 = 25.4$.
Since $x_0 > X_0$, go to Step 3.

Step 3.   Integer conditions not satisfied. Go to Step 4.

Step 4.   Choose (arbitrarily) x_1 for branching. Create and add two new problems to the list.
Problem 2: (8–40) through (8–42) and $0 \leq x_1 \leq 3$; $0 \leq x_2 \leq 5$.
Problem 3: (8–40) through (8–42) and $4 \leq x_1 \leq 5$; $0 \leq x_2 \leq 5$.

Step 1.   Remove Problem 2 from the list.

Step 2.   Solution is: $x_1 = 3$, $x_2 = 3\%$, $x_0 = 25.125$.
Since $x_0 > X_0$, go to Step 3.

Step 3. Integer conditions not satisfied. Go to Step 4.

Step 4. Choose x_2 for branching. Create and add two new problems to the list.
Problem 4: (8–40) through (8–42) and $0 \le x_1 \le 3;\ 0 \le x_2 \le 4$.
Problem 5: (8–40) through (8–42) and $0 \le x_1 \le 3;\ 5 \le x_2 \le 5$:

Step 1. (List now contains Problems 3, 4, and 5) Remove Problem 4.

Step 2. Solution is: $x_1 = 3$, $x_2 = 4$, $x_0 = 24$.
Since $x_0 \ge X_0$, go to Step 3.

Step 3. Integer restrictions are satisfied. Set $X_0 = x_0 = 24$. Go to Step 1.

Step 1. Remove Problem 5 from list (leaving just Problem 3).

Step 2. Solution is: $x_1 = 1\frac{6}{7}$, $x_2 = 5$, $x_0 = 24.1428$.
Since $x_0 > X_0$, go to Step 3.

Step 3. Integer restrictions not satisfied. Go to Step 4.

Step 4. Choose x_1 for branching. Create and add to the list the following problems.
Problem 6: (8–40) through (8–42) and $0 \le x_1 \le 2;\ 5 \le x_2 \le 5$.
Problem 7: (8–40) through (8–42) and $3 \le x_1 \le 3;\ 5 \le x_2 \le 5$.

Step 1. (List contains Problems 3, 6, and 7). Remove Problem 6.

Step 2. Solution is: $x_1 = 2$, $x_2 = 5$, $x_0 = 23$.
Since $x_0 < X_0$, return to Step 1.

Step 1. Remove Problem 7.

Step 2. Problem has no feasible solution. Return to Step 1.

Step 1. Remove Problem 3.

Step 2. Solution is: $x_1 = 4$, $x_2 = 3$, $x_0 = 25$.
Since $x_0 > X_0$, go to Step 3.

Step 3. Integer restrictions are satisfied. Set $X_0 = x_0 = 25$. Go to Step 1.

Step 1. Terminate since the list is empty.
The optimal solution is $x_1 = 4$, $x_2 = 3$, $x_0 = 25$.

This solution process can be summarized by the tree structure shown in Figure 8–4. In the figure, node numbers denote problem numbers for our list of problems. The numbers above the nodes are the LP solution values associated with each node. Note that if Problem 3 had been chosen instead of Problem 2 initially, Problems 6 and 7 would never have been created. In general, the manner in which the list of problems is managed and the branching decisions are made has a tremendous impact on the time it takes the algorithm to solve a given problem. Commercial computer codes have sophisticated "list management" and branching rules to intelligently guide the algorithm.

The relationship between the tree and the general branch-and-bound procedure should be clear. Each node represents the integer problems defined over a particular subset of the original set of possible solutions. An upper bound for each subset is found by solving the LP relaxations associated with each node. If at any given node, the upper bound is greater than the current lower bound (X_0), the tree structure must be further developed by connecting two new nodes with branches emanating from the node at hand. The new nodes are called descendants, and

FIGURE 8–4

Tree Structure Associated with the Branch-and-Bound Solution of Example Problem

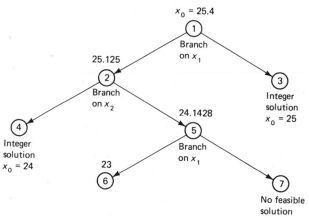

the original node is called the predecessor. If the LP solution at a given node is integer valued or less than X_0, then no descendants from the node need be considered (because neither could possibly yield integer solutions as attractive as we currently have.) In such a case, we work our way back up the tree and look for some other node from which to branch. The tree construction (and the algorithm) stops when no such node can be found.

8.5. CONCLUSION AND SUMMARY

Integer and mixed integer models are natural and powerful extensions of linear programming models. They enable a decision maker to model many important problems outside the realm of linear programming.

Often alternative models exist for the same problem. For such cases an important rule of thumb is that the model with the fewest integer variables should be chosen for solving. Generally speaking, experience indicates that computational burden grows quickly as the number of integer variables in a model grows. (Unlike linear programming, in which the critical item is the number of constraints.)

EXERCISES

8.1.   Consider a plant location and distribution problem with the following information. Five potential sites have been identified for consideration. The sites chosen are to serve eight demand zones. The unit shipping costs along with estimated yearly demand, the fixed charges, and capacities are

Site	Zone								Fixed Charge	Capacity
	1	*2*	*3*	*4*	*5*	*6*	*7*	*8*		
1.........	1	2	$\frac{1}{2}$	$\frac{1}{2}$	1	2	1	1	75	300
2.........	2	1	$\frac{1}{2}$	3	1	1	2	1	60	400
3.........	1	2	1	1	2	1	1	2	100	500
4.........	$\frac{1}{2}$	$\frac{1}{2}$	1	$\frac{1}{2}$	$\frac{1}{2}$	2	1	1	200	500
5.........	1	2	$\frac{1}{2}$	2	1	1	$\frac{1}{2}$	$\frac{1}{2}$	100	400
Demand......	100	200	100	150	80	200	300	150		

a.   Write out the cost-minimization model for this problem.
b.   Modify the model to ensure that no more than three sites are chosen.
c.   Modify the model to ensure that Sites 3 and 4 are not both chosen.

8.2.   A space official must decide which of n proposed experiments should be included in the nose cone of a given rocket. A panel of experts studied the experiments and were able to associate a "scientific value," denoted by sv_j, with each experiment, $j = 1, 2, \ldots, n$. The nose cone has a usable volume of v_1 cubic feet. Furthermore, the electrical system can provide no more than v_2 volts. Assume the volume and electrical requirements of experiment j are v_{1j} and v_{2j} respectively.

a.   Formulate the model that would help choose experiments so that the total scientific value of the flight is maximized.
b.   Suppose experiments k and l (from research groups at different universities) are very similar and a policy decision is made that not both experiments should be taken aboard. Modify your model of part (a) to ensure this condition.
c.   Modify your model to include the condition that if experiment k is chosen, then experiment p should also be chosen.

8.3.   Set up the mathematical programming problem to choose the set of capital budgeting projects that will maximize the net present value of the projects selected, but not violate the budget available in any of the three years:

Project No.	Net Present Value ($000 omitted)	Expenditure		
		Year 1 ($000 omitted)	Year 2 ($000 omitted)	Year 3 ($000 omitted)
1	25	30	80	10
2	40	40	70	40
3	70	50	60	70
4	10	60	50	0
5	20	80	40	0
6	35	10	30	80
7	60	20	50	0
8	75	25	80	60
9	15	40	10	5
10	45	50	10	40
Budget		300	320	220

8.4.   A distributing company has six customers to deliver goods to daily.

Customer	Weight of Goods
1	1
2	3
3	2
4	4
5	8
6	5

The company has four trucks that may be assigned to the delivery of these goods. Once a truck is loaded, however, it will not return for the rest of the day.

Truck	Cost per Day	Capacity
1	$ 5	6
2	$12	8
3	$10	10
4	$16	20

a. Build a cost-minimization model to determine which trucks should serve which customers, assuming that a given customer is served from only one truck.

b. Modify your model to ensure that a given truck serves at most two customers.

c. Modify your model to allow for more than one truck serving the same customer (that is, splitting up an order).

8.5.   A plumbing company has five men who handle all their house plumbing work. The five men live in different places throughout the city and drive directly from their homes to the house they will work on. Today the firm has five jobs scheduled to be performed. Each job will take a whole day. The men are paid for driving, so the company wants to minimize the entire distance all the men have to travel.

The following distances constitute all possible driving:

	House				
Plumber	Jones	Smith	Snyder	Daly	Simpson
Joe.....................	10	7	3	5	11
Al......................	8	4	11	10	5
Mack..................	4	3	12	7	6
Bill....................	17	11	1	4	2
Herman...............	2	8	12	3	12

Set up the zero-one assignment model. Discuss the relationship of this model to a "transportation" model.

8.6.　Jones Manufacturing Company faces the following problem. Should they make or buy each of several products? The company policies specify that they will either make or buy the whole lot of each product in a complete lot. The company has four products to make or buy with six machines involved in making these products if they are made in the shop. The times per unit produced follow:

	Machine					
Product	A	B	C	D	E	F
1.............	0.04	0.02	0.02	0	0.03	0.06
2.............	0	0.01	0.05	0.15	0.09	0.06
3.............	0.02	0.06	0.00	0.06	0.2	0.20
4.............	0.06	0.04	0.15	0	0	0.05

Forty hours are available on each machine. One hundred and ten units of each product are needed. The costs of making and buying products are listed below.

Product	Make	Buy
1.....................	$2.25	$3.10
2.....................	2.22	2.60
3.....................	4.50	4.40
4.....................	1.90	2.25

a.　Formulate the relevant model assuming that all 110 units of a given product are either made or purchased.

b.　Modify the model to allow for purchasing less than 110 units of a given product.

c. Suppose there is a set-up cost of F_{ij} for getting machine j ready for product i. Modify your model to allow for these set-up costs.

8.7. Consider a traveling salesman problem with the following distance matrix.

From	To					
	1	2	3	4	5	6
1...................	0	3	2	1	5	4
2...................	3	0	1	2	3	1
3...................	2	1	0	2	2	2
4...................	1	2	2	0	1	5
5...................	5	3	2	1	0	2
6...................	4	1	2	5	2	0

Write out the model that could be used to determine a minimum cost route for this problem.

8.8. Solve the traveling salesman problem of Exercise 8.7 using the nearest neighbor heuristic. Show how your solution satisfies the integer programming formulation of the problem.

8.9. Consider a machine shop faced with scheduling production runs on five different products. Once the shop is set up for a given product, the entire lot is run. The set-up costs are substantial and depend upon what product the shop was previously set up for. Denote by F_{ij} the set-up cost for product j, given that the previous set-up was for product i. Build a model that could be used to determine the order in which the products should be made so that total set-up costs are minimized. (Hint: Formulate this as a traveling salesman problem.)

8.10. Consider an assembly line balancing problem with six tasks and a desired system output rate of five completed units per hour. The task time and precedent data is as follows:

Task	Completion Time	Predecessor
1........................	5	none
2........................	2	none
3........................	8	1
4........................	2	1, 3
5........................	6	2, 4
6........................	7	5

a. Write the model that would determine the minimum number of work stations needed.
b. Modify your model of Part (a) to include the requirement that no more than two tasks be scheduled for a given work station.

8.11. Consider a product-mix problem where two products are made by blending different proportions of two inputs. Assume that the market price is fixed at \$10 and \$6 per unit for Products 1 and 2 respectively, but that the cost of each of the inputs depends on the volume we purchase as shown below. (For example, we must pay \$4 per unit for anything from 0 to 1,000 units of Input 1 we buy, \$3 per unit for any we buy beyond 1,000 but less than 2,000, and \$2 per unit for any units we buy in excess of 2,000 up to 5,000).

Input 1		Input 2	
Volume	*Unit Price*	*Volume*	*Unit Price*
0–1,000...............	\$4	0–500................	\$4
1,000–2,000..............	3	500–1,000..............	3
2,000–5,000..............	2	1,000–3,000..............	1.5

For quality reasons the ratio of Input 1 to Input 2 for product 1 must be at least 0.6. Product 2 is required to be at least 30 percent Input 2. Our marketing department forecasts that we could not sell more than 1,500 units of Product 1 nor more than 1,000 units of Product 2. However, we have firm commitments to make available at least 500 units of each product.

Formulate the mixed integer programming model that would help us assess the maximum profit production mix.

8.12. Solve, using branch-and-bound:

Maximize

$$x_0 = 6x_1 + 4x_2$$

subject to

$$2x_1 + x_2 \le 10$$
$$x_1 + x_2 \le 8$$
$$0 \le x_i \le 8; \quad x_i \text{ integer.}$$

"Round" your first LP solution and compare with the optimal solution.

8.13. Solve, using branch-and-bound:

Maximize

$$x_0 = 50x_1 + 60x_2 + 2x_3 + 4x_4 + 4x_5 + 2x_6$$

subject to

$$-100x_1 \qquad\qquad + x_3 + x_4 \qquad\qquad \le 0$$
$$-100x_2 \qquad\qquad + x_5 + x_6 \le 0$$
$$x_3 \qquad + x_5 \qquad = 50$$
$$x_4 \qquad + x_6 = 50$$
$$x_j \ge 0; \quad j = 3, 4, 5, 6$$
$$x_1, x_2 \text{ binary.}$$

(If possible, use a computer to solve your LP problem.)

8.14. Solve, using branch-and-bound:

Maximize

$$x_0 = 5x_1 + 6x_2 + 4x_3$$

subject

$$x_1 + 2x_2 + x_3 \leq 20$$
$$0 \leq x_j \leq 6$$
$$x_j \text{ integer.}$$

8.15. Consider the problem:

Maximize

$$x_0 = 4x_1 + 6x_2 + 8x_3$$

subject to

$$2x_1 + x_2 + x_3 \leq 8$$
$$-x_1 \qquad + x_3 \leq 3$$
$$0 \leq x_j \leq 4; \quad x_j \text{ integer.}$$

a. Solve as an LP problem and round your solution to get a feasible integer solution.

b. Check your result of Part (*a*) with the branch-and-bound algorithm.

8.16. Consider the problem of assigning four workers to four jobs in such a way that the total time to complete all jobs is minimized. The time (in days) for Worker *i* to do Job *k* is given below.

	Job			
Worker	*1*	*2*	*3*	*4*
1	3	1	2	2
2	2	2	4	2
3	1	5	1	1
4	4	3	2	3

a. Formulate the integer programming model for this assignment problem.

b. Solve the problem using the branch-and-bound "approach." (Note that there are 4! = 24 feasible assignments. Enumerate a few of these to yield a good objective function bound before applying the branch-and-bound algorithm. Note that no LP's need be solved.)

SUGGESTIONS FOR FURTHER STUDY

Darnell, D. W., and Loflin, C., "National Airlines Fuel Management and Allocation Model," *Interfaces,* vol. 7, no. 2, February 1977.

Garfinkel, R. S., and Nemhauser, G. L., *Integer Programming.* New York: Wiley, 1972.

Geoffrion, A. M., "Better Distribution Planning with Computer Models," *Harvard Business Review*, vol. 54, no. 4, July–August 1974.

———— "A Guided Tour of Recent Practical Advances in Integer Linear Programming," *OMEGA*, April 1976.

Glover, F., and Sommers, D., "Pitfalls of Rounding in Discrete Management Decision Problems," *AIDS*, vol. 6, no. 2, May–June 1975.

Henderson, W. B., and Berry, W. L., "Determining Optimal Shift Schedules for Telephone Traffic Exchange Operators," *AIDS*, vol. 8, no. 1, January 1977, pp. 239–55.

Noonan, F., and Giglio, R. J., "Planning Electric Power Generation: A Nonlinear Mixed Integer Model Employing Bender's Decomposition," *Management Science*, vol. 23, no. 9, May 1977, pp. 946–56.

Plane, D., and McMillan, C., *Discrete Optimization: Integer Programming and Network Analysis for Management Decisions.* Englewood Cliffs, N.J.: Prentice-Hall, 1971.

Salkin, H. M., *Integer Programming.* Reading, Mass.: Addison-Wesley, 1975.

Taha, H. A., *Integer Programming Theory, Applications and Computations.* New York: Academic Press, 1975.

Thesen, A., "Heuristic Scheduling of Activities Under Resource and Precedence Restrictions," *Management Science*, vol. 23, no. 4, December 1976, pp. 412–22.

Warner, D. M., "Scheduling Nursing Personnel According to Nursing Preference: A Mathematical Programming Approach," *Operations Research*, vol. 24, no. 5, September–October 1976, pp. 842–56.

Zionts, S., *Linear and Integer Programming.* Englewood Cliffs, N.J.: Prentice-Hall, 1974.

9

Markov Chains

9.1. INTRODUCTION

THIS CHAPTER, in contrast to Chapters 4 through 8, deals with random phenomena. The processes involved here are *stochastic* rather than *deterministic*. The models treated in this and the next chapter will deal with stochastic processes where certain assumptions lead to specific types of processes. The models of this chapter are the *Markov chain models* and deal with processes where the process "moves" from one outcome (or realization) to another outcome according to set of probabilities. The next chapter deals with *waiting-line models* where the "service" and "waiting for service" are subject to random variations.

A *stochastic process* is a collection of random variables whose values are observed at certain points in time. Such processes are very general in nature and some specific assumptions must be imposed in order to yield a tractable model. Since the processes are evolving over time there are two classes of models: *discrete-time*—the values of the random variables are or can be observed only at particular points in time, usually denoted as 0, 1, 2 . . . ; and *continuous-time*—the values are or can be observed at *any* point in time. For the remainder of this chapter only discrete-time processes are considered. Some examples of stochastic processes are:

1. The price of a stock is observed at the opening of the stock market every day for a calendar year.
2. The weather is observed and recorded at noon of each day at a particular location.

3. The market share of a particular product in a certain location is recorded at the end of each quarter.

Another characteristic of a stochastic process is the set of possible
values of the random variables.[1] Random variables can take on any set
of specified values, however, for the remainder of this chapter our attention is restricted to random variables that take on values from the set
$\{1, 2 \ldots\}$. These values will be referred to as the *states* of the process.

In addition to the above characteristics, the *history of the process*
will be of interest. The random variable X_0 refers to the initial state of
the process, so that the history refers to the states of the process from
the initial state to the current state.

Finally, the *movement* of the process from one state to another is of
concern. That is, it is necessary to know how the history of the process
is generated.

A *Markov chain*, for our purposes,[2]

a. is a discrete-time process—it is observed at times $t = 0, 1, 2 \ldots$;
b. is a finite-state process—the random variables take on values $X_t =$
   $1, 2, \ldots, N$ for each t;
c. is governed by transition probabilities p_{ij}—the movement from state
   i to state j is given by the probability p_{ij};
d. exhibits the *Markov property*—any future state of the process depends only on the current state and is independent of the past history of the process.

The Markov property is often referred to as the "lack of memory."
More formally, if the process has the history

$$X_0 = i_0 \quad \text{(initial state)}$$
$$X_1 = i_1$$
$$X_2 = i_2 \tag{9-1}$$
$$\cdot$$
$$\cdot$$
$$\cdot$$
$$X_n = i_n \quad \text{(current state)},$$

then the probability of any future state $X_{n+1} = j$ can be given as

$$P(X_{n+1} = j | X_n = i_n, \ldots, X_2 = i_2, X_1 = i_1, X_0 = i_0) = p_{ij}$$
$$= P(X_{n+1} = j | X_n = i). \tag{9-2}$$

Since the p_{ij} are probabilities they must satisfy the properties

$$p_{ij} \geq 0; \quad i, j = 1, 2, \ldots, N \tag{9-3}$$

---

[1] The reader is referred to the introduction of Chapter 2 for a brief discussion of
random variables. More detail can be found in the references following that chapter.

[2] The definition of a Markov chain given here is not the most general definition of
either a Markov chain or a Markov process. More general definitions can be found in
the references at the end of the chapter.

and

$$\sum_{j=1}^{N} p_{ij} = 1 \text{ for each } i = 1, 2, \cdot \ldots, N. \qquad (9\text{--}4)$$

In terms of Markov chains the property given by (9–4) can be interpreted as: Given that the process is in state i, the process must "move" to some state j. Note that it is possible to have $p_{ii} = 1$—the process stays in state i.

The probabilities, p_{ij}, referred to in(c) are called *transition probabilities* and are assumed to be the same for each time period. This property is referred to as *stationarity* of the transition probabilities and is one of the major limitations on the applicability of Markov chains. Some results for nonstationary probabilities are available but are beyond the level of this text.[3] In other words, if the transition probabilities are stationary, then

$$P(X_{n+t} = j | X_n = i) = P(X_t = j | X_0 = i) \qquad (9\text{--}5)$$

must hold for all choices of n. To illustrate the nature of this statement consider the probability of failure of a light bulb in the next week, given that it is currently operating. Defining the states 1 as operating and 2 as failure, Equation (9–5) says that the probability of failure after one week's use ($X_1 = 2$), given a brand new bulb ($X_0 = 1$), is the same as the probability of failure in week 100 ($X_{100} = 2$), given that the bulb is operating in week 99 ($X_{99} = 1$). Clearly this is not the case since 99 weeks of use have caused some deterioration of the light bulb and hence increased the probability of its failure. Thus in all applications of Markov chains one must realize the implications of stationarity when dealing with long time-horizons.

In summary a Markov chain is a stochastic process $\{X_t\}$ satisfying:

1. The process is discrete time; $t = 0, 1, 2 \ldots$ where $t = 0$ defines the initial time period, and X_0 the initial state.
2. The process has a finite state space $X_t = \{1, 2, \ldots, N\}$ for each t.
3. There is a set of stationary transition probabilities, p_{ij}, for $i, j = 1, 2, \ldots, N$.
4. The process satisfies the Markov property—the future state depends only on the current state.

In addition to these aspects of a Markov chain there are two additional aspects that will aid in dealing with the examples and applications of Markov chains that follow. The first of these aspects is the grouping of

---

[3] Such results refer to the behavior of the Markov chain when considered over a long time span. For a model that simply considers the behavior of a process over a single time period, stationarity is not necessary.

the transition probabilities into a matrix.[4] This matrix will be used to describe the *one-step* transitions from one state to another; that is, p_{ij} is the movement of the process from State i to State j during two adjacent observations. This transition matrix will be written as:

$$
P = \begin{pmatrix}
p_{11} & p_{12} & p_{13} & \cdots & p_{1N} \\
p_{21} & p_{22} & p_{23} & \cdots & p_{2N} \\
\cdot & & & & \\
\cdot & & & & \\
\cdot & & & & \\
p_{N1} & p_{N2} & p_{N3} & \cdots & p_{NN}
\end{pmatrix}
\tag{9-6}
$$

where p_{11} = probability of going from State 1 to State 1 (probability of staying in State 1),

p_{12} = probability of going from State 1 to State 2,

p_{21} = probability of going from State 2 to State 1,

p_{22} = probability of going from State 2 to State 2 (probability of staying in State 2),

and so on.

This matrix is *descriptive* in that it details the potential movements from one state to another.

The second property that is important in the following sections is the notion of an *initial probability distribution*. This distribution gives, probabilistically, the initial state of the system. Knowing the initial position of the process and the transition probabilities one can readily compute the position of the process after one transition or time period.

9.2. SOME EXAMPLES

Example 1. The weather in State College has been observed to follow the pattern:

If it is clear today the probability of clear weather tomorrow is 0.6.
If it is clear today the probability of cloudy weather tomorrow is 0.2.
If it is clear today the probability of rain tomorrow is 0.2.
If it is cloudy today the probability of clear weather tomorrow is 0.1.
If it is cloudy today the probability of cloudy weather tomorrow is 0.2.
If it is cloudy today the probability of rain tomorrow is 0.7.
If it is raining today the probability of clear weather tomorrow is 0.1.
If it is raining today the probability of cloudy weather tomorrow is 0.8.
If it is rainy today the probability of rain tomorrow is 0.1.

From this information the weather process is described as a Markov chain in which:

---

[4] Recall that a matrix is a rectangular array of numbers. A brief review of matrix algebra is given in Appendix C.

The time intervals are days;
The states are the types of day: clear, cloudy, rain;
The transition probabilities are given by:

$P =$

Today's Weather	Tomorrow's Weather		
	Clear	Cloudy	Rain
Clear	0.6	0.2	0.2
Cloudy	0.1	0.2	0.7
Rain	0.1	0.8	0.1

(9–7)

The Markov property is satisfied by the definition of the process since today's weather is the only information needed to determine the probability of tomorrow's weather. Note that the entries in each row sum to 1; that is

$$p_{clear, clear} + p_{clear, cloudy} + p_{clear, rain} = 1,$$

and so on. It is important to notice that the columns *do not* necessarily sum to 1. The first column sum is $p_{clear, clear} + p_{cloudy, clear} + p_{rain, clear}$, which need not equal one since the weather need not be clear tomorrow.

If in addition, the initial state of the weather is taken to be equally likely among the three $(\frac{1}{3}, \frac{1}{3}, \frac{1}{3})$ then the probability of the weather on the next day is computed as:

The probability of clear weather tomorrow is equal to

(the probability of clear today) times (the probability of remaining clear)

$$\left(\frac{1}{3}\right) \qquad \times \qquad (0.6 = p_{clear, clear})$$

plus

(the probability of cloudy today) times (the probability going from cloudy to clear)

$$\left(\frac{1}{3}\right) \qquad \times \qquad (0.1 = p_{cloudy, clear})$$

plus

(the probability of rain today) times (the probability of going from rain to clear)

$$\left(\frac{1}{3}\right) \qquad \times \qquad (0.1 = p_{rain, clear})$$

$$= \frac{1}{3}(0.6) + \frac{1}{3}(0.1) + \frac{1}{3}(0.1) = 0.267.$$

Similarly, the probability of cloudy weather tomorrow is:

$$p_{\text{clear}} \times p_{\text{clear, cloudy}} + p_{\text{cloudy}} \times p_{\text{cloudy, cloudy}} + p_{\text{rain}} \times p_{\text{rain, cloudy}}$$
$$= \frac{1}{3}(0.2) + \frac{1}{3}(0.8) + \frac{1}{3}(0.2) = 0.4;$$

and the probability of rain tomorrow is:

$$p_{\text{clear}} \times p_{\text{clear,rain}} + p_{\text{cloudy}} \times p_{\text{cloudy, rain}} + p_{\text{rain}} \times p_{\text{rain, rain}}$$
$$= \frac{1}{3}(0.2) + \frac{1}{3}(0.1) + \frac{1}{3}(0.7) = 0.333.$$

The above procedures can be neatly summarized as follows. If $p^{(0)} = (p_1^{(0)}, p_2^{(0)}, p_3^{(0)})$ represent the initial probabilities of being in each state and

$$P = \begin{pmatrix} p_{11} & p_{12} & p_{13} \\ p_{21} & p_{22} & p_{23} \\ p_{31} & p_{32} & p_{33} \end{pmatrix}$$

is the transition matrix, then the probabilities of each of the states at the next time period $p^{(1)} = (p_1^{(1)}, p_2^{(1)}, p_3^{(1)})$ are given by

$$\begin{aligned} p_1^{(1)} &= p_1^{(0)} \; p_{11} + p_2^{(0)} \; p_{21} + p_3^{(0)} \; p_{31} \\ p_2^{(1)} &= p_1^{(0)} \; p_{12} + p_2^{(0)} \; p_{22} + p_3^{(0)} \; p_{32} \\ p_3^{(1)} &= p_1^{(0)} \; p_{13} + p_2^{(0)} \; p_{23} + p_3^{(0)} \; p_{33}. \end{aligned} \qquad (9\text{-}8)$$

The general form for (9-8), given the $i, j = 1, \ldots, N$ is:

If $p^{(0)} = (p_1^{(0)}, p_2^{(0)}, \ldots, p_N^{(0)})$ and $p^{(1)} = (p_1^{(1)}, p_2^{(1)}, \ldots, p_N^{(1)})$

and

$$P = \begin{pmatrix} p_{11} & p_{12} & \cdots & p_{1N} \\ p_{21} & p_{22} & \cdots & p_{2N} \\ \cdot & \cdot & & \cdot \\ \cdot & \cdot & & \cdot \\ \cdot & \cdot & & \cdot \\ p_{N1} & p_{N2} & & p_{NN} \end{pmatrix}, \qquad (9\text{-}10)$$

then

$$p_1^{(1)} = p_1^{(0)} \; p_{11} + p_2^{(0)} \; p_{21} + \cdots + p_N^{(0)} \; p_{N1} = \sum_{i=1}^{N} p_i^{(0)} \; p_{i1}$$

$$p_2^{(1)} = p_1^{(0)} \; p_{12} + p_2^{(0)} \; p_{22} + \cdots + p_N^{(0)} \; p_{N2} = \sum_{i=1}^{N} p_i^{(0)} \; p_{i2} \quad (9\text{-}11)$$

$$\vdots$$

$$p_N^{(1)} = p_1^{(0)} \; p_{1N} + p_2^{(0)} \; p_{2N} + \cdots + p_N^{(0)} \; p_{NN} = \sum_{i=1}^{N} p_i^{(0)} \; p_{iN}$$

The above computations can be expressed compactly using matrix notation. With this notation (9–11) can be written as:

$$p^{(1)} = p^{(0)}P \tag{9-12}$$

where (9–9) and (9–10) define the appropriate terms. Performing the matrix multiplication indicated in (9–12) results in the formulas of (9–11). The reader familiar with matrix algebra will recognize (9–11) as the definition of the multiplication of a row vector times a matrix. The formulas given by (9–11) are sufficient for the remainder of the chapter, although the equation (9–12), which is equivalent, will be used as a shorthand notation for the chapter.

Example 2. Probably the most widely known example of Markov chains in a decision making setting is that of *Brand Switching.* Consider the situation faced by the manufacturers of three competing products. As a result of certain marketing surveys the consumers' loyalty to the various brands has been determined for some time period. For example, as a result of a survey following information has been determined:

Of 100 customers currently using Brand A, 84 will stay with A, 9 will switch to Brand B, and 7 will switch to Brand C;

Of 100 customers currently using Brand B, 78 will stay with B, 14 will switch to A, and 8 will switch to C;

Of 100 customers currently using Brand C, 90 will stay with C, 4 will switch to A, and 6 will switch to B.

Past experience has shown that a customers' loyalty or propensity to switch brands depends only on the brand the customer currently owns and not on any previous purchases.

Based on this information the preceding example is modeled as a Markov chain where:

States: The brands of product.

Time period: Interval between purchases.

Transition probabilities:

$$
P = \begin{array}{c} \\ A \\ B \\ C \end{array}
\begin{array}{ccc} A & B & C \\ \begin{pmatrix} 0.84 & 0.09 & 0.07 \\ 0.14 & 0.78 & 0.08 \\ 0.04 & 0.06 & 0.90 \end{pmatrix} \end{array}.
$$

If the current share of the market is given by:

$$p^{(0)} = (0.39, 0.32, 0.29) = (\text{A's share, B's share, C's share}),$$

then the market shares after one time period are computed according to (9–8) as:

$$(0.39 \ 0.32 \ 0.29) \begin{pmatrix} 0.84 & 0.09 & 0.07 \\ 0.14 & 0.78 & 0.08 \\ 0.04 & 0.06 & 0.90 \end{pmatrix} = (0.384, \ 0.302, \ 0.314).$$

Just as with the previous example the computations can be explained as follows:

For Brand A:

$$
\begin{aligned}
0.39 \times 0.84 &= \text{(probability of starting in } A) \\
&\quad \times \text{(probability of staying in } A) \\
+0.32 \times 0.14 &= \text{(probability of starting in } B) \\
&\quad \times \text{(probability of switching to } A) \\
+0.29 \times 0.04 &= \text{(probability of starting in } C) \\
&\quad \times \text{(probability or switching to } A) \\
\hline
&= \text{probability of being in } A \text{ at end of period 1} \\
&= 0.384.
\end{aligned}
$$

For Brand B:

$$
\begin{aligned}
0.39 \times 0.09 &= \text{(probability of starting in } A) \\
&\quad \times \text{(probability of switching to } B) \\
+0.32 \times 0.78 &= \text{(probability of starting in } B) \\
&\quad \times \text{(probability of staying in } B) \\
+0.29 \times 0.06 &= \text{(probability of starting in } C) \\
&\quad \times \text{(probability of switching to } B) \\
\hline
&= \text{probability of being in } B \\
&\quad \text{at end of period 1} \\
&= 0.302.
\end{aligned}
$$

A similar analysis holds for Brand C.

This example serves to point out one of the main concerns when applying a Markov chain analysis: *The process being modeled must satisfy the Markov property.* In the above model of brand switching one might very well argue that the process is better described by a model that takes into consideration more than one past brand; however, such a model could not satisfy the Markov process in its current form. In the next example this type of consideration is taken into account by proper definition or redefinition of the states of the process.

Example 3. Reconsider the brand switching model of Example 2 and suppose that a more sophisticated predictor has observed that the loyalty of customers are more accurately forecast if the two previous purchases are taken into account. In particular the following data has been collected concerning the customers' loyalty given the last two brands purchased.

Last Purchase	Current Purchase	Probability of Next Purchase		
		A	B	C
A.............. A		0.9	0.05	0.05
A.............. C		0.5	0.1	0.4
A.............. B		0.3	0.4	0.3
B.............. A		0.5	0.1	0.4
B.............. C		0.4	0.2	0.4
B.............. B		0.1	0.8	0.1
C.............. A		0.5	0.05	0.45
C.............. C		0.1	0.05	0.85
C.............. B		0.2	0.5	0.3

By the very nature of the process if the state of the process is defined to be the brand purchased the Markov property cannot be satisfied. That is, the fact that the next brand purchased depends on two previous brands can be expressed as

$$P\{X_{n+1} = i_{n+1}|X_n = i_n, X_{n-1} = i_{n-1}\} \qquad (9\text{--}13)$$

where X_k is the brand purchased. However, the above process can be transformed to a Markov chain by defining a state as the two previous purchases, thus creating a Markov chain with nine states. The corresponding transitions matrix is:

	AA	AC	AB	BA	BC	BB	CA	CC	CB
AA	0.9	0.05	0.05	0	0	0	0	0	0
AC	0.0	0	0	0	0	0	0.5	0.4	0.1
AB	0.0	0	0	0.3	0.3	0.4	0	0	0
BA	0.5	0.4	0.1	0	0	0	0	0	0
$P =$ BC	0.0	0	0	0	0	0	0.4	0.4	0.2
BB	0.0	0	0	0.1	0.1	0.8	0	0	0
CA	0.5	0.05	0.45	0	0	0	0	0	0
CC	0.0	0	0	0	0	0	0.1	0.85	0.05
CB	0.0	0	0	0.2	0.3	0.5	0	0	0

The above entries are computed keeping in mind that states consist of two purchases. For example, from AA to AC means that, given the previous two purchases were A and A, then the next purchase must be C. The entire sequence is AAC of which the last two entries, AC, are of interest. From BC to BC means that, given the last two purchases were BC, the possibilities for the entire sequence are BCA, BCB or BCC. The last two entries do not contain the desired sequence (BC) and hence the transition probability is 0.

As the reader can see, this redefinition of the states of the process allows for the Markov property to hold but causes an expansion of the number of states. The number of states of these compound models increases as the square of the number of states for a one time-period model if the states are redefined as the two previous outcomes. The increase is as the cube of the number if the states are redefined as the three previous outcomes, and so on.

As another example for which the definition of the states of the process is important, consider a simplified gambling model.

Example 4. You and another person are flipping coins with the bet that if the coins match (HH or TT) you win $1; if the coins do not match (HT or TH) you lose $1. Repeated flips of a coin constitute a sequence of independent events and hence the sequence of outcomes *does not* constitute a Markov chain. That is, future states do not depend on any previous states. However, suppose each gambler starts with $K and the game ends if the bankroll is exhausted or reaches some fortune $N. If the states of the process are defined to be the gambler's worth then a Markov chain[5] can be constructed where:

States: Gambler's worth $(0, 1, 2, \ldots, N)$.

Time periods: Each bet.

Transition probabilities: If the coin is fair the probability of a win is $\frac{1}{2}$ (HH, TT) which results in an increase in worth. Thus $p_{i, i+1} = \frac{1}{2} = p_{i, i-1}$, where $i = 1, 2, \ldots, N - 1$, is the gambler's worth. Also $p_{00} = p_{NN} = 1$ describe the end of the process and are referred to as *absorbing states*.

The model is a special case of a more general Markov chain model known as the *random walk model*. The general random walk model can be described as a process which remains in the current state with probability p_1 and transitions to either of two adjacent states with probabilities p_2 and p_3 where $p_1 + p_2 + p_3 = 1$. The random walk model has had many applications in diverse fields; for example: to model particle movements in physics, to describe certain gambling situations, as a method of analyzing the stock market. The analysis of waiting-line models is dealt with in the next chapter. This last example has received a good deal of attention in the literature and the reader is referred to the references for additional information. As our final example we present a simplified model of the analysis of stock market transactions.

Example 5. Stock market analysis by Markov chain methods presents the same problem of definition of state as described for the brand switching model. These models also have raised questions regarding the stationarity of the transition matrix, which will be discussed in the next

---

[5] A moment's reflection will reveal that the gambler's worth after the next gamble depends only on the current worth.

section. For the purposes of this example suppose that the future price of a particular stock, given the current price, is of interest.[6] In order to construct a Markov chain model of the process, define

States: The price of the stock. The possible prices are restricted to $5 increments: $0, $5, $10, $15, $20. The inclusion of other price increments would greatly increase the state space.

Time increment: Opening price of the stock on successive trading days. Again finer increments are possible and would make the model more realistic.

Transition probabilities: It is assumed the stock price moves from one price to either of the neighboring prices as in the random walk example. That is, the price goes up $5 with a certain probability a_i, decreases by $5 with probability b_i, and remains the same with probability c_i, where $a_i + b_i + c_i = 1$. These probabilities are dependent upon the current price; specifically, suppose these probabilities are:

$$
P = \begin{array}{c} \\ \$\,0 \\ \$\,5 \\ \$10 \\ \$15 \\ \$20 \end{array}
\begin{array}{ccccc}
\$0 & \$5 & \$10 & \$15 & \$20 \\
1 & 0 & 0 & 0 & 0 \\
\tfrac{1}{2} & \tfrac{1}{4} & \tfrac{1}{4} & 0 & 0 \\
0 & \tfrac{1}{6} & \tfrac{2}{6} & \tfrac{3}{6} & 0 \\
0 & 0 & \tfrac{1}{4} & \tfrac{1}{4} & \tfrac{1}{2} \\
0 & 0 & 0 & \tfrac{1}{2} & \tfrac{1}{2}
\end{array}
$$

The stock price of $0 is an absorbing state, for once entered it cannot be left. As in the previous examples, if some initial probability distribution of the current price is specified one can easily find the future state (the price distribution at the opening of tomorrow's market).

These examples are simplified examples of some applications of Markov chain analysis. Several additional examples are presented in the last section of this chapter. Some questions that were raised during the above discussion need to be answered, however.

9.3. CHARACTERIZATIONS AND LONG-TERM BEHAVIOR OF MARKOV CHAINS

This section provides a more formal definition and explanation of the basic properties of Markov chains. Some of the discussion of the preceding examples touched very briefly on the topics to be discussed in this section.

---

[6] This is a simplification of a particular type of Markov chain model. Other types have been extensively discussed in the literature.

The first additional property to be discussed is that of n-step transition probabilities. A review of the previous examples will reveal that they were all stated in terms of one-step transitions. That is, given a transition matrix and the current state, we develop the distribution for the state at the *next time period*. It is natural to ask whether one can extend the analysis to more than one time period. The answer is that the analysis can be extended rather readily, but the extension requires an understanding of the underlying assumptions. One critical assumption is that of *stationarity* of the transition probabilities; that is, the transition matrix P remains the same for each time period. Whenever something other than one-step transitions are computed, the stationarity property must hold.

In terms of the weather example (Example 1) of the previous section the transition matrix is:

$$P = \begin{array}{c} Clear \\ Cloudy \\ Rain \end{array} \begin{array}{ccc} Clear & Cloudy & Rain \\ \begin{pmatrix} 0.6 & 0.2 & 0.2 \\ 0.1 & 0.2 & 0.7 \\ 0.1 & 0.8 & 0.1 \end{pmatrix} \end{array},$$

relating one-step movements. Now we are interested in the probabilities of two-step movements; that is, if the current state is clear weather, what is the probability of being in state clear after *two* transitions. Such a transition would involve the sequence:

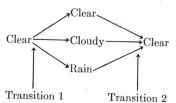

$$(p_{clear,\ clear})(p_{clear,\ clear}) + (p_{clear,\ cloudy})(p_{cloudy,\ clear})$$
$$+ (p_{clear,\ rain})(p_{rain,\ clear})$$
$$= (0.6)(0.6) + (0.2)(0.1) + (0.2)(0.1) = 0.4.$$

Similarly, the probability of going from Cloudy to Rain in two steps is given by:

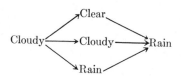

or

$$(p_{cloudy,\ clear})(p_{clear,\ rain}) + (p_{cloudy,\ cloudy})(p_{cloudy,\ rain})$$
$$+ (p_{cloudy,\ rain})(p_{rain,rain})$$
$$= (0.1)(0.2) + (0.2)(0.7) + (0.7)(0.1) = 0.23.$$

In general if the current state is i and it is desired to compute the two-step probabilities to state j, the following equation is valid:[7]

$$\sum_{k=1}^{N} p_{ik}p_{kj} = p_{ij}^{(2)} \text{ for each } i \text{ and } j = 1, \ldots, N. \qquad (9\text{--}14)$$

This equation simply states that to get from i to j in two steps, go from i to k (in one step) and then from k to j (in one step) for each of all possible intermediate states k. Using equation (9–14) the two-step transition probabilities for the weather example can be computed as:

$$P^{(2)} = \begin{pmatrix} 0.4 & 0.32 & 0.28 \\ 0.15 & 0.62 & 0.23 \\ 0.15 & 0.26 & 0.59 \end{pmatrix}.$$

As the reader can readily verify, the above matrix can be obtained by multiplying P by itself. That is:

$$P^{(2)} = P \cdot P. \qquad (9\text{--}15)[8]$$

From equation (9–15) it is straightforward to show that

$$P^{(3)} = P^{(2)} \cdot P = P \cdot P \cdot P \qquad (9\text{--}16)$$

and hence

$$P^{(n)} = P^{(n-1)} \cdot P = \underbrace{P \cdot P \cdot \ldots \cdot P}_{n \text{ times}}. \qquad (9\text{--}17)$$

That is to say: The n-step transition matrices (which give the probabilities of going from i to j in n steps) are given by raising P to the nth power. Recall again that for these probabilities to be meaningful the transition probabilities must be *stationary*.

It is of interest to note the effect of computing the n-step probabilities for several values of n.

$$P^{(3)} = \begin{pmatrix} 0.3 & 0.368 & 0.332 \\ 0.175 & 0.338 & 0.487 \\ 0.175 & 0.554 & 0.271 \end{pmatrix} \quad P^{(4)} = \begin{pmatrix} 0.25 & 0.3992 & 0.3508 \\ 0.1875 & 0.4922 & 0.3203 \\ 0.1875 & 0.3626 & 0.4499 \end{pmatrix}.$$

As can be seen, calculations are time consuming and prone to errors. Also it appears that the values of the probabilities are approaching some common values as n increases. Since n represents time periods the transition matrices will be referred to as *long-term probabilities* for large values of n. Before discussing this topic further it is necessary to identify

---

[7] This equation is a specific example of the *Chapman-Kolmogorov Equations*, which describe the general relationships for n-step transition probabilities.

[8] The $\cdot$ denotes matrix multiplication, and Equation (9–14) is simply the formula for obtaining the results of the multiplication of two matrices.

certain properties of Markov chains for which this type of analysis is meaningful.

At this point it is possible for the discussion to become very technical; to avoid this situation we will briefly discuss those properties of a Markov chain that lead to meaningful long-term analyses. For complete details the reader is referred to the more technical references. *This is not meant to undermine the importance of what follows for without considerations of these properties it may well be that any attempt to compute long-run probabilities is meaningless.*

In order for long-run analysis of Markov chains to have meaning, the following properties must be verified:

1. *Irreducible:* A Markov is said to be irreducible if it is possible to start from State i and reach State j in some finite number of transitions for all States i and j. That is

$$p_{ij}^{(n)} > 0 \text{ for some } n, \text{ for all } i \text{ and } j. \tag{9-18}$$

In terms of the previous examples:

Example 1 is an *irreducible* Markov chain since $p_{ij}^{(1)} > 0$ for all i and j.

Example 2 is an *irreducible* Markov chain since $p_{ij}^{(1)} > 0$ for all i and j.

Example 3 is an *irreducible* Markov chain. This is not obvious from $P^{(1)}$ but requires the computation of $P^{(2)}$, in which all $p_{ij}^{(2)} > 0$.

Example 4 has the transition matrix

$$
P = \begin{array}{c}
\\
\$0 \\
\$1 \\
\$2 \\
\vdots \\
\\
\$N
\end{array}
\begin{array}{c}
\$0 \quad \$1 \quad \$2 \quad \cdots \quad \$N
\end{array}
\left(
\begin{array}{ccccc}
1 & 0 & 0 & \cdots & 0 \\
\frac{1}{2} & 0 & \frac{1}{2} & \cdots & 0 \\
0 & \frac{1}{2} & 0 & \cdots & 0 \\
\vdots & \vdots & \vdots & & \vdots \\
0 & 0 & 0 & \cdots & 1
\end{array}
\right),
$$

from which it is evident that if the process starts in either state $0 or state $N no other state can be reached. Thus it is *not irreducible.*

Example 5 is also *not irreducible* since State $0 is absorbing.

2. *Periodic:* A state, i, is said to be periodic with period $t > 1$ if it is possible for the chain to be in state i only for multiples of t. In other words $p_{ii}^{(n)} = 0$ whenever n is *not* a multiple of t. If $t = 1$ the Markov chain is said to be *aperiodic.* The idea of periodicity relates to a cyclic

nature with which the process returns to certain states. For example if a process has the transition matrix

$$P = \begin{array}{cc} & \begin{array}{cc} 1 & 2 \end{array} \\ \begin{array}{c} 1 \\ 2 \end{array} & \begin{pmatrix} 0 & 1 \\ 1 & 0 \end{pmatrix} \end{array}$$

and starts in state 1 then the process will be in state 1 after 2,4,6 . . . transitions and in state 2 after 1,3,5, . . . transitions. Clearly the period is two (2).

These properties are summarized as: If a finite Markov chain is irreducible and aperiodic, it is *ergodic*.[9]

Ergodic chains are important because for such a chain it can be shown that the long-run probabilities exist and are uniquely determined. That is

$$\lim_{n \to \infty} p_{ij}^{(n)} = \pi_j; \quad j = 1, \ldots, N; \quad (9\text{--}19)$$

where the π_j satisfy the so called *Steady State Equations:*

$$\pi_j \geq 0 \quad (9\text{--}20)$$

$$\sum_{j=1}^{N} \pi_j = 1 \quad (9\text{--}21)$$

$$\pi_j = \sum_{i=1}^{N} \pi_i p_{ij}; j = 1, \ldots, N. \quad (9\text{--}22)$$

These probabilities, π_j, are called steady state probabilities for they are the probability of finding the process in state j after the process has gone through a large number of transitions.

The relationships given by (9–20), (9–21), and (9–22) have a rather simple interpretation. Equations (9–20) and (9–21) are simply conditions that guarantee that the π_j are probabilities. For example see Section 12 of Chapter 2. The Equations (9–22) are characteristic of a system in steady state or equilibrium. That is, once a system has reached a steady state, the probability of finding the system in a state, say π_1, equals the probability of the system's moving to that state: $\pi_1 p_{11} + \pi_2 p_{21} + \pi_3 p_{31}$. Similar results apply to the other states.

The system of linear equations given by (9–21) and (9–22) provides a convenient means of computing these long-run or steady-state probabilities. For the weather example, (9–21) and (9–22) become:

$$\pi_1 = 0.6\pi_1 + 0.1\pi_2 + 0.1\pi_3 \quad (9\text{--}23)$$
$$\pi_2 = 0.2\pi_1 + 0.2\pi_2 + 0.8\pi_3 \quad (9\text{--}24)$$
$$\pi_3 = 0.2\pi_1 + 0.7\pi_2 + 0.1\pi_3 \quad (9\text{--}25)$$
$$1 = \pi_1 + \pi_2 + \pi_3. \quad (9\text{--}26)$$

---

[9] In general in order for a Markov chain to be ergodic it must also be *positive recurrent*. However, for finite state chains irreducibility is equivalent to this condition. More details are found in the Hillier and Lieberman or Ross references.

Solving equations $(9–24)–(9–26)$, we obtain:

$$\pi_1 = 0.2; \quad \pi_2 = 0.425; \quad \pi_3 = 0.375.$$

Earlier the matrix of four-step transitions, $P^{(4)}$, was determined. As can be seen, the above steady-state results are approximately the same though $P^{(4)}$ has not yet "settled down." If one were to form $P^{(8)} = P^{(4)} \cdot P^{(4)}$ a pattern very close to the steady-state probabilities would develop.

At this point it should be noted that in general Equations $(9–21)–(9–22)$ will contain $N + 1$ equations and N variables. Since the system must have a unique solution, any one of the equations in $(9–22)$ can be disregarded. However, $(9–21)$ must always be maintained as part of the system that is solved since this equation, along with $(9–20)$, guarantees that the resulting π_j are probabilities.

The steady state probabilities were applicable to Example 1 because it was determined that $p_{ij}^{(2)} > 0$ for all i, j, and thus it is an irreducible finite Markov chain. As a counter example consider the transition matrix

$$P = \begin{pmatrix} 1.0 & 0.0 & 0.0 \\ 0.0 & 0.5 & 0.5 \\ 0.0 & 0.6 & 0.4 \end{pmatrix}.$$

The Markov chain is *not* ergodic because of state 1 (which is absorbing), and if $(9–21)–(9–22)$ are applied:

$$\begin{aligned} \pi_1 &= \pi_1 \\ \pi_2 &= 0.5\pi_2 + 0.6\pi_3 \\ \pi_3 &= 0.5\pi_2 + 0.4\pi_3 \\ 1 &= \pi_1 + \pi_2 + \pi_3, \end{aligned}$$

which does not have a unique solution, since the second and third equations are identical (after some algebra).

Once again it is important to realize that these steady-state probabilities rely on the stationarity of the process, which may be difficult to verify in many applications. For example, in the brand switching model, changes in the transition probabilities could be due to changes in advertising policies, consumer behavior and so on; for the stock market model, the changing nature of market conditions can easily change the probabilities. Given these reservations, the steady-state probabilities are important and can be used in the decision making process as: "What will be the case if nothing is done?" This type of analysis can be illustrated in connection with Example 2, the brand switching model.

The transition matrix is:

$$P = \begin{pmatrix} 0.84 & 0.09 & 0.07 \\ 0.14 & 0.78 & 0.08 \\ 0.04 & 0.06 & 0.9 \end{pmatrix},$$

and the initial market shares are $(0.39\ 0.32\ 0.29)$. One can verify that the Markov chain is ergodic since $P_{ij}^{(2)} > 0$ for $i,j = 1,2,3$. Assuming the transition matrix is stationary, the steady-state equations are:

$$\pi_1 = 0.84\pi_1 + 0.14\pi_2 + 0.04\pi_3$$
$$\pi_2 = 0.09\pi_1 + 0.78\pi_2 + 0.06\pi_3$$
$$\pi_3 = 0.07\pi_1 + 0.08\pi_2 + 0.9\pi_3$$
$$1 = \pi_1 + \pi_2 + \pi_3.$$

The solution to this system yields the steady state probabilities:

$$\pi_1 = 0.325; \quad \pi_2 = 0.249; \quad \pi_3 = 0.426.$$

Thus if the situation remains stationary, Brands A and B can expect to lose approximately 7 percent of their market shares (from 39 percent and 32 percent to 32 percent and 25 precent, respectively). There are several strategies available to A and B to alter the results; for example, they might try to increase their retention of their original customers; or they might try to increase their gains from their competitors. Suppose the Brand A company decides to adopt an advertising campaign designed to alter the transition probabilities. Because of market conditions and budget considerations, a campaign of Type 1 will increase the retention of Brand A customers but will not attract new customers from B and C; a campaign of Type 2 is aimed at increasing the number of customers who switch to A from B and C.

For the type 1 campaign, the new transition matrix is determined to be:

$$P = \begin{pmatrix} 0.9 & 0.06 & 0.04 \\ 0.14 & 0.78 & 0.08 \\ 0.04 & 0.06 & 0.9 \end{pmatrix},$$

The steady-state probabilities for this case are:

$$\pi_1 = 0.347; \quad \pi_2 = 0.214; \quad \pi_3 = 0.439.$$

For Type 2, the new transition matrix is determined to be:

$$P = \begin{pmatrix} 0.84 & 0.09 & 0.07 \\ 0.2 & 0.75 & 0.05 \\ 0.14 & 0.06 & 0.8 \end{pmatrix},$$

from which the steady-state probabilities are

$$\pi_1 = 0.52; \quad \pi_2 = 0.24; \quad \pi_3 = 0.24.$$

As can be seen from the results, the campaign aimed at attracting new customers has a much greater effect on A's market share. This knowledge can be used in conjunction with the cost of the campaign to determine which strategy to use. Some additional aspects of this type of analysis are contained in the exercises.

9.4. ABSORBING STATES

Many of the important applications of Markov chain analysis deal with situations in which there is one or more absorbing states in the process. An *absorbing state* is a state which, once entered, cannot be left; thus such states absorb the process. In the examples of the previous section there are two instances of absorbing states—in Example 4 the states corresponding to a worth of $0 or N are absorbing; in Example 5 a stock price of $0 is absorbing. Other instances of absorbing states include: in manpower planning models, leaving the firm (retirement, termination, job change) is an absorbing state; in the study of hospital admissions systems, the arrival of the patient at the assigned room is an absorbing state; in models of student flow within an education system, graduation or flunking out are absorbing states. Thus with so many potential applications of such chains the analysis of Section 3 needs to be expanded to include such models.

A Markov chain with one or more absorbing states can be readily identified by entries in the transition matrix. In particular, a state i is absorbing if

$$p_{ii} = 1, \qquad (9\text{--}27)$$

and any state for which (9–27) holds will be called *absorbing*. In Example 4, $p_{00} = p_{nn} = 1$, and in Example 5, $p_{00} = 1$.

Absorbing states do not allow for the computation of steady-state probabilities as in the last section. The reason for this is that if a state is absorbing and can be reached from other states, then the steady-state probability is 1 for that state. This is certainly reasonable, and formal arguments can be found in the references.[10]

In the presence of absorbing states there are some questions of interest concerning the long-range behavior of the process. These questions are:

1. What is the expected time the process is in a non-absorbing state before it enters an absorbing state?
2. What is the total time before absorption for each non-absorbing state?
3. What is the probability of absorption starting from each non-absorbing state?

As stressed in the preceding sections the stationarity of the process is essential if the long-range probabilities are to be meaningful. Such an assumption is equally important in the presence of absorbing states. The

---

[10] Chapter 3 of the Kemeny, Snell reference is a particularly lucid exposition of this material. It should be noted that most of the material that follows is applicable to more general situations than absorbing versus non-absorbing states. In particular for finite Markov chains the analysis can be applied to those processes that contain *transient states* and ergodic states where transient states are those states that are eventually left and not reentered. The determination of transient states in general is not pursued here.

relevance of these questions to management decision making is brought to light in Application 5 in Part II of this book. The remainder of this section is devoted to the procedures for dealing with Markov chains with absorbing states. The first step is to rearrange the states so that the absorbing states are grouped at the top-left of the transition matrix; the remaining states are then adjoined in any order. For Example 5 the transition matrix is already in the appropriate form; for Example 4 the rearranged matrix is:

$$
P = \begin{matrix} & \begin{matrix} 0 & N \end{matrix} & \begin{matrix} 1 & 2 & 3 \end{matrix} \\ \begin{matrix} 0 \\ N \\ 1 \\ 2 \\ 3 \\ \cdot \\ \cdot \end{matrix} & \left(\begin{matrix} 1 & 0 \\ 0 & 1 \\ \frac{1}{2} & 0 \\ 0 & 0 \\ 0 & 0 \\ \cdot & \cdot \end{matrix} \right. & \left. \begin{matrix} 0 & 0 & 0 & \cdots \\ 0 & 0 & 0 & \cdots \\ 0 & \frac{1}{2} & 0 & \cdots \\ \frac{1}{2} & 0 & \frac{1}{2} & \cdots \\ 0 & \frac{1}{2} & 0 & \cdots \\ \cdot & & & \end{matrix} \right) \end{matrix}
$$

Arranging the states in this manner yields the *canonical form*

$$
P = \left(\begin{array}{c|c} I & O \\ \hline A & T \end{array} \right), \tag{9–28}
$$

where I is an $r \times r$ identity matrix for a total of r absorbing states; O is an $r \times (n - r)$ matrix of all zeros; A has dimension $(n - r) \times r$ and represents the transitions from non-absorbing states to absorbing states; and T has dimension $(n - r) \times (n - r)$ and represents transitions among the non-absorbing states. The results that follow are based on the components of (9–28). To illustrate the following developments we will use the transition matrix:

$$
P = \begin{matrix} & \begin{matrix} I \end{matrix} & \begin{matrix} II & III \end{matrix} \\ \begin{matrix} I \\ II \\ III \end{matrix} & \left(\begin{array}{c|cc} 1 & 0 & 0 \\ \hline \frac{1}{2} & 0 & \frac{1}{2} \\ 0 & \frac{1}{2} & \frac{1}{2} \end{array} \right), \end{matrix}
$$

which could be viewed as a modified version of Example 5.

For any absorbing Markov chain written in the form (9–28) we define a *fundamental matrix*

$$
F = (I - T)^{-1}, \tag{9–29}
$$

where F has dimension $(n - r) \times (n - r)$ and its entries represent *the mean or expected number of times the process is in each non-absorbing state before being absorbed.*[11]

---

[11] The notation M^{-1} for a square $n \times n$ matrix M denotes the inverse of the matrix M. Recall that the inverse of a matrix has the property: $MM^{-1} = M^{-1}M = I$.

For the above example the computations are:

$$F = \left(\begin{pmatrix} 1 & 0 \\ 0 & 1 \end{pmatrix} - \begin{pmatrix} 0 & \frac{1}{2} \\ \frac{1}{2} & \frac{1}{2} \end{pmatrix} \right)^{-1} = \begin{pmatrix} 1 & -\frac{1}{2} \\ -\frac{1}{2} & \frac{1}{2} \end{pmatrix}^{-1} = \begin{pmatrix} 2 & 2 \\ 2 & 4 \end{pmatrix}.$$

Thus if the process started in State II, the expected number of time periods in State II until absorption is 2, and the expected number of periods in State III is also 2. If the process started in State III, the expected number of periods in States II and III are 2 and 4, respectively.

Since the rows of F represent the absorption of the process from various states *the sum of each row of F represents the total expected time until absorption from each non-absorbing state.* That is:

$$t_i = \sum_{j=i}^{n-r} f_{ij} \tag{9-30}$$

is the sum of each row of F, with elements f_{ij}. In terms of the previous example, $t_{II} = 2 + 2 = 4$, and $t_{III} = 2 + 4 = 6$, which are the expected numbers of time periods in States II and III, respectively, until absorption.

Another point of interest is *the determination of which absorbing state will capture the process.* These probabilities are given by

$$B = FA, \tag{9-31}$$

where F is the fundamental matrix of (9–29) and A is the appropriate portion of (9–28). The matrix B has dimension $(n - r) \times r$, and each column corresponds to absorption of the non-absorbing states by a particular absorbing state. In terms of the example, the computations are:

$$B = FA = \begin{pmatrix} 2 & 2 \\ 2 & 4 \end{pmatrix} \begin{pmatrix} \frac{1}{2} \\ 0 \end{pmatrix} = \begin{pmatrix} 1 \\ 1 \end{pmatrix}.$$

Since there is a single absorbing state, the probability of absorption from the non-absorbing states must be 1. Put another way, *each of the rows of B represents the probability of absorption of a non-absorbing state by each of the absorbing states.*

While the arguments presented here have been largely algebraic, the discussion of Application 5 contains some probabilistic arguments concerning these computations.

9.5. SOME APPLICATIONS OF MARKOV CHAINS

In addition to the previous example relating to the application of Markov chains, several additional applications are now presented.

Equipment Replacement

In many settings there is a need to review material or equipment on a periodic basis and to make some decision concerning the replacement of

the equipment based on the outcome of the review. This type of problem can be formulated in terms of a Markov chain. To illustrate this
application, consider the problem faced by the intramural department of
a large university with regard to its tennis program. The athletic department has a central pool of tennis racquets used in instruction. After
heavy use the racquets are being evaluated for repair or scrap. In addition, new racquets are required to meet current demand. The initial pool
consists of 150 racquets. New racquets are purchased at a cost of $5.29
each. Repairing of racquets by the staff costs an average of $2.00 per
racquet. Scrapped racquets are sold for $0.50 each.

In the analysis of the racquets and their use the diagram in Figure 9–1
was constructed. For this diagram the states were defined as:

State 1: New racquet.

State 2: One year old, no repairs.

State 3: Two years old, no repairs.

State 4: Repaired once.

As a result of heavy use it was decided to not repair racquets more
than once. Also, racquets were to be scrapped after one year's use after
repair or after three years' use.

FIGURE 9–1

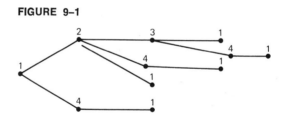

Past records were used to supply the following probabilities to the above
diagram. The probabilities p_{11}, p_{21} represent rackets that must be replaced because of "borrowing of equipment."

$$
P = \begin{array}{c} 1 \\ 2 \\ 3 \\ 4 \end{array}
\begin{pmatrix}
0.05 & 0.75 & 0.0 & 0.2 \\
0.05 & 0.0 & 0.4 & 0.55 \\
0.5 & 0.0 & 0.0 & 0.5 \\
1.0 & 0.0 & 0.0 & 0.0
\end{pmatrix}
\begin{array}{cccc} 1 & 2 & 3 & 4 \end{array}
$$

Using the steady state equations, one would expect the various states
of the system to be:

$$\pi_1 = 0.355; \quad \pi_2 = 0.271; \quad \pi_3 = 0.107; \quad \pi_4 = 0.267.$$

On the average, the expected cost of a policy of repairing as needed
would be:

$$0.355(150)(\$5.29) = \text{cost of new racquets each year} = \$281.69$$
$$+0.267(150)(\$2.00) = \text{cost of repairs each year} = \$80.10$$
$$-(0.107 + 0.267)(150)(\$0.50) = \text{profit from scrapped racquets} = \$28.05.$$

Thus the total cost per year is $333.74 for the policy of repairing as stated earlier. The above analysis could be used to evaluate different repair policies.

Population Mobility

This set of examples deals with application of Markov chains to studying the transition of a population from one state to another. The term population is used rather loosely here; for example, recent studies have attempted to model successive generations of forest contents as Markov chains.[12] That is, by sampling successive generations of the contents of a forest one can construct a Markov chain model that reflects these transitions or "forest successions." As a simplified example, suppose a forest consists of four major species: aspen, birch, oak, and maple. As a result of samplings the matrix of transition probabilities is:

$$
P = \begin{array}{c c} & \begin{array}{cccc} Aspen & Birch & Oak & Maple \end{array} \\ \begin{array}{c} Aspen \\ Birch \\ Oak \\ Maple \end{array} & \left(\begin{array}{cccc} 0.04 & 0.07 & 0.03 & 0.86 \\ 0.0 & 0.0 & 0.8 & 0.2 \\ 0.0 & 0.1 & 0.35 & 0.55 \\ 0.05 & 0.0 & 0.1 & 0.85 \end{array}\right) \end{array}.
$$

Such analysis could be used as a planning tool to predict what type of forest will result from various types of starting population.

Markov chain models have also been used to analyze the movement of human populations, a phenomenon of growing importance in regional land-use planning. Changes in the population of a city, county, or state are difficult to predict. Markov chain models have been used to model the movement of populations and to predict the effect of certain types of assumptions on the population of a region.

For example, for a particular area define the population states to be:

State 1: No movement.

State 2: Movement *within* region.

State 3: Movement *out of* region (deaths, transfers, etc.).

State 4: Movements *into* a region (births, new family, etc.). with associated probabilities:

$$
P = \begin{array}{c c} & \begin{array}{cccc} 1 & 2 & 3 & 4 \end{array} \\ \begin{array}{c} 1 \\ 2 \\ 3 \\ 4 \end{array} & \left(\begin{array}{cccc} 0.80 & 0.1 & 0.05 & 0.05 \\ 0.60 & 0.20 & 0.1 & 0.1 \\ 0.0 & 0.0 & 0.5 & 0.5 \\ 0.5 & 0.3 & 0.15 & 0.05 \end{array}\right) \end{array},
$$

_____
[12] H. S. Horn, "Forest Succession," *Scientific American*, May 1975.

where these probabilities characterize various movements given the current state of the family.

This type of model is typically applied in the prediction of the movements of students through an educational institution or the movement of personnel through a business organization.

Finally, we conclude with a small example that will serve to introduce the topic of the next chapter—waiting lines. Consider the situation often faced in banks: A customer arrives and joins a line in front of a teller's window and waits for service (check cashing, deposit, and so on). One way of measuring the effectiveness of the bank is to describe such things as average waiting time, average time when tellers are idle, and so on. Models of such situations, called Waiting-Line Models, use some ideas from Markov chains. For example, we may define the states of the system as the number of customers in the system. The "transitions" among states are then defined in terms of probability of a customer arriving (the states increases by 1) or a customer being served (the state decreases by 1). These ideas form the basis for Chapter 10.

EXERCISES

9.1.   A simple model of the economy of a country represents the state of the economy as a Markov chain. In particular, there are three possible states —inflation (I), recession (R) and stagnation (S)—and the probabilities of transitions between states are given by

$$
\begin{array}{c}
\begin{array}{ccc} I & \quad S & \quad R \end{array} \\
\begin{array}{c} (I) \\ (S) \\ (R) \end{array}
\begin{pmatrix}
0.5 & 0.0 & 0.5 \\
0.4 & 0.6 & 0.0 \\
0.0 & 0.4 & 0.6
\end{pmatrix}.
\end{array}
$$

Given that the economy is in a state of recession, what is the probability of each state after one period? Two periods? Answer the same questions if the current state is stagnation.

9.2.   Your company and its two competitors currently have 40, 40, and 20 percent market shares of the local market for a particular product. A recent market survey has yielded the following information: Your company retains 80 percent of its current customers while losing 5 percent to Competitor 1 and losing 15 percent to Competitor 2. Competitor 1 retains 85 percent of its customers while losing 5 percent to your company and 10 percent to Competitor 2. Competitor 2 retains 80 percent of its customers and loses 10 percent to each of its competitors.

Construct the appropriate transition matrix for these data. What will the market shares be after one period? At equilibrium?

9.3.   The behavior of a customer at an ice cream store has been observed to be a Markov process, for the purchase of ice cream today depends on whether or not ice cream was purchased yesterday. In particular, the transition matrix is:

	Today	
Yesterday	*Purchases*	*Does not Purchase*
Purchased	0.25	0.75
Did not Purchase.............	0.8	0.2

For each starting state find the probability of purchase tomorrow, the next day, and at equilibrium.

9.4.   The failure of a machine in a production line has been observed to be a Markov process with transition probabilities:

	Next Week	
This Week	*Failure*	*No Failure*
Failure................	0.1	0.9
No failure.............	0.3	0.7

If the machine is currently operating what is the probability of no failure in the long run?

9.5.   A game consists of locating a pea under one of four shells arranged in a circle. Once every minute the pea is secretly moved among the shells according to the following diagram:

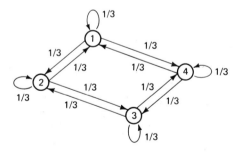

That is, the pea is moved to an adjacent shell or stays where it is with equal probabilities. If the game has been going on for a long time, what is the probability of the pea being under each of the shells?

9.6.   On the basis of previous data a company has modeled its sales forecasts as a Markov process. The company has chosen sales levels of 100, 200, and 400 units as states and has constructed a transition matrix of the form:

Last Year's Sales	This Year's Sales		
	100	200	400
100..............	0.5	0.5	0.0
200..............	0.3	0.6	0.1
400..............	0.05	0.25	0.7

From this data the company wants to answer the following:

a. What are the expected sales for this year for each of the sales levels for last year?

b. If last year's sales were 100 units, what is the probability of sales of 400 units in two years?

c. If these probabilities represent a stationary process, what are the long-run expected yearly sales?

9.7. A market survey company has completed a testing program for two different advertising campaigns for a product. The product (Brand A) has two major competitors, Brands B and C. Initially the market shares of the products are 30, 36 and 34 percent for A, B, and C, respectively. If the current model uses a transition matrix

$$
\begin{array}{c} \\ A \\ B \\ C \end{array}
\begin{array}{ccc} A & B & C \\ \begin{pmatrix} 0.65 & 0.15 & 0.2 \\ 0.3 & 0.65 & 0.05 \\ 0.1 & 0.15 & 0.75 \end{pmatrix} \end{array} ,
$$

and the proposed campaigns would alter this to

Campaign 1

$$
\begin{array}{c} A \\ B \\ C \end{array}
\begin{array}{ccc} A & B & C \\ \begin{pmatrix} 0.75 & 0.1 & 0.15 \\ 0.3 & 0.65 & 0.05 \\ 0.1 & 0.15 & 0.75 \end{pmatrix} \end{array}
$$

Campaign 2

$$
\begin{array}{c} A \\ B \\ C \end{array}
\begin{array}{ccc} A & B & C \\ \begin{pmatrix} 0.5 & 0.1 & 0.2 \\ 0.35 & 0.6 & 0.05 \\ 0.15 & 0.15 & 0.7 \end{pmatrix} \end{array} ,
$$

which campaign would be chosen?

9.8. Determine the steady-state probabilities for each of the following:

a.
$$
\begin{pmatrix} 0.8 & 0.1 & 0.1 \\ 0.05 & 0.75 & 0.2 \\ 0.0 & 0.6 & 0.4 \end{pmatrix}
$$

b.
$$
\begin{pmatrix} 1.0 & 0.0 & 0.0 \\ 0.8 & 0.1 & 0.1 \\ 0.5 & 0.0 & 0.5 \end{pmatrix}
$$

9.9. A corporation has classified its sales trainees as to their potential in the organization into three groups as a result of an initial questionnaire.

Of the current group 24 percent are classified as high potential, 41 percent as average, and 35 percent as below average. Past experience has shown the company that by the end of the training period the evaluations become

	High	Average	Below Average
High::::..............	0.7	0.25	0.05
Average................	0.25	0.6	0.15
Below average..........	0.1	0.4	0.5

a. What will the profile of the current group look like after the training period?
b. If the above transitions remain constant what is the equilibrium profile of trainees?

9.10. A manufacturing company currently has 40 percent of the market against 30 percent for each of its competitors. If the company and the competitors are designated as A, B, C and the current customer switching of brands is estimated to be:

$$
\begin{array}{c c c c}
 & A & B & C \\
A & 0.7 & 0.25 & 0.05 \\
B & 0.1 & 0.8 & 0.1 \\
C & 0.05 & 0.05 & 0.9
\end{array}.
$$

a. Evaluate the effect of a 10 percent underestimate in company A's original market share on A's market share: after one time period; at equilibrium. You can assume the market shares of B and C are reduced by equal amounts.
b. Evaluate the effect of a 10 percent underestimate on the retention of A's customers: after one time period; at equilibrium. Switches to B and C are reduced by equal amounts.
c. How much would company B be willing to pay, in terms of market share, in order to increase its retention rate by 5 percent? Perform this analysis for one time period and for equilibrium.

9.11. For

$$
P = \begin{pmatrix} \frac{1}{3} & \frac{1}{3} & \frac{1}{3} \\ \frac{1}{3} & \frac{1}{3} & \frac{1}{3} \\ 0 & 0 & 1 \end{pmatrix},
$$

compute F, t, and B of Section 4.

9.12. For Example 4 of Section 2 with $N = 3$, compute the appropriate long-term probabilities.

9.13. Past data at a college have shown that the student movement from class to class is a Markov chain with transition matrix

$$P = \begin{array}{c} \\ s_1 \\ s_2 \\ s_3 \\ s_4 \\ s_5 \\ s_6 \end{array} \begin{array}{cccccc} s_1 & s_2 & s_3 & s_4 & s_5 & s_6 \\ \left(\begin{array}{cccccc} 1.0 & 0.0 & 0.0 & 0.0 & 0.0 & 0.0 \\ 0.0 & 1.0 & 0.0 & 0.0 & 0.0 & 0.0 \\ 0.25 & 0.0 & 0.15 & 0.6 & 0.0 & 0.0 \\ 0.15 & 0.0 & 0.0 & 0.1 & 0.75 & 0.0 \\ 0.1 & 0.0 & 0.0 & 0.0 & 0.1 & 0.8 \\ 0.05 & 0.9 & 0.0 & 0.0 & 0.0 & 0.05 \end{array}\right) \end{array},$$

where s_1 represents flunking out, s_2 graduation, s_3 freshman class, s_4 sophomore class, s_5 junior class, s_6 senior class. Notice that for each state it is possible to remain in that state—this represents a grade deficiency that must be corrected.

a. Determine the probability of graduation and flunking out for each class.
b. Suppose 1,000 new students are admitted. What is the long-run distribution of these students?
c. Suppose the transition probabilities for the freshman year become (0.15 0.0 0.15 0.7 0.0 0.0). How does this affect the answers for (a) and (b)?

SUGGESTIONS FOR FURTHER STUDY

Billingsley, F., *Statistical Inference for Markov Processes.* Chicago: The University of Chicago Press, 1961.

Carey, K. J., and Sherr, L. A., "Market and Price Factors in Transaction-to-Transaction Price Change Behavior of Common Stocks," *Applied Economics,* vol. 6, 1974.

Chung, K. H., "A Markov Chain Model of Human Needs: An Extension of Maslow's Need Theory," *Academy of Management Journal,* vol. 12, 1969.

Chung, K. L., *Markov Chains with Stationary Transition Probabilities.* New York: Springer-Verlag, 1960.

Davies, R., Johnson, D., and Farrow, S., "Planning Patient Care with a Markov Model," *Operational Research Quarterly,* vol. 26, 1975.

Dynkin, E. B., *Markov Processes.* Englewood Cliffs, N.J.: Prentice-Hall, 1965.

Gregory, G., and Litton, C. D., "A Markov Analysis of a Single Conveyor System," *Management Science,* vol. 22, November 1975.

Grinold, R. C., "Manpower Planning with Uncertain Requirements," *Operations Research,* vol. 24, May–June 1976.

Hillier, F. S., and Lieberman, G. J., *Introduction to Operations Research.* San Francisco: Holden-Day, 1967.

Howard, R. A., *Dynamic Programming and Markov Processes.* New York: Wiley, 1960.

Kemeny, J. G., and Snell, J. L., *Finite Markov Chains.* Princeton, N.J.: Princeton University Press, 1960.

Kolesar, P., "A Markovian Model for Hospital Admission Scheduling," *Management Science,* vol. 16, 1970.

Lilien, G. L., and Rao, A. G. "A Model for Manpower Management," *Management Science*, vol. 21, no. 12, August 1975.

Luce, R. D., and Raiffa, H., *Games and Decisions*. New York: Wiley, 1957.

Parzen, E., *Stochastic Processes*. San Francisco: Holden-Day, 1962.

Ross, S. M., *Introduction to Probability Models*. New York: Academic Press, 1972.

Schachtman, R. H., and Hogue, C. J., "Markov Chain Model for Events Following Induced Abortion," *Operations Research*, vol. 24, September–October 1976.

Simmons, D. M., "Common-Stock Transaction Sequences and the Random-Walk Model," *Operations Research*, vol. 19, 1971.

Valliant, R., and Milkovich, G. T., "Comparison of Semi-Markov and Markov Models in a Personnel Forecasting Application," *Decision Sciences*, vol. 8, 1977.

10

Waiting-Line Models

10.1 INTRODUCTION

THE MODELS presented in this chapter are considerably different from those presented in the preceding chapters with the exception of Chapters 2 and 3. In Chapters 4 to 8 the models were *prescriptive*, that is, their solution prescribed an optimal course of action. In Chapters 2 and 3 and in this chapter the models are mainly *descriptive* in that they serve to characterize the system but do not in general provide an optimal course of action. Certainly, the stochastic or random or probabilistic nature of the processes involved accounts for the lack of an optimal solution, since we do not know what state of the world will occur. That is, the best we can do is talk in terms of the expected value of the variables involved.[1] In Chapter 3 we characterized the decision making process according to probabilities of various events and the decision maker's criteria. In this chapter we will study the behavior of waiting-line systems, in which the random nature of the process is exhibited in the rates of arrivals and service.

Almost everyone is familiar with waiting lines, since at one time or another he or she has been involved in one. Waiting for service at a gasoline station, waiting for a hamburger at the local fast food outlet, waiting in line at registration or at a check-out counter at a store, and so on, are examples of waiting lines. In general, the models deal with situations where there are customers in need of some service or product arriving

---

[1] This class of models is known as Stochastic Programming. The reader is referred to Wagner's book referenced in Chapter 4 for more detailed discussion.

at a service facility where the service or product is dispensed. If there is someone ahead of the arriving customer, a line forms and grows and shrinks according to how fast the service is dispensed and how fast customers are arriving. We want to determine such things as "How long is the line?", "How long does a customer have to wait?", "Suppose the service rate in increased; how does that affect the waiting line?" and so on. In order to be able to answer these and other questions a more formal definition of a waiting-line model is needed. As in each of the preceding chapters the study of a model will involve definition of the components of the model, a list of assumptions about the model, and a method of obtaining numerical results.

10.2. COMPONENTS OF WAITING-LINE SYSTEMS

What follows is a list of the essential elements of a waiting-line model and the characteristics of these elements.

A. *Calling Population:* The set of potential customers to the system to receive the service. This set has the following *characteristics:*
   1. *Size: a. Finite*—the number of potential customers is limited to some fixed number. For example, the number of airplanes requiring landing space at O'Hare Field is determined by the number of airplanes in the "nearby" air space.
   b. *Infinite*—the number of potential customers is essentially unlimited. Since we occupy a finite planet it is difficult to find actual infinite populations; however in the context used here, we mean very large relative to the rest of the system. For example, the number of potential customers for a dentist in New York City could be estimated to be 2,500; while this number is finite, it provides an essentially infinite population for the study of the waiting room behavior of a dentist's office.
   2. *Generation Pattern:* The pattern by which customers are generated for the system. In the models that follow we will use a probability distribution to describe this pattern—called the *arrival rate.* Thus we will be dealing with random variations or a stochastic model. The most common assumption about the generating pattern is that the distribution of the time between arrivals (interarrival time) is the exponential distribution to be described in the next section.

B. *Waiting-Line System:* That portion of the model that deals with the waiting line and the service facility. This portion has the following *characteristics:*

1. *Waiting Line:* The actual line that is formed by customers waiting for service. The waiting line will be characterized by its length. It may be either a finite waiting line or a potentially infinite line. In most real applications of queuing models the waiting line in finite, such as the number of people that can physically fit into a waiting room. Potentially infinite waiting line models provide some important results as well.

2. *Waiting-Line Discipline:* The rule that describes how customers get from the waiting line to the service facility. The most common rules for selecting customers for service are:

    a. FIFO (First in–first out, also known as first-come, first-served): This is certainly the most common and is used implicitly in all models of this chapter.

    b. LIFO (Last in–first out): This rule characterizes the waiting lines formed in many manufacturing systems where the output of a machine (arrivals) is put into a stack and the top of the stack is taken to the next machine for further work.

    c. RANDOM: The arrivals are chosen at random for service. Again such a system is more common in manufacuring systems where parts are drawn at random from the waiting line or pool of arrivals.

3. *Service Facility:* The manner in which the service is dispensed to the customers. The characteristics of the service facility are:

    a. Number of Servers: The number of positions of people dispensing the required product or service. There may be a *single server* or *multiple servers.*

    b. Arrangement of Servers: If there is more than one server they may be arranged in terms of two different patterns: *PARALLEL*—servers side by side each dispensing the same service, such as tellers in a bank; or *SERIES*—In order to receive complete service a customer must pass through several servers, such as a car going through a car wash.

    c. Service Pattern: The probability distribution associated with the rate at which the service is dispensed. The usual assumption is that the service time conforms to the exponential distribution.

4. *Exits From System:* Those means by which a customer (arrival) can leave the waiting line system. There are three such exits:

    a. Completion of service: the customer passes completely through the system.

    b. Balking: the customer observes the size of the waiting line and decides not to join the system.

    c. Reneging: The customer joins the system but becomes impatient with waiting and exits before receiving or completing service.

FIGURE 10–1

Waiting-Line Model

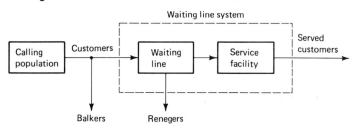

For most waiting-line models we want to consider those exits made by customers who complete service; the behavior of the impatient customer is important, though, and the procedures to be described later in this chapter enable one to deal with such problems.

Combining the preceding components, we obtain the general representation of a waiting-line model in Figure 10–1.

In Figure 10–1 we have made a distinction between the entire model and the waiting-line system, which is the portion enclosed in the dotted lines. The *waiting-line system* comprises the waiting line and the service facility while specifically excluding the calling population and balkers. Within

FIGURE 10–2

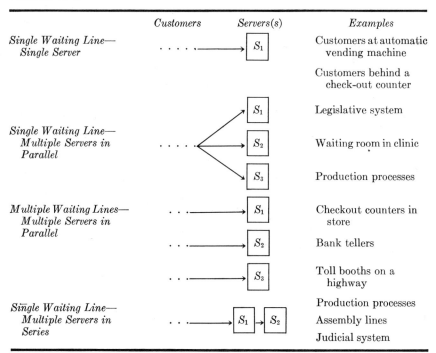

the waiting-line system several possible representations are possible depending on the configuration of the waiting-line and service facilities. The most common are shown in Figure 10–2.

10.3. ASSUMPTIONS IN WAITING-LINE MODELS

Since we are dealing with stochastic or random processes we need to make some assumptions about the process so that we are able to study it in a systematic fashion. Recall that in Chapters 4, 5, and 6 we assumed specific forms of the functions involved in the models and by relaxing those assumptions obtained different models. Similarly, in this chapter we will place assumptions on the probability distribution that represents the rate at which customers enter the system and on the probability distribution that determines the rate at which service is dispensed. Some of these assumptions will be relaxed in Chapter 11. The first three assumptions are related to the probability distribution; assumption 4 relates to the stability of the system.

Assumption 1. If the probability density function with parameter λ is given by

$$f(t) = \begin{cases} \lambda e^{-\lambda t} & t \geq 0 \\ 0 & t < 0, \end{cases} \tag{10–1}$$

then the *interarrival times* (times between arrivals) are said to have an *exponential distribution. We will assume the interarrival times are exponentially distributed.* This assumption has several implications for waiting-line models in terms of some key properties of the exponential distribution.[2]

Property 1. For time periods of fixed length the probability of an arrival is equal for each such interval. In other words, the probability of an arrival is dependent upon the length of the interval, not upon when the interval occurs. Intuitively, this means we need be concerned only with the length of an arrival and not where in the process it occurs or when other arrivals take place. Sometimes arrivals are said to occur *randomly,* which means according to an exponential distribution.

Property 2. The exponential distribution *is memoryless;* that is, it does not depend on the past history of arrivals. This is a valuable property for it allows us to ignore past data of the process since the next arrival is independent of all previous arrivals. If this were *not* the case, we would have to keep records of arrivals since the probability of a current arrival would depend on this past history.

Property 3. If the *interarrival time* has an exponential distribution

---

[2] These are not all properties of this distribution. For complete details see the text of Hillier and Lieberman or that of Parzen cited in the references.

with parameter λ then the *number of arrivals* over a specific time interval has a *Poisson distribution* with parameter λt. That is:

$$P(n) = (\lambda t)^n e^{-\lambda t}/n! \tag{10–2}$$
$$n = 0, 1, 2 \ldots \text{ for } t > 0 \text{ fixed but arbitrary.}$$

where the expected number of arrivals per unit time $(t = 1)$ is λ, the same parameter as that given in (10–1).

As a result of this observation we will refer to λ as the *arrival rate* (customers per unit time).

The Poisson distribution is defined over the integers $n = 0, 1, 2, \ldots$ and hence is valuable when studying arrivals and it also serves as a *counting* process for the number of arrivals.

Assumption 2. The service times at a *busy* service facility have an exponential distribution with parameter μ. That is:

$$g(t) = \begin{cases} \mu e^{-\mu t} & t \geq 0 \\ 0 & t < 0, \end{cases} \tag{10–3}$$

where μ is the service rate, that is, the number of customers served per unit time when the server is busy. We note that each of the properties associated with Assumption 1 holds for the service times as well; in addition we list one more important property with respect to service times.

Property 4. The minimum of several independent exponential random variables is also exponentially distributed. This property is important for those models where we have more than one server in parallel and each server has the same exponential service time distribution with service rate μ. As a result of this assumption it is possible to consider such a system (with n servers) as a system with a single server with service rate $n\mu$ when there are n or more customers in the system.[3]

Assumption 3. Only one event can occur at a time. That is, there cannot be more than one arrival in a small time period; similarly for service completions.

Assumption 4. The waiting-line model has reached a *steady state* or *state of equilibrium*. That is, the system has been operating under the previous assumptions for enough time so that the system has become stable and does not depend on how much time has elapsed since the system started. The condition of the system prior to steady state is *transient* and rather difficult to analyze. Some analysis of such systems will be discussed in the next chapter.

10.4. MODEL CHARACTERISTICS

The characteristics of a waiting-line model are a probabilistic description of the waiting line and the service facility. Since we usually have

---

[3] A complete discussion of the derivation of this result can be found in the references.

only probabilistic information about the components of the model, we should not be surprised to find that our characterizations of the model will also be in terms of probabilities.

A key term in the analysis of waiting-line models is that of *the state of the system*, which is defined as the number of customers in the waiting line *and* in the service facility. Thus if the system is in state 0 there are no customers in the system and the service facility is said to be *idle*; if in state 1, there is one customer in the service facility; if in state 2, there are two customers in the system, and so on. In Section 5e we will redefine the state of the system to study more general models.

Once the probabilities of being in the various possible states of the system are determined one can determine the system characteristics of interest. These characteristics include:

L: The expected number of customers in the entire waiting-line system.

W: The expected waiting time of a customer in the entire system.

L_q: The expected number of customers in the waiting line itself— the expected length of the waiting line.

W_q: The expected waiting time in the waiting line (excluding service time).   (10–4)

These are important characteristics because they will enable us to apply economic information to determine the cost of a particular system or a particular configuration. This information, as we will see in a later section, will be useful for system design and operation.

In order to be consistent and properly identify these characteristics we define some notation which will be used in the remainder of this chapter and in portions of Chapter 11:

n: State of system—number of customers in the system $n = 0,1,2, \ldots$

P_n: Probability of being in state n.

λ: Average arrival rate of customers (expected number of arrivals per unit time).

μ: Average service rate of customers (expected number of service completions per unit time for a busy server).

$\rho = \dfrac{\lambda}{\mu}$: Utilization factor (expected time server is busy).

The development that follows differs considerably from the usual introduction to waiting-line models. In most introductions the development at this point is based on developing formulas for various types of models, usually beginning with a single-server, infinite-state model. Our development will be based on recent developments and will require but one formula.[4] The only required formula is:

$$L = \lambda W, \tag{10-5}$$

called Little's formula,[5] which relates the expected waiting time and the expected number of customers in the *entire system*. This formula (10-5) can be justified by the following argument. On the average, λ arrivals will occur in a unit of time. Each of these will expect an amount of time equal to W. Thus, the total amount of waiting time accrued in one unit of time is given by the product of λ and W. To illustrate this numerically, suppose that we define an hour to be the period of time. Also suppose that λ is equal to 2, and that W is equal to 4. This means that, on the average, two customers will arrive per hour, and each will expect to wait four hours. Thus, during a one-hour period of time (with an average of two arrivals) the total waiting time accumulated will be eight hours. If the system is experiencing waiting time at the rate of eight hours every hour, this must mean that there are eight customers in the system, on the average. Thus, L, the average number of customers in the system, would be equal to eight. Hence, it is reasonable to state that $L = \lambda W$.

We could use the same argument to describe only the waiting line itself. This would lead us to this relationship:

$$L_q = \lambda W_q. \tag{10-6}$$

There is a very simple relationship between W and W_q. The expected total time in the system must be equal to the expected time in the queue plus the expected time in the service facility. From our discussion of service times we know that the expected time in the service facility is $1/\mu$. Thus, it is obvious that

$$W = W_q + \frac{1}{\mu}. \tag{10-7}$$

With these three expressions, once we have found either L, W, L_q, or W_q it is easy to find the remaining three system properties.

10.5. THE RATE DIAGRAM AND BALANCE EQUATIONS

The development of waiting-line models and their numerical analysis will be based on two ideas: the *rate diagram* and the *balance equations*.

---

[4] For example see the works of Ross and Hillier and Lieberman given at the end of this chapter.

[5] The formula bears the name of the author of an important paper in waiting-line theory. The complete reference is given at the end of the chapter.

The analysis will be aimed mainly at finite-state waiting lines, which are more realistic. As some of the development and the exercises show, we will be able to recover the usual waiting-line formulas from our approach. To repeat briefly, the main assumptions are:

1. Poisson Arrivals.
2. Exponential Service.
3. Only one event (arrival or service) can occur at a time.
4. The system is in steady state or equilibrium.

The use of the third and fourth assumptions will become clear as the discussion proceeds. The need for the assumption of Poisson arrivals and the exponential service, however, requires some discussion. A complete discussion would take us far afield, but some remarks can lead to useful insights. The development of waiting-line models is based on a more general process known as a *continuous-time Markov chain.* As was mentioned briefly at the end of Chapter 9, the waiting-line models fit the general framework of a random walk Markov chain with appropriate assumptions. The main assumption is that the process satisfies the Markov property.[6] Certainly one way to guarantee this is to require that the model move between states (undergo transitions) according to an exponentially distributed random variable. The fact that the inter-arrival times and the service times are exponentially distributed is enough to satisfy the requirement.[7] Since the exponential distribution has the memoryless property required of Markov chains the analysis that follows can be related to the Markov chain example of Chapter 9.

The basic elements of the development are:

1. *The Rate Diagram:* A conceptual model that describes the possible states of the model and the transitions from one state to another. Initially we will assume that the state of the system is the number of customers in the system. This will be relaxed in the next section. Associated with each state is:

    A probability of being in that state

    An arrival rate: either constant for each state or perhaps state-dependent

    A service rate: either constant or state-dependent.

2. *The Balance Equations:* A system of equations that state that: *for any state of the model the rate of flow into that state must equal the rate of flow out of that state.*

---

[6] A second assumption requires that the process being studied can be characterized in terms of "states." These states are completely analogous to the states of a Markov chain.

[7] While this may be intuitively clear the reasoning is much more demanding than it appears. The interested reader is referred to the bibliography at the end of the chapter for more details of exponential processes.

In other words, the expected rate of arrivals into any state must equal the expected rate of service completions in order that the system be in equilibrium. These balance equations will be used to compute the state probabilities mentioned earlier.

The idea of the rate diagram can be seen as follows: Suppose there is a gas station with one waiting place and one service place at the pump. Arrivals are Poisson with rate of λ per hour; service is exponential with rate of μ per hour.

The states of the system (numbers of customers) are 0, 1, 2. The rate diagram is:

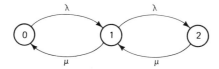

where the nodes represent system states. The arrows represent possible movements among the states with the arrow pointing in the direction of movement. We will follow the convention that arrivals are given on top and departures on the bottom of the diagram. Each arrow will have an arrival or service rate associated with it.

The balance equations can be explained as follows: Suppose the states correspond to reservoirs and the arrows to a hydraulic system. If the flow into a reservoir were greater than the flow out, then after enough time had passed all the fluid in the system would collect in that reservoir. Similarly if the flow out of a reservoir were greater than the flow into it eventually there would be no fluid in that reservoir. Thus when we say the system is in equilibrium we have described the possible states, which must have probabilities greater than 0 but less than 1.

These two basic ideas begin our study of waiting-line models, which will concentrate on model development for realistic situations to include finite state systems, finite populations, and state-dependent arrival and service rates. The first model is:

a. Single Server—Finite Waiting Line—Poisson Arrivals, Exponential Service

This general class of models is characterized by the fact that there is a limit on the number of customers who wait in line. This is a realistic situation since almost every situation can tolerate only a finite number of waiting customers. To illustrate the model construction suppose there is a gasoline station with a single pump (server) and enough space for one car (customer) at the pump and for two additional cars to wait for service. The arrival rate is 20 cars per hour and the service rate is 30 cars per hour.

We let $n = 0,1,2,3$ represent the states of the system—that is, the numbers of cars waiting for service. The *rate diagram* for the steady state model is:

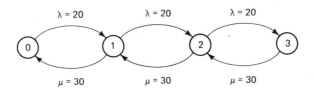

The balance equations can be constructed as:

For State 0: For the rate in to equal the rate out,

$$\mu P_1 = \lambda P_0. \tag{10-8}$$

To go from State 0 to State 1 the system must have been in State 0 and had an arrival; since the arrival rate is $\lambda(=20)$ and the probability of being in State 0 is P_0, the expected *rate out* of State 0 is λP_0. Likewise the expected *rate in* to State 0 is μP_1, which is the service rate for State 1 times the probability of being in State 1.

For State 1: The system can enter State 1 either by being in State 0 and having an arrival (λP_0) or by being in State 2 and having a service completion (μP_2). Thus the *expected rate in* to State 1 is the *sum* of these expected rates: $\lambda P_0 + \mu P_2$. Similarly the system leaves State 1 by an arrival (λP_1), which moves the system to State 2, or by the completion of service (μP_1), which moves the system to State 0. The total *expected rate out* of the state is $\lambda P_1 + \mu P_1 = (\lambda + \mu)P_1$.

State	*General* Rate In = Rate Out	*Example* Rate In = Rate Out	
0	$\mu P_1 = \lambda P_0$	$30P_1 = 20P_0$	(10-9)
1	$\lambda P_0 + \mu P_2 = \lambda P_1 + \mu P_1$	$20P_0 + 30P_2 = (20+30)P_1$	(10-10)
2	$\lambda P_1 + \mu P_3 = \lambda P_2 + \mu P_2$	$20P_1 + 30P_3 = (20+30)P_2$	(10-11)
3	$\lambda P_2 = \mu P_3$	$20P_2 = 30P_3.$	(10-12)

In addition, since P_0, P_1, P_2, and P_3 are probabilities of being in the various states, they must sum to 1:

$$P_0 + P_1 + P_2 + P_3 = 1. \tag{10-13}$$

These five equations determine a solution for the various probabilities. To determine this solution note that each balance equation can be solved in terms of one of the probabilities. It is usual to solve all the equations in terms of P_0; this is merely convention.

From (10–9),

$$P_1 = (\tfrac{2}{3})P_0. \tag{10–14}$$

From (10–10),

$$P_2 = (\tfrac{5}{3})P_1 - (\tfrac{2}{3})P_0;$$

substituting (10–14),

$$P_2 = (\tfrac{5}{3})(\tfrac{2}{3})P_0 - (\tfrac{2}{3})P_0$$
$$= (\tfrac{4}{9})P_0. \tag{10–15}$$

From (10–11),

$$P_3 = (\tfrac{5}{3})P_2 - (\tfrac{2}{3})P_1;$$

substituting (10–14) and (10–15),

$$P_3 = (\tfrac{5}{3})(\tfrac{4}{9})P_0 - (\tfrac{2}{3})(\tfrac{2}{3})P_0$$
$$= (\tfrac{8}{27})P_0. \tag{10–16}$$

From (10–12),

$$P_3 = (\tfrac{2}{3})P_2;$$

substituting (10–15),

$$P_3 = (\tfrac{2}{3})(\tfrac{4}{9})P_0 = (\tfrac{8}{27})P_0. \tag{10–17}$$

Note that (10–16) and (10–17) are precisely the same, and one can be omitted. This will always be the case, and in order to obtain a numerical solution one need consider only equations (10–14), (10–15), and (10–16) along with (10–13).[8] Substituting these equations into (10–13) yields:

$$P_0 + (\tfrac{2}{3})P_0 + (\tfrac{4}{9})P_0 + (\tfrac{8}{27})P_0 = 1$$

or

$$P_0 = {}^{27}\!/_{65}.$$

Thus

$$P_1 = (\tfrac{2}{3})({}^{27}\!/_{65}) = {}^{18}\!/_{65}$$
$$P_2 = (\tfrac{4}{9})({}^{27}\!/_{65}) = {}^{12}\!/_{65}$$
$$P_3 = (\tfrac{8}{27})({}^{27}\!/_{65}) = {}^{8}\!/_{65}$$

are the probabilities of being in the various states. Because P_0 is the probability of no customers in the system—that is, that the system is empty—P_0 is the probability that the server is idle. For this example the server is idle approximately 41.5 percent of the time $({}^{27}\!/_{65})$. To complete the characterization of the system we want to determine the quanti-

---

[8] Alternatively we could consider (10–14), (10–15), and (10–17) along with (10–13). It is clear that the result would be exactly the same.

ties of Section 3. Namely, the expected number of customers in the system is:

$$L = E(n) = \sum_{n=0}^{3} nP_n$$

$$= 0(27\!\!/\!_{65}) + 1(18\!\!/\!_{65}) + 2(12\!\!/\!_{65}) + 3(8\!\!/\!_{65})$$

$$= {}^{66}\!\!/\!_{65} = 1.015 \text{ cars.}$$

The expected waiting time of a customer is:

$$W = L/\lambda,$$

where λ is the expected arrival rate $= 20/\text{hour}$; therefore,

$$W = (66/65)(1/20) = 0.0508 \text{ hours, or } 3,048 \text{ minutes.}$$

A technicality at this point is what is meant by a customer; that is, do we count those arrivals that find the system full and hence spend no time in the system, or do we want to count only those who actually join the system? The above formula is counting *all* arrivals. *To compute the waiting time for only those who actually join the system,* note that the probability that an arrival can join is $1 - P_3 = 1 - 8\!\!/\!_{65} = {}^{57}\!\!/\!_{65}$. The expected waiting time for those who enter the system is based on the arrival rate for those who *can* enter; this rate is

$$\hat{\lambda} = \lambda(1 - P_3) = 20(57/65) = 17.538,$$

and the waiting time for these arrivals is

$$\hat{W} = L/\hat{\lambda} = (66/65)/17.538 =$$

$$= 0.05789 \text{ hour, or } 3.47 \text{ minutes.}$$

Thus whenever dealing with finite-capacity waiting lines one must be specific about which type of customer is being referred to when dealing with waiting times. For the remainder of the chapter an arrival rate λ will indicate *all* arrivals while $\hat{\lambda}$ will denote the rate for those who enter the system:

The system has been completely characterized; in summary:

$P_0 = 27/65$	Probability of idle server
$P_1 = 18/65,$	
$P_2 = 12/65,$	
$P_3 = 8/65$	Probability system is full
$L = 1.015$ cars	Expected line length
$W = 3.05$ minutes	Expected waiting time for all arrivals
$\hat{W} = 3.47$ minutes	Expected waiting time for those that join the system.

The reader is asked in Exercise 1 to show that the above approach can be used to derive the general result

$$P_n = [(\lambda/\mu)^n(1 - \lambda/\mu)]/[1 - (\lambda/\mu)^{N+1}]; \quad n = 0,1, \ldots , N \quad (10\text{-}18)$$

for a system with a finite waiting-line length N, arrival rate of λ, service rate of μ; the reader also is asked to derive a general expression for L and W.

b. Single Server—Finite Capacity—State-Dependent Rates

In the previous example the arrival and service rates were the same for each state of the system, but in many instances these rates vary depending on the state of the system. There are several applications for state-dependent rates (of either arrival or service or both); by incorporating such rates in the model, we can allow for balking and reneging, and we can provide for increasing or decreasing the number of servers if the system requires it.

To illustrate these remarks add the following additional assumptions to the previous model. Whenever a customer arrives and sees one customer waiting, he fails to join the waiting line 20 percent of the time; if there are two waiting, he fails to join the line 50 percent of the time. In addition, the gas station owner has an assistant who aids in service whenever there are three cars in the system. The assistant raises the service rate to 45 cars per hour. The *rate diagram* now is:

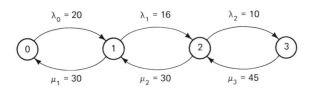

and the *balance equations* are:

State	General Rate In = Rate Out		Example Rate In = Rate Out	
0..............	$\mu_1 P_1$	$= \lambda_0 P_0$	$30P_1$	$= 20P_0$
1..............	$\lambda_0 P_0 + \mu_2 P_2$	$= \lambda_1 P_1 + \mu_1 P_1$	$20P_0 + 30P_2$	$= 16P_1 + 30P_1$
2..............	$\lambda_1 P_1 + \mu_3 P_3$	$= \lambda_2 P_2 + \mu_2 P_2$	$16P_1 + 45P_3$	$= 10P_2 + 30P_2$
3..............	$\lambda_2 P_2$	$= \mu_3 P_3$	$10P_2$	$= 45P_3$

Since the rates may depend on the states, we have identified with each rate the state it corresponds to; for example, $\lambda_2 = 10$ means that when there are two customers in the system the arrival rate is 10 cars per hour (50 percent of the original rate).

The solution to these equations is:

$$P_1 = (2/3)P_0$$
$$P_2 = (23/15)P_1 - (2/3)P_0 = (16/45)P_0$$
$$P_3 = (8/9)P_2 - (16/45)P_1 = (32/405)P_0,$$

which implies

$$P_0 + (2/3)P_0 + (16/45)P_0 + (32/405)P_0 = 1$$

or

$$P_0 = 405/851$$

and hence

$$P_1 = 270/851; \quad P_2 = 144/851; \quad P_3 = 32/851.$$

The expected number of customers is

$$L = 0(405/851) + 1(270/851) + 2(144/851) + 3(32/851)$$
$$= 654/851 = 0.768 \text{ car.}$$

Since there are different arrival rates for some of the states an *expected arrival rate* is used:

$$\bar{\lambda} = \lambda_0 P_0 + \lambda_1 P_1 + \lambda_2 P_2$$
$$= 20(405/851) + 16(270/851) + 10(144/851)$$
$$= 13860/851 \cong 16.287$$
$$W = L/\bar{\lambda} = (654/851)(851/13860) = 0.0472 \text{ hours} = 2.832 \text{ minutes.}$$

In Exercise 2 the reader is asked to develop general formulas for such a system. The above model can be used to interpret two situations that have been treated jointly: (1) finite systems *with balking;* that is, interpret the state dependent arrival rates as *balking* on the part of potential customers; and (2) systems where the number of servers depends on the number of customers in the system.

c. Multiple Servers—Finite Waiting Line

As noted in Section 2, the exponential distribution of service times is important when dealing with multiple-server waiting lines. That is, if there are s servers, each with the same exponential distribution, with parameter μ, then the service rate for the entire system is $s\mu$. In other words, the system is equivalent to one server with rate $s\mu$. For example, if we had three servers the rate diagram for a finite system with four states would be:

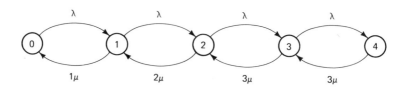

This diagram reflects Property 4 of Section 2. That is, the service rate when the system has three or more customers is 3μ, but when the system has less than three customers the service rate reflects the number of customers. It is as if the single server has three components and the number that are busy depends on the number of customers. In Exercise 3 the reader will be asked to develop the following general results for such a system, in which n represents the state of the system with arrival rate λ, and s is the number of servers or channels with service rate μ:

$$P_0 = \left(\sum_{n=0}^{s-n} \frac{\rho^n}{n!} + \frac{\rho^s}{s!} + \frac{1}{1 - \rho/s}\right)^{-1} \qquad (10\text{-}19)$$

$$L_q = \frac{P_0\rho^s\rho/s}{s!(1 - \rho/s)^2} \qquad (10\text{-}20)$$

$$\rho = \lambda/\mu.$$

The computation of P_0 from (10-19) is not particularly attractive; Figure 10-3 supplies these probabilities for various values of s and $\lambda/s\mu$. Once P_0 is known the remaining system characteristics can be computed.

d. Infinite Capacity—Single Server—Poisson/Exponential Models

We close our discussion of the usual waiting-line models by considering the "classic" example for which certain system characteristics are readily available. This model has the characteristic that the number of possible states (number of customers in the system) is infinite.

Also we use this model to demonstrate the validity of the balance equation approach with respect to the usual probability approach. The rate diagram for such a model is:

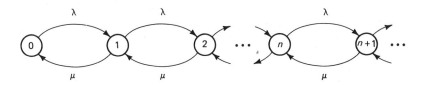

and the balance equations are:

State	Rate In	= Rate Out	(10-21)
0.	μP_1	$= \lambda P_0$	
1.	$\lambda P_0 + \mu P_2$	$= \lambda P_1 + \mu P_1 = (\lambda + \mu)P_1$	
2.	$\lambda P_1 + \mu P_3$	$= \lambda P_2 + \mu P_2 = (\lambda + \mu)P_2$	
. . . .	.		
. . . .	.		
. . . .	.		
n.	$\lambda P_{n-1} + \mu P_{n+1}$	$= \lambda P_n + \mu P_n = (\lambda + \mu)P_n$	

FIGURE 10–3

Multi-Server Poisson/Exponential Queuing System: Probability that the System is Idle, P_0

$\dfrac{\lambda}{s\mu}$	Number of Channels, s								
	2	3	4	5	6	7	8	10	15
.02	.9608	.9418	.9231	.9048	.8869	.8694	.85214	.81873	.74082
.04	.9231	.8869	.8521	.8187	.7866	.7558	.72615	.67032	.54881
.06	.8868	.8353	.7866	.7408	.6977	.6570	.61878	.54881	.40657
.08	.8519	.7866	.7261	.6703	.6188	.5712	.52729	.44933	.30119
.10	.8182	.7407	.6703	.6065	.5488	.4966	.44933	.36788	.22313
.12	.7857	.6975	.6188	.5488	.4868	.4317	.38289	.30119	.16530
.14	.7544	.6568	.5712	.4966	.4317	.3753	.32628	.24660	.12246
.16	.7241	.6184	.5272	.4493	.3829	.3263	.27804	.20190	.09072
.18	.6949	.5821	.4866	.4065	.3396	.2837	.23693	.16530	.06721
.20	.6667	.5479	.4491	.3678	.3012	.2466	.20189	.13534	.04979
.22	.6393	.5157	.4145	.3328	.2671	.2144	.17204	.11080	.03688
.24	.6129	.4852	.3824	.3011	.2369	.1864	.14660	.09072	.02732
.26	.5873	.4564	.3528	.2723	.2101	.1620	.12492	.07427	.02024
.28	.5625	.4292	.3255	.2463	.1863	.1408	.10645	.06081	.01500
.30	.5385	.4035	.3002	.2228	.1652	.1224	.09070	.04978	.01111
.32	.5152	.3791	.2768	.2014	.1464	.1064	.07728	.04076	.00823
.34	.4925	.3561	.2551	.1821	.1298	.0925	.06584	.03337	.00610
.36	.4706	.3343	.2351	.1646	.1151	.0804	.05609	.02732	.00452
.38	.4493	.3137	.2165	.1487	.1020	.0698	.04778	.02236	.00335
.40	.4286	.2941	.1993	.1343	.0903	.0606	.04069	.01830	.00248

.42	.4085	.2756	.1834	.1213	.0800	.0527	.03465	.01498	.00184
.44	.3889	.2580	.1686	.1094	.0708	.0457	.02950	.01226	.00136
.46	.3699	.2414	.1549	.0987	.0626	.0397	.02511	.01003	.00101
.48	.3514	.2255	.1422	.0889	.0554	.0344	.02136	.00820	.00075
.50	.3333	.2105	.1304	.0801	.049	.0298	.01816	.00671	.00055
.52	.3158	.1963	.1195	.0721	.0432	.0259	.01544	.00548	.00041
.54	.2987	.1827	.1094	.0648	.0381	.0224	.01311	.00448	.00030
.56	.2821	.1699	.0999	.0581	.0336	.0194	.01113	.00366	.00022
.58	.2658	.1576	.0912	.0521	.0296	.0167	.00943	.00298	.00017
.60	.2500	.1460	.0831	.0466	.0260	.0144	.00799	.00243	.00012
.62	.2346	.1349	.0755	.0417	.0228	.0124	.00675	.00198	.00009
.64	.2195	.1244	.0685	.0372	.0200	.0107	.00570	.00161	.00007
.66	.2048	.1143	.0619	.0330	.0175	.0092	.00480	.00131	.00005
.68	.1905	.1048	.0559	.0293	.0152	.0079	.00404	.00106	.00004
.70	.1765	.0957	.0502	.0259	.0132	.0067	.00338	.00085	.00003
.72	.1628	.0870	.0450	.0228	.0114	.0057	.00283	.00069	.00002
.74	.1494	.0788	.0401	.0200	.0099	.0048	.00235	.00055	.00001
.76	.1364	.0709	.0355	.0174	.0085	.0041	.00195	.00044	
.78	.1236	.0634	.0313	.0151	.0072	.0034	.00160	.00035	
.80	.1111	.0562	.0273	.013	.0061	.0028	.00131	.00028	
.82	.0989	.0493	.0236	.0111	.0051	.0023	.00106	.00022	
.84	.0870	.0428	.0202	.0093	.0042	.0019	.00085	.00017	
.86	.0753	.0366	.0170	.0077	.0035	.0015	.00067	.00013	
.88	.0638	.0306	.0140	.0063	.0028	.0012	.00052	.00010	
.90	.0526	.0249	.0113	.0050	.0021	.0009	.00039	.00007	
.92	.0417	.0195	.0087	.0038	.0016	.0007	.00028	.00005	
.94	.0309	.0143	.0063	.0027	.0011	.0005	.00019	.00003	
.96	.0204	.0093	.0040	.0017	.0007	.0003	.00012	.00002	
.98	.0101	.0045	.0019	.0008	.0003	.0001	.00005	.00001	

Solving these equations reveals the following general pattern:

$$P_1 = \frac{\lambda}{\mu} P_0 \tag{10-22}$$

$$P_2 = \frac{(\lambda + \mu)}{\mu} P_1 - \frac{\lambda}{\mu} P_0 = \left(\frac{\lambda}{\mu}\right)^2 P_0$$

.
.
.

$$P_n = \frac{(\lambda + \mu)}{\mu} P_{n-1} - \frac{\lambda}{\mu} P_{n-2} = \left(\frac{\lambda}{\mu}\right)^n P_0$$

In order to determine a value for P_0 we make use of the fact that

$$P_0 + P_1 + \cdots + P_n \cdots = \sum_{n=0}^{\infty} P_n = 1; \tag{10-23}$$

that is:

$$1 = \sum_{n=0}^{\infty} P_n = \sum_{n=0}^{\infty} \left(\frac{\lambda}{\mu}\right)^n P_0 = P_0 \sum_{n=0}^{\infty} \left(\frac{\lambda}{\mu}\right)^n. \tag{10-24}$$

Recognizing that, if $|a| < 1$,

$$\frac{1}{1-a} = 1 + a + a^2 + a^3 + \cdots = \sum_{x=0}^{\infty} a^x,$$

Equation (10-24) becomes, if $\lambda/\mu < 1$,

$$1 = P_0 \left(\frac{1}{1 - \frac{\lambda}{\mu}}\right). \tag{10-25}$$

Thus, if $\lambda/\mu < 1$,

$$P_0 = 1 - \frac{\lambda}{\mu}. \tag{10-26}$$

The ratio λ/μ, or ρ, is called the *intensity* or *utilization factor* of the waiting line. We also remark that *we did not need to impose the restriction that $\lambda/\mu < 1$ in the previous models*; that is, it is relevant only for that system with infinite states.

By substituting (10-26) into (10-22) the general form is:

$$P_n = \left(1 - \frac{\lambda}{\mu}\right)\left(\frac{\lambda}{\mu}\right)^n. \quad n = 0, 1, 2. \ldots$$

The system characteristics are

$$L = E(n) = \sum_{n=0}^{\infty} nP_n = \sum_{n=0}^{\infty} n(1 - \rho)\rho^n.$$

We can verify by division that

$$\frac{\rho}{(1 - \rho)^2} = \rho + 2\rho^2 + 3\rho^3 + \cdots = \sum_{n=0}^{\infty} n\rho^n,$$

so that

$$L = (1 - \rho) \sum_{n=0}^{\infty} n\rho^n = (1 - \rho) \frac{\rho}{(1 - \rho)^2} = \frac{\rho}{(1 - \rho)}$$

or

$$L = \frac{\lambda}{\lambda - \mu}, \qquad (10\text{--}27)$$

which is the number expected in the system.

Also $L = \lambda W$ implies:

$$W = \frac{L}{\lambda} = \frac{\lambda}{\mu - \lambda}\frac{1}{\lambda} = \frac{1}{\mu - \lambda} = \text{Expected waiting time in system.} \qquad (10\text{--}28)$$

$$W_q = W - \frac{1}{\mu} = \frac{\lambda}{\mu(\mu - \lambda)} = \text{Expected waiting time in line itself.} \qquad (10\text{--}29)$$

$$L_q = \lambda W_q = \frac{\lambda^2}{\mu(\mu - \lambda)} = \text{Expected number in the line itself.} \qquad (10\text{--}30)$$

These results $(10\text{--}27)$–$(10\text{--}30)$ are the usual results associated with this type of model. They are useful in certain situations, but it is important to remember that they depend on two key assumptions: (1) there is an infinite number of states, and (2) $\lambda/\mu < 1$. These assumptions are often violated in real applications, so that these results must be used with caution.

As an example consider a barber shop where there is one chair and Poisson arrivals at four customers per hour and exponential service at six customers per hour. The infinite-state results are, from equations $(10\text{--}27)$–$(10\text{--}30)$:

$$\rho = \tfrac{4}{6} = \tfrac{2}{3} < 1$$
$$L = 2 \text{ customers}$$
$$W = \frac{1}{2} \text{ hour in system}$$
$$L_q = \frac{4}{3}$$
$$W_q = \frac{1}{3} \text{ hour.}$$

If on the other hand the barber shop is assumed to have finite capacity, the results are dependent on the capacity; for example, if N is the system capacity, then:

	N			
	2	*3*	*4*	*6*
L (customers)...............	0.737	1.015	1.242	1.565
W (hour).................	0.184	0.254	0.311	0.392
$\hat{W}$ (hour)................	0.233	0.289	0.336	0.404

e. Generalized State Spaces

In many situations the definition of the state of the system as the number of customers in the system is not satisfactory. For example consider the rate diagram

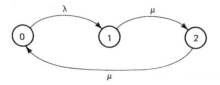

If the state of the system is defined to be the number of customers, this is *not* an allowable model, since it requires two simultaneous service completions for transition to State 0 from State 2 (see Assumption 3). However, the above diagram corresponds to the following model.

In a production process there is a portion of the job to be done in sequence (servers in series) with the restriction that new jobs enter only when there are no other jobs in process. The arrival rate of jobs into the process is Poisson with rate λ and the exponential service rates of the machines are μ_1 and μ_2 respectively.

If we define the state of the system to be 0 when the system is empty; 1 when a job is in machine 1; and 2 when a job is in machine 2, we see that the above description is valid *and* that the assumption concerning only one event occurring at a time is satisfied. Applying the balance equations we obtain:

State	Balance Equation
0.....................	$\mu_2 P_2 = \lambda P_0$
1.....................	$\lambda P_0 = \mu_1 P_1$
2.....................	$\mu_1 P_1 = \mu_2 P_2,$

which can be solved to characterize the system (see Exercise 11). This example could also be a case of a single server giving two different types of service to each customer. In general there is no way to specify what definition of the state of the system will be appropriate for the preceding analysis. Some rather general guidelines *may* help in such situations:

1. The definition must be consistent with the assumptions of Section 2.
2. The states of the system must *accurately* reflect the true nature of the problem. For example, if in the preceding example we had assumed only two states (busy and idle), we would not have had an exponential service model. Combining the two service rates by adding the results gives what is called a *gamma* distribution of service times.
3. In some cases defining the state of a system as a *position* in the process will result in a correct formulation. This will not always be the case, so caution is advised.

As an illustration of the type of complex problem that can be considered by the previous model, consider the following situation.

A machine shop has two machines with exponential service rates of μ_1, μ_2 respectively. A job to be processed goes first to Machine 1 and then to Machine 2 if idle or will wait in Machine 1 until Machine 2 is free. A job will enter the process even if 2 is occupied while 1 is free.

State	Definition
0.....	System empty.
1.....	Job in Machine 1.
2.....	Job in Machine 2, none in Machine 1.
3.....	Job in both.
4.....	Job in Machine 1 done, waiting for Machine 2 to empty.

The rate diagram is:

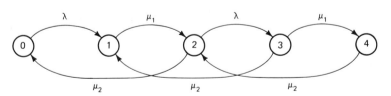

From which the balance equations are constructed as:

State	Rate In	= Rate Out
0...............	$\mu_2 P_2$	$= \lambda P_0$
1...............	$\lambda P_0 + \mu_2 P_3$	$= \mu_1 P_1$
2...............	$\mu_1 P_1 + \mu_2 P_4$	$= \lambda P_2 + \mu_2 P_2 = (\lambda + \mu_2) P_2$
3...............	λP_2	$= \mu_1 P_3 + \mu_2 P_3 = (\mu_1 + \mu_2) P_3$
4...............	$\mu_1 P_3$	$= \mu_2 P_4.$

While the above system, along with $P_0 + P_1 + P_2 + P_3 + P_4 = 1$, can be solved, the results are somewhat complicated and not given here.

10.6. NONEXPONENTIAL DISTRIBUTIONS

To this point all the models under consideration have been assumed to be of the exponential type. The example of the last section showed how a seemingly nonexponential model could be converted into the appropriate form. As noted in Section 4, however, this procedure will not always resolve the difficulty; that is, there are many situations that do not satisfy the assumption of an exponential model. As mentioned earlier in the chapter, the assumption of Poisson arrivals implies that *arrivals occur randomly;* similarly, exponential service times imply *random service times*. While these may be accurate approximations of real-world problems in many settings, it is not difficult to think of settings for which these assumptions are not appropriate. For example, consider a situation when the *service-time is constant*. This would be the case when the service requirements are essentially the same for each customer. As a second case, consider a situation where the number of arrivals is controlled or regulated. Such situations are found in many production processes.

Since there are many situations for which the exponential assumptions do not hold the question arises as how to deal with such models. The derivations of the results necessary to study such situations as arbitrary service times, non-Poisson input, and priority discipline waiting lines are much more complex than that of the previous section.[9] The results of these derivations, however, are rather easily stated and applied. The discussion that follows presents only a few of the potential additional models that can be studied. Other results for nonexponential systems can be found in the references.

a.   Poisson Input and Erlang Service

Consider the case of a waiting line model where there is a single server, the arrival process is Poisson with parameter λ, and the service time has an Erlang distribution.

The probability density function for the Erlang distribution is:

$$f(t) = \frac{(\mu t)^{k-1}}{(k-1)!} \mu e^{-\mu t}; \quad t \geq 0 \tag{10-31}$$

---

[9] The statement of the derivations would take us too far afield, although many of the results require only a minimum of mathematical background. For example, Wagner presents derivations within the framework of differential and integral calculus.

where μ and k are the parameters, with k a positive integer. The mean of the Erlang distribution is $1/\mu$ and the variance is $\sigma^2 = 1/k\mu^2$.

The Erlang distribution is important because of its relationship to the exponential distribution. In particular, if there are k independent exponentially distributed random variables, each with parameter μ, then their *sum* has an Erlang distribution with parameters μ and k. If the service required by a customer requires the completion of a sequence of k identical tasks, the Erlang distribution would be the appropriate distribution for the service times. The system characteristics for a single server, Poisson input with parameter λ, Erlang service with parameters μ and k are:

$$L_q = \frac{\lambda^2\sigma^2 + \rho^2}{2(1 - \rho)} = \frac{1 + k}{2k}\frac{\lambda^2}{\mu(\mu - \lambda)} ; \qquad (10\text{--}32)$$

$$W_q = \frac{1 + k}{2k}\frac{\lambda}{\mu(\mu - \lambda)} ;$$

$$W = W_q + \frac{1}{\mu} ;$$

$$L = \lambda W.$$

A discussion of other situations involving Erlang service times is too advanced for this chapter. The reader is referred to the reference for further information. As a point of information, note from (10–31) and (10–1) that the exponential distribution is a special case of the Erlang distribution with $k = 1$.

b. Poisson Input—Arbitrary Service

Another nonexponential model of importance is the case where there are no restrictions on the service time distribution. Such situations would occur whenever the *service time fluctuates greatly from customer to customer* or even when the *service time is the same for each customer*. Just as for the previous model the derivations are complex. Consider a system with a Poisson input, parameter λ, and a single server with arbitrary service times, and infinite states. Suppose the mean service time is $1/\mu$ with variance σ^2. If the utilization factor, $\rho = \lambda/\mu$, is less than one, then the system characteristics are:

$$P_0 = 1 - \rho; \qquad (10\text{--}33)$$

$$L_q = \frac{\lambda^2\sigma^2 + \rho^2}{2(1 - \rho)} ;$$

$$W_q = L_q/\lambda;$$

$$L = \rho + L_q;$$

$$W = L/\lambda.$$

A special case of the arbitrary service time distribution is that of *constant service times*. Suppose in the previous model it is assumed that there is no variation in service times, that is, $\sigma^2 = 0$. In this case the results of (10–33) hold, but

$$L_q = \frac{\rho^2}{2(1 - \rho)}.$$

(10–34)

c. Other Types of Models

Three additional models that seem to follow naturally from the preceding discussion involve the relaxation of the assumption on exponential arrivals while retaining exponential service time. Unfortunately, the results for this situation are much more complex than for the situations of the preceding section. To date, some analytical results are available along with tables of computational results.

In addition to these types of models, several other types of models are of interest in applications of waiting lines. Such models include: arbitrary arrival, arbitrary service; Erlang arrivals, Erlang service; balking and reneging within these models; priority service disciplines, and so on. For the most part limited analytical results are available for these models, and there are some tabulations of computational results. As an alternative to the development of general results, general waiting-line models can be analyzed using *simulation techniques*. Simulation will be discussed in Chapter 11, and many of the applications given there will concern waiting-line models.

10.7. DECISION MAKING WITH WAITING-LINE MODELS

The discussion of waiting-line models to this point has described the characteristics of the model; for example, the various state probabilities, the expected number of customers in line, and so on. In addition to these descriptive results it is useful to consider some decision making aspects of the model and its results. In particular we want to look at the implications of increased (and decreased) service facilities in terms of additional (or fewer) servers; changing arrival rates, and so on.

There are two types of decision making processes to be considered. First of all, what is the effect of changing service and/or arrival rates on the system characteristics? Secondly, what is the effect of such changes on the cost of the system?

There are many types of decision making settings to be considered, some of which can be answered using calculus; others require a simulation approach (based on the results of the previous section). The several brief examples presented here are meant as only an introduction to some of the potential analyses.

Example 1. Consider the gas station example of Section 4(a). The owner is considering hiring an assistant, thereby raising the service rate to 45 cars per hour. (a) First of all the owner wants to know what percentage of time the assistant will be idle, if hired on a full-time basis; (b) second, the owner wants to know the effect on the system if the assistant works only when the system is in State 3. (c) Third, the completion of a new highway will increase the expected arrival rate to 50 per hour, and the owner wants to know the potential effect of the increased rate on the business. For part (a) the equations (10–14) to (10–16) can be modified by letting $\mu = 45$ to yield

$$P_1 = (4/9)P_0 \qquad\qquad (10\text{–}35)$$
$$P_2 = (16/81)P_0$$
$$P_3 = (64/729)P_0.$$

Or, alternatively, one can employ equation (10–18) to obtain

$$P_0 = (1 - 4/9)/[1 - (4/9)] = 0.5781,$$

which is the same result that would be obtained from (10–35) by requiring $P_0 + P_1 + P_2 + P_3 = 1$. As one would expect, an increase in the service rate (from 30 to 45 cars per hour) results in an increase in idle time (from $P_0 = 0.4154$ to $P_0 = 0.5781$).

To deal with part (b) one need only modify (10–17) to read

$$P_3 = (20/45)\, P_2 = (16/81)\, P_0.$$

From the procedure of Section 4a, the system characteristics are:

$$P_0 = 81/187 = 0.4332,$$
$$P_1 = 0.2888,$$
$$P_2 = 0.1925,$$
$$P_3 = 0.0855,$$

$$L = \sum_{n=0}^{3} nP_0 = 0.9305,$$

$$W = 0.9305/20 = 0.0465 \text{ hours or } 2.7914 \text{ minutes,}$$
$$\hat{W} = 0.05088 \text{ hours or } 3.0528 \text{ minutes.}$$

Finally, if $\lambda = 50$ and $\mu = 30$, Equation (10–18) becomes

$$P_n = (5/3)^n(27/272) \quad \text{for } n = 0, 1, 2, 3,$$

which yields the state probabilities:

$$P_0 = 0.0993; \quad P_1 = 0.1654; \quad P_2 = 0.2757; \quad P_3 = 0.4596.$$

The other system characteristics are:

$$L = 2.096 \text{ cars}; \quad W = 2.515 \text{ min.}; \quad \hat{W} = 4.65 \text{ min.}$$

This example is particularly important because it shows the importance of computing W and $\hat{W}$ for finite state waiting lines. The reason for the increase in waiting time for customers who actually join the system is that for such customers the effective arrival rate is:

$$\hat{\lambda} = \lambda(1 - P_3) = 50(1 - 0.4596) = 27.02.$$

This example also illustrates that waiting-line analysis is descriptive rather than prescriptive. That is, while the analysis provides the system characteristics under various operating settings, it does not prescribe an optimal course of action. The decision maker must evaluate these system characteristics and select an operating policy that meets the appropriate criteria. It is clear from Figure 10–4 that some of the system characteristics are conflicting. For example increasing the service rate, at the appropriate cost, will increase the idle time (P_0) of the service facility but will decrease the waiting time.

FIGURE 10–4

System Characteristics	Original Model $\lambda = 20,$ $\mu = 30$	$\lambda = 20,$ $\mu = 45$	$\lambda = 20,$ $\mu_1 = \mu_2 = 30,$ $\mu_3 = 45$	$\lambda = 50,$ $\mu = 30$
P_0	0.415	0.578	0.433	0.099
P_1	0.277	0.257	0.289	0.165
P_2	0.185	0.114	0.193	0.276
P_3	0.123	0.051	0.085	0.460
L	1.015 cars	0.637	0.931	2.096
W	3.048 min.	1.91	2.791	2.515
$\hat{W}$	3.473 min.	2.01	3.052	4.65

In an attempt to evaluate such criteria consider a second example for which we construct a cost function associated with the waiting-line system.

Example 2. A grocery store employs a single check-out person and is considering hiring a second. The pay rate for checkers is $2.25 per hour. The system has room for at most three customers. If each lost customer represents $5 worth of business, evaluate the addition of a second checker for Poisson input with parameter $\lambda = 10$, and exponential service with parameter $\mu = 4$ for a single server and $\mu = 8$ for two servers. In the development of decision rules when we have costs involved we will assume there are two types of costs: cost of the servers and waiting cost. The cost of servers will usually be expressed as a wage rate; the waiting cost can have several interpretations: lost future business due to waiting, lost work time while waiting, and so on. In what follows we will assume the costs are known and that the total cost of the system is their sum;

Total cost (TC) = Service Cost (SC) + Waiting Cost (WC).

For the single server equation (10–18) yields:

$$P_n = \frac{(2.5)^n \, (-1.5)}{1 - (2.5)^4} = (2.5)^n \, (0.03941); \quad n = 0, 1, 2, 3.$$

Thus the probability that the system is full is $P_3 = 0.61576$. Using P_3 and the cost of lost customers, the total cost per hour of a single server is·

$$TC = \$2.25 + \$10 \, [\lambda - \hat{\lambda}] = \$5 \, [10 - 10(1 - P_3)] = \$2.25 + \$30.79$$
$$= \$33.04,$$

where $\lambda - \hat{\lambda}$ represents the number of customers turned away. For two servers with total service rate of $\mu = 8$ the result of (10–18) is:

$$P_n = \frac{(1\%)^n \, (-\frac{1}{4})}{1 - (1\%)} = (1\%)^n \, (0.17344); \quad n = 0, 1, 2, 3.$$

The probability of a full system is $P_3 = 0.33875$, and the total system cost is:

$$TC = 2(\$2.25) + \$5 \, (3.3875) = \$21.44 \text{ per hour}.$$

Comparing these results, the cost of two servers is considerably less than that of one server because fewer customers will be lost. If the owner of the grocery store is satisfied with the cost estimates and system parameters, the appropriate decision can be made. If, on the other hand, the owner feels unsure of the estimates the above model can be used to test the sensitivity of the solution to various changes.

Example 3. An infinite state, Poisson input, exponential service model has been constructed of a waiting-line situation with parameters $\lambda = 4$, $\mu = 6$. Based on past data the cost of keeping a customer waiting is \$3 per hour. Currently the model assumes a single server and the analyst wants to evaluate the effect of hiring a second server, at a cost of \$2 per hour, thus raising the service rate to $\mu = 8$.

To perform this analysis the expected number of customers and the expected waiting time are computed from (10–27) and (10–28) as:

$$W = 1/(\mu - \lambda) = 1/(6 - 4) = \frac{1}{2};$$
$$L = \lambda/(\mu - \lambda) = \frac{4}{2} = 2.$$

The expected waiting cost of the single server model is:

$$E(WC) = (\$3/\text{hour}/\text{customer})(\tfrac{1}{2} \text{ hour})(2 \text{ customers}) = \$3.$$

For the model with $\mu = 8$ the above equations become

$$W = 1/(8 - 4) = \tfrac{1}{4},$$
$$L = \tfrac{4}{4} = 1,$$

and the expected waiting cost is:

$$E(WC) = (\$3)(\tfrac{1}{4})(1) = \$0.75.$$

The total cost for the additional server is:

$$TC = \$2 + \$.75 = \$2.75.$$

This total cost, being less than the *waiting cost* for the single server model, implies the saving of $0.25 per hour by raising the service rate to $\mu = 8$.

10.8. SUMMARY

The preceding discussions only begin to touch on the vast body of literature available on the subject of waiting-line models. A look at the bibliographies of the references at the end of the chapter indicates the widespread interest in waiting-line models. Much of this interest is directed toward models other than the exponential models and involves either complex derivations or compilations of numerical studies. The reason for this interest is that many real-world models are not exponential. Of what use are the exponential models? Initially, the exponential models can provide an approximation to the real-world system that is rather easily analyzed. Also the exponential model provides the ability to change the system parameters and determine the new system characteristics. Just as the linear models of Chapter 4 may be an approximation to the real-world situation, so too the exponential model may be an approximation of the true situation. As long as this fact is recognized and taken into account in the final decision making process, the results can be of use as an aid in this process.

Another important issue in the application of waiting-line models is the relationship of data to the assumptions. In particular, if data are collected in some waiting-line setting, when do these data fit the exponential assumptions? Some of the examples of the preceding sections illustrated cases in which the exponential model assumptions do not hold—constant service times, regulated arrivals, and so on. In many situations, however, one can rule out these cases and return to the original question: "If data are collected on the arrival rate of customers and on the service times, when is the use of the exponential model justified?" One way to answer this question is through the use of "goodness-of-fit" tests. That is, the data collected regarding the arrival and service times are regarded as a sample of the true distribution. To test the goodness of these data with respect to the Poisson and exponential distributions, one can employ certain statistical tests. For example, the chi-squared (χ^2) test could be used to test the sample and population means. A complete discussion of the area is not appropriate at this point, but it is important to note that for applications of waiting-line models, one must deal with the issue of whether or not the exponential assumptions hold.

Finally we note that waiting-line models present an important application of multiple-criteria decision making. That is, some of the system characteristics developed in Sections 3 and 4 are conflicting and hence an analysis of the system requires developing trade-offs between these criteria. For example, the idle time of the system (P_0) is inversely related to the waiting time of customers and the length of the waiting line. For a given system one can improve the service characteristics but usually at the expense of increased idle time. At some point the decision maker must decide between these two criteria. The last example of Section 7 presented an attempt to convert both criteria to a single dimension, dollars. A cost function for the entire system was developed reflecting the operating cost (cost per hour for the server) and the waiting cost. While this is certainly a feasible approach, it is more than likely that the determination of the waiting costs is difficult and may or may not be realistic. In some settings, such as retail stores, past data may be used as an estimate to the value of lost business. When dealing with public services, however, such as hospitals, such costs are difficult to quantify. An alternative approach is to adapt the multiple-criteria approaches of Chapter 7 to such models.

EXERCISES

10.1.   Consider a model characterized by a single server, finite capacity, Poisson arrivals (arrival rate λ), and exponential service (service rate μ). Show that the following general results are obtainable (let $N =$ number of states of system and $\rho = \lambda/\mu$):

$$P_0 = \frac{1 - \rho}{1 - \rho^{N+1}}$$

$$P_n = \frac{(1 - \rho)\rho^n}{1 - \rho^{N+1}}, \text{ where } n = 0, 1, \ldots, N$$

$$L = \frac{\rho}{1 - \rho} - \frac{(N + 1)\rho^{N+1}}{1 - \rho^{N+1}}$$

$$W = \frac{L}{\hat{\lambda}}, \hat{\lambda} = \begin{cases} \lambda & \text{for all arrivals} \\ \lambda(1 - P_N) & \text{for customers entering the system.} \end{cases}$$

10.2.   For a model characterized by a single server, finite capacity, Poisson arrivals, and exponential service with state-dependent rates, show that the following results hold (let $N =$ number of states and μ_n and λ_n be the state-dependent rates):

$$P_0 = 1/\left[1 + \frac{\lambda_0}{\mu_1} + \frac{\lambda_0 \lambda_1}{\mu_1 \mu_2} + \cdots + \frac{\lambda_{N-1}\lambda_{N-2}\cdots\lambda_0}{\mu_N \mu_{N-1}\cdots\mu_1}\right];$$

$$P_n = \frac{\lambda_{n-1}\lambda_{n-2}\cdots\lambda_0}{\mu_n \mu_{n-1}\cdots\mu_1}; n = 1, 2, \ldots, N$$

$$W = \frac{L}{\bar{\lambda}}.$$

where $\bar{\lambda}$ is the expected arrival rate.

10.3. For a waiting-line model characterized by a single server, finite population, Poisson arrivals, and exponential service (let $M = $ size of population), show that:

$$P_0 = 1 \Big/ \sum_{n=0}^{M} \left[\frac{M!}{(M-n)!} \left(\frac{\lambda}{\mu}\right)^n \right];$$

$$P_n = \frac{M!}{(M-n)!} \left(\frac{\lambda}{\mu}\right)^n P_0, \ n = 1, 2, \ldots M;$$

$$L = L_q + (1 - P_0);$$

$$L_q = M - \frac{\lambda + \mu}{\lambda}(1 - P_0);$$

$$W = L/\hat{\lambda}, \ \hat{\lambda} = \Sigma(M-n)\lambda P_n = \lambda(M-L).$$

10.4. For a waiting-line model characterized by multiple servers, infinite waiting line, Poisson arrivals and exponential service (let $s = $ number of servers and $\rho = \lambda/\mu$), show that:

$$P_0 = 1 \Big/ \left[\sum_{n=0}^{s-1} \frac{\rho^n}{n!} + \frac{\rho^s}{s!}\left(\frac{1}{1 - \rho/s}\right) \right];$$

$$P_n = \begin{cases} \dfrac{\rho^n}{n!} P_0 \text{ if } 0 \le n \le s \\[2mm] \dfrac{\rho^n}{s!s^{n-s}} P_0 \text{ if } n \ge s \end{cases};$$

$$L_q = \frac{P_0 \rho^s \rho/s}{s!(1 - \rho/s)^2}.$$

10.5. An information booth at a department store handles an average of 10 calls per hour. The single attendant can answer an average of 15 calls per hour. Assuming Poisson arrivals and exponential service times:

a. What is the average number of people waiting for questions to be answered?
b. What is the average number of people standing in the line (counting the customer whose question is being answered)?
c. On the average, how long does it take from the time a person gets to the booth or line until he leaves the booth?
d. On the average, how long does a person wait before he starts asking his question?

10.6. Answer Question 5, assuming that every question requires exactly four minutes to answer. (Hint: the standard deviation of a constant is zero.)

10.7. Answer Question 5, assuming that there is room for only four people (three waiting, one talking) around the booth.

a. What percentage of the customers who approached the booth will have their questions answered?

b. How long can these customers expect to wait?

10.8. Answer Question 5, assuming there are now two attendants (taking customers from the single line). Each attendant can handle an average of 15 calls per hour.

10.9. A machinist has five machines to service. Each machine requires service, on the average, once every four running hours. The machinist requires an average of 30 minutes to service a machine. (Note the service rate is 1/0.5 hr. or 2 per hour.) Assume Poisson arrivals (an arrival is a machine needing service) and exponential service times.

a. How much time elapses (on the average) between the time a machine needs service and the time its service is completed?

b. How much of the elapsed time (from part a) is waiting for the machinist? How much of the time is actually spent being serviced?

c. How many machines, on the average, are not running?

10.10. In an infinite-state model of a waiting room, the Poisson arrival rate is six per hour, the Exponential service rate is eight per hour. The cost of waiting has been estimated at $5 per person per hour. Find the expected waiting cost associated with this model.

10.11. Using the information given in Section 5e of the text, determine the system characteristics for the example given there.

10.12. The QRZ Company currently has two office copying machines; one is located in each of the two separate office areas. For each machine, the service rate (exponential) is 15 orders per hour. (An order may be anywhere from one to several hundred copies.) The clerks bring material to be copied, arriving at the rate of 8 per hour (Poisson-distributed). Some people have noticed that one machine may be swamped while the other is idle; they have suggested moving the two machines to a central location, so the clerks would wait for whichever machine is available first. This would entail an additional cost of $2.40 per hour for the entire company. Clerk time costs $4.00 per hour. Evaluate the proposal to consolidate copying in one place.

10.13. A bank drive-in window can service customers at a rate of one every four minutes, or 15 per hour. Customers arrive at an average of 12 per hour. There is room for only three cars, plus the car being served. The bank values its customers; they feel it costs $1.00 each time a customer leaves and parks elsewhere because there is no space to wait. Assuming a 30-hour week, 52-week year, what would be the annual value to the bank of expanding the waiting space by one car? Two cars? Three cars?

10.14. In an infinite-state model, a decision must be made between two servers. The appropriate data for each server (assumed exponential) is:

Server	Service Rate, μ	Cost
A....................	20/hour	$3/hour
B....................	30/hour	$4/hour

The arrivals are Poisson-distributed ($\lambda = 10$ per hour). The customer waiting cost is $1 per hour. Which server should be hired?

10.15. A barber shop with a single barber has room for at least two customers. The system is assumed to have Poisson input ($\lambda = 3$ per hour) and exponential service ($\mu = 4$ per hour). Find:

    a. Expected number of customers in the shop.
    b. Expected time spent in the shop.
    c. If $\mu = 8$ per hour, how much more business would be done?

10.16. For a single-server, Poisson input ($\lambda = 20$ per hour), exponential service ($\mu = 12$ per hour), finite state ($N = 2$) model, find:

    a. Probability the system is idle.
    b. Probability the system is full.

10.17. A gas station has a single pump and three waiting positions. Assume an exponential model with parameters $\lambda = 30$ cars per hour and $\mu = 20$ per hour. Also customers balk (will not enter the system) according to:

    100 percent will join if system empty or one car at pump,
     80 percent will join if one car is waiting and one car at pump,
     50 percent will join if two cars are waiting and one car at pump,
      0 percent will join if three cars are waiting and one car at pump.

    a. Characterize the system using the rate diagram approach.
    b. If each customer turned away represents $5 worth of sales, what is the expected cost of the current system?

10.18. A new drive-in bank is being opened and the management wants to study the effect of various size waiting lines. The model is exponential with parameters $\lambda = 15$ per hour, $\mu = 20$ per hour. Not including the car being serviced, the waiting-line sizes being considered are (*a*) 1 car (*b*) 2 cars, (*c*) 4 cars. For each, compute the percentage of customers lost because of inadequate space.

10.19. Several alternate schemes have been proposed for processing orders at QRS Company. It is important to give prompt service, and the company feels that the cost, in dollars, delay order is equal to $1000 n^2$ where n is the number of days between receiving an order and processing it. For example, a one-day delay costs $1000, but a five-day delay costs $25,000.

    Evaluate the following systems for processing orders, given that an average of 100 orders per day (Poisson-distributed) occur.

System	Average Processing Rate	Standard Deviation of Processing Time (days)	Daily Cost
A	105	0	$100
B	110	0	110
C	120	0	140
D	120	0.001	115
E	120	0.002	110
F	120	0.005	105
G	120	0.1	50
H	200	0	300

10.20. Compare the waiting time for two single-channel Poisson/exponential systems, one of which permits no more than two in the system, the other permitting no more than ten in the system. The arrival rate is 4; the service rate is 10. Should limits *always* be placed on queues to reduce waiting time? Why or why not?

10.21. A car-wash with three waiting places has Poisson input ($\lambda = 8$ per hour) and exponential service ($\mu = 10$ per hour). The owner believes each lost customer costs $2, and is considering the addition of new equipment that will raise the service rate to $\mu = 12$ per hour. This new equipment costs $1 per hour. Should it be added?

10.22. For a single-server Poisson/exponential system with $\lambda = 10$, sketch the relationship between the number of customers in the system and the mean service time. Let $\mu = 10.1, 10.2, 10.5, 11, 12, 13, 15, 15, 16, 18$, and 20. What observations can you make about the effect of small changes in the service rate (a) When ρ is near unity, and (b) When ρ is near 0.5?

10.23. Consider an inventory system for a camera store that operates as follows: Whenever a customer buys a camera, another camera is immediately reordered. There is no other such camera in stock. The delivery time on these orders averages 10 days, exponentially distributed. Customers come to buy a camera at a rate (Poisson-distributed) of once every 30 days. A customer who comes when no camera is in stock, however, will wait until the camera arrives from the distributor, and invariably buys it when the store calls to say the camera is in.

a. How long does it take for a buyer to get a camera, on the average?
b. On the average, how many people are waiting for cameras?

10.24. Although it is known that customers at Lou's knitting shop arrive according to the Poisson distribution at the rate of four per hour, Lou does not know the form of the probability distribution of her service times. Lou's advisor has obtained the following information in such a fashion that customers were unaware of being observed.

Number of Customers	Service Time (minutes)	
	At Least	*But Less Than*
40................	0	2
90................	2	4
16................	4	6
110................	6	8
40................	8	10
10................	10	12
0................	12	

a.   Estimate the average service time per customer.

b.   Estimate the variance of service times,

$$\sigma^2 = \frac{\Sigma(x - \bar{x})^2}{n - 1}.$$

c.   Estimate the system parameters and describe their meaning.

10.25   The two machine model of Section 10.5(*e*) can be viewed as a two-server-in-series model. By an appropriate definition of the states of the system, extend the model to include a finite waiting line *between* the servers. Conceptually the model is:

SUGGESTIONS FOR FURTHER STUDY

Bleuel, W. H., "Management Science's Impact on Service Strategy," *Interfaces,* vol. 6, no. 1, pt. 2, November 1975, pp. 4–12.

Bolling, W. B., "Queueing Model of a Hospital Emergency Room," *Industrial Engineering,* September 1972.

Cooper, J. K., and Corcoran, T. M., "Estimating Bed Needs by Means of Queueing Theory," *New England Journal of Medicine,* vol. 291, 1974, pp. 404–5.

Driscoll, M. F., and Weiss, N. A., "An Application of Queueing Theory to Reservation Networks," *Management Science,* vol. 22, January 1976.

Foote, B. L., "A Queueing Case Study of Drive-In Banking," *Interfaces,* vol. 6, no. 4, August 1976, pp. 31–37.

Gross, D., and Harris, C. N., *Fundamentals of Queuing Theory.* New York: Wiley, 1974.

Gupta, I., Zareda, J., and Kramer, N., "Hospital Manpower Planning by Use of Queuing Theory," *Health Services Research,* vol. 6, 1971.

Harris, C. M., and Thiagarajan, T. R., "Queueing Models of Community Correctional Centers in the District of Columbia," *Management Science,* vol. 22, October 1975.

Hillier, F. S., and Lieberman, G. J., *Introduction to Operations Research.* 2nd ed. San Francisco: Holden-Day, 1974.

Jackson, J. R., "Job Shop-Like Queueing Systems," *Management Science,* vol. 10, 1963.

Jaiswal, N. K., *Priority Queues.* New York: Academic Press, 1968.

Keller, T. F., and Laughhunn, D. J., "An Application of Queuing Theory to a Congestion Problem in an Outpatient Clinic," *Decision Sciences,* vol. 4, 1973.

Koenigsberg, E., and Lam, R. C., "Cyclic Queue Models of Fleet Operations," *Operations Research,* vol. 24, no. 3, May 1976, pp. 516–29.

Kolesar, P. J., Rider, K. L., Crabill, T. B., and Walker, "A Queueing-Linear Programming Approach to Scheduling Police Patrol Cars," *Operations Research,* vol. 23, no. 6, November 1975, pp. 1045–62.

Little, J. D. C., "A Proof for the Queueing Formula $L = \lambda w$," *Operations Research,* vol. 9, 1061.

Newell, G. F., *Applications of Queueing Theory.* Chapman and Hall, 1971.

Panico, J. A., *Queueing Theory.* Englewood Cliffs, N.J.: Prentice-Hall, 1969.

Parzen, E., *Stochastic Processes.* San Francisco: Holden-Day, 1962.

Rosenshine, M., "Queueing Theory: The State-of-the-Art," *AIIE Transactions,* vol. 7, September 1975.

Ross, S. M., *Applied Probability Models with Optimization Application.* San Francisco: Holden-Day, 1970.

———, *Introduction to Probability Models.* New York: Academic Press, 1970.

Stidham, S., "A Last Word on $L = \lambda w$," *Operations Research,* vol. 22, 1975.

Wagner, H. M., *Principles of Operations Research.* Englewood Cliffs, N.J.: Prentice-Hall, 1969.

11

Simulation

11.1 INTRODUCTION

THE DECISION-MAKING TECHNIQUES discussed thus far have been analytical techniques. That is, they have been techniques that an analyst can use in direct calculation of values (often optimal) for the decision variables at hand. Such approaches have been very useful in aiding decision makers in a host of different real-world decision problems. Many such examples have been discussed in previous chapters. Still, it is true that there are many important decision problems that do not lend themselves to analysis by straightforward analytical techniques. Recall that the essence of modeling is to capture the essential features of the system at hand. Frequently, systems of interest are so complex that their essential features cannot be represented by mathematical models that can be analyzed by direct analytical techniques. Simple optimization techniques are not powerful enough to yield solutions to such complex problems. In such cases, we must be satisfied with "usable" solutions obtained by "experimenting" on the model. For our purposes, we will define simulation to be the act of performing experiments on a model in some orderly fashion. These experiments are designed and performed toward the end of enhancing understanding of the behavior of a system. In short, simulation is an evaluative technique for complex systems. It is an important tool for both system design and system analysis.

As the complexity of the system at hand increases, simulation becomes more and more attractive as a decision making aid. This is particularly true for dynamic and/or probabilistic systems. One of the most attractive features of a simulation approach is the opportunity it gives the analyst to understand the dynamic nature of a system. Most simple analytical techniques are ill-equipped to do this—their application is most often found in "static" problems. With simulation, though, we can "move" the model through time and observe how the system behaves in a dynamic sense. Furthermore, a simulation approach can deal with probabilistic elements that are often difficult if not impossible to handle analytically.

Examples of simulation applications are extremely widespread. Some illustrative examples are:

a. Simulation games designed to improve managerial performance in complex decision-making environments.
b. Simulation of the world's weather patterns to predict weather changes.
c. Simulation of waterway systems to evaluate flood control proposals.
d. Simulation of inventory systems to determine optimal inventory policies.
e. Simulation of large queuing systems (like job shops, banks, computer centers) to determine optimal system configurations.
f. Simulation of hospital systems to examine resource allocation trade-offs.
g. Simulation of transportation systems to evaluate design changes and determine optimal traffic control policies.
h. Simulation of communication networks to evaluate routing, capacity, and expansion alternatives.
i. Simulation of the United States' energy production and distribution system to evaluate policy and technology changes.

Many other examples exist. A common attribute of the examples listed above is a high level of complexity. The systems exhibit nonlinear relationships and/or several probabilistic elements.

Before discussing a general framework for simulation, we would do well to keep in mind a few of the unattractive features of simulation. Unlike some analytical techniques, like linear programming, that yield optimal solutions to problems, a simulation approach guarantees nothing more than a usable solution. For certain systems, it may be difficult to determine how close the solution we have is to the "true" optimal solution. Furthermore, most sizable simulation studies are carried out on modern computers. The amount of computer programming and computer execution time required to perform a particular analysis might be very large. Still, simulation may be the most attractive, if not the only, way to analyze certain systems. Its power and versatility often outweigh its shortcomings.

11.2. A GENERAL SIMULATION PROCEDURE

The methodology involved in designing a simulation analysis of a system is very much like the classical scientific method. There are certain steps that every complete study should contain:

1. A model should be developed that attempts to capture the essential features of the system under question. In developing such a model, it is helpful to think in terms of controllable variables (also called decision variables), uncontrollable variables, and the relationships that exist between these variables.

2. The second step is to validate the model that has been developed. Models are often operated and compared with past system behavior and with the analyst's expectations. Any necessary modifications must be made before usable results are obtained from the model.

3. Having completed the validation step, the analyst then designs and performs experiments on the model. Given values or other representations for the uncontrollable variables, we experiment with the decision variables and observe how the system responds. A flow diagram of this procedure is given in Figure 11–1.

FIGURE 11–1

A Flow Diagram for a Simulation Procedure

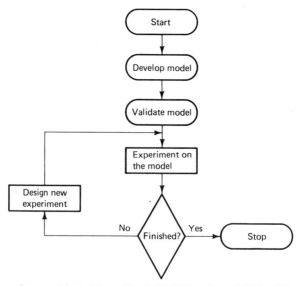

Source: Adapted from Claude McMillan, Jr. and Richard F. Gonzalez, *Systems Analysis: A Computer Approach to Decision Models*, 3d ed. (Homewood, Ill.: Richard D. Irwin, Inc., 1973), p. 26.

11.3. THE MONTE CARLO METHOD FOR REPRESENTING STOCHASTIC ELEMENTS IN SIMULATION MODELS

A useful tool in many simulation studies is the Monte Carlo method of generating random variables from probability distributions. The technique is both simple and powerful, as the following example will illustrate. Assume that the output (X) from a given probabilistic process is an integer between 0 and 39, inclusive. Furthermore, assume that we are concerned about X falling in certain intervals (0–9, 10–19, 20–19, 30–39), and that we know the corresponding probability of X being in any given interval at a given time. This information is displayed in Figures 11–2A and 11–2B.

FIGURE 11–2A	**FIGURE 11–2B**
Hypothetical Probability Distribution	**Hypothetical Distribution along with Two-Digit Integer Assignments**

a, b	$p(a \leq X \leq b)$		a, b	$p(a \leq X \leq b)$	*Two-Digit Integers*
0, 9	0.15		0, 9	0.15	00–14
10, 19	0.20		10, 19	0.20	15–34
20, 29	0.50		20, 29	0.50	35–84
30, 39	0.15		30, 39	0.15	85–99
	1.00			1.00	

In Figure 11–2B we associate with each event the number of uniformly distributed (that is, equally likely) two-digit integers that correspond to the probability of the event. For example, the event $0 \leq X \leq 9$ has a probability of 0.15 of occurring. Thus we associate 15 two-digit random integers (00–14) with this event. The consecutive numbering of the allocated random integers is purely for convenience. Likewise, for the event $20 \leq X \leq 29$, we allocate 50 two-digit random numbers (35–84). Note that the total number of random numbers used for all four events is 100. The idea is that the ratio of the number of random numbers assigned to an event to the total number of random numbers assigned to the whole distribution is equal to the probability of the event occurring. Had we chosen to allocate three-digit random numbers instead, we would have needed 1,000 numbers in all. Whether one uses two-, three-, or four-digit random numbers (or whatever) is a matter of convenience and the precision of the probability distribution. There must be at least as many digits as positions after the decimal point in the probability distribution.

Having made the random number assignments, the output of this process is simulated by picking numbers from a random number table and simply determining the corresponding event. For example, suppose we went to a two-digit random number table and got the number 27. This would indicate that the event $10 \leq X \leq 19$ occurred. We can think of this as one simulation of a process whose output is a random variable that is described (modeled) by the probability distribution in Figure 11–2A. If we continue to "simulate" this process, and if we keep track of the frequency with which each event occurs, we would expect that the relative frequency of occurrence of each event would approach, in the limit as the number of trials in the simulation grows without bound, the probability of each event occurring. Figure 11–3 shows the results for 100 trials. We should expect that a larger number of trials would produce relative frequencies that are closer to the original probability numbers. The reader is encouraged to use the random number table in Appendix B and perform a 100-trial simulation of the distribution shown in Figure 11–2A. Why are your results slightly different from those shown in Figure 11–3?

FIGURE 11–3

Results from 100 Monte Carlo Simulations of the Distribution shown in Figure 11–2A

a, b	$p(a \leq X \leq b)$	*Integer Assignments*	*Number of Occurrences*	*Relative Frequency*
0, 9.	0.15	00–14	13	0.13
10, 19.	0.20	15–34	21	0.21
20, 29.	0.50	35–84	54	0.54
30, 39.	0.15	85–99	12	0.12

11.4. THE PRETZEL SALESMAN

Let us now consider a simple example to demonstrate the use of the Monte Carlo technique in a decision problem. W. W. Lattimer operates a corner pretzel stand. Each night he must decide how many pretzels he will make for the following day's business. Since there is no market for leftover pretzels, preparing too many is wasteful. On the other hand, preparing too few causes Lattimer to forgo some sales. Currently, he has the policy that he prepares for the next day the number of pretzels that were demanded today. Lattimer was not completely happy with this "order quantity" policy of his, but he really had no reason to believe (since he knew nothing about expected payoffs) that some other policy would yield better results. Eventually he heard through the grapevine that his competition across the street determined the next day's quantity by averaging the last two days' demand. It was claimed that the act of averaging ironed out abnormal fluctuations and resulted, over the long run, in higher average daily profits. This idea seemed to make sense to

Lattimer, but he was reluctant to give up the present policy without further examination; and he was not quite sure how to evaluate the two policies.

One way to resolve the dilemma faced by this decision maker is to simulate the operation of the business for some time period (say, 20 days) for both policies and compare the results. Assume that pretzels cost $0.05 each to make, and that they are sold for $0.20 each. Furthermore, assume that past experience indicates that the demand for pretzels on any day is described by the probability distribution shown in Figure 11–4. Note that the uncontrollable variable in this problem is "demand." The controllable variable is "supply"—how many pretzels are prepared for a given day's business. These variables interact to produce various levels for the measure of effectiveness, which in this case is average daily

FIGURE 11–4

Daily Demand Distribution for Pretzels

Number Demanded	Probability
20	0.10
21	0.20
22	0.40
23	0.15
24	0.10
25	0.05
	1.00

profits. We need to develop a model that explicitly represents the relationships between these variables.

Let D represent daily demand, Q represent the quantity of pretzels prepared for a given day, and S represent the quantity of pretzels sold in a given day. Then the following relationships must be valid;

$$\text{If } D \leq Q, \text{ then } S = D. \tag{11-1}$$
$$\text{If } D > Q, \text{ then } S = Q.$$

The profit derived from a day's operation is

$$(\text{Price}) \times (\text{Number Sold}) - (\text{Cost}) \times (\text{Number Prepared})$$

$$\text{Profit} = 0.2S - 0.05Q. \tag{11-2}$$

To complete our mathematical model, we need to represent mathematically the two supply policies.

Policy 1. Supply for tomorrow the quantity that was demanded today. Symbolically we can represent this policy by the equation

$$Q_{t+1} = D_t \tag{11-3}$$

where Q_{t+1} is the quantity to be supplied for day $t + 1$ and D_t is the demand at day t.

Policy 2. Supply for tomorrow the average of today's and the previous day's demand. This relationship becomes

$$Q_{t+1} = (D_t + D_{t-1})/2. \qquad (11-4)$$

Having formulated the relevant relationships, we are ready to simulate the operation of this business. Figure 11–5 shows a general flow-chart that we will follow in these simulations. The "boxes" in Figure 11–5 serve the following purposes:

Box 1. Simply pick an initial demand value so that we can start the simulations.

Box. 2. Depending on which policy we are testing, use Equations 11–3 or 11–4 to calculate the quantity of pretzels to be supplied for the next day.

Box 3. To generate a daily demand figure for a given day, we will use the Monte Carlo method previously described. Figure 11–7 shows the demand distribution of Figure 11–4 together with random number

FIGURE 11–5

A General Flowchart for Simulating 20 Days' Operation of the Pretzel Business

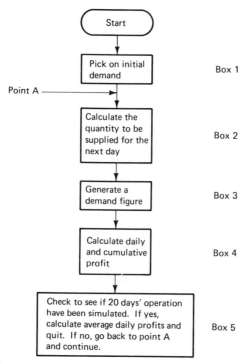

assignments for each possible demand. A daily demand can thus be generated by obtaining a two-digit random integer from a random number table and assessing to which particular demand that number corresponds.

Box 4. Having values for demand and supply, we can calculate the

FIGURE 11–6

Flowchart for Simulating Operation under Policy 1 where: (a) t **Implies the "Day" involved, (b) Total,** $=$ **Total Profits as of Day** t

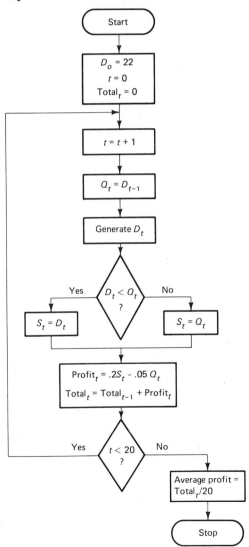

FIGURE 11–7

Daily Demand Distribution along with Two-Digit Integer Assignments for the Monte Carlo Method

Number Demanded	Probability	Two-digit Integers
20......................	0.10	00–09
21......................	0.20	10–29
22......................	0.40	30–69
23......................	0.15	70–84
24......................	0.10	85–94
25......................	0.05	95–99
	1.00	

quantity sold by the relationships shown in Equation 11–1. Then the profit equation (11–2) can be used to calculate the daily profit.

Box 5.   Here we simply check to see if we have simulated enough days' operation. If we have, we want to summarize our results and stop. If we have not, we want to continue with our simulations. Figure 11–6 contains a more explicit version of the flow diagram for simulating this business under Policy 1. Using Figure 11–6 and a random number table, we can carry out the desired calculations. Figure 11–8 is a work sheet showing a few of the trials; the second column contains two-digit random numbers, which are used to generate the demand values. These random numbers were obtained by taking the first two digits from the first column in Appendix B. Any arbitrarily chosen set of two digit integers from Appendix B could be used for this simulation. Assuming an initial value for D of 22, the reader should verify the values in the table. For instance, for day $t = 1$, we have $Q_1 = D_0 = 22$. Now we need to generate D_1. The random digit 54 corresponds (from Figure 11–7) to a demand of 22. Therefore, $D_1 = 22$, and thus $S_1 = D_1 = 22$. Knowing S_1 and Q_1, we can calculate the corresponding profit by

$$\text{Profit} = 0.2S_1 - 0.05Q_1$$
$$= 0.22(22) - 0.05(22) = \$3.30.$$

FIGURE 11–8

A Partial Listing of the Simulation Results for Policy 1 of the Pretzel Example

t	Random Number	Q_t	D_t	S_t	$Profit_t$	Total $Profit_t$
0............	—	—	22	—	—	0
1............	54	22	22	22	3.3	3.3
2............	02	22	20	20	2.9	6.2
3............	98	20	25	20	3.0	9.2
4............		25				

The other values in the table can be verified in a similar fashion. Problem 4 at the end of the chapter asks the reader to complete the simulation for Policy 1, do the simulation for Policy 2, and compare the results.

Although the pretzel example is very simple, it adequately demonstrates the essential ideas behind Monte Carlo simulation. This procedures has widespread application to many managerial systems. In particular, it is often employed to help analyze stochastic inventory systems as demonstrated in Section 11.5. The pretzel example just presented had the characteristics of many simulation studies. A stochastic process was integrated into the model via the Monte Carlo method and the model was "moved through time" day by day. The measure of effectiveness (profits) was explicitly present in the model and was monitored day by day.

The reader should be careful, though, not to equate simulation with Monte Carlo. It is often necessary to simulate completely deterministic models—models that are free of probabilistic elements. Furthermore, many stochastic elements in models have probability distributions or densities that can be represented by some standard theoretical distribution. In such cases there are simpler ways for generating outputs from such processes. These process generators will be discussed later in the chapter.

11.5. INVENTORY SYSTEMS

The design, analysis, and management of inventory systems are important issues for decision makers in a wide variety of institutional settings. Inventory problems exist in private industry, government, hospitals, universities, and virtually all other institutions. Inventory systems are usually managed by implementing some controlling policy such as: When the inventory level drops to a predetermined re-order level, R, replenish inventory by placing an order for Q units. Alternatively, review the inventory level every T days; if, at a review, the level is less than a predetermined amount, s, place an order such that the inventory level will be restored to S units; otherwise, do not place an order at a review. Normally the review period, T, is given. For instance, we might review at the end of every week.

The first policy described above is called a "re-order point" system and the second policy is an example of a "periodic review" system. Other types of inventory policies exist but these (with minor variations) are the most widely used in practice. Notice that for each type of policy there are two important decision variables. For the re-order point system, we need to determine R and Q. For the periodic review system, we need to determine s and S. Having these values, inventory management can be automated.

In choosing numerical values for these decision variables, we try to find an optimal trade-off among the cost of carrying inventory, the cost of placing orders to replenish inventory, and the cost associated with being caught short when demand exceeds available inventory. These cost components are usually added together to yield a total variable cost function for some time period, a week, a month, or a year. Management's objective is to determine a policy that causes the average value of the total cost function to be minimized.

Although such cost models are relatively easy to develop, they are often very difficult to solve mathematically. Models corresponding to most real-world inventory systems usually contain nonlinear functions of the decision variables. Moreover, they usually contain one or more stochastic elements that result from demand and/or lead-time considerations.[1] As a result, the mathematical analysis required to compute an opti-

FIGURE 11–9

Demand Distribution for Inventory Example

Demand	Probability	Random Number Assignment
0......................	0.1	0
1......................	0.3	1, 2, 3
2......................	0.5	4, 5, 6, 7, 8
3......................	0.1	9
	1.0	

mal policy is often extremely difficult. For many systems, mathematical analysis is impossible.

Simulation, however, can easily cope with the complexities of inventory systems. We can simulate the behavior of a system for a variety of candidate policies. Then, management can choose the policy that yields the most desirable system behavior on the average. Complex mathematics are not needed.

To illustrate the approach, consider an inventory system for which the daily demand is uncertain but can be represented probabilistically by the distribution shown in Figure 11–9. Assume that

a. When demand exceeds inventory, backordering is allowed but a stockout cost of $1 per unit is charged for each unit backordered.

b. Lead-time is constant at two days.

c. The cost of placing an order to replenish inventory is $10 (regardless of the amount ordered).

---

[1] Lead-time is defined to be the time between placement and receipt of an inventory-replenishing order.

d. The cost of carrying inventory is 50¢ per day for each unit in inventory at the beginning of the day.

Suppose management wants to install a re-order point policy but is uncertain about the values to use for R and Q. This issue could be resolved by simulating the cost behavior of the system for a variety of possible policies and choosing the policy that yields a minimum cost. For example, we could test the policy "Whenever the inventory on hand at the beginning of a day is less than or equal to $R = 2$, place an order for $Q = 6$ units." Assume that we allow only one order to be outstanding at a time.

Using the Monte Carlo approach, we can generate daily demands, keep track of inventory levels and backorders, and compute corresponding daily costs. These daily costs can be cumulated and averaged to estimate the cost behavior of the system for the $R = 2$, $Q = 6$ policy. Figure 11–10 is a worksheet used to carry out (in conjunction with Figure 11–9) the simulation for three weeks. The random numbers used in the simulation were arbitrarily taken from the first column in Appendix B. Day 1 of the simulation starts with an inventory level of six units. Zero units are ordered since our inventory on hand is greater than R, and zero units are received since no order was outstanding. The random number 5 gives us a demand of two units. No units need to be backordered and we begin Day 2 with four units on hand. The cost associated with our Day 1 experience is simply the $3 inventory-holding cost since no stockout or ordering costs were incurred. The reader should verify the other entries on the worksheet.

Summing the cost results in the worksheet and averaging over the three weeks yields an average cost of $28.5 per week for the $R = 2$, $Q = 6$ policy. Cost estimates for other policies could be obtained in a similar fashion and used to compare policies. To improve the reliability of the comparisons, however, we should examine the system for more than three weeks. More will be said about this issue later in the chapter.

11.6. QUEUING SYSTEMS

In the previous two examples, we were primarily concerned with system behavior along a single dimension of performance—profits for the pretzel example and costs for the inventory example. For many systems, though, we are interested in several aspects of system behavior rather than a single measure of effectiveness. This is certainly true for queuing systems, where we are often concerned with the average time a customer spends in a queue, the average time a customer spends in the system, the average length of the queues, and the percentage utilization of the service facilities, as well as other system characteristics.

The multi-dimensional aspect of system performance can readily be examined by simulation. We simply monitor the various performance

FIGURE 11–10

Worksheet for Inventory Simulation

Day	Starting Inventory	Units Ordered	Units Received	Random Number	Units De-manded	Units Back-ordered	Holding Cost	Stockout Cost	Ordering Cost	Total Cost
1	6*	0	0	5	2	0	$3.0	0	0	$ 3.0
2	4	0	0	0	0	0	2.0	0	0	2.0
3	4	0	0	9	3	0	2.0	0	0	2.0
4	1	6	0	1	1	0	0.5	0	10.0	10.5
5	0	0	0	9	3	3	0	3.0	0	3.0
6	0	0	6	8	2	0	0	0	0	0.0
7	1	6	0	5	2	1	0.5	1.0	10.0	11.5
8	0	0	0	5	2	2	0	2.0	0	2.0
9	0	0	6	2	1	0	0	0	0	0
10	2	6	0	6	2	0	1.0	0	10.0	11.0
11	0	0	0	4	2	2	0	2.0	0	2.0
12	0	0	6	9	3	0	0	0	0	0
13	1	6	0	0	0	0	0.5	0	10.0	10.5
14	1	0	0	3	1	0	0.5	0	0	0.5
15	0	0	6	7	2	0	0	0	0	0
16	4	0	0	1	1	0	2.0	0	0	2.0
17	3	0	0	9	3	0	1.5	0	0	1.5
18	0	6	0	7	2	2	0	2.0	10.0	12.0
19	0	0	0	2	1	1	0	1.0	0	1.0
20	0	0	6	3	1	0	0	0	0	0
21	2	6	0	5	2	0	1.0	0	10.0	11.0

* Initial inventory arbitrarily assigned.

measures we are interested in as the simulations proceed and summarize the results when finished. Different choices for decision variables may well affect the various performance measures differently. Simulation gives us insight into performance trade-offs and allows us to do some crude (but useful) "goal programming" type of analysis on complex systems.

In the preceding chapter, the basic elements of queuing theory were explored, and some simple queuing models were discussed. For several sets of classical assumptions, simple formulas were developed to predict mean time in the system, mean queue length, percentage utilization of service facility, and so forth. However, many real queuing systems do not satisfy these assumptions. As a result, some of the formulas we developed in the previous chapter have limited real-world application.

Real queuing systems that are too complex to be analyzed analytically are best explored by simulation. The basic ideas involved in such simulations are developed in the example below. So that the details won't get in the way of the ideas, the example is kept very simple. The approach presented here, however, is readily applied to more complex systems.

Consider an infinite population, first come-first serve single-channel queuing system in which the time between arrivals is uniformly distributed between 0 and 20 minutes with a mean of 10 minutes, and the service time is uniformly distributed between 0 and 16 minutes with a mean of 8 minutes. Suppose we are interested in the average behavior of the system as described by the mean time a customer spends in the system and the percentage utilization of the service facility. We could assess these measures by simulating the behavior of the system for a large number of customers. If we simply keep track of how long each customer spends in the system and how many hours the service facility is actually used, we can compute the performance measures we want when we have finished looking at the experience of a predetermined number of customers.

The ideas involved are rather simple. We will need two random variable generators—one for time between arrivals and one for service times. Furthermore, we will need some variables or locations in which to store intermediate results, and the appropriate logic to link the variables together.

Let us denote the state of this queuing system at any point in time by the number of people in the system. Let the variable T denote the time since the last change in the state of the system occurred. Such a change of state can occur in either of two ways: when a person enters the system, or when a person is finished being serviced and leaves the system. Determining which event (arrival or departure) will happen next is the crux of the simulation procedure. Once we have resolved this issue, we simply increment the appropriate counters for intermediate results, obtain new values for our random variables (time between arrivals and/or service time), and repeat the process. This procedure is described by the flow diagram in Figure 11–11.

For instance, if the next event that is destined to occur is an arrival into the system, we would follow the left-hand branch shown in Figure 11–11. Since one more person has entered the system, we add one to a counter used to keep track of the number of arrivals. The "system time" (T) is then updated by "advancing" it to the time of this arrival. If the system was not empty when the customer arrived, the customer would enter a queue. We would then generate the time the next arrival will occur, and return to the top of the diagram for the next trial. On the other hand, if this customer entered an empty system, he would go directly into the service facility. We would then have to determine how long his service is going to take, in addition to the time of the next arrival, before returning to start the next trial.

Suppose now that the next system-disturbing event is a departure. As

FIGURE 11–11

General Flow Diagram for Queuing Simulation

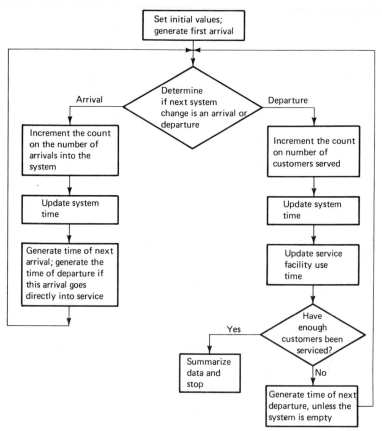

before, a counter for the number of departures from the system is incremented by one and the system time is updated. Since a customer has just left the system, the service facility was just used and we add to our cumulative total of service facility use the time this customer spent in the facility. If the last departure left the system empty, we temporarily set the time of the next departure to plus infinity and return for the next trial. Such a step is needed to insure that the next event that occurs will be an arrival. On the other hand, if the system currently is not empty, so that the first person in line moved into the service facility when the last person departed, we simply determine the time the next departure will occur and return for the next trial.

By going through many trials, insight into the behavior of the system can be gained. Note that the procedure described above requires that times for the status-disturbing events be determined in each trial. These times are determined in practice by "generating" them from their corresponding random distributions. For instance, we stated earlier that the

FIGURE 11–12

Uniformly Distributed Random Numbers

	$\Delta T1 =$ Time between Arrivals (0–20)	$\Delta T2 =$ Service Times (0–16)
1	15.49	2.09
2	16.23	11.11
3	17.24	14.75
4	15.45	5.37
5	1.27	9.38
6	7.20	14.09
7	5.59	3.22
8	7.99	0.34
9	13.75	5.02
10	13.82	5.16
11	14.35	6.40
12	18.85	0.88
13	16.97	9.51
14	18.66	3.95
15	1.71	15.32
16	5.75	6.23
17	3.17	4.52
18	6.62	9.83
19	11.23	2.42
20	3.86	6.21
21	18.93	15.52
22	6.55	9.69
23	4.65	1.05
24	9.00	1.88
25	11.73	11.80

time between arrivals into the queuing system was a uniformly distributed random variable with a mean of ten minutes. So, a particular "time between arrivals" could be generated by taking numbers from a random number table with numbers between zero and twenty. Short segments of such random numbers are displayed in Figure 11–12 (longer lists could be obtained from Appendix B by dividing the numbers found there by 1,000 and then ignoring those numbers that are outside the desired intervals).

Before we can go through the details of simulating our queuing system, we must assign names to the various variables needed. Assume the following:

$T =$ System time (denotes time when the state of the system changes)

$\Delta T_1 =$ Interval of time between last arrival and next arrival (a random variable).

$\Delta T_2 =$ Duration of next servicing operation (a random variable).

$TS =$ Cumulative time service facility has been used.

$NARR =$ Number of arrivals into the system.

$NDEP =$ Number of departures = number that have completed service.

$TAR_{NARR+1} =$ Time of next arrival (since time 0).

$TDP_{NDEP+1} =$ Time of next departure (since time 0).

Using these variables and the logic just discussed, we can add more detail to our flow diagram and obtain the flow diagram shown in Figure 11–13. (The reader should study the two diagrams carefully. Make sure you understand the various relationships calculating TDP and TAR. Note that statements like $NARR = NARR +1$ simply mean that the count on the number of arrivals is the old count plus one.)

We are now ready to simulate our queuing system. Assume that we want to continue the simulation until $N = 10$ customers have been serviced. At such a time, we will stop the simulation and compute the percentage utilization of the service facility and the average time a customer spends in the system. As shown in Figure 11–13, the percentage utilization figure is obtained by computing what percentage the cumulative service facility usage time (TS) is of the total system time (T). The average time in the system is also easy to compute. Throughout the simulation, we will record the time each customer enters and leaves the system. Thus, we can easily calculate the time each particular customer spent in the system. The mean time in the system will simply be the average of these numbers.

Figure 11–14 contains a worksheet on which we can record our experiences, trial by trial, throughout the simulation. Since we start at time equal to zero with the system empty, we must give our variables ap-

FIGURE 11–13

Specific Flow Diagram for Queuing Simulation

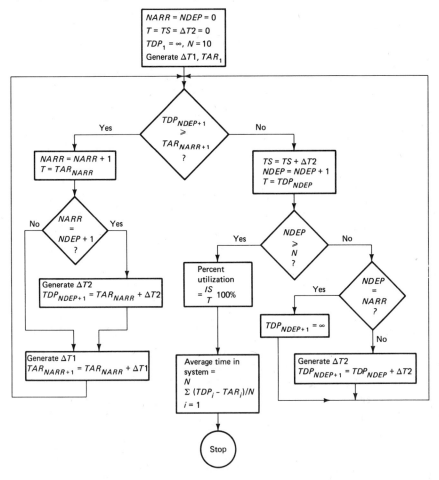

propriate initial values and make sure that the *first event* that occurs is an arrival. Hence, we set

$$
\begin{aligned}
NARR &= 0 \\
NDEP &= 0 \\
T &= 0 \\
TS &= 0 \\
\Delta T2 &= 0 \\
TDP_1 &= \infty \\
N &= 10
\end{aligned}
$$

and we generate (from our random number table of Figure 11–12) ΔT_1, which is also equal to the time of the next (first) arrival. These initial

FIGURE 11–14

Work Sheet for Queuing Simulation

Trial	System Time T	ΔT_1	ΔT_2	$NARR$	$NDEP$	TAR_{NARR+1}	TDP_{NDEP+1}	TS
1	0	15.49	—	0	0	15.49	∞	0
2	15.49	16.23	2.09	1	0	31.73	17.58	—
3	17.58	—	—	—	1	—	∞	2.09
4	31.73	17.24	11.11	2	—	48.97	42.84	—
5	42.84	—	—	—	2	—	∞	13.20
6	48.97	15.45	14.75	3	—	64.42	63.72	—
7	63.72	—	—	—	3	—	∞	27.96
8	64.42	1.27	5.37	4	—	65.69	69.79	—
9	65.69	7.20	—	5	—	72.89	—	—
10	69.79	—	9.38	—	4	—	79.17	33.33
11	72.89	5.59	—	6	—	78.48	—	—
12	78.48	7.99	—	7	—	86.47	—	—
13	79.17	—	14.09	—	5	—	93.26	42.71
14	86.47	13.75	—	8	—	100.22	—	—
15	93.26	—	3.22	—	6	—	96.49	56.80
16	96.49	—	0.34	—	7	—	96.82	60.02
17	96.82	—	—	—	8	—	∞	60.36
18	100.22	13.82	5.02	9	—	114.04	105.24	—
19	105.24	—	—	—	9	—	∞	65.38
20	114.04	14.35	5.16	10	—	128.39	119.21	—
21	119.21	—	—	—	10	—	∞	70.55

conditions are recorded on trial 1 of the work sheet. Following Figure 11–13, we now compare TDP_1 with TAR_1 to determine whether a departure or an arrival will occur next. Of course, an arrival will occur first (because of our initial conditions) and we move down the left-hand branch (the "arrival" side) of the flow diagram. We increment $NARR$ from 0 to 1 and advance the system time (T) to the time of this arrival. Since $NARR$ *does* equal ($NDEP + 1$), which means the first arrival went directly into the service facility, we generate ΔT_2 (from Figure 11–12) and then determine the time of the next departure as well as the time of the next arrival before returning for the next trial. The results obtained for this trial are recorded on line two of the work sheet. The

FIGURE 11–15

Work Sheet Showing "Summary" Calculations

i	TAR_i	TDP_i	DIF_i
1	15.49	17.58	2.09
2	31.73	42.84	11.11
3	48.97	63.72	14.75
4	64.42	69.79	5.37
5	65.69	79.17	13.48
6	72.89	93.26	20.37
7	78.48	96.49	18.01
8	86.47	96.82	10.35
9	100.22	105.24	5.02
10	114.04	119.21	5.17
			105.72

From Figure 11–14 we see that $TS = 70.55$, $T = 119.21$, so that

$$\text{Percent utilization} = \frac{70.55}{119.21} \times 100 \text{ percent}$$
$$= 59.18 \text{ percent.}$$
$$\text{Average time in system} = \frac{105.72}{10} = 10.572 \text{ minutes.}$$

reader should continue in this fashion and verify all the figures on the work sheet. Note that it took 21 trials to get $N = 10$ customers through the system.

We are now ready to summarize our results. Figure 11–15 shows the required calculations. When the simulation was terminated, the system time was 119.21 minutes, while the cumulative facility use time was 70.55 minutes. Hence, the utilization of the service facility was 59.18 percent. Now, from Figure 11–14 we see that Customer 1 entered the system at time 15.49 minutes and left at time 17.58 minutes. Thus, Customer 1 was in the system for 2.09 minutes. The "in system" time for all ten customers can be calculated in a similar fashion. The sum of these "in system" times is 105.72 minutes, and thus the mean time spent in the system is 10.57 minutes. These calculations are displayed in Figure 11–15.

Note that there are several performance measures (like queue length, average time spent in queue, etc.) that we did not keep track of in the preceding simulation. Doing so will be left for the exercises at the end of the chapter.

In the above example, only one system configuration was simulated. One purpose of simulation, however, is to analyze several different configurations in order to predict the behavior of the real system under similar conditions. For example, the following questions might be investigated by a series of simulation experiments:

What would be the effect of instituting a schedule so that an arrival occurs every ten minutes?

What would be the effect of adding a second server whenever the queue exceeds two customers?

What would be the effect of starting the queue with ten customers, reflecting overnight arrivals?

Would it be advantageous to hire a slower but more consistent server?

Answers to these questions would aid management considerably in making decisions about the queueing system.

11.7. TRANSIENT AND STEADY-STATE BEHAVIOR

With more patience, we could have simulated the behavior of the queuing system over a larger number of customers (N). Doing so is fruitful, as we will soon discover. The queuing simulation was re-run four times for different values of N. The results were:

	\multicolumn{4}{c}{N}			
	200	*300*	*400*	*500*
Percentage utilization	78.88	76.30	76.08	77.31
Average time in				
system, minutes	18.09	16.06	15.98	16.58

Note that these results are fairly consistent, but differ drastically from the results shown in Figure 11–15 that we obtained for $N = 10$. How can this be explained? We know that by the very nature of a simulation study, results obtained are not as precise as results obtained from an analytical approach. But the $N = 10$ and $N = 500$ results differ by approximately 50 percent.

The large discrepancy between the $N = 10$ and $N = 500$ results is due to a phenomenon characteristic of the behavior of most dynamic systems. If we start looking at time equal to zero at the behavior of a system and continue to observe the behavior for a considerable length of time, we will notice that the output can be roughly characterized by two phases—a transient phase and a steady state phase. This behavior is illustrated in Figure 11–16. Roughly, the steady-state phase refers to the behavior of a system after the system "settles down," or stabilizes. The transient phase refers to that period of time between time zero and time of stability. Of course, there are some systems that never reach steady state—they never stabilize. For instance, if the mean service time in our queuing example is greater than or equal to the mean time between arrivals, the queue length will grow without bound and never stabilize. Other examples are abundant.

FIGURE 11–16

Hypothetical Example of Transient and Steady-State Behavior of Queuing System

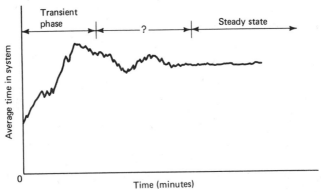

If a system is going to stabilize, it may do so fairly quickly. But the transient time varies considerably from system to system, and even for the same system with parameter changes. The point at which we say the system enters "steady state" is largely a matter of judgment. The inconsistency we apparently encountered with the figures for percentage utilization and average time in the system for small and large values of N is really not an inconsistency at all.[2] Rather, the figures are results from two different phases of the system's behavior. The $N = 10$ results occurred during the transient stage, while the large N results ($N = 200, 300, 400,$ and 500) correspond more closely to the steady-state phase.

Many times decision makers are concerned only with the behavior

---

[2] Some of the difference may be due to sampling error. Simulation trials can be viewed as samples from a population and thus subject to statistical sampling error. Most of the discrepancy here, however, is due to the transient–steady-state consideration.

in the steady state. When this is the case, it is common practice to throw away the results from the transient phase trials and base calculations only on the "steady-state" trials. Doing so gives a more accurate representation of steady-state conditions. Thus, the transient phase data can be identified and excluded from the calculations. If, however, the duration of the transient time is small compared to the length of time the simulation is run, the steady-state data will overwhelm the transient data, and the error due to the transient data will be small. Of course, it may be that a decision maker is mainly concerned with the transient phase. Many queuing systems (like queues in banks and grocery stores) essentially start at time zero every day, or every time the demand process changes, such as the start of lunch hour. In such cases, transient behavior is very important. In fact, it does a decision maker very little good to know what the steady-state conditions of a queuing system are if for the greater part of the "operating time" the system is in a transient state.

11.8. STATISTICAL ISSUES

There are some particularly difficult statistical problems that arise in the analysis of simulation experiments. Many of these problems arise because the observations in the output time series are not independent of each other; this is called autocorrelation or serial correlation. Autocorrelation causes difficulties when the analyst is interested in measuring the precision of the estimates derived from the simulation; knowing the precision of the estimates is helpful in determining the length of the simulation run, and in determining significant differences among the outputs of several experiments. Because one observation in a serially correlated time series depends upon the previous observation (or upon some other past observation), there is not as much information contained in one observation of a serially correlated time series as there is in a series of independent observations. Thus, the ordinary statistical techniques, which require independence of observations, are not directly applicable in most simulation studies.

The issues of sample size determination and of precision and reliability of simulation results are beyond the scope of this text. For these topics the reader is referred to the literature on experimental design aspects of simulation.

11.9. PROCESS GENERATORS

We have seen the importance of having at our disposal a generator of uniformly distributed random numbers. All three examples considered in this chapter employed such generators. As mentioned earlier, though, many probabilistic processes can be described by mathematical distributions. For example, queuing problems often involve the exponential distribution. Scheduling systems often involve a normal distribution. With the aid of a random fraction generator, random variables from these and other theoretical distributions can be readily generated. For example, if y is a random fraction from a uniform distribution, and λ is the average arrival rate into a queuing system, then a generator that will yield times between arrivals that are negative-exponentially distributed is

$$t = -\frac{1}{\lambda} \log_e y.$$

Of course, such a process could be simulated by the Monte Carlo method we discussed earlier. Recall, though, that this would require a sequence of logic in addition to a random fraction generator to produce a value for t. The above generator accomplishes the same thing with a single equation.

In a like manner, random variables from normal, gamma, and other standard distributions can be easily generated. Details can be found in the references at the end of the chapter.

11.10. THE ROLE OF THE COMPUTER

For the examples presented in the chapter, the simulations were carried out manually. In principle any system could be simulated manually, but in practice simulation is almost always done on a computer. Computers are ideally suited for making large numbers of calculations and doing the bookkeeping functions required of simulation studies.

The widespread interest in the use of simulation as a means of analyzing large complex systems has given rise to the development of several special purpose simulation languages for computer programming. These languages are structured so that certain operations that are commonly needed in simulation studies can be carried out very easily and quickly. Although FORTRAN is capable of doing almost anything that these special purpose languages can do, FORTRAN is often more difficult to work with. Representative of the popular special purpose languages are SIMSCRIPT, GPSS (General Purpose Systems Simulator), and DYNAMO. Although other simulation languages exist, SIMSCRIPT, GPSS, and DYNAMO have had the most application to date. Both SIMSCRIPT and GPSS offer the analyst broad simulation capabilities. SIMSCRIPT requires more programming knowledge to use than does GPSS, but in several ways is more powerful. Either will suffice for most problems.

DYNAMO is a language written specifically to accommodate the development called industrial dynamics by Jay W. Forrester. Industrial dynamics is a scheme for modeling the dynamic behavior of an entire organization. Forrester's work concentrates on the information flow system within an organization and the way this system relates to decision making and organization activities. DYNAMO is designed specifically to facilitate the study of the behavior of these complex interactions.

11.11. SUMMARY

This chapter has presented some of the basic notions of simulation. While the ideas are simple, they can be extremely powerful when put to creative use. Complex systems can be designed and/or analyzed using simulation. Stochastic components of systems can be incorporated into the analysis by Monte Carlo or some other generation scheme. The ability to deal efficiently with stochastic elements and portray the complete dynamic behavior of a system are major advantages of simulation.

EXERCISES

11.1.   Discuss some system that would be best analyzed via simulation. What are the controllable and uncontrollable variables? What are the relationships between variables, and between the variables and the system's environment? In what way is your model only an approximate representation of the real system? What measures of effectiveness would you be interested in exploring? What difficulties do you foresee in modeling the system?

11.2.   Discuss simulation possibilities for the following systems:

    a.   Job shops
    b.   Transportation networks
    c.   Stock market
    d.   Stream pollution
    e.   Horse races

11.3.   For the following arrival distribution, use a random number table to generate arrivals for 5, 10, 20, and 40 time periods. From the results of each of the four simulations, compute the average number of arrivals in a period. Compare the results with the expected value of the probability distribution. Comment on any discrepancies that you find.

Number of People Arriving in a Period	*Probability*
1	0.10
2	0.20
3	0.35
4	0.20
5	0.10
6	0.05
	1.00

11.4. Refer to the pretzel example in Section 11.4.

    a. Complete the 20-day simulation under Policy #1.
    b. Do the simulation using Policy #2.
    c. Which of the two policies should be implemented?

11.5. Refer to the inventory example of Section 11.5. Continue the simulation for five more weeks and compare the average cost estimate with that given in the chapter.

11.6. Refer to the inventory system of Section 11.5.

    a. Compare the $R = 1$, $Q = 8$ policy with the $R = 2$, $Q = 6$ policy.
    b. Determine the optimum policy.

11.7. Refer to the inventory example of Section 11.5. Simulate the behavior of the system for the $R = 2$, $Q = 6$ policy when lead-time is not constant but described by

Lead-Time	*Probability*
1.....................	0.4
2.....................	0.6

(Hint: Use two sets of random numbers—one for generating demands and one for generating lead-times. Generate a lead-time when an order needs to be placed. Otherwise, proceed as before.)

11.8. Consider the following communications network with five nodes.

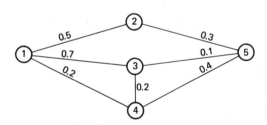

The numbers associated with the branches represent the probability that the branch is *busy* at any instant of time. Management is concerned about the quality of service between Node 1 and Node 5.

    a. Use Monte Carlo to estimate the probability that a call placed at any given time will go through (use 30 trials).
    b. Calculate the probability precisely.

11.9. Ships arrive at a port with an inter-arrival time given by probability distribution p_o. The port has three docks, and ships randomly choose an unloading dock. A special crew is required to *prepare* the ship for unloading and this preparation time is distributed according to p_1. Once a ship is ready for unloading, the regular dock crew completes the unloading. (Each dock has its own regular crew, but the special crew works on all three docks.) The unloading time at each dock is probabilistic and described by p_j, $j = 2$, 3, 4. Prepare a flow diagram to simulate the operation of this port. Assume that all crews treat ships on a first-come, first-serve basis. Ignore transportation time for the special crew. Provide for keeping track of

a. How long a ship (on the average) waits to get into a dock.
b. How long a ship (on the average) takes to get unloaded.
c. The percentage of the time each crew is busy.

11.10. Would the system of Problem 9 readily lend itself to mathematical queuing theory methods? Discuss.

11.11. Consider a corner hot dog stand where hot dogs sell for 30 cents each, and have a unit cost of 10 cents. The demand for hot dogs on a given day is given by

Number of Hot Dogs per Day	Probability
0	0
1	0.05
2	0.10
3	0.15
4	0.20
5	0.25
6	0.15
7	0.05
8	0.05
	1.00

Let D_t denote the number of hot dogs demanded on day t, and assume that Q_{t+1}, the quantity available for sale on a given day $t + 1$, is determined by

$$Q_{t+1} = 1.1D_t.$$

Simulate the daily profitability of this enterprise for 20 days, starting with $D_o = 5$.

11.12. Consider a two-stage queuing problem as shown below:

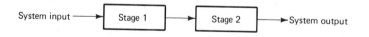

System inputs have a uniformly distributed inter-arrival time distribution (time between arrivals) with a mean of ten minutes. The service times for stages 1 and 2 (t_1 and t_2) are uniformly distributed with means of eight and six minutes, respectively.

a. Compose a flow diagram to simulate the behavior of this system. Keep track of the percent utilization of each stage and the queue lengths at each stage.

b. Simulate the systems behavior until the system produces 20 outputs.

c. Experiment with the sensitivity of the system's behavior to change in the service time distributions for the two stages.

11.13. Two mechanics service seven machines. Service times are uniformly distributed between zero and four hours. Breakdowns occur randomly, and the time between breakdowns for each machine is uniformly distributed with a mean of eight hours. When more than one machine is waiting for service, the one with the shortest repair time is serviced first.

a. Develop a flow chart that could be used to assess the average waiting time for this system of seven machines.

b. Use Monte Carlo simulation to calculate the average waiting time.

11.14. Consider an inventory system for a single product in which daily demand is a random variable that can be modeled using a Poisson distribution with a mean of four units. As demand is satisfied, the inventory level drops until a predetermined reorder point is reached. At such a time, the company places an order to replenish its inventory. The time period between placing and receiving such an inventory replenishing order (called the lead-time) is probabilistic and described by the following distribution:

Days	*Probability*
1....................	0.5
2....................	0.3
3....................	0.2

Currently, the company is operating using the following decision rule: When the inventory level drops to or below 12 units, place an order for 10 units. Assume that demand that cannot be satisfied when initially encountered is lost (that is, no backordering is allowed).

a. Develop a flowchart that could be used to determine the average number of inventory replacement orders made per month, the average inventory level, and the number of units of lost demand.

b. For a three-month (90-day) period, simulate the behavior of this inventory system.

c. Suppose the cost of placing an order is $5, the average unit holding cost is $1, and the unit stockout cost (what it costs the company for each unit of demand it is unable to fill) is $20.00. Compute the average daily inventory cost based on a 90-day simulation.

d. Consider now the decision rule: "When the inventory levels drop to or below eight units, place an order for ten units." Use simulation to compare this operating rule with the previous rule.

11.15. A quick-food home-delivery restaurant guarantees it can deliver orders within two hours after they are placed. If a customer is forced to wait more than two hours, he gets his order free. The average profit margin on orders placed is $3.00, and the average cost to the restaurant is $2.00. Orders are called in in a Poisson fashion, with an average rate of six per hour. The restaurant has but one employee, who is both cook and delivery boy. The delivery truck has a telephone so that orders can be received while a delivery is in progress. Service time (which includes food preparation and delivery) is exponentially distributed, with a mean service time of 15 minutes. Can the restaurant operate profitably under its current free meal policy?

SUGGESTIONS FOR FURTHER STUDY

Abranovic, W. A., and Wallace, W. A., "A Computer Simulation Approach for Planning in Hospital Ancillary Services," *Socio-Econ. Plan. Sci.*, vol. 5, 1971, pp. 429–88.

Alexander, L. P., III, *Dynamo User's Manual*. 2d ed. Cambridge, Mass.: M.I.T. Press, 1963.

Emshoff, J. R., and Sisson, R. L., *Design and Use of Computer Simulation Models*. New York: Macmillan, 1970.

Forrester, J. W., *World Dynamics*. Cambridge, Mass.: Wright-Allan Press, 1973.

Frerichs, R. R., and Prawda, J., "A Computer Simulation Model for the Control of Rabies in an Urban Area of Colombia," *Management Science*, vol. 22, 1975, pp. 411–21.

Gordon, G., *The Application of GPSS V to Discrete System Simulation*. Englewood Cliffs, N.J.: Prentice-Hall, 1975.

Hancock, W., Dissen, R., and Merten, A., "An Example of Simulation to Improve Plant Productivity," *AIIE Transactions*, vol. 9, no. 1, March 1977, pp. 2–10.

Hirsch, G., and Miller, S., "Evaluation of H.M.O. Policies with a Computer Simulation Model," *Medical Care*, vol. 12, 1974, pp. 668–81.

Jain, S. K., "A Simulation-Based Model for Scheduling and Management Information for a Machine Shop," *Interfaces*, vol. 6, no. 1, November 1975.

McMillan, C., and Gonzalez, G. F., *Systems Analysis*. 3d ed. Homewood, Ill.: Richard D. Irwin, Inc., 1973.

Naylor, T. H., *Computer Simulation Experiments with Models for Economic Systems*. New York: Wiley, 1971.

Schellenberger, R. E., "Criteria for Assessing Model Validity for Managerial Purposes," *Decision Sciences*, vol. 5, no. 4, October 1974, pp. 644–53.

Shannon, R. E., "Simulation: A Survey with Research Suggestions," *AIIE Transactions*, vol. 7, no. 3, September 1975, pp. 289–301.

———, *Systems Simulation: The Art and Science*. Englewood Cliffs, N.J.: Prentice-Hall, 1975.

Shepard, K. W., "Applying Simulation Techniques to Legislative Analysis: The Veterans and Survivors Pension Reform Act," *Interfaces*, vol. 7, no. 1, November 1976.

Smith, V. K., Webster, D. B., and Heck, N. A., "The Management of Wilderness Areas: A Simulation Model," *AIDS*, vol. 7, no. 3, July 1976, pp. 524–37.

Wyman, F. P., *Simulation Modeling: A Guide to Using Simscript.* New York: Wiley, 1970.

12

Critical Path Methods for
Project Management

12.1. INTRODUCTION

CRITICAL PATH METHODS deal with the planning, scheduling, and controlling of activities required to complete some (typically large) project. Generally these projects consist of many distinct but interrelated components. For instance, the construction of a large building is such a project. Many activities (excavation, pouring concrete, erecting walls, etc.) must be completed in order to complete the project. Although certain activities may be undertaken concurrently, many activities cannot be started until others have been finished (for example, walls cannot be erected until the foundation has been laid). Thus, the managerial issues concerning such projects can be very complex.

Critical path methods[1] are designed to aid management by:

a. Providing a means for graphically portraying the entire project in a manner that enhances understanding of the interrelationships among all the component activities.

b. Estimating when each activity should begin so that the project can be completed by some target date (or at minimum cost).

c. Identifying those particular activities that are critical in the sense that if they are delayed the entire project will be delayed.

---

[1] There are many techniques that come under the general heading of "critical path" methods. PERT (*Program Evaluation and Review Technique*) is the word usually associated with the approach presented in this chapter. The other techniques are much the same, being either small variations or extensions.

d. Providing a convenient means for monitoring and reporting on the progress of the project.

e. Providing a means for assessing the effect on total project time of delays in certain activities, changes in resource levels allocated to certain activities, and the rescheduling of certain activities.

This information is extremely useful and greatly simplifies the planning, scheduling, and controlling aspects of project management. One of the early successful applications concerned the development of the Polaris submarine system by the United States Navy; critical path methods are credited with shortening the original expected completion time by approximately two years. Other important application areas include: planning and developing new products; managing a major maintenance project in high-technology industries; and planning and conducting large research projects. Many other applications exist (even writing mystery novels).

12.2. NETWORK DIAGRAMS

An integral part of any critical path analysis is the construction of a network depicting the various activities required for project completion and the precedence relationships among the activities. Typically, the nodes in the network denote events and the arcs (branches) of the network represent the various activities. Events, which occur at specific points in time, refer to the completion and/or beginning of one or more activities. A "path" through the network is a connected sequence of nodes and arcs.

The construction of a network diagram is very important in itself. This operation requires the analyst to carefully define all the activities required for project completion, the precedence relationships between the activities, and time estimates for each activity. Having this data, the analyst can then construct the diagram, which gives a visual display of the entire project. This network construction phase of the analysis usually deepens one's understanding of the project.

Aside from yielding a better understanding of the project, the network diagram provides a convenient framework from which we can make several simple, yet extremely useful, calculations about when certain events should (or could) take place. From these results we can readily compute possible starting times for the various activities. Moreover, we can identify which path through the network is most critical in the sense that it requires the most time. Since the project is not completed until *all* activities are completed, this critical path determines the length of the project. Of course, there could be ties so that a project has more than one critical path.

Note that all these results provide useful managerial information. They enable us to plan and schedule activities wisely. Moreover, they aid in the control function in that we can make periodic progress reports comparing actual event times with computed event times in an attempt to keep the project on schedule. Discrepancies and their effect on the project completion time can be assessed with the aid of the diagram.

Guidelines for Constructing a Network Diagram

1. One and only one activity connects any given pair of events. Moreover, one and only one arc in the network is used to denote a given activity.
2. Often we must introduce "dummy" activities into the network in order to show the required precedence relationships or to deal with situations that would otherwise violate rule (1) above. These dummy activities have zero duration times associated with them.
3. Typically we label the arcs in the network with the appropriate activity duration times. Nodes are usually numbered starting with "1" for the first node and continuing in a natural fashion. The last node (denoting the end of the project) is given the largest number. Intermediate nodes are numbered as they are encountered. Thus, different people may number the intermediate nodes differently.

Consider for example a project consisting of four activities. Figure 12–1 shows the duration times along with the precedence requirements

FIGURE 12–1

Data for Example Project

Activity	Immediate Predecessor	Time (days)
A_1	—	2
A_2	—	3
A_3	A_2	2
A_4	A_1, A_2	3

for the activities. Figure 12–2 shows the corresponding network diagram. Since activities A_1 and A_2 have no predecessors, they can begin the project and be undertaken concurrently. Event (node) one denotes the "beginning of the project" and the activities (arcs) corresponding to A_1 and A_2 emanate from Node 1 and terminate at nodes arbitrarily numbered three and two respectively.[2] Node 2 denotes the completion of activity A_2. From Figure 12–1, we see that A_3 can begin once A_2 is

---

[2] The numbering of these nodes could have been reversed.

FIGURE 12–2

Network Diagram for Example Project

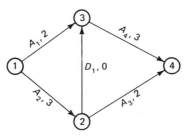

completed. Thus, an arc labeled A_3 is created emanating from Node 2. Figure 12–1 also indicates that activity A_4 cannot begin until both A_1 and A_2 have been completed. To impose this joint prerequisite for A_4, we must create a "dummy" activity, D_1, going from Node 2 to Node 3. Node 3, then, denotes the completion of both A_1 and A_2. Thus activity A_4 can be depicted beginning at Node 3. The project is completed when both A_3 and A_4 are completed. Thus, both A_3 and A_4 terminate at Node 4, which denotes the event "project complete."

Note that in the diagram of Figure 12–2, no two activities appear with the same beginning and ending nodes. This must always be the case if we are to easily identify the event corresponding to a given node. It is this requirement that created the need for the dummy activity from Node 2 to Node 3. Without D_1, the proper relationship would not exist among A_1, A_2, and A_4. Note also in Figure 12–2 that the activity duration times are listed on the network arcs along with the activity identification. It is convenient to have these times displayed in this fashion when we are making various calculations concerning the network. Finally, note that there are three paths from the beginning of the project, Node 1, to the

FIGURE 12–3

Data for House Construction Project

Activity	Immediate Predecessor	Time (days)	Activity Description
A_1	—	7	Excavate and foundation
A_2	A_1	3	Frame
A_3	A_2	4	Rough wall and siding
A_4	A_2	4	Electrical
A_5	A_2	6	Plumbing
A_6	A_3	2	Roof
A_7	A_4, A_5	8	Plaster
A_8	A_7	8	Finishing
A_9	A_6, A_8	5	Painting

FIGURE 12–4

Network for House Construction Project

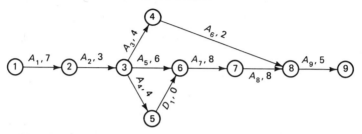

Note that D_1 is a dummy activity.

end of the project, Node 4.[3] Saying that all activities must be completed (before the project is complete) is the same as saying that all three paths must be traveled. Clearly then the finishing time for the project is determined by the path with the longest associated time. The determination of this "critical" path is one of our prime objectives.

Before turning to the calculations we can make with the aid of a network diagram, it would be useful for the reader to study another example of network construction. Figure 12–3 describes a house construction project consisting of nine activities. Using the guidelines put forth and demonstrated on the previous example, the reader should produce a network diagram equivalent to that of Figure 12–4.

12.3. EARLY EVENT TIMES

The "early event time" for a given event is defined to be the earliest possible time the event could occur. It is the time the event should occur if all preceding events occur as early as possible. These times are computed by assigning a starting time of zero for event number one and working sequentially until the early event time for the final event is computed. Specifically, the procedure is as follows: To find the early event time for a given event, first identify all the immediately preceding events. To the early times for these events, add the duration times for the activities connecting the relevant pairs of events. Since the event at hand cannot occur until all of the connecting activities are completed, the *greatest* of these numbers is the early event time.

Let's use the above procedure to calculate the early event times for our first example (Figure 12–2). For convenience, denote the early event time for event j by E_j and the duration of the activity connecting Nodes i and j by d_{ij}. Then we have the following:

---

[3] The paths are: (1) Node 1 to Node 3 to Node 4; (2) Node 1 to Node 2 to Node 4; (3) Node 1 to Node 2 to Node 3 to Node 4.

For Event 1:

$$E_1 = 0 \text{ (starting time for project)} \qquad (12\text{–}1)$$

For event 2:

$$E_2 = E_1 + d_{12} = 0 + 3 = 3 \qquad (12\text{–}2)$$

For event 3:

$$\begin{aligned}
E_3 &= \max \{E_1 + d_{13}, E_2 + d_{23}\} \\
&= \max \{0 + 2, 3 + 0\} = 3
\end{aligned} \qquad (12\text{–}3)$$

For Event 4:

$$\begin{aligned}
E_4 &= \max \{E_2 + d_{24}, E_3 + d_{34}\} \\
&= \max \{3 + 2, 3 + 3\} = 6.
\end{aligned} \qquad (12\text{–}4)$$

Recall that Node 4 denotes the event "project finished." We now know that the earliest possible completion time for the project is six days.

From the early event times we can readily determine the "earliest start" and "earliest finish" times for all the project activities. The early event time for a given event is also the earliest possible starting time for all activities emanating from that event. The earliest possible finishing times for these activities are given by adding the corresponding activity duration times to the relevant early event time. (Actually, these earliest finish times were computed in computing the early event times.)

If we let ES_{ij} denote the earliest start time for the activity connecting Nodes i and j and EF_{ij} be the corresponding earliest finishing time, then we have

$$ES_{ij} = E_i \qquad (12\text{–}5)$$

and

$$EF_{ij} = E_i + d_{ij} \qquad (12\text{–}6)$$

for all node pairs (i, j) connected by activities in the network.

Thus, we see that the earliest start times for the activities A_1, A_2, D_1, A_3, and A_4 are 0, 0, 3, 3, and 3, respectively. The earliest finish times for these activities are 2, 3, 3, 5, and 6, respectively.

The earliest start and finish times for all the activities provide management with useful information concerning planning and coordinating the flow of resources throughout the project.

12.4. LATE EVENT TIMES

In addition to the early event times, it is useful to know the latest event times for all events in a network. The latest event time for a given event is defined to be the latest possible time the event could occur without delaying the project beyond its target date. Typically the target date is taken to be the earliest possible completion time for the project.

These latest event times are computed by starting with the last event (project finished) and working sequentially toward Node 1 until all events have been treated. For a given event, the latest event time is found by subtracting from the latest time for each immediately following event the duration times of the connecting activities. The smallest of the resulting numbers is the desired result. Denoting by L_j the latest time for event j, we then have

$$L_4 = E_4 = 6 \tag{12-7}$$
$$L_3 = L_4 - d_{34} = 6 - 3 = 3 \tag{12-8}$$
$$L_2 = \min \{L_3 - d_{23}, L_4 - d_{24}\}$$
$$= \min \{3 - 0, 6 - 2\} = 3 \tag{12-9}$$
$$L_1 = \min \{L_2 - d_{12}, L_3 - d_{13}\}$$
$$= \min \{3 - 3, 3 - 2\} = 0. \tag{12-10}$$

For this simple example under consideration, these latest event times happen to be identical to the early event times we found previously. In general this will not be the case. More commonly, some but not all of the corresponding early and latest event times will be identical.

From the latest event times, we can easily compute latest start (LS_{ij}) and latest finish (LF_{ij}) times for all the activities in a network. The latest start time for an activity is defined to be the latest possible time the activity could begin without causing a delay in the project beyond its current target completion date. The latest finish time is similarly defined.

Since an event denotes the completion of one or more activities (except for event number one) the latest finish times for all project activities are simply given by the appropriate latest event times. The latest starting times for the activities are given by subtracting from the latest event times the appropriate activity duration times. That is

$$LF_{ij} = L_j \tag{12-11}$$

and

$$LS_{ij} = L_j - d_{ij} \tag{12-12}$$

for all node pairs (i, j) connected by activities in the network. Continuing with our small example we have that the latest finish times for the activities A_1, A_2, D_1, A_3, and A_4 are 3, 3, 3, 6, and 6, respectively. The latest starting times for these activities are 1, 0, 3, 4, and 3, respectively.

As with the early start and finish times, the late start and finish times for the various activities are of considerable aid to management. For instance, our target date for project completion for our example is six days. That is, if all events occur as early as possible, event number four (project finished) will occur in six days. We have some discretion, however, over when certain activities can be undertaken without changing the project completion time. Consider activity A_1, for instance. We found that the early start time for A_1 was at time zero, while the latest possible start time (if the project is to stay on schedule) is at time one. Thus we have some flexibility concerning the starting time for activity A_1. For activity A_2, however, we found that both the earliest and latest start times were at time zero. Thus we have no choice concerning the beginning time for activity A_2. If we do not start A_2 at time zero, the project will not be completed in six days!

12.5. ACTIVITY SLACK

The "slack" associated with an activity is the amount by which the starting (or finishing) time for the activity could slip without causing a delay in the project completion time. Above, we found that the slack for activity A_1 was one day but that activity A_2 had zero slack. In general the slack for an activity is given by the difference between its earliest and latest starting time. This, in turn, is identically equal to the difference between the earliest and latest finishing times.

12.6. CRITICAL PATH

In general a network diagram contains many paths from the beginning to the ending node. All paths must be traversed before the project can be completed. If we take the target date to be the earliest possible completion date for the project, there will exist at least one path through the network consisting entirely of activities with zero slack.[4] Such a path is called a "critical path."[5] If any activity on the critical path is delayed, the project completion time will be delayed.

Figure 12–5 shows a summary of the calculations made concerning the example of Figure 12–2. Note that the path consisting of activities A_2, D_1, and A_4 is the critical path for the network. If any of these activities is delayed, the project will not be completed on schedule.[6] At the same time, if the duration times for any of these activities can be reduced, it may be possible to hasten the project completion date.

Often the information summarized in Figure 12–5 is also put on the network diagram for convenient reference. Moreover, the critical path throughout the diagram is often singled out by using broader or different colored arrows. Other schemes have also been used. Regardless of how the critical path is denoted, its meaning is the same. The critical path identifies the bottleneck activities—those activities that must be monitored most closely if the project is to be completed on schedule.

---

[4] If the target date is later than the earliest possible completion date, the critical path will consist of activities with the smallest slack values.

[5] All events on the critical path will also have zero slack, where "event slack" is defined to be the difference between the earliest and latest event times.

[6] Of course, D_1 is a dummy activity and cannot really be delayed. But A_2 and A_4 could be delayed by weather or for many other reasons.

FIGURE 12–5

Summary of Calculations for Example Project (activities with zero slack are "critical" activities)

Activity	ES_{ij}	EF_{ij}	LS_{ij}	LF_{ij}	Slack
A_1 (1, 3)......................	0	2	1	3	1
A_2 (1, 2)......................	0	3	0	3	0
D_1 (2, 3)......................	3	3	3	3	0
A_3 (2, 4)......................	3	5	4	6	1
A_4 (3, 4)......................	3	6	3	6	0

Note that the activities are denoted by beginning and ending node as well as their original designation.

12.7. CRASHING ACTIVITIES

What if the scheduled project completion time is larger than desired? The only way it can be reduced is to shorten one or more activities. "Crashing" refers to reducing the duration time of an activity. This can be accomplished by shifting resources from other activities or by obtaining additional resources and, thus, adding to the cost of the project. Normally we think of crashing one or more activities on the critical path. Crashing noncritical activities could not help reduce the project completion date since these activities already have positive slack.

When the critical path contains many activities, it may not be obvious at all which activities should be crashed. Often crashing is available only in discrete amounts and at considerable cost. Candidate activities should be compared on the basis of their crashing cost as well as the amount by which they reduce project completion time. Moreover, crashing decisions should not be made without assessing their potential impact on the various noncritical paths in the network. If the length of the critical path is reduced enough, some other path may become critical. Thus, part of the cost incurred to reduce the length of the critical path may be wasted.

To illustrate the idea of crashing, return to the network of Figure 12–2. Recall that the current project completion date is six days from time zero, and that the activities on the critical path are A_2, D_1, and A_4. Nothing can be done about D_1, since it is a dummy activity. Suppose it is possible to crash A_4 from three to two days at a certain cost and A_2 from three days to one at a considerably higher cost. Further assume that not both activities can be crashed.

If A_4 is crashed, the project time is reduced from six to five days and the current critical path remains critical, although the path consisting of A_2 and A_3 also becomes a critical path. On the other hand, if A_2 is crashed and reduced by two days, the project completion time is reduced only by one day since the path consisting of A_1 and A_4 becomes the critical path with a length of five days.

In either case, the project completion time is reduced from six to five days. Thus, we should choose to crash A_4 because of cost considerations.

12.8. TIME-COST TRADE-OFFS

The above discussion dealt with time-cost trade-offs in an after-the-fact sense. Once the critical path had been determined, crashing was considered to reduce the project completion to a more satisfactory level.

An alternative to this would be to consider from the outset the duration times for all activities to be variable (within limits). Over these limits we can approximate each activity cost by a linear cost function. Then, given a pre-specified project completion date, we can use linear programming to compute the minimum-cost way to meet the target date. Note that since activity duration times are variable, the earliest event times will also be variable.

To build the LP model, define

t_{ij} = Duration time of the activity connecting nodes i and j. (a decision variable).

T_j = Earliest time for event j (a decision variable).

L_{ij}, U_{ij} = Lower and upper bounds, respectively, on the duration of activity (i, j).

c_{ij} = Unit variable cost associated with activity (i, j). (Reduction in activity cost per unit increase in activity time.)

F_{ij} = Cost axis intercept of linear cost function for activity (i, j).

The cost associated with a given activity (i, j) can then be represented by

$$\text{Cost}_{ij} = F_{ij} - c_{ij} t_{ij} \qquad (12\text{–}13)$$

as depicted in Figure 12–6. Over the range from L_{ij} to U_{ij} this is usually a reasonable cost model.[7] In practice, the constants c_{ij} and F_{ij} can be estimated as follows. Obtain estimates for the activity cost associated with the smallest and largest activity times under consideration for a given activity. Denote these values by c_L and c_U, respectively. From c_L and c_U we can easily determine c_{ij} and F_{ij} since our cost function is a straight line.

---

[7] In certain situations, other functional forms might better represent activity cost than do the linear equations shown here. Moreover, in some cases the t_{ij} variables might be required to be discrete. The linear programming formulation shown here, however, is often a reasonable approximation.

FIGURE 12-6

Activity Cost Approximated by a Linear Function of Activity Duration Time

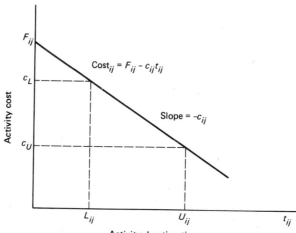

Notation: t_{ij} = Activity duration time.
U_{ij} = Upper bound on activity time.
L_{ij} = Lower bound on activity time.
c_{ij} = *Reduction* in activity cost per unit *increase* in activity time.
F_{ij} = Cost axis intercept.
c_L = Activity cost when $t_{ij} = L_{ij}$.
c_U = Activity cost when $t_{ij} = U_{ij}$.

The constant c_{ij} (the negative of the slope) is given by

$$c_{ij} = (c_L - c_U)/(U_{ij} - L_{ij}). \tag{12–14}$$

Having this value, F_{ij} is given by (12–13) to be

$$F_{ij} = c_L + c_{ij}L_{ij}. \tag{12–15}$$

Given these definitions, the linear programming model is:

Minimize cost

$$\sum_{(i,j)} (F_{ij} - c_{ij}t_{ij}) = \sum_{(i,j)} F_{ij} - \sum_{(i,j)} c_{ij}t_{ij} \tag{12–16}$$

subject to

$$T_i + t_{ij} \le T_j \tag{12–17}$$
$$T_n \le \text{Target} \tag{12–18}$$
$$0 \le L_{ij} \le t_{ij} \le U_{ij} \tag{12–19}$$

plus nonnegativity conditions on the T_j. The first summation in the objective function is a constant and can be dropped from the optimization problem. Note that the summation in the objective function as well as all the constraints are intended for all meaningful pairs (i, j) in the network. Furthermore, note how the constraints denoted by (12–17) force the T_j to assume the appropriate early event times. Finally, note that (12–18) plays the role of forcing the project to be completed on or before the target date. Solving the model several times for various values for the target date would yield considerable insight into the issue of time-cost trade-offs.

12.9. UNCERTAIN ACTIVITY TIMES

So far we have assumed that activity duration times were deterministic—that either they were known with certainty or they were LP decision variables to be chosen by management. For many projects, the duration times for most (or all) activities are uncertain and usually viewed as being probabilistic rather than deterministic. This is particularly true for large, first-time projects for which past experience is only a crude guide because nothing very similar has been undertaken before.

When duration times are uncertain, we make the same types of calculations as we did with the certainty case (early and late event times, activity start and end times, critical path, etc.). Here these calculations are based on the "expected" duration time for each activity. Moreover, we calculate the variance of each activity duration time and use it to determine the variance of the length (that is, time) of the expected critical path. Then in addition to having an estimate of when the project is expected to be completed, we have an estimate of the variance associated with this figure. Therefore, we can then compute the probability that the project will be completed by any specified date. This additional information is extremely useful to management.

Common practice is to assume that the activity duration times may be characterized by Beta distributions and that the duration times for different events are independent.[8] For each activity we will require three time estimates denoted by a, m, and b:

- a: Optimistic estimate—not likely but possible if everything goes well.
- m: Most likely estimate—the mode of the distribution.
- b: Pessimistic estimate—not likely but possible if everything goes wrong.

From these estimates the mean and variance of the time for each activity can be computed using the equations

---

[8] The Beta distribution assumption is not essential, however, in that the expressions for mean and variance can be derived using intuitive arguments without reference to any distribution.

$$\mu = \frac{1}{6}(a + 4m + b) \tag{12-20}$$

$$\sigma^2 = \left(\frac{b - a}{6}\right)^2. \tag{12-21}$$

Using these values, the critical path and its variance can readily be computed. Since the activities are assumed to be independent, the variance associated with the critical path is given by the sum of the variances of the activities comprising the critical path. The probability of completing the project by some given date can then be computed using a "normal" probability table. The use of a normal distribution to describe the project completion time follows from the Central Limit Theorem. Since the project completion time is the sum of several independent random variables, it is approximately normal.

To illustrate the calculations, lets consider the example shown in Figure 12-7. The network diagram for this example is shown in Figure

FIGURE 12-7

Data for Example with Uncertain Duration Times

Activity	Immediate Predecessor	Days a	Days m	Days b	μ	σ^2
A_1......................	—	2	3	4	3	0.1111
A_2......................	A_1	1	3	4	2.833	0.2500
A_3......................	A_1	2	3	4	3	0.1111
A_4......................	A_2	2	4	6	4	0.4444
A_5......................	A_3	1	3	5	3	0.4444

12-8. Note that the expected duration times as well as the variances are shown on the activity arcs. Using the expected activity times in our calculations, we see that the earliest time for Event 5 is 9.833 days. The critical path is the path consisting of activities A_1, A_2, and A_4 and the variance associated with this path is $0.1111 + 0.25 + 0.4444 = 0.8055$. Thus, our expectation is that the project will be completed in 9.833 days with a variance of 0.8055.

Suppose we feel that a project length greater than 12 days would be excessive and we want to know the probability that the project will be completed in less than 12 days. Now that we know the mean and variance of the finishing time, we can easily compute the probability. The standard deviation for the finishing time is

$$\sigma = \sqrt{0.8055} = 0.8975 \text{ day.}$$

Thus the standard Z value corresponding to 12 days is

$$Z = \frac{12 - 9.833}{0.8975} \simeq 2.4145.$$

FIGURE 12–8

Network Diagram for Example with Uncertain Activity Times

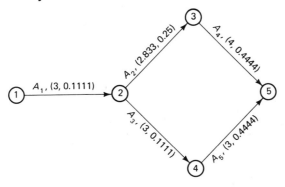

Then from the normal table found in Appendix A, we see that the probability is approximately

$$1.0 - 0.008 = 0.992.$$

Thus, even though the activity times are uncertain, we are virtually certain that the project will be completed within 12 days.

It must be pointed out, however, that the above probability analysis assumes that the critical path remains in fact the limiting path through the network. Because of the random nature of the duration times, some apparently noncritical path may in fact emerge as the real critical path. If this is likely to happen, the approach outlined above may not be attractive because the calculations would have to be made for each candidate path. In such cases it is usually better to use Monte Carlo simulation to determine various statistics and make probability statements about the project completion date.

12.10. SUMMARY

Critical path analysis is useful in several different ways. The development and visual reinforcement of a network diagram enhances one's understanding of the "systems" aspect of the project at hand. The identification of the critical path enables management to focus attention on those activities most likely to influence the project completion date. Thus management is forewarned of bottleneck activities and can be prepared to deal effectively with them. The calculation of slack for each activity enables management to make intelligent decisions on when certain activities should begin. If an activity has zero slack, its beginning time is fixed. If an activity has positive slack, however, management has some freedom in setting the starting date. This flexibility could be used to minimize fluctuations in work schedules and possibly to avoid re-source crises.

When opportunity exists for reducing an activity duration time by applying more resources to the activity, the cost-benefit aspects of crashing should be closely considered. One of the major contributions of critical path analysis is the framework it provides for investigating the advisability of shifting resources among activities. This aids in planning for the flow and better use of resources. In those cases where duration time is totally open to managerial discretion, linear programming can be used to assess minimum-cost duration times that will lead to project completion by some specified date.

Finally, when there is considerable doubt about duration times, the three-estimate approach enables management to plan and control the project even though faced with this uncertainty. The network diagram still provides a framework facilitating planning and controlling. Probability statements about the project completion time can be based on direct calculations or upon Monte Carlo simulation techniques.

EXERCISES

For Problems 12.1, 12.2, 12.3, and 12.4, first construct a network diagram and then complete a table like that shown in Figure 12–5 summarizing your calculations. Clearly identify the critical path in each case.

12.1.

Activity	Immediate Predecessor	Duration (Days)
A_1	—	6
A_2	A_1	8
A_3	A_1	10
A_4	A_3	3
A_5	A_2, A_4	6

12.2.

Activity	Immediate Predecessor	Duration (Days)
A_1	—	12
A_2	—	4
A_3	A_1, A_2	6
A_4	A_2	7
A_5	A_4	8
A_6	A_3, A_5	5

12.3.

Activity	Immediate Predecessor	Duration (Days)
A_1	—	6
A_2	—	8
A_3	—	4
A_4	A_1, A_2	10
A_5	A_1, A_3	3

12.4.

Activity	Immediate Predecessor	Duration (Days)
A_1...................	—	8
A_2...................	—	4
A_3...................	—	3
A_4...................	A_1, A_2	5
A_5...................	A_2, A_3	10
A_6...................	A_1, A_3	4

12.5. Consider again the project described in Problem 12.1. Suppose we have the option to crash any of the activities. The reduced activity times and the corresponding costs are given below:

Activity	Duration time		Direct Cost	
	Regular	Crash	Regular	Crash
A_1.................	6	4	300	400
A_2.................	8	7	200	250
A_3.................	10	8	500	600
A_4.................	3	2	800	950
A_5.................	6	5	500	700

   a. Construct a time-cost trade-off curve for this project. (Enumerate and evaluate the relevant options. Then plot the results.)

   b. Suppose it has been estimated that each day cut off the completion time is valued at $100. What is the optimal time-cost trade-off?

12.6. *a.* Consider the following project where the activity duration times can be approximated by bounded continuous decision variables. Following the development in the chapter (Equations (12–16) through (12–19)) write out in detail the LP model. Use a "Target" date of 15 days.

Activity	Immediate Predecessor	Lower Bound	Upper Bound	Activity Cost Lower Bound	Upper Bound
A_1............	—	4	6	$100	80
A_2............	—	3	7	200	150
A_3............	A_1	5	7	150	140
A_4............	A_2, A_3	4	6	220	150
A_5............	A_1	3	5	300	250

   b. Solve the model and discuss the results.

   c. Test the sensitivity of project cost to various target dates.

12.7. Consider again the project described in Problem 12.6. Suppose management has a budget of $800. Construct an LP model that could be used to determine the activity duration times that minimize project completion time while satisfying the budget constraint.

12.8. Discuss how an LP model of the type discussed in the chapter (Equations (12–16) through (12–19)) could be used to help analyze problems like that of Problem 12.5. Be specific with respect to Problem 12.5.

12.9.   Analyze the house construction project described by Figures 12–3 and 12–4.

12.10.   Consider a multinational firm that is eager to build and operate a manufacturing facility in some new country.

a.   Enumerate a set of likely activities required for this expansion.

b.   Develop a network diagram for your activities.

12.11.   An electronics firm is planning on moving into the pocket calculator market. Since this is a new product area for the firm, there is considerable uncertainty about how long it will take to complete certain activities before the proposed product can become a reality at the retail level. The activities and their estimated times are:

			Times in Months		
		Immediate	*Opti-*	*Most*	*Pessi-*
Activity	*Description*	*Predecessor*	*mistic*	*Likely*	*mistic*
A_1..........	Design circuits	—	2	3	4
A_2..........	Test prototype	A_1	1	3	5
A_3..........	Manufacture for test market	A_2	2	3	5
A_4..........	Develop marketing plan	—	4	5	8
A_5..........	Develop instruction manual	A_2	1	2	3
A_6..........	Advertise	A_2, A_4	2	3	5

How long will it be before the calculator is on the shelf in the test market area? How could this time be shortened?

12.12.   Publishing a textbook is a multi-activity project that can be analyzed using critical path methods. Consider the following similified example:

			Times in Months		
		Immediate	*Opti-*	*Most*	*Pessi-*
Activity	*Description*	*Predecessor*	*mistic*	*Likely*	*mistic*
A_1..........	Write manuscript	—	8	10	20
A_2..........	Review and edit	A_1	4	6	8
A_3..........	Copy edit	A_2	1	2	3
A_4..........	Prepare artwork	A_2	2	3	5
A_5..........	Set galleys	A_3	2	3	4
A_6..........	Check galleys	A_5	1	2	3
A_7..........	Prepare page proofs	A_4, A_6	1	2	3
A_8..........	Check page proof	A_7	1	2	3
A_9..........	Prepare and set index	A_7	1	2	3
A_{10}..........	Print book	A_8, A_9	1	2	3
A_{11}..........	Bind book	A_{10}	1	2	3

Estimate the probability that the book will be on the market within two years of starting to write.

The following three problems concern projects with uncertain activity time. For each problem:

a. Determine the mean and variance of each activity time.
b. Identify the apparent critical path. Comment on how likely it is that some other path will in fact turn out to be critical.
c. Determine the expected project completion time and its variance.
d. Answer the probability question listed with the problem.

12.13.

Activity	Immediate Predecessor	Days		
		a	m	b
A_1................	—	10	12	15
A_2................	—	8	10	15
A_3................	A_1	6	9	13
A_4................	A_2, A_3	8	8	8
A_5................	A_2	12	15	18

What is the probability that the project could be completed within 30 days?

12.14.

Activity	Immediate Predecessor	Days		
		a	m	b
A_1................	—	2	4	7
A_2................	—	4	5	8
A_3................	A_1	1	3	6
A_4................	A_2, A_3	3	5	7
A_5................	A_4	5	7	8
A_6................	A_1	2	4	6

What is the probability that the project will be completed between 15 and 20 days after starting.

12.15.

Activity	Immediate Predecessor	Days		
		a	m	b
A_1................	—	4	6	10
A_2................	—	4	5	7
A_3................	—	6	9	11
A_4................	A_1	2	4	7
A_5................	A_2	5	7	9
A_6................	A_3, A_4, A_5	3	5	6
A_7................	A_1	3	4	7
A_8................	A_3	4	6	10

What is the probability that the project will be completed in less than 20 days?

12.16. Discuss how simulation could be used to study the project described by Problem 12.14. Develop a flow diagram for the simulation.

SUGGESTIONS FOR FURTHER STUDY

Merton, W., "PERT and Planning for Health Programs," *Public Health Reporter*, vol. 81, 1966, pp. 449–54.

Moder, J., and Phillips, C. R., *Project Management with CPM and PERT*. New York: Reinhold, Inc., 1970.

Ringer, L. J., "Statistical Theory for PERT in which Completion Times of Activities are Interdependent," *Management Science*, July 1971.

Robillard, P., and Trahan, M., "The Completion Time of PERT Networks," *Operations Research*, vol. 25, no. 1, January–February 1975, pp. 15–29.

Strenski, J. B., "PERT Charting Public Relations," *Public Relations Journal*, February 1975, pp. 22–23.

Swanson, L. A., and Pazer, H. L., "Implications of the Underlying Assumptions of PERT," *Decision Sciences*, October 1971.

Wiest, J. D., and Levy, F. K., *A Management Guide to PERT/CPM*. 2d ed. Englewood Cliffs, N.J.: Prentice-Hall, 1977.

d7

PART II
Applications

THE PURPOSE of these applications is to present several ways in which quantitative methods have been used in aiding managerial decisions. The cases illustrate some of the difficulties that are encountered in implementation, as well as discuss ways the researchers assisted in implementation of the findings. The quantitative methodologies illustrated range in sophistication from arithmetic to mathematical programming. The purpose of this diversity is to indicate that useful operations research need not necessarily be complicated. It is often true that the simpler methodologies have a higher chance of implementation, and are therefore more useful in the long run. Some of the cases illustrate that *usefulness* may be more important than *optimality*. Sometimes it is said that "the best is the enemy of the good." When the costs of research and implementation are included, what is apparently non-optimal may quickly become optimal or very close to it.

For the seven applications that are included here, the problem being addressed and the techniques of analysis that were used are summarized.

Application 1: A results measurement system for the California Public Employment Service. Problem: Devise a scheme for measuring the output of a public service organization. Techniques used: arithmetic, the Delphi method, common sense, managerial skill. An important part of this case is the involvement of the managers in practically all phases of the research.

Application 2: An application of decision analysis. Problem: Decide whether to build a new production facility for producing a chemical product. Techniques used: probability assessment, sensitivity studies, decision analysis, value of information, decision trees. May be used following Chapter 3.

Application 3: A linear programming model to evaluate the economics of water use and wastewater treatment in ammonia production. Problem: Evaluate the economic and environmental impact of measures intended to control water usage and quality in ammonia production. Technique used: Linear programming. May be used following Chapter 6.

Application 4: Mathematical programming and the location of fire companies for the Denver fire department. Problem: Where should fire stations be located? Techniques used: Integer programming, goal programming, data capture, regression analysis. An important part of the discussion deals with the merger of judgment and optimization results. May be used following Chapter 8.

Application 5: A Markov model of professional flows in a CPA firm. Problem: Describe staff flows between the various levels within a CPA firm, in order to evaluate implication of personnel policies. Technique used: Markov analysis. May be used following Chapter 9.

Application 6: A waiting-line integer programming approach to scheduling police patrol cars. Problem: Generate a methodology for scheduling police patrol cars, so that there is a reasonable correspondence between the number of cars on duty and the demands for service placed upon those cars, while paying attention to constraints such as start time and meal times. Techniques used: Steady-state and dynamic waiting-line analysis, integer programming, simulation. Of particular importance is the way a simple model is assumed, even though it is obviously wrong; then the usefulness of the simple approach is validated by a more thorough model. This simple model also provides input data to other models. May be used following Chapter 10.

Application 7: A simulation of a fire alarm system. Problem: As the alarm rate increases, what is the effect upon the time required to dispatch fire trucks? Technique used: simulation. May be used following Chapter 11.

Application 1

A Results Measurement System for the California Public Employment Service*

THE READER OF THIS TEXT might have reached the opinion that operations research is almost completely involved with theoretical concepts that can easily be quantified and that are then immediately implemented in the organization for which they were developed. Nothing is further from the truth! The application of operations research in economic-based organizations involves applications from the very simple to the very complex, dealing with many organizational problems that affect people's jobs and livelihood.

There need not be an automatic relationship between the mathematical complexity of an application and the importance of that application in the organization. This first case study is designed to illustrate these points:

1. A mathematically simple application that has had a substantial effect upon the organization.
2. Some methods of data collection that were used in the application.
3. The importance of project involvement for those who will be affected by the application of operations research.

The Employment Development Department (EDD) of the state of California administers the public employment service (ES) within

---

* This case discussion was developed from Gene L. Gallagher, "A Results Measurement System for the California Public Employment Service," presented to the Northwest Chapter, The Institute of Management Sciences, May 1975. Mr. Gallagher developed this application with the Operations Research Group, Employment Development Department, State of California.

California. The major objective of the ES is to provide job placement and related employment services to the unemployed and under-employed. The final delivery of these employment services is performed by more than 100 local field offices in major towns and cities of the state.

Historically the output of each field office was measured by counting the number of job placements that office produced. But as additional emphasis was placed upon Special Applicant Groups (SAG), such as veterans, minorities, unemployment insurance claimants, handicapped, etc., it was recognized that this historical method of counting the number of placements as the output measure was not sufficient. In order to broaden the output measure, an operations research group was assigned to develop what was to be called a Balanced Placement Formula (BPF), which would state the contributions toward the overall objectives of the employment service for each of three factors:

Quantity, or the number of placements made by the field office
Quality, or how long the job placement was expected to last
Priority, or recognizing additional credit that should be given for placements of job applicants belonging to the Special Applicant Groups

The development of this balanced placement formula system was constrained by two very important factors:

1.   The formula must be simple!
2.   The formula must utilize only existing data sources.

The initial formula for calculating the balanced placement score was stated in terms of a work sheet, similar to Figure A1–1. (This work sheet

FIGURE A1–1

Original BPF Worksheet

Placement Category	(1) Placements	(2) Weighting Value	(3) Score (1) × (2)
Total	X_0	1.0	
Veterans	X_1	a_1	
Poor	X_2	a_2	
Minorities	X_3	a_3	
U.I. Claimants	X_4	a_4	
Handicapped	X_5	a_5	
4–150 Days	X_6	a_6	
Permanent	X_7	a_7	

Total Balanced Placement Score _____

is a modification of a somewhat more extensive work sheet that was actually used initially.) In this work sheet, the field office needed to provide only the values for the X's, which represented the total number of placements for the time period, the number of placements for each special applicant group, and the number of placements in the two categories for job duration. The coefficients, or weighting values, a_1 through a_7, were the additional credit that each placement was to be given if it fell into one of the special applicant groups or one of the longer job durations. The procedure for determining the values of these coefficients will be discussed later.

The balanced placement formula could have been communicated to the users in the form:

$$\text{BP Score} = X_0 + \sum_{j=1}^{7} a_j X_j$$

where

$X_0 =$ Total number of placements
$X_1 =$ Number of veteran placements
$X_2 =$ Number of poor placements
$X_3 =$ Number of minority placements
$X_4 =$ Number of unemployment insurance claimant placements
$X_5 =$ Number of handicapped placements
$X_6 =$ Number of 4–150 day placements
$X_7 =$ Number of permanent placements
$a_j =$ Weighting factor for category j.

But it is worthwhile to ask whether the work sheet of Figure A1–1 or the formula shown above is more understandable to the users of balanced placement output measurement system!

After the general form of the measurement system had been established, it was decided to have a demonstration test using ten representative field offices. But before a demonstration could be accomplished, it was necessary to find usable values for the coefficients a_j, which represent the additional credit to be given for each special placement category. These values were determined by applying the Delphi technique for obtaining group consensus opinions. The Delphi technique is a questionnaire procedure that is designed to give participants the benefit of sharing ideas and beliefs, but at the same time avoiding the dominance of a discussion group by a small number of "strong" personalities.[1] This questionnaire procedure was used with all field office managers for two reasons:

---

[1] For a discussion of the Delphi Method, see Olaf Helmer, *Social Technology*, New York: Basic Books, Inc., 1966, pp. 108; and Andre L. Delbeca, Andrew H. Van de Ven, and David H. Gutafson, *Group Techniques for Program Planning*, Glenview, Ill.: Scott, Foresman and Company, 1975.

1. The eventual implementation of this system would have a substantial influence on field office operations.

2. The administrators of the department had a diverse range of opinions as to what the coefficient values should be.

Perhaps a third and unstated reason for using this "grass roots" technique for coefficient evaluation is to give the field office managers a sense of genuine involvement and participation in the project. This involvement and participation is very important in final implementation of operations research projects.

An explanation of the BPF and a questionnaire were sent to each field office manager. Filling out the questionnaire, each manager indicated his or her feelings about the correct value of each coefficient. After the questionnaires were returned, the results were compiled to see if a consensus was reached. Analysis of the data revealed that no consensus had been reached. For example, nearly 40 percent of the respondents indicated that the value of a_3 should be between 0 and 0.2, about the same number between 0.3 and 0.7, with the remainder of the responses indicating values greater than 0.7. This information for all coefficients was coherently summarized, and returned to the respondents with a second questionnaire. The respondents to the second questionnaire were able to ascertain whether their initial responses were reasonable after looking at the group view, or if they were substantially out of line. The second questionnaire showed a closer consensus. Looking at the coefficient for minorities, as an example, a closer consensus had been reached. The results of the first and second questionnaire are shown in Figure A1–2.

The procedure could have been repeated, hoping for closer consensus. However, the analyst made the decision that there was a high enough degree of consensus; the median value for each coefficient from the second questionnaire was used as the value for the a's in the Balanced Placement Formula. If this decision is not satisfactory, that fact should be revealed by a lack of acceptance of the BPF among its users.

At this point there is sufficient information available for the demonstration test using ten field offices. In addition to the BPF, other output measures were to be observed during the tests, so that judgments could be made as to whether field offices maintain balance in their efforts while using the Balanced Placement Formula. Among these other output measures were the total number of placements (X_0 in the formula given above) and the total number of individuals placed, which may be less than the total number of placements because one person may be placed several times. The output measures were converted to productivity measures by dividing the output measures by the input measure, which was the total number of staff members for the particular office.

FIGURE A1–2

Results of Questionnaire—Minorities

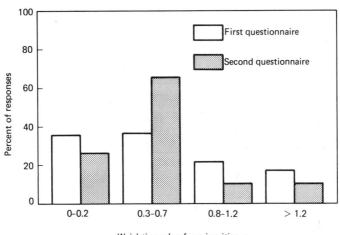

Weighting value for minorities, a_3

Prior to and during the test, substantial contact between the operations research group and the field offices was necessary. An orientation package was prepared for each office manager. Monthly reports were provided so that each office could compare its own performance with both its region and the state. A monthly visit was made by the project team to the test field offices. Additionally, interim and final meetings of the test office managers were held.

Initially, the test office managers had difficulty accepting and implementing the balanced placement formula. But at the end of the test they unanimously endorsed BPF as an equitable method of measuring overall placement performance. From a qualitative standpoint, these results were observed from the tests:

There was a general consensus that BPF is more equitable than strict numerical count in measuring field office effectiveness.

The BPF created increased awareness of overall placement objectives.

The BPF simplified the multiple placement priorities. Prior to BPF, it was necessary for a manager to look at many output measures to judge performance. BPF provided a unified, simplified measure.

From a quantitative standpoint, the test group improved its performance over the base period substantially more than the control group, which comprised the remaining field offices in the state. This improvement is shown in Figure A1–3. The opponents of BPF had maintained that test offices might increase their BPF score but decrease the total

FIGURE A1–3

Change from Base to Test Period

	Placements per Staff Member	BPF Score per Staff Member
Control group.............	+20%	+31%
Test group...............	+28%	+60%

number of placements. In fact, the test offices experienced a greater increase in total placements per staff member than the control group!

The result of the test was that BPF was recommended for state-wide implementation. The version that was recommended for implementation was slightly different in that three additional special applicant groups

FIGURE A1–4
Final BPF

Category	Performance Item	(1) Number Accomplished	(2) Weight	(1) × (2) Score
Total	*Placement Transactions*		1.0	
Special Applicant Groups	Individuals Placed:			
	Veteran		0.5	
	Viet-Vet		0.3	
	Minority		0.5	
	Poor		0.5	
	Handicapped		1.0	
	UI claimant		0.2	
	Youth		0.3	
	Older worker		0.3	
Job Duration	4–150 days		0.2	
	Permanent		0.4	
Employment Assistance	Individuals placed after job development attempts		1.0	
			Total score	_____

were included, primarily because of the existence of data that had not been available at the beginning of the test. Another modification was that credit was given for special applicant group and job duration only once for an individual during a fiscal year; under the original design, an applicant belonging to several special groups could receive the extra credits for as many jobs as that person was placed in during the year. Finally, the coefficient values were changed slightly to account for anticipated federal emphasis for various employment situations. Figure A1–4 shows the final work sheet that was used for computing the balanced placement formula. As a part of the BPF implementation, regular reports are sent to each field office to permit each field office manager to compare the performance of that office with the region and with the state. Auxiliary tables are also provided giving detailed information on job duration, special applicant group placement, and other factors. As of this writing, the implementation is called an "Interim Decision," suggesting that further modifications will be made as additional experience is gained with the BPF. But in spite of this "go slow" implementation, the BPF is being used as the performance measure in a performance incentive system for allocating staff among the several regions in the state of California.

Application 2

An Application of Decision Analysis

THE EXAMPLES of decision theory in the chapters of this text have dealt with quite small problems. In every case, the decision problem could be represented in either a payoff table or a decision tree, either of which could easily fit within one page. However, decision analysis is not necessarily limited to such small problems. In the words of Ramon Zamora,[1]

> Decision analysis is an emerging discipline that combines the philosophy, theory, methodology, and professional practice necessary to formalize the analysis of important decisions. It is the latest step in a sequence of quantitative advances in the operations research/management science field. Specifically, decision analysis is the result of combining the fields of systems analysis and statistical decision theory. Systems analysis captures the interactions and dynamic behavior of complex situations. Statistical decision theory deals with logical decisions in simple, uncertain situations. The conscious blending of these concepts gives a methodology for analyzing decision in complex, dynamic, and uncertain situations.

Because decision analysis typically deals with decisions that are strategically important to a firm, specific applications are seldom published in their original form. This case study will demonstrate the analysis of a decision in simplified form. All of the computations are original for this text presentation; the scenario is simplified from an actual decision analysis application performed by the Stanford Research In-

---

[1] Ramon M. Zamora, "Recent Applications of Decision Analysis," Stanford Research Institute, Menlo Park, Calif., October 1972.

stitute. A disguised version of the actual application is presented in Zamora's publication, cited in Footnote 1.

THE CASE STUDY

The decision that is being analyzed is whether to build a production facility and produce a chemical product called "X-27." This particular production process is a capital-intensive operation, with relatively small labor inputs required. There are many uncertainties in the situation. The price at which the product can be sold, the cost of obtaining the raw materials, future price changes both for raw materials and for X-27, labor costs, and labor productivity, are all uncertain. In spite of these uncertainties, the firm is interested in pursuing the opportunity to build the new production facility.

One way of performing a decision analysis is to divide the effort into three phases: a deterministic phase, a probabilistic phase, and an information phase.[2] For the X-27 decision, these three phases will be explored.

The Deterministic Phase

The first phase in a decision analysis is to determine the relationships among variables of concern in the problem. Uncertainty is not considered in this phase of the analysis. For the X-27 decision, the problem is structured as a discounted cash flow problem. A "best guess" (called the base case) is made about each of the inputs required to calculate the cash flow for a future year, if the production process is constructed. By knowing the price of each of the inputs, the market price of the output, the amount of output, and the rate of change of each of these variables from one year to the next, the future cash flow in any year may be calculated. By knowing the cost of the production facility, the life of the production process, and the discount rate, the net present value of the decision to build the new production process can be calculated.

At this point, the primary usefulness of the deterministic model is to conduct a sensitivity analysis on the uncertain quantities that are in the model. The purpose of the sensitivity analysis is to determine which variables are important in determining the desirability of the investment, and which variables are relatively unimportant. To answer this question, a "best case" and a "worst case" value are assigned to each variable. The sensitivity study is performed, one variable at a time, in the follow-

---

[2] Ronald A. Howard, "The Foundations of Decision Analysis," *I.E.E.E. Transactions on Systems Science and Cybernetics*, vol. SSC-4, no. 3, September 1968.

FIGURE A2–1

Variables Considered in the X–27 Cash Flow Model

Variable	"Best Guess" (base case)
Product/process life	10 years
Market price of X-27	$10/lb.
Cost of raw materials	$2/lb. of X-27
Labor cost	$17/hr.
Labor productivity	10 lb. of X-27/hr.
Cost of X-27 production facility	$4,000,000
First year production of X-27	80,000 lb.
Annual change in X-27 market price	+4%
Annual change in raw material cost	+5%
Annual change in labor cost per hour	+6%
Annual change in labor productivity	+1%
Annual change in output of X-27	+3%

ing manner: All variables are set at their base case values, shown in Figure A2–1. The one variable being studied is set first at its worst value, and the deterministic cash flow model is used to calculate the present value of building the X-27 facility. Then this variable under study is set to its best value, while all other variables remain at their base case values. The net present value is then calculated, using the deterministic model. This procedure is repeated for each of the uncertain variables. By finding the difference between the net present value, using the best case and worst case, a measure of the importance of knowing the exact value of each variable is obtained. In Figure A2–2 the results of this deterministic sensitivity analysis of each of the variables are shown. The variables are ranked according to the difference in net present value from the best to worst case for each variable.

From the listing in Figure A2–2, the next step is to determine the *crucial variables*. The crucial variables are those variables that have the most effect upon the profitability of the decision to build the X-27 facility. In Figure A2–2 the variables at the top of the list are most influential, while the variables at the bottom of the list have the least effect. It was decided that the first seven variables should be considered crucial. In each case, the change in net present value from the worst case to the best case exceeds $500,000. Furthermore, the noncrucial variables, when each is at its worst case individually, do not cause a negative net present value for the decision to build the X-27 facility.

The Probabilistic Phase

The deterministic phase has resulted in a net present value cash flow model to calculate the net present value for any set of values for the variables. In addition, the deterministic phase has identified seven vari-

FIGURE A2–2

Results of Deterministic Sensitivity Analysis

				Net Present Value ($000)		
Variable	Base Case	Worst Case	Best Case	Worst Case	Best Case	Difference
1. Annual change in X-27 market price........	+4%	−3%	+9%	−1,354	2,042	3,396
2. Product/process life........	10 yrs.	8 yrs.	17 yrs.	−388	2,691	3,079
3. First year production of X-27........	80,000 lb.	60,000 lb.	95,000	−717	1,198	1,915
4. Market price of X-27........	$10/lb.	$9/lb.	$11/lb.	−335	1,089	1,424
5. Cost of X-27 production facility........	$4,000,000	$4,800,000	$3,700,000	−423	677	1,100
6. Annual change in X-27 output........	+3%	+1%	+6%	35	960	925
7. Labor productivity........	10 lb./hr.	7 lb./hr.	12.5 lb./hr.	−162	629	791
8. Cost of raw materials........	2 lb. of X-27	$2.40/lb.	$1.80/lb.	80	526	446
9. Labor cost........	$17/hr.	$21/hr.	$15/hr.	81	525	444
10. Annual change in raw material cost........	+5%	+9%	+3%	104	494	390
11. Annual change in labor cost per hour........	+6%	+9%	+5%	210	428	218
12. Annual change in labor productivity........	+1%	0	+3%	321	478	157

ables as crucial variables; these crucial variables will be further considered in the probabilistic phase. For each of the crucial variables, it is
necessary to assess the probability distribution for the values that the
variable might attain. Since each of the variables can take on any value
between the worst and best cases already identified in the deterministic
phase, a continuous probability distribution, such as shown in Figure
A2–3, is developed, using a probability assessment technique. It is necessary, for computational purposes, to break the continuous distribution
into a small number of discrete steps. This approximate discrete distribution is also shown in Figure A2–3. Similar procedures are followed for
each of the crucial variables. The resulting three-step discrete distributions are shown in Figure A2–4.

At this point, the decision to build the production facility can be
viewed as a decision tree with 3^7, or 2,187, end points, since each crucial
variable has three values. The decision problem has one additional end
point, a net present value of $0 if the facility is not built. For each of
the 2,187 points resulting from a decision to build the plant, the deterministic model can be used to calculate the present value of the cash
flow for that set of values of the crucial variables, while all other variables are set at their base-case values. The probability for each of the

FIGURE A2–3

Probability Distribution for First-Year Output

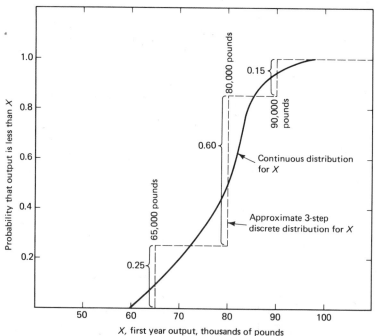

X, first year output, thousands of pounds

FIGURE A2–4

Probabilities For Crucial Variables

Variable	Values	Probabilities
1. Annual change in X-27 market price................	−2%	0.2
	+4%	0.6
	+7%	0.2
2. Product/process life............................	9	0.2
	11	0.7
	15	0.1
3. First year production of X-27......................	65,000	0.25
	80,000	0.60
	90,000	0.15
4. Market price of X-27.............................	$ 9.20	0.25
	10.00	0.50
	10.80	0.25
5. Cost of X-27 production facility....................	$3,800,000	0.1
	4,000,000	0.8
	4,600,000	0.1
6. Annual change in X-27 output.....................	+2%	0.3
	+3%	0.4
	+5%	0.3
7. Labor productivity..............................	8.5	0.25
	9.5	0.6
	11.0	0.15

end points can easily be calculated by multiplying the probabilities for the individual values for a particular set of values. These 2,187 cases also can be used to find what is called a *profit lottery,* a probability distribution for the net present value that will result if the decision is made to build the X-27 facility. This lottery is shown in Figure A2–5. The worst case is a present value of −$2.9 million. The best case is a net present value of +$8.3 million. From the profit lottery, it is apparent that the probability is approximately 40 percent that the net present value will be negative and approximately 60 percent that it will be positive. There are about equal chances that the net present value will be above or below $4,000,000. Other probability statements can be made from the profit lottery diagram. The expected value of the lottery is $418,000. If the decision maker is willing to use expected net present value as the decision criterion, the current information indicates that the plant should be built. If expected net present value is not the criterion desired by the decision maker, risk preference analysis may be used in place of expected monetary value. For the rest of this discussion, it will be assumed that expected net present value is the criterion desired by the decision maker.

The final step in the probabilistic phase is a probabilistic sensitivity analysis. This sensitivity analysis answers the question, "How important

FIGURE A2–5

Profit Lottery if X-27 Facility is Constructed

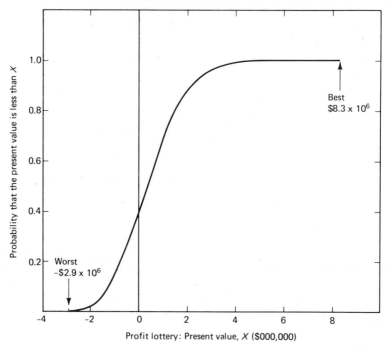

Profit lottery: Present value, *X* ($000,000)

is the value of a particular crucial variable when all other crucial variables are permitted to vary probabilistically?"

As an example of probabilistic sensitivity, consider the crucial variable, first-year production of X-27. When this first-year production is 65,000 lbs., only 729 of the 2,187 end points in the tree need be looked

FIGURE A2–6

Partial Decision Tree

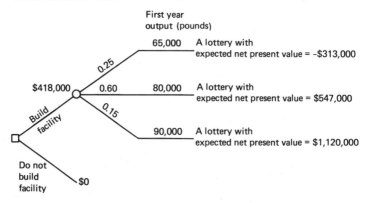

at. These 729 end points all have 65,000 lbs. first-year output. The profit lottery for these 729 end points has an expected net present value of $-\$313,000$. The partial decision tree is shown in Figure A2–6.

The Informational Phase

The probabilistic sensitivity analyses conducted in the probabilistic phase are primarily designed to aid in answering the question of whether additional information should be obtained before the decision is made to build the X-27 facility. Information from Figure A2–6, showing the probabilistic sensitivity of first-year output, can also be represented in the payoff table of Figure A2–7. The calculations alongside the payoff

FIGURE A2–7

Calculation of EVPI

	Profit, given Output		
First-Year Output	*Build*	*Don't Build*	*Probability*
65,000..............	$-\$ \ 313,000$	0*	0.25
80,000..............	547,000*	0	0.60
90,000..............	1,120,000*	0	0.15

Without information about output,
$$EMV^* = 0.25(-\$313,000) + 0.60(\$547,000) + 0.15(\$1,120,000)$$
$$= \$418,000.$$
With information,
$$EPC = 0.25(0) + 0.60(\$547,000) + 0.15(\$1,120,000) = \$496,000.$$
$$EVPI = EPC - EMV^* = \$78,000.$$

table show that the expected value of perfect information for first-year output is $78,000. There are three other variables for which it is conceivable that additional information could be obtained. Knowing the first-year market price of X-27 has an expected value of perfect information of $45,000. The cost of the production facilities has a perfect information value of $14,000; perfect information on labor productivity has no value. (The other three crucial variables, annual change in market price, product/process life, and the annual change in X-27 output, are of such a nature that it is not feasible to resolve much of the uncertainty existing at this point.)

It is interesting to note that labor productivity is not a variable for which the resolution of uncertainty has economic value, using the three-step discretized probabilities. This illustrates some of the possible differences between deterministic and probabilistic sensitivity studies. In the deterministic sensitivity, labor productivity at its worst value caused the plant not to be built, but when profit lotteries are calculated, labor productivity is not a variable that can change the decision. For any of its three values in the three-step discrete probability distribution for labor productivity, the expected net present value is positive.

The next step in the informational phase of the decision analysis is to compare the expected value of perfect information for the three variables (initial output, market price, and the cost of production facility) with the cost of resolving some of the uncertainty in these variables. Since finding out more about the cost of the production facility would involve substantial engineering and architectural drawings, it would not be possible to resolve that uncertainty for $14,000, which is the expected value of that information. If pilot plant operation could determine initial output of X-27, such a step might be desirable, depending upon its price; EVPI = $78,000 for initial output. Similar discussions could be made for the market price of X-27.

COMMENTS ON THIS CASE STUDY

This case study, though relatively simple, has been intended to illustrate the manner in which relatively complex problems can be broken down and analyzed with the tools of operations research. In the study reported by Zamora, several additional factors were considered. The initial decision was not a simple yes/no decision. Rather, a two-stage expansion into X-27 was possible. In addition, Zamora illustrates the importance the decision makers' time preference (reflected in the discount rate) and risk preference. The concept of sensitivity can be applied to each of these aspects of the decision as well.

Application 3

A Linear Programming Model to Evaluate the Economics of Water Use and Waste Water Treatment in Ammonia Production[*]

THE PAST DECADE has been a period of legislation and demands for legislation to control the use of natural resources. Among these natural resources is the water in streams, rivers, and lakes. But as the demand for controlling water use and prescribing standards for dumping industrial effluent into bodies of water increases, it is important to be able to evaluate the consequences of water quality standards. Will the standards result in serious economic disruptions caused by drastically higher product prices? How can this question be answered other than by intuition?

This case study describes how a linear programming model of an ammonia plant has been used to evaluate the impact of measures to control water use and quality. An optimization model, linear programming, is used to answer questions that are important from a public policy standpoint. The underlying assumption of this application is that firms producing ammonia will act rationally (that is, to maximize profits) when water control measures are adopted. The linear programming model is used to describe what this profit-maximizing behavior might be under proposed control procedures.

Ammonia, the subject of this case study, is an extremely important commodity. Considerably more than half of the ammonia production in the United States is used for fertilizer production. There are also

---

[*] James A. Calloway, "The Economics of Water Use and Wastewater Treatment in Ammonia Production." Unpublished doctoral dissertation, College of Business, University of Houston, 1974.

important industrial applications. The ammonia used for fertilizer has an important effect upon the cost of food, because the cost of fertilizer is an important contribution to the cost of food production.

THE LINEAR PROGRAMMING MODEL OF AN AMMONIA PLANT

The ammonia production model is basically a series of flows. There are flows of river water used for steam, production, and cooling; flows of wastewater that results from the production process; flows of solid wastes removed from the river water; and flows of energy used in the processes. The activities or variables of the model are the components of the production process. These components include:

1. The ammonia plant itself, which combines hydrogen (from natural gas, a "feedstock") and nitrogen (from the air) into ammonia.
2. Various water cooling devices, such as cooling towers of various designs.
3. Demineralizers, which remove minerals from various water flows in the system.
4. A clarifier, which removes solid material from river water and produces sludge for disposal.

Each of these components represents an activity that must be accomplished to produce ammonia. Performing each activity has a cost that is reflected in the objective function coefficient for that activity. Each activity also has inputs and outputs. Figure A3–1 shows a portion of the flows in a simplified diagram of an ammonia plant. For example, consider the clarifier; the amount of clarifier activity is defined as X_1. When $X_1 = 1$, the flow diagram indicates that an input of 1,000 gallons of river water is required, and 970 gallons of clarified water along with 200 pounds of sludge are produced. With the assistance of Figure A3–1, the following constraint equations can be established:

Ammonia production must equal 10,000 tons:

$$X_3 = 10,000. \qquad \text{(A3–1)}$$

River water used by clarifier must equal river water withdrawn:

$$1,000X_1 = 1,000X_{12}. \qquad \text{(A3–2)}$$

Clarified water from clarifier and from ammonia plant must equal the amount of clarified water used by demineralizer:

$$970X_1 + 600X_3 = 1,000X_2. \qquad \text{(A3–3)}$$

Demineralized water produced by demineralizer must equal demineralized water used by ammonia plant:

$$910X_2 = 620X_3. \qquad \text{(A3–4)}$$

FIGURE A3–1

Partial Flow Diagram of Ammonia Production (The numbers alongside the inputs and outputs of each activity represents the amount required or produced at each flow.)

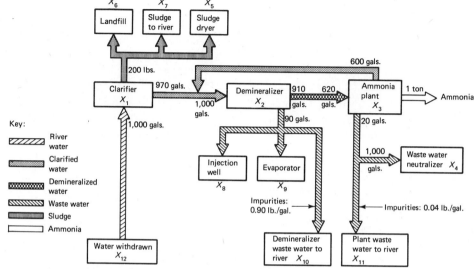

X_1: Amount of water input to clarifier (thousands of gallons).
X_2: Amount of water input to demineralizer (thousands of gallons).
X_3: Amount of ammonia produced (tons).
X_4: Amount of waste water neutralized (thousands of gallons).
X_5: Amount of sludge processed by dryer (pounds).
X_6: Amount of sludge disposed at landfill (pounds).
X_7: Amount of sludge dumped into river (pounds).
X_8: Amount of demineralizer waste pumped into injection well (gallons).
X_9: Amount of demineralizer waste treated by evaporator (gallons).
X_{10}: Amount of demineralizer waste water to river (gallons).
X_{11}: Amount of plant waste water to river (gallons).
X_{12}: Amount of water withdrawn from river (thousands of gallons).
Note: Coefficients showing flows are for pedagogical purposes; they are not actual flows for an operating ammonia plant.

Wastewater generated in ammonia plant must equal amount of wastewater sent to neutralizer or to river:

$$20X_3 = 1,000X_4 + X_{11}. \qquad (A3-5)$$

Demineralizer wastewater generated must equal amount sent to injection well, evaporator, or to river:

$$90X_2 = X_8 + X_9 + X_{10}. \qquad (A3-6)$$

Sludge generated by clarifier must equal amount sent to landfill, river, or dryer:

$$200X_1 = X_5 + X_6 + X_7. \qquad (A3-7)$$

There is a legislated limit on sludge sent to river:

$$X_7 \leq \text{Limit}. \tag{A3-8}$$

There is a legislated limit on the impurities in the water returned to the river:

$$0.90X_{10} + 0.04X_{11} \leq \text{Limit}. \tag{A3-9}$$

These constraints represent only a portion of the constraints in the full-scale model of an ammonia plant. This illustration has omitted many pieces of equipment and the entire cooling, steam, and fuel flows. However, this set of equations does illustrate many of the concepts required for modeling this process. Furthermore, with this simplified model of an ammonia production system, the technical details needed to reach conclusions about the effectiveness of various water quality control measures can be investigated.

In his study, Calloway investigated the effects of various water control policies on energy consumption, cost of ammonia production, and effectiveness. The methodology was to find the least-cost method of production when there are no constraints on the effluent streams being dumped into the river. Then these control procedures were established:

Limits were set upon the amount of sludge that could be deposited in the river. This was accomplished directly with the limit in constraint (A3-8).

The effect of a tax on water withdrawn from a river was investigated. This was accomplished by increasing the objective function coefficient for X_{12} by the amount of the imposed tax. (The other component of the objective function coefficient for water withdrawn is the cost of pumping.)

Limits were placed on the amount of impurities in the water returned to the river.

Calloway reached the following conclusions about these control procedures. Placing a limit on the sludge deposited in the river had no effect on amount of water withdrawn, and had a very small effect (less than 0.1 percent) on the production cost of ammonia. The landfill alternative was selected by the cost-minimizing model when river disposal was not permitted.

When a tax was placed on water withdrawn, the production process was modified by choosing alternatives that do not require as much water. For example, cooling methods that re-use the cooling water from the river were used in place of those cooling methods that do not re-use the cooling water. This reduced the amount of river water withdrawn, reduced the amount of impurities deposited in the river (because all of the impurities originate from water withdrawn from the river), increased the energy consumption, and increased the production cost. The amount of these changes depends upon the amount of the tax. For example, a tax of about 2¢ per 1,000 gallons reduced the amount of river water withdrawn by about 50 percent, reduced the impurities by about 50 percent, and increased energy consumption by about 1 percent. A tax of about 50¢ per 1,000 gallons reduced the impurities and water withdrawn by about 90 percent, with a 3 percent cost increase and an 8 percent energy increase.

Reducing the amount of impurities that may be deposited in the river had the anticipated effects of increased cost, increased energy consumption, and reduced withdrawals of water. Requiring zero discharge of impurities into the river resulted in a 95 percent reduction in water use, a 3 percent increase in ammonia production cost, and a 2 to 3 percent increase in energy consumption, depending upon the geographical location of the plant.

A particularly important result is some of the information available from the optimal tableaus of the various problems. For example, the shadow price (dual variable) for constraint (A3–9) (impurities limit) shows the added cost if the limit on impurities were reduced by one pound. This value is the amount of tax on impurities in effluent streams that would have the same effect on impurities as the constraint. This gives the regulatory/legislative body two approaches to effluent control: outright restrictions, or taxation of effluents. With the ammonia model, policies could be devised to have the same effect using either restrictions or taxes. Calloway has constructed models for ammonia plants in four different regions; there are substantial geographical differences in the amount of tax that would be required to achieve zero discharge of impurities; hence, a uniform national tax would not have uniform effects on water quality.

Study of this model made it obvious that there would be no extreme price changes in ammonia if strict effluent controls were implemented. Without a formal approach of this type, such a conclusion would be more difficult to reach and perhaps more arguable after being reached.

Application 4

Mathematical Programming and the Location of Fire Companies for the Denver Fire Department*

THE PROBLEM AND ITS ECONOMICS

FIRE PROTECTION for urban areas is an expensive service. For many cities with paid fire departments, the fire department budget will typically be in the neighborhood of 10 percent of the city's general revenue funds. Commonly, more than 90 percent of the fire department budget represents salaries of firefighters and administrators. One of the important controllable variables affecting the level of expenditures for fire protection is the number of fire companies; a company is a major fire-suppression vehicle, such as a pumper (engine) or a ladder (truck), and its around-the-clock complement of firefighters. Moreover, if there are exogenous factors, such as a labor contract that specifies the number of firefighters to be assigned to a company, the most important factor in determining the size of a fire department's budget is the number of fire companies that the city employs. There are two major types of fire-suppression companies; a pumper or engine company is primarily responsible for putting water on a fire (or other means of extinguishment, as appropriate). A ladder or truck company is primarily responsible for rescue; it also serves as a "water tower" for directing a stream of water (provided by a pumper) down onto a fire. Typically, a city will have more pumpers than trucks.

* This application is abstracted from T. E. Hendrick, D. R. Plane, et al., *An Analysis of the Deployment of Fire-Fighting Resources in Denver, Colorado,* Santa Monica, Calif.: The Rand Corporation, R-1566/3-HUD, 1975.

The major cost of a firefighting company is labor costs, and not the more visible costs of the fire station and the fire suppression vehicle. As an example, the fire department of the City and County of Denver, Colorado, estimates that the annual cost for one company of firefighters is about a quarter of a million dollars, which is approximately the same as the capital costs required for a firehouse with a fire-suppression vehicle. Thus, very high payoffs may be associated with moving a fire station, when such a change can reduce the annual labor costs by reducing the number of fire companies needed to provide a specified level of fire suppression protection.

THE OBJECTIVE OF THE DENVER RESEARCH PROJECT

A major objective of this research, as stated by the City Council and the Mayor of the City and County of Denver, was to find a method of providing the then-current level of fire suppression service (which was generally considered acceptable) at a reduced cost. To achieve this objective, several steps were necessary:

1. Determination of a criterion for measuring the level of fire suppression services provided by any geographic configuration of fire companies.
2. Using this criterion, measure the current level of fire-suppression services in Denver.
3. Apply an appropriate optimization technique to hold the level of service constant, while lowering the cost of providing that service.
4. Explicitly consider the imperfections in the criterion by utilizing judgmental inputs from experienced firefighters and city administrators.
5. Explicitly consider political factors that might have only minor effects on either costs or level of service, but that might substantially affect the likelihood of implementation of the recommendations of the research.

MEASUREMENT OF THE LEVEL OF FIRE SUPPRESSION SERVICES

The ultimate measure of the level of fire-suppression services would be measurements including loss of life, personal injury, and property damage caused by fire; the difficulties of quantifying such global measures necessitates a surrogate measure of performance. Hence, the *response time* of fire suppression vehicles, defined in this study as the elapsed time from the end of the dispatching operation to the arrival of each suppression vehicle at the scene of an incident, has been taken as the surrogate measure of performance for this research. (Other studies define response time to include slightly different elements of time from the receipt of an alarm to the arrival of the fire-suppression vehicle.) Various aspects of response time are investigated; for example, the response times of the first pumper (to many points in the city) are averaged and compiled into a frequency distribution. The second pumper, third, and so on, are similarly considered throughout the research. Although the location of ladder truck companies was considered in the project, this case study describes only the location of pumper companies. Throughout this paper the term firehouse or fire station is, therefore, interchangeable with the location of a pumper company.

To use response time as an appropriate measure of performance under alternative proposals for fire protection, it is necessary for other factors to be similar. Thus, the manning levels of the fire suppression vehicles and the level of ancillary activities relating to fire protection, such as arson investigation, building codes and their enforcement, and fire prevention, are held constant in all alternatives considered in the research.

By holding constant both the vehicle manning levels and activities such as fire prevention, only one important variable affects costs for fire services: the number and location of fire companies. Hence, the major effort of this project was the development of a proposal for fire company locations that will leave the level of service (as measured by response time) approximately unchanged by closing mislocated stations and opening new stations where required, while reducing the number of companies and thereby reducing costs.

The decision to use response time for fire-suppression vehicles as the criterion or measure of performance for a fire station configuration requires more specific definition. Two aspects of response time are considered at various points:

1. The maximum permissible response time for the pumper closest to each of 246 "focal points" throughout the city. (A focal point, which will be formally defined later, is a location or structure in the city at which point, for purposes of analysis, fires in the vicinity of the focal point are assumed to occur.) Thus, the first use of response time relates to specifying the *maximum* permissible response time to focal points.

2. The *average* and the distribution of the response times for the pumper closest (first-due pumper) to each of the 246 focal points is also considered as a measure of performance for a fire-suppression system. Similar measures were investigated for the second closest pumper, etc.

AN INTEGER PROGRAMMING FORMULATION OF THE FIRE STATION LOCATION PROBLEM

If it is possible to specify the maximum permitted response time for the closest pumper to each focal point, the fire station location problem can be formulated as an integer programming problem. The special form of this problem is called a *set-covering* problem. The objective function for this problem is to minimize the number of fire stations; the constraints require that each focal point is to be covered by at least one fire station within the time requirement specified for that focal point. Symbolically, this becomes:

Minimize

$$x_o = \sum_{j=1}^{n} x_j \qquad (A4\text{--}1)$$

subject to

$$\sum_{j=1}^{n} a_{ij}x_j \geq 1, i = 1, 2, \ldots, m$$

$$x_j = 0 \text{ or } 1$$

where all

$$a_{ij} = 0 \text{ or } 1.$$

In the fire station location problem, the set of all potential locations is identified as the n activities or variables. If a variable, such as x_3, has a value of 0, it means that a fire station shall not be placed at Location 3; if $x_3 = 1$, it means that a fire station is to be placed at Location 3. The description of those potential locations that serve each focal point is contained in the coefficient matrix; $a_{ij} = 1$ indicates that the Focal Point i can be served by a pumper company at Location j within the response time specified for Focal Point i; $a_{ij} = 0$ indicates that the Focal Point i

FIGURE A4–1

Response Time Requirements and Response Time Data for a Hypothetical City

Focal Point	Maximum Response Time Requirement for First Due Pumper (seconds)	Expected Response Time Fire Station Locations (seconds)			
		1	*2*	*3*	*4*
1	120	150	110	90	140
2	90	60	200	120	80
3	90	100	120	200	80
4	180	150	170	90	100

cannot be served by Location j within the response time specified for Focal Point i.

As a hypothetical example, suppose that a city under consideration has only four focal points and four possible fire station locations. Figure A4–1 shows the maximum permissible response time for each focal point and the expected response time for each focal point/fire station location pair. The formulation of the problem to minimize the number of stations while meeting the response time requirements is:

Minimize $x_1 + x_2 + x_3 + x_4$

subject to

$$x_2 + x_3 \geqq 1 \qquad \text{(Focal Point 1 is served by Location 2 or 3)}$$

$$x_1 + x_4 \geqq 1 \qquad \text{(Focal Point 2 is served by Location 1 or 4)}$$

$$x_4 \geqq 1 \qquad \text{(Focal Point 3 is served by Location 4)}$$

$$x_1 + x_2 + x_3 + x_4 \geq 1 \quad \text{(Focal Point 4 is served by any location)}$$

$$x_1, x_2, x_3, x_4 = 0, 1.$$

AN OBJECTIVE FUNCTION WITH TWO GOAL LEVELS

A major difficulty encountered in the above formulation is that it does not differentiate between fire station sites that have existing fire stations, and fire station sites that require the construction of a fire station. If a particular data set yields multiple optima, it is desirable to choose the solution (or those solutions) that utilizes the maximum number of existing fire stations. This desirability rests upon two factors. The first is the economic desirability of avoiding capital expenditures where possible. The second, and perhaps more important, is the often very large political "cost" of moving a fire station. Hence, it is desirable to maximize the use of existing fire stations, as long as such a solution can be found that does not expand the total number of fire stations beyond that required by the optimizing procedure. To include these two goal levels in the model, a hierarchical objective function was developed for the set-covering problem. Minimizing number of stations is the first priority, and maximizing the number of existing locations is the second priority.

This hierarchical formulation solves the goal-programming problem with a simple numerical modification of the objective function. The set-covering problem with a hierarchical objective function is:

Minimize

$$x_o = \sum_{j=1}^{r} x_j + \sum_{j=r+1}^{n} (1 + \epsilon)\, x_j \qquad \text{(A4-2)}$$

subject to

$$\sum_{j=1}^{n} a_{ij} x_j \geq 1,\ i = 1, 2, \ldots m$$

$$x_j = 0 \text{ or } 1$$

where all

$$a_{ij} = 0 \text{ or } 1$$

and ϵ is any number between 0 and $1/n$.

The existing station locations are indexed from 1 to r. The purpose of the term ϵ is to make it more costly to build a new station, but not so costly that additional companies are needed. No solution requiring $h + 1$ stations can be preferred to a solution requiring h stations.

DATA REQUIREMENTS FOR THE OPTIMIZATION MODEL

Measurement and Prediction of Response Time

To measure and predict response times for Denver, approximately 1,600 actual fire vehicle responses were measured. The timing was accomplished by dispatchers at Fire Alarm Headquarters; these response times were matched with response distances calculated from coordinates of the fire stations and the incidents. The response times were measured from the end of the dispatch operation to the radio message indicating that the first vehicle had arrived at the scene of the incident. Response distances were measured by assuming that the fire suppression vehicle traveled along a right-angle path, corresponding to the typical north-south, east-west street network in most of the city. One major section of Denver, the downtown area, has a street grid that is at a 45° angle to the grid of the rest of the city. Because of the location of the current fire stations, it was reasonable to assume that any responses into the downtown district with its angled streets would utilize only streets with the angled orientation. Since it would be unusual for a response to be made over a combination of north-south, east-west and angled streets, this possibility was not considered in the experiment. Hence, by knowing the coordinates of the beginning and the end of the response and the street orientation at the end of the response, it was a simple calculation to find the estimated travel distance for the vehicle.

A regression analysis was performed using these paired time/distance observations to build a predictive model for the response time for fire vehicles in the city of Denver. A linear relationship, a square root transformation on distance, and a logarithmic transformation on distance were investigated; the data were also classified by time of day (rush hour and non-rush hour) and by responding stations. The general conclusions from these analyses were:

1. There was no difference in response velocity for rush hour and non-rush hour responses.
2. The linear relation between time and distance yielded a fit as good as or better than the curvilinear models.
3. The only important geographical difference in response velocity was that between downtown areas and the other parts of the city.

From these observations, two predictive equations were determined from the observations on two groups of stations. For the downtown area,

$$\text{Time (seconds)} = 18.213 + 0.022846 \text{ distance (feet).}$$

For the remainder of the city,

$$\text{Time (seconds)} = 26.292 + 0.019326 \text{ distance (feet).}$$

Alternative Locations for Fire Stations

The next step in the analysis was the development of a set of possible locations for fire stations. The assistant chief for each district was asked to suggest a number of places that he would consider for locating fire stations if there were no existing fire stations in the city. This yielded a list of 100 candidate sites including the existing 27 stations. These candidate sites were located on a map so that their spatial distribution could be studied. Since a few areas of the city did not contain enough alternative locations, additional sites were added at locations suggested by fire department personnel. This provided a total of 112 candidate sites for fire stations.

Identification of Fire Hazards, Focal Points, and Time Differentials

In order to determine the points in Denver at which the level of fire-suppression service (as measured by maximum permissible response time) was to be established, an inventory of fire hazards throughout the city was developed by the firefighters. This inventory of hazards contained more than 800 structures. The next step was to group these hazards into classes that had similar response time requirements. Five classes were established; super-red (most hazardous), red, yellow, green, and blue (least hazardous). The classification of each of the 800 hazards into one of these five categories was performed by the assistant fire chiefs, and was reviewed by a group of senior assistant chiefs and fire prevention personnel.

If two hazards from this inventory are located very close to each other, it is not necessary to specify explicitly the protection for each of the adjacent or nearby structures. If the time requirements for a red hazard are met, it is obvious that a less severe hazard located across the street or within a few blocks will also receive adequate fire protection. Hence, the 800 hazards were reduced to 246 *focal points*. A focal point is, therefore, a collection of nearby hazards; the response time classification of the focal point is the classification of the most severe hazard belonging to the focal point.

The next input into the set covering formulation of the fire station location problem is the determination of the time requirement for each of the focal points, or for each class of focal points. Instead of specifying specific time requirements for each class, which would have been inconsistent with the objective of this research (reduce the cost of main-

FIGURE A4–2

taining approximately the current level of fire suppression services), attention was focused upon determining appropriate response time differentials for each focal point class. The fire department members of the research team were initially reluctant to provide these differentials. Statements such as "I want to be able to get every place as quick as I can" were the typical response to questions about the relative importance, in terms of response time differentials, between the color-coded focal points. When the question was rephrased to "If you only had one station to protect a new shopping center and a hospital, where would you build the station?", the previous egalitarian answer was changed to place the station nearer the hospital. As a result, a policy capturing experiment was designed in terms of an abstract fire station location problem rather than seeking a time differential directly.[1]

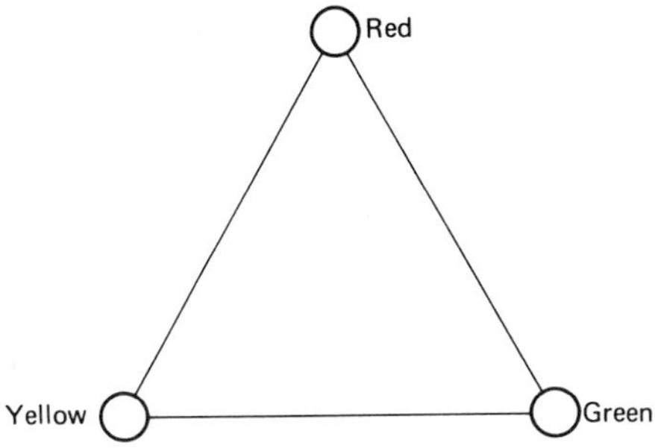

All assistant fire chiefs were given a diagram similar to Figure A4–2. These diagrams were labeled with a red dot, a yellow dot, and a green dot at the three vertices of the triangle. The assistant chiefs were told

---

[1] This experiment was designed by Dr. David E. Monarchi.

the distance between the focal points and that a road network would be constructed connecting each focal point to the one fire station they were permitted to locate. They were then asked to indicate with a dot where they would build one fire station to serve these three hazards. Nineteen of the twenty-one responses indicated that the fire station should be located in the upper left part of the triangle, closest to the red, second closest to the yellow, and farthest from the green focal point. The centroid of this cluster indicated these time differentials: a 90-second differential between red and yellow and a 30-second differential between yellow and green. Although there are many pitfalls in this procedure, it did yield a consensus of respected officers that was readily accepted by fire department personnel. An interesting aspect of these data is that they were obtained by rephrasing the question into a familiar terminology. Instead of speaking in terms of response time differentials (which is not a common area of thought for firefighters), the question was rephrased in terms of station location, which is a typical matter of concern. After this experiment had been completed, the fire chief and his staff (using the information from the experiment) determined that these two empirical differentials—augmented by the chief's judgmentally determined differentials of one minute between super-red and red focal points and no differential between blue and green—would be fire department policy.

The time differentials were obtained so that a series or sweep of solutions could be obtained. For example, the problem was solved with the time requirement for super-red focal points of 1.8 minutes, then 1.9 minutes, and so on, yielding a broad range of alternative station configurations.

Converting the Data to a Mathematical Programming Problem

All of the information now exists to formulate a mathematical programming problem. The coefficient matrix was formed with one row for each of the 246 focal points. For a focal point, the element in that row is 1 for any column (fire station candidate site) that satisfies the focal point response time requirement for the particular problem being solved, and a 0 in any column representing a site that cannot meet the time requirement for that focal point. The response times were calculated from the regression equations described earlier in this paper. The hierarchical objective function, (A4–2), with a sufficiently small value of ϵ, such as 0.005, was solved with an integer programming algorithm.[2]

---

[2] The computer code which solved these problems was developed by Dr. Fred Glover.

"Solutions" from the Optimizing Algorithm

Nine different problems were solved with this data base. The maximum time to super-red focal points was varied from 1.8 minutes to 2.6 minutes in increments of 0.1 minute. The results of these solutions are indicated in Figure A4–3.

FIGURE A4–3

Solutions from the Optimizing Algorithm

Maximum Time to Super-Reds	Total Number of Locations*	Number of New Locations†
1.8	36	21
1.9	36	20
2.0	32	17
2.1	28	14
2.2	27	12
2.3	25	14
2.4	23	14
2.5	23	10
2.6	22	9

* Note that this is $INT(x_o)$, where x_o is the objective function value.
† Note that this can be found as $(x_o - INT(x_o))/\epsilon$.

Since there were 27 firehouses in the city of Denver at the time, it was obvious that the current level of fire suppression services would be somewhere in the range of 2.1 to 2.5 minutes, or from 28 to 23 locations. These five configurations were displayed on maps, and discussed with the fire chief and several officers. Their general reaction was: "That computer is stupid!" These "solutions" were deficient in at least two areas. First, the model tended to draw stations to the extreme corners of the city boundaries, in response to super-red focal points located nearby. This was not acceptable to the fire chief and his staff. Second, the protection in the downtown area was insufficient. This was anticipated by the research team because no special consideration had been given for the requirements for more than one vehicle at fires in the congested downtown area.

ADDITIONAL INFORMATION TO BLEND ANALYTICS AND JUDGMENTS

Parallel to the optimization model, an information model was developed. This relatively simple computer program provided several reports to describe the consequences of any locational configuration of fire companies. Much of the data from the optimization model was used;

specifically, the lists of focal points and classifications, the list of potential fire stations, and the travel time between each candidate site and each focal point were used in the information model. The user needs to specify only the location of the fire companies in the configuration of interest, and the desired maximum response time to each focal point class. The information provided is:

1. An exception listing of focal points for which maximum permissible response time requirements are not met in the configuration.
2. The average response time of first-due pumpers, the average response time of second-due pumpers, etc. These averages are calculated for each focal point class, and for the city as a whole.
3. A frequency distribution, by half-minute intervals, for each of the fire-suppression vehicles mentioned above, by class of focal point.
4. A company report that shows the specific focal points served by each company to which it is the first-due pumper; the second- and third-due pumpers for each focal point are also listed.

In order to use this information to blend experience into the results of the optimization analysis, the fire chief and his staff were asked to compose a configuration of fire stations utilizing both their experience and the insights gained from the optimization output. The first step in combining the judgment contained in this configuration with the optimization results was the decision of the research team to accept the department's recommended configuration in the downtown area as a constraint. Although questions of the "optimality" of the research recommendations could arise, the team recognized that the methodology did not explicitly account for vehicles other than the first-due to the focal points. (These considerations can be employed in the set-covering formulation of the problem, but only by increasing the cost of obtaining the optimal solution.)

The second step in infusing judgment into the decision process utilized the information model with the configuration of stations suggested by the fire chief and his staff. This configuration left 30 focal points uncovered within the department's target response times of two minutes for super-red, three minutes for red, four and one-half minutes for yellow, and five and one-half minutes for blue or green. Each focal point for which the time requirement was not satisfied was examined by the chief and his staff. For every such focal point, the department was satisfied with the protection provided for that focal point. In making these determinations, specific streets and their traffic conditions and directions were considered; these elements were beyond the scope of the regression analysis used to predict response time. Additionally, the specific hazards were reviewed by the department to determine whether fire protection problems would result from their proposed configuration of stations; this review revealed that all "violated" constraints in their configuration could be "violated" safely.

This outcome provided a way to relax certain constraints in the optimization technique. In effect, the department's proposed configuration yielded a set of constraints that could be relaxed to the response times provided by their configuration. Additional constraints perhaps could also have been relaxed through an individual study of each constraint, but there was no practical way to reassess each focal point without repeating the entire process of focal point determination.

The focal point data base, with the constraints relaxed as indicated by the department's solution, was used as input to the optimization model. The optimization model produced a solution with one less pumper than the department's judgmental configuration. Furthermore, the output from the optimization model (with an added policy requirement that all newer stations be included) was identical with the department's configuration except that one particular station (No. 7) was not included in the optimization solution.

WHAT WAS THE VALUE OF THE OPTIMIZATION MODEL?

At this point, an assessment of the usefulness of the optimization model in Denver's fire station location study is in order. The first usefulness of the optimization procedure was observed when the fire chief and his staff included some of the locations suggested by the initial runs of the optimization model in their judgmental configuration, which has been discussed above. Specifically, two new locations in newer parts of the city were suggested by the optimization model. Only one of these two new locations that were incorporated by their judgmental configuration had been previously discussed. A third "suggestion" arising from the initial runs of the optimization model was one that the fire chief and his staff immediately understood, but that the analysts lacked sufficient insight to comprehend. The optimization model suggested that an existing station was not necessary and that a new fire station should be constructed several blocks away. To the analysts, this appeared to be an unrelated closing and opening. To the department, with their experience, it was a logical location change. This change was included by the chief and his staff in their judgmental configuration; it had not been discussed prior to this phase of the research.

The second useful aspect of mathematical programming is the relaxation of constraints, which led to the recommended removal of one pumper company. If mathematical programming had suggested nothing other than this one deletion, the cost of the analysis would have been recovered from this one change; the cost saving from one company for six months approximates the cost of this research.

To recapitulate, we have gone through these steps: First, a series of solutions was developed using the mathematical programming model. Second, the chief and his staff prepared a configuration that they could support, which incorporated some of the ideas of the mathematical programming solutions. Third, information from this configuration was used to relax some of the constraints, and the mathematical programming problem was solved again. The result was a reduction of one pumper company.

The output of this third iteration was not yet a suitable recommendation; additional judgment was merged into the analysis. The firefighters who were involved in the research project felt that the abolition of Station No. 7, suggested by the procedures above, left a "hole" in the fire coverage for the city. In other words, at this point they could not agree that the data that had been used in solving the problem was an adequate representation of the hazards in that particular part of the city. Several suggestions were made by various members of the research team, including several rearrangements of the configuration of stations in the sector of the city being studied. One of these judgmental configurations, which did not increase the number of companies required, became the basis of the recommendation of the research project.

SYSTEM PERFORMANCE AND RECOMMENDATIONS

The combination of mathematical programming and judgment described above resulted in a set of recommendations for the location of pumper companies in the City and County of Denver; this proposed configuration calls for 25 pumper companies rather than the 27 companies existing at the beginning of this project. For purposes of comparison, three configurations have been selected for presentation; these three represent only a small portion of the configurations that were investigated in the research. These three configurations are the existing configuration (27 pumpers), the proposed configuration (25 pumpers), and the 25-pumper configuration that resulted from the optimization problem requiring a 2.3-minute maximum response time to super-red focal points (see line 6 of Figure A4-3). Figure A4-4 shows the average response time for the various classes of focal points for the three configurations. From this comparison, it is apparent that the proposed configuration has average response times at least as good as, and in some cases better than, the existing configuration—and this is accomplished with two fewer pumpers. Another useful comparison is the optimization configuration versus the proposed configuration. Although there are differences in emphasis between the proposed and the optimization configurations, there is no city-wide difference in the average response time. The effect of the infusion of the department's judgment has been to increase the

FIGURE A4–4

Comparison of Response Times for First-Due Pumper

	Average First-Pumper Response Time (minutes)		
Focal Point	*Existing Configuration (27 pumpers)*	*Proposed Configuration (25 pumpers)*	*Optimization Configuration (25 pumpers)*
Super-red......................	1.8	1.7	1.9
Red...........................	2.3	2.3	2.1
Yellow........................	2.2	2.2	2.3
Blue, Green...................	2.5	2.5	2.7
City-wide.....................	2.3	2.2	2.2

emphasis given to super-red focal points, at the expense of the red and yellow focal points. Figure A4–5 compares the percentage of focal points that meet the department's "target" maximum response times of two minutes for super-red focal points, and appropriate differentials for the other classes. This table shows results similar to those observed in average response time: The proposed configuration is at least as good as, and in some cases better than, the existing configuration. The comparison between the optimization configuration and the proposed configuration is not as favorable, indicating that the infusion of judgment has had some adverse effects on this measure. This aspect is not surprising, in that the optimization solution was derived using maximum response time constraints.

The evaluation of the proposed configuration (and others) did not stop at this point. A simulation model, developed by the New York City Rand Institute and adapted to Denver as a part of this research, was utilized to test the dynamic behavior of alternative configurations under various alarm rates.

FIGURE A4–5

Percentage of Focal Points Where First-Due Pumper Response Time is Less than or Equal to Targets on Maximum Response Time

			Percentage of Focal Points Meeting Target		
Focal Points		*Target Response Time (minutes)*	*Existing Configuration (27 pumpers)*	*Proposed Configuration (25 pumpers)*	*Optimization Configuration (25 pumpers)*
Class	*Number*				
Super-red......	20	2.0	65%	75%	60%
Red...........	117	3.0	80	81	88
Yellow.........	69	4.5	96	97	100
Blue, Green....	40	5.0	98	98	100
City-wide......	246		86	88	91

HOW ARE THESE RESULTS BEING USED BY THE CITY AND COUNTY OF DENVER?

Based on the research described in this case study the finance director of the City and County of Denver and his Budget and Management Office prepared a multi-year plan for fire services for the City and County of Denver. The first year of this plan has been explicitly included in the Mayor's budget for the years 1975 and 1976. This plan calls for an eventual reduction of two pumper companies, as described in this paper, and a reduction of three ladder companies. This reduction, if fully implemented in future budget decisions, will result in an accumulated net cost reduction of $2.3 million over a six-year period, and a continuing annual cost reduction of about $1.2 million, based on 1974 wage rates.

Application 5

A Markov Model of Professional Staff Flows in a CPA Firm[*]

MOST OF THE TEXT EXAMPLES of Markov chains deal with irreducible chains, in which it is possible to move between any pair of states in some finite number of transitions. The case study being illustrated here is not an irreducible Markov chain; it has two absorbing states. Once a Markov chain has reached an absorbing state, it remains there. The approach for this case study is to illustrate the results using probability reasoning. Not every result will be so derived, but a sufficient number is included to present the flavor of the development.

The purpose of this case study is to examine staff flows between the various levels within a CPA firm. The four levels are junior, senior, manager, and partner. There are two absorbing states: (1) leave the firm (not as a partner), and (2) leave the firm as a partner. A transition matrix is shown in Figure A5–1. These data were obtained for a five-year period, showing the proportion of each category of employee that moved to the next level or to one of the absorbing states. (The data are also disguised slightly because of the confidential consideration of the firm.) Note that in the transition matrix, which is based on a calendar year, an employee can move only one level at a time, and demotions are not possible. To illustrate some of the numbers, the probability that a junior will remain a junior after one year is 0.57, regardless of how long the employee has been a junior. That same junior has a 0.27 probability of

* Adapted from "A Model of Professional Staff Flows in a CPA Firm," by Jackson F. Gillespie and Wayne E. Leininger, in *Proceedings*, American Institute for Decision Sciences, November 1975.

FIGURE A5–1

Transition Matrix for a CPA Firm

		Transient States				Absorbing States	
		Junior	Senior	Manager	Partner	Leave	Leave as Partner
Transient states	Junior	0.57	0.27	0.0	0.0	0.16	0.0
	Senior	0.0	0.57	0.17	0.0	0.26	0.0
	Manager	0.0	0.0	0.81	0.05	0.14	0.0
	Partner	0.0	0.0	0.0	0.96	0.0	0.04
Absorbing states	Leave	0.0	0.0	0.0	0.0	1.0	0.0
	Leave as partner	0.0	0.0	0.0	0.0	0.0	1.0

becoming a senior at the end of a year, and a 0.16 probability of leaving the firm.

It is apparent that the flows of personnel in a firm do not follow the Markov property; a person who is promoted from one level to the next in a very short time has a better than average chance of an early promotion to the next level. It is also apparent that the assumtion of stationarity does not apply; different economic conditions, for example, may cause different promotion policies to be used by the firm. However, in spite of the obvious nonapplicability of these important assumptions, the results of the model with the assumptions were subjected to tests of reasonableness, which will be described below.

One of the predictions that can be made from this model is the proportion of current juniors who will leave the firm and the proportion of current juniors who will eventually leave the firm as partners. In the long run all juniors will leave the firm, so they must leave by way of one of the absorbing states; leave, or leave as partner. (According to the model there is a nonzero probability that a person will never leave even after a very large number of transitions. This probability becomes inconsequentially different from zero when the number of transitions is large.) By finding, for example, the two-step transition probabilities, obtained by multiplying the transition probability matrix by itself, one can find the probability that a junior will still be a junior after two years, the probability that a junior will have become a senior in two years, etc. The two-step transition probabilities are shown in Figure A5–2. The transition matrix reaches a steady state after a large number of transitions. The many-step transition matrix has all zeros except at the absorbing states, as shown in Figure A5–3. This shows, for each skill level, the proportions who will leave the firm and who will leave as partner.

It is also possible to find the expected number of years that a person

FIGURE A5–2

Two-Step Transition Probabilities

		Transient States				Absorbing States	
		Junior	Senior	Manager	Partner	Leave	Leave as Partner
Transient states	Junior	0.3249	0.3078	0.0459	0	0.3214	0
	Senior	0	0.3249	0.2346	0.0085	0.4320	0
	Manager	0	0	0.6561	0.0885	0.2534	0.0020
	Partner	0	0	0	.9216	0	0.0784
Absorbing states	Leave	0	0	0	0	1	0
	Leave as partner	0	0	0	0	0	1

at each level will remain at each of the levels. For example, a junior might remain a junior one year, two years, three years, four years, and so on for as many years as one cares to consider. From the transition probability matrix, the probability that a junior will be a junior for exactly one year is $1 - 0.57 = 0.43$. A junior may be a junior exactly two years by transition from junior to junior at the first move, and from junior to senior at the second year. The probability of this happening is 0.57×0.43. A junior may remain a junior for exactly three years by these transitions: junior to junior, junior to junior, junior to senior. This will happen with the probability of $0.57 \times 0.57 \times 0.43$. By expanding this reasoning, Figure A5–4 shows the number of years as a junior and the probability distribution for that random variable. The expected value of this probability distribution can easily be found to be 2.3256 years, which is the expected (or average) number of years that a person who is now

FIGURE A5–3

Many-Step Transition Probabilities

		Transient States				Absorbing States	
		Junior	Senior	Manager	Partner	Leave	Leave as Partner
Transient states	Junior	0	0	0	0	0.935	0.065
	Senior	0	0	0	0	0.896	0.104
	Manager	0	0	0	0	0.737	0.263
	Partner	0	0	0	0	0	1
Absorbing states	Leave	0	0	0	0	1	0
	Leave as partner	0	0	0	0	0	1

FIGURE A5–4

Number of Years as a Junior

X, *Number of Years*	$P(X)$, *Probability*	$X\ P(X)$
1	0.43	0.43
2	0.57×0.43	0.4902
3	$0.57^2 \times 0.43$	0.4191
4	$0.57^3 \times 0.43$	0.3185
5	$0.57^4 \times 0.43$	0.2270
6	$0.57^5 \times 0.43$	0.1552
. . .	. . .	. . .
. . .	. . .	. . .
. . .	. . .	. . .

Expected years as a junior, for those currently junior. $= 2.3256$

a junior will be a junior. Similar results can be obtained for the number of years a person who is now a junior can expect to spend as a senior, as a manager, and as a partner. These are shown in Figure A5–5.

These two characteristics that have been developed are indicative of the kinds of reasonableness tests to which the model could be subjected. Personnel data would be available to indicate the number of juniors who would leave before they reached partner. This could be compared with the prediction from the model, 0.935 (Figure A5–3). Similarly, one could use personnel data to find the number of years that a group of juniors spent in each of the various ranks. The researchers in this case used tests of reasonableness to determine that the model was a useful representation of staff flows within the firm.

The next use of the model was to aid in predicting the number of staff personnel in each of the levels in future years. For example, one can use the framework of Markov chains to investigate what will happen if the firm starts with a specified number of employees in each level, and hires

FIGURE A5–5

Expected Number of Years at Each Level, for Each Starting Level

Starting Level	*Years in Level*			
	Junior	*Senior*	*Manager*	*Partner*
Junior	2.33	1.46	1.31	1.63
Senior	0	2.33	2.08	2.60
Manager	0	0	5.26	6.58
Partner	0	0	0	25

a specified number into each of the levels in each year. For example, suppose the firm starts with the following distribution:

2,000 juniors   (49 percent)
1,000 seniors   (25 percent)
750 managers   (19 percent)
300 partners   (7 percent),

and then hires 1,000 new juniors each year. To illustrate the calculations, consider first the 2,000 juniors at the beginning of the year. Of these, 57 percent will remain juniors, or 1,140 will go from junior to junior. With the influx of 1,000 new juniors, the number of juniors at the end of the period is 2,140. Similarly, begin with 1,000 seniors, of which 0.57 or 570 will remain seniors, and add 0.27 of the 2,000 beginning juniors (540) who become seniors. This gives a total of 1,110 seniors at the end of the first year. Continuing this procedure, the expected staff levels at the end of the first year will be:

2,140 juniors   (49 percent)
1,110 seniors   (25 percent)
777 managers   (18 percent)
326 partners   (8 percent).

The same procedure can be used to find the staffing levels at the end of the second year, assuming 1,000 new hires at the junior level. These results are:

2,220 juniors   (48 percent)
1,210 seniors   (26 percent)
818 managers   (18 percent)
351 partners   (8 percent).

Using this procedure, one can assertain what will happen to the mix of skill levels within the firm for this anticipated hiring level of 1,000 new juniors each year, if the transition matrix remains stationary. Figure A5–6 shows the proportion of employees that will be in each of the four levels at various points in the future. This points out that the mix of various levels will change substantially as time passes, if the hiring policy and promotion policies remain as postulated. One can also obtain information about the speed of these changes, to investigate whether difficulties caused by such a change would be short-run, long-run, or so far in the future that they do not matter. For example, this policy shows severe long-run change in the proportion of partners, but very little change in the first five years. This gives some idea of when the problem of changing staff mixes needs to be addressed. Since the long-run behavior is substantially different from the short-run (that is, the skill mix has a large proportion of partners in the long run) it is perhaps un-

FIGURE A5–6

Long Run Skill Mix if 1000 Juniors Are Hired Each Year (percentages)

Year	Junior	Senior	Manager	Partner
1	49	25	18	8
2	48	26	18	8
3	47	27	18	8
4	46	27	19	8
5	45	27	19	9
10	42	26	21	11
15	40	25	22	13
20	39	24	22	15
40	36	23	20	21
Infinite	35	22	19	24

realistic to assume that the firm will allow the transition probabilities to remain constant. Hence, these long-run behavior patterns are tentative at best.

This same method of analysis is applicable to many organizations. For example, a university faculty could also be very well described by a process such as this.

Application 6

A Waiting-Line Integer Programming
Approach to Scheduling
Police Patrol Cars*

THE PURPOSE OF THIS STUDY is to illustrate a way in which waiting-line models (also called queuing theory) and mathematical programming have been combined to develop schedules for police car patrols. It is particularly interesting to note the way in which waiting-line theory has been used for a case in which it is obvious that the assumptions of the steady-state waiting-line model are not met. Hence, a part of this case study is a description of the manner in which the appropriateness of the model was validated. This case study also illustrates use of one technique of operations research, waiting-line models, as a data source for another tool, mathematical programming.

The purpose of the analysis is to assure that there is a reasonable correspondence between the number of cars on duty and the demands for service placed upon these cars. There are two distinct phases of the methodology that is developed: a descriptive model (steady-state queuing models later validated by dynamic queuing analysis) to show the probability that no cars will be available to answer a call for service; and an optimizing algorithm (integer programming) to devise a schedule that minimizes the number of cars required while meeting service standards.

A group of police cars may be viewed as the servers in a multi-channel waiting-line system. Calls for service (the customers) are transmitted by

---

* This application is based on P. J. Kolesar, K. L. Rider, T. B. Crabill, and W. E. Walker, "A Queueing-Linear Programming Approach to Scheduling Police Patrol Cars," The Rand Corporation P-5260-1, 1975.

FIGURE A6–1

Arrival Rate of Calls for Service

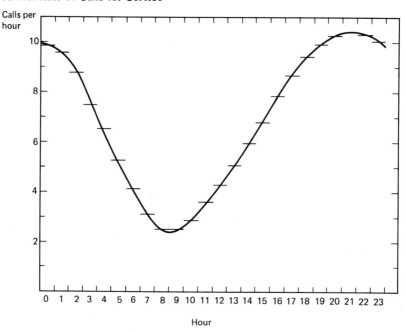

radio to the patrol cars. If there is a car available to respond to a call when it is received by the dispatcher, that car is sent to the address requesting service. If there is no car available, the call may be held in a queue until it can be served. (In some cases a high-priority call, such as a robbery in progress, may interrupt a less important call, such as investigation of a burglary that occurred the night before.) The arrival rate of calls for service varies throughout the day, with a high point in the hours before midnight and the low point during the hours around 7 A.M. The steps in devising the scheduling methodology of this case study are:

1. Partition a day into a series of time periods, such as one-hour periods, during which it is assumed the arrival rate for calls for service remains constant.

2. Specify a service requirement. For this case study, the service requirement is that the probability that there will be no cars available to respond to a call for service must not exceed 0.10.

3. Use steady state queuing analysis, as described in Chapter 10 of this text, to determine the number of cars necessary to meet the service level constraint in each time period.

4. Use integer programming to find the schedule of assignments that provides the required number of cars in each time period while also minimizing the number of cars needed.

5. Because the assumptions employed in the steady-state queuing analysis (Step 2 above) are violated by the changing call rate and nonexponential service time, investigate whether the violation of these assumptions affects the model's usefulness.

The first step (breaking the day into a series of "steady-state" periods) is shown in Figure A6–1. This figure shows how the arrival rate for calls for service varies during the course of a day in a particular precinct. The horizontal lines in the same figure show a series of one-hour periods during which the call rate is assumed to be stable. The arrival rates for calls are tabulated in Figure A6–2. If it is assumed that the number of calls for service during any hour is described by a Poisson distribution with the mean appropriate to that time period (which is supported by the data described in the case study) and that service times for calls are described by an exponential distribution (which is definitely not the case) then the equations shown in Chapter 10, Exercise 4, of the text can be used to describe the probabilities of the system being in each of its states. Later in the case study the impact of violating the assumptions for this queuing model will be discussed. The necessary equations are:

$$P_0 = \cfrac{1}{\left[\left(\displaystyle\sum_{n=0}^{s-1} \frac{\rho^n}{n!}\right) + \frac{\rho^s}{s!}\left(\cfrac{1}{1 - \rho/s}\right)\right]}$$

$$P_n = \frac{\rho^n}{n!} P_0; \quad 1 \le n \le s$$

where

P_n = Probability of n calls in the queuing system at any point in time
λ = Arrival rate of calls for service
μ = Service rate per channel (car)
$\rho = \lambda/\mu$
s = Number of channels (cars).

With these equations, the number of cars necessary to assure the required probability (assumed to be 0.1) that there will be no car available when a call arrives can be determined. For example, if $\lambda = 5.0$, $\mu = 2.0$, and $s = 4$ cars, the following system characteristics hold:

$\rho = 5/2 = 2.5$

$$P_0 = 1 \left/ \left[\frac{2.5^0}{0!} + \frac{2.5^1}{1!} + \frac{2.5^2}{2!} + \frac{2.5^3}{3!} + \frac{2.5^4}{4!}\left(\frac{1}{1 - 2.5/4}\right)\right]\right. = 0.0737$$

$$P_1 = \frac{2.5^1}{1!} (0.0737) = 0.1842$$

$$P_2 = \frac{2.5^2}{2!} (0.0737) = 0.2303$$

$$P_3 = \frac{2.5^3}{3!} (0.0737) = 0.1919.$$

Since a car is available when there are four cars assigned and there are 0, 1, 2, or 3 calls for service in the system, the probability of an available car is:

$$P_0 + P_1 + P_2 + P_3 = 0.0737 + 0.1842 + 0.2303 + 0.1919 = 0.6801$$

and the probability of no car available is

$$P(\text{no car available}) = 1 - 0.6801 = 0.3199.$$

The resulting probability that no car is available is greater than the acceptable probability (0.1), so it is obvious that four cars is not a sufficient number of cars for a period with an average arrival rate of five per hour and a ½-hour service time.

With $s = 5$ cars:

$$P_0 = 1 \bigg/ \left[\frac{2.5^0}{0!} + \frac{2.5^1}{1!} + \frac{2.5^2}{2!} + \frac{2.5^3}{3!} + \frac{2.5^4}{4!} + \frac{2.5^5}{5!} \left(\frac{1}{1 - 2.5/5} \right) \right] = .0801$$

$$P_1 = \frac{2.5^1}{1!} (0.0801) = 0.2003$$

$$P_2 = \frac{2.5^2}{2!} (0.0801) = 0.2503$$

$$P_3 = \frac{2.5^3}{3!} (0.0801) = 0.2086$$

$$P_4 = \frac{2.5^4}{4!} (0.0801) = 0.1304$$

$$P(\text{available}) = P_0 + P_1 + P_2 + P_3 + P_4 = 0.8696$$

or

$$P(\text{no car available}) = 1 - 0.8696 = 0.1304,$$
which fails to meet the standard, 0.1.

With $s = 6$ cars:

$$P_0 = 1 \bigg/ \left[\frac{2.5^0}{0!} + \frac{2.5^1}{1!} + \frac{2.5^2}{2!} + \frac{2.5^3}{3!} + \frac{2.5^4}{4!} + \frac{2.5^5}{5!} \right.$$
$$\left. + \frac{2.5^6}{6!} \left(\frac{1}{1 - 2.5/6} \right) \right] = 0.08162$$

$$P_1 = \frac{2.5^1}{1!} (0.08162) = 0.2041$$

$$P_2 = \frac{2.5^2}{2!} (0.08162) = 0.2551$$

$$P_3 = \frac{2.5^3}{3!} (0.08162) = 0.2126$$

$$P_4 = \frac{2.5^4}{4!} (0.08162) = 0.1328$$

$$P_5 = \frac{2.5^5}{5!} (0.08162) = 0.0664$$

$$P(\text{available}) = P_0 + P_1 + P_2 + P_3 + P_4 + P_5 = 0.9526,$$

which satisfies the service requirement.

This same technique can be used to find the number of cars necessary to satisfy the service requirements for any arrival rate for calls for service. Figure A6–2 shows, for this sample precinct, the arrival rate and the number of cars required to achieve no more than a 0.1 probability of no car available, given this arrival rate, and an average service time of one-half hour per call.

If each car were on duty only one hour per day, the value of r_t in Figure A6–2 would be the number of cars to place on duty each hour of the day. In many cities, however, patrols are on duty for eight-hour

FIGURE A6–2

Call Arrival Rate and Number of Cars Required

	t	*Arrival Rate of Calls,* λ_t	$r_t,$ *Number of Cars*
Midnight–1 A.M.	0	9.8	9
1– 2 A.M.	1	9.6	9
2– 3 A.M.	2	8.7	8
3– 4 A.M.	3	7.4	8
4– 5 A.M.	4	6.7	7
5– 6 A.M.	5	5.3	6
6– 7 A.M.	6	4.1	5
7– 8 A.M.	7	3.3	4
8– 9 A.M.	8	2.5	4
9–10 A.M.	9	2.5	4
10–11 A.M.	10	2.9	4
11–12 noon	11	3.8	5
Noon–1 P.M.	12	4.3	5
1– 2 P.M.	13	5.0	6
2– 3 P.M.	14	5.9	6
3– 4 P.M.	15	6.6	7
4– 5 P.M.	16	7.8	8
5– 6 P.M.	17	8.6	8
6– 7 P.M.	18	9.4	9
7– 8 P.M.	19	9.8	9
8– 9 P.M.	20	10.2	9
9–10 P.M.	21	10.4	9
10–11 P.M.	22	10.2	9
11–12 midnight	23	10.0	9

FIGURE A6–3

Shift Schedules

Hour	Start 0800 Meal Hour				Start 1600 Meal Hour				Start 2400 Meal Hour			
	3	4	5	6	3	4	5	6	3	4	5	6
0									1	1	1	1
1									1	1	1	1
2										1	1	1
3									1		1	1
4									1	1		1
5									1	1	1	
6									1	1	1	1
7									1	1	1	1
8	1	1	1	1								
9	1	1	1	1								
10		1	1	1								
11	1		1	1								
12	1	1		1								
13	1	1	1									
14	1	1	1	1								
15	1	1	1	1								
16					1	1	1	1				
17					1	1	1	1				
18						1	1	1				
19					1		1	1				
20					1	1		1				
21					1	1	1					
22					1	1	1	1				
23					1	1	1	1				
Shift number	1	2	3	4	5	6	7	8	9	10	11	12

shifts, and are given one hour off during the shift for meals. Therefore, an integer programming problem was developed to minimize the number of cars required while still satisfying various requirements. To illustrate how this may be accomplished, consider two scheduling variables: The time a shift may begin, and the time for meal break for each car. If it is possible to begin shifts only at three times, 0800 (8 A.M.), 1600 (4 P.M.), and 2400 (midnight), and if meal times can only be taken at the third, fourth, fifth, or sixth hour of a shift, the hours covered by each of these 12 possible shifts are shown in Figure A6–3. A blank in a particular hour for a shift indicates that the shift will not place a car on duty during that hour, while a 1 indicates that the shift will place a car on duty during that hour. If we let x_j be the number of cars to be assigned to shift j, and if we let a_{tj} be a zero or one, depending upon the coefficient in Figure A6–3, the integer programming problem to be solved is:

Minimize

$$x_1 + x_2 + x_3 + x_4 + x_5 + x_6 + x_7 + x_8 + x_9 + x_{10} + x_{11} + x_{12}$$

subject to

$$
\begin{aligned}
x_9 + x_{10} + x_{11} + x_{12} &\geq 9 \quad \text{(For hours 0 and 1, which require nine cars)} \\
x_{10} + x_{11} + x_{12} &\geq 8 \quad \text{(Hour 2)} \\
x_9 \qquad + x_{11} + x_{12} &\geq 8 \quad \text{(Hour 3)} \\
x_9 + x_{10} \qquad + x_{12} &\geq 7 \quad \text{(Hour 4)} \\
x_9 + x_{10} + x_{11} \qquad &\geq 6 \quad \text{(Hour 5)}
\end{aligned}
$$

and so on, for the remaining hours;
all $x = 0, 1, 2, 3, \ldots$ (that is, an integer number of cars must be assigned to each shift.)

More succinctly, this problem is stated as:

Minimize

$$\sum_{j=1}^{12} x_j$$

subject to

$$\Sigma \, a_{tj} x_j \geq r_t \quad \text{for each hour, } t = 0, 1, \ldots, 23$$
all x_j integers ≥ 0.

The solution to this integer programming problem is $x_1 = 2$; $x_2 = 2$; $x_3 = 2$; $x_4 = 1$; $x_5 = 3$; $x_6 = 3$; $x_7 = 3$; $x_8 = 3$; $x_9 = 1$; $x_{10} = 2$; $x_{11} = 3$; $x_{12} = 4$. (For example, $x_1 = 2$ means that two cars are assigned to Shift 2, starting at 0800 and taking meals at the third hour.) This solution requires 29 car-shifts.

From the queuing relationships, the probability that a car is available for each of the hours is shown in Figure A6–4. Of course the constraint of never having more than a 0.1 probability of no car available has been met. And there is no other schedule requiring fewer car-shifts that would meet all the constraints. But what would be the effect of easing some of the constraints? For example, what if cars could start a shift at any hour of the day instead of only at three different hours?

In order to investigate the effects of easing the constraints, the researchers solved the integer programming problem with all possible shift starting times (24 possibilities) and all possible meal times (8 possible start times per shift), which would produce 192 columns in Figure A6–3. The optimal solution to this program with the same service requirement as above (no more than a 0.1 probability of no car available) required 24 cars (as compared with 29 for the three start times and four meal time schedules), but it also required 13 different shift start times, which would be administratively burdensome. After some experimentation, a schedule using five shift start times and all possible meal

FIGURE A6–4

Schedule from Integer Progamming

Hour	r_t, Cars Required	Cars Assigned	Probability of No Car Available
0........................	9	10	0.032
1........................	9	10	0.028
2........................	8	9	0.038
3........................	8	8	0.040
4........................	7	7	0.063
5........................	6	6	0.060
6........................	5	10	0.000
7........................	4	10	0.000
8........................	4	7	0.000
9........................	4	7	0.000
10........................	4	5	0.018
11........................	5	5	0.049
12........................	5	5	0.077
13........................	6	6	0.047
14........................	6	7	0.035
15........................	7	7	0.059
16........................	8	12	0.001
17........................	8	12	0.002
18........................	9	9	0.058
19........................	9	9	0.073
20........................	9	9	0.089
21........................	9	9	0.098
22........................	9	12	0.007
23........................	9	12	0.006

times was devised that also used 24 cars. This solution would be administratively reasonable, except for the meal times. Other schedules could be generated with this procedure using judgment to facilitate the selection of administratively realistic shifts.

It should be mentioned that solving integer programming problems of the size described in this case study may be a difficult and/or expensive task, because of the large number of variables in the problem. The authors of the original paper present an alternative formulation of the problem that requires more variables but has a special structure that makes solution easier. The authors prove that, in their formulation, only a portion of the variables need to be specified to be integers and the remaining variables will automatically be integers. This structure is exploited in solving the mixed-integer programming problem with a branch-and-bound algorithm.

Model Validation

The use of the steady-state, multi-channel, Poisson arrivals, exponential service times, infinite queue model has required some assump-

FIGURE A6-5

Dynamic and Steady-State Waiting-Line Models (three shift start-times, four meal times, 29 cars)

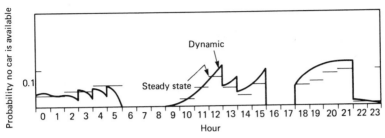

tions, many of which may not be correct. The assumptions were investigated in two steps. The first step was to build a dynamic queuing model (not discussed in the text) that permits the arrival rate for calls for service to vary over time. It solves the time-dependent queuing equations for the system using numerical integration to determine $P_n(t)$, the state probabilities as a function of time. It permits an investigation of the effect of the assumption that the arrival rate is constant during each hour. Referring to Figure A6-1, it uses the curve instead of the disjointed horizontal lines. The dynamic queuing model showed that when the probability that a call will wait in queue for service is quite small, the assumption of a constant arrival rate within an hour is reasonable, because there would tend to be a very small queue at the beginning of each hour. Although the results of dynamic queuing theory have not been discussed in this text, analyses are described in the paper from which this study is abstracted; these results are presented in Figures A6-5 and A6-6. For the example with 29 cars, Figure A6-5 compares the probability of no car available from steady-state analysis with the corresponding result from dynamic analysis. Note that the two methods give reasonably similar results. Since, in this case, cars are typically available when a call is received, there is not much chance of the system having a big backlog of unserved calls. Figure A6-6 makes a similar comparison for the actual schedule being used by the police department being studied. Note that the steady-state approximation is not as good in this case, which has many more delayed calls.

A second level of validation was used in this case study. A large-scale simulation model of police department operations was available to the researchers.[1] This model could consider actual arrival rates for calls for service as they varied over time, and also the various priorities of

---

[1] P. Kolesar and W. Walker, "A Simulation Model of Police Patrol Operations: Executive Summary," R-1625/1. Santa Monica, Calif.: The Rand Corporation, March 1975.

FIGURE A6–6

Dynamic and Steady-State Waiting-Line Models (existing schedule, 24 cars)

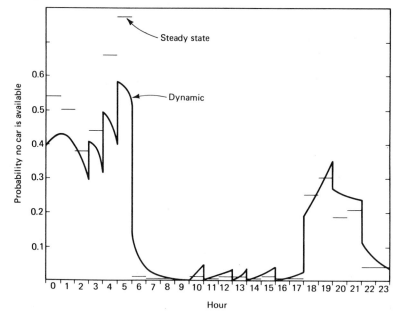

Hour

calls. Furthermore, travel time from call to call or from patrol to call could be modeled explicitly. The need for two cars on some kinds of service calls could also be considered. A simulation of this size is very difficult to construct and requires a great amount of data, but the results of the dynamic queuing model compared favorably with the results of the simulation.

Uses of the Model

The authors report using the model to develop alternative schedules for the New York City Police Department. Alternatives were generated using data for various seasons, various precincts, week-days vs. week-ends, and various shift starting times. Schedules appeared attractive were subjected to further analysis with the dynamic queuing model. This series of schedules permitted insight into questions about the improvements possible by mealtime flexibility, by added times for the start of shifts, week-day vs. week-end schedules, and the usefulness of insight from one precinct to other precincts.

Application 7

A Simulation of a Fire Alarm System*

For several years in the early 1970s, the Denver Fire Department was involved in developing a concept of computer assisted dispatch for fire alarms. There are many potential advantages to such a system. Written communication may replace vocal communications; the information retrieval capabilities of a computer may be used in conjunction with computer-assisted dispatch to provide useful information to the fire-fighters. The computer system could also provide a useful data base for many kinds of analysis, such as that described in another application in this text. But one of the primary reasons promulgated for installation of such a system (which would cost much more than a million dollars) was the fear that the current manual dispatching system would become inadequate if the rate of fire alarms continues to grow. The personnel at fire alarm headquarters felt that alarms would begin to "stack" in the dispatch operation, and that the delays would substantially impair the capabilities of the Denver Fire Department. This problem was investigated by assessing the effect of increased alarm rates on the time required to dispatch vehicles.

The current dispatch operation is a manual operation. The typical dispatch team consists of three members; two of them usually answer telephone calls, while the third serves as the dispatcher, notifying vehicles of the alarms to which they are to respond. Any of the three

---

* This application is abstracted from T. E. Hendrick and D. R. Plane, *Denver Fire Services Project Report*, Denver Urban Observatory, 1974.

members of the team may pull the "running card" from the card file. This card contains the information necessary for determining the vehicles to be dispatched to a specific address. The companies to respond are notified by voice over the direct wire "vocalarm" system. The vocalarm communication system is located in front of an equipment status board, which provides the information necessary for correct dispatching.

The Fire Department has suggested that, if the current dispatch procedures are to be maintained, it would be necessary to duplicate the status board and part of the communications equipment, in order to avoid dispatch delays at higher alarm rates. These expenditures would not be necessary if a computer assisted dispatch system is installed.

No attempt was made by the research team to establish "tolerable" delays in the dispatching operation. Rather, the approach was descriptive; procedures were devised for describing the relationship between the alarm rate and delays encountered in the dispatching operation. There was no attempt to assess whether current or anticipated delays are acceptable.

The description of the relationship between alarm rate and dispatch delays was provided by a simulation of the dispatching operation. The purpose of the simulation experiment was to keep track of delays in the dispatching operation. For these purposes, a delay was considered to have been encountered if some function of the dispatching operation could not be performed as soon as the information was available for its performance. A delay occurs because of the unavailability of personnel or equipment for the necessary operation.

The basic structure of the simulation is to divide the operations necessary for dispatching into three functions: the alarm function, the card-pull function, and the dispatch function. The alarm function begins with the receipt of an alarm (a telephone ring, an alarm box signal) and ends when there is enough information available to pull the running card. The card-pull function follows at once and ends when the running card has been pulled. The dispatch function then begins; it ends at the time of the third announcement of the address and incident type to the responding vehicles over the vocalarm system. In this description of these three functions, the beginning times that have been described assume that an operator and the facilities are always available to begin that particular function. If this is not the case, the particular function cannot begin: a delay is encountered. It is these delays that the simulation experiment was designed to measure.

Data were gathered by observing the dispatch operations at fire alarm headquarters. The average times to perform each of the three functions ranged from 15 to 28 seconds. The complete distribution of times for each of the functions was maintained and used in the simulation. The logic of the simulation was to select at random a time for each of the three functions (according to the observed historical data); assign a function to an operator when the operator, the necessary equipment, and the necessary information were available so that the function could be performed; and then keep track of any delays that were encountered.

The arrival of fire alarms at fire alarm headquarters in the simulation was generated by a Poisson process (exponentially distributed inter-arrival times). This probability distribution has been shown to be a useful description of the arrival of fire alarms, for short periods of time (such as an hour or two) during which the arrival rate is approximately constant. This does not mean to imply that the arrival rate is the same at 5 A.M. and 5 P.M.; rather, it is useful to think of the process that generates fire alarms as being a series of successive steady states, with each successive steady-state period having a somewhat different rate of arrivals for fire alarms.

In Denver the rate of arrivals of fire alarms varies from about one an hour to six an hour, depending upon the season of the year and the time of day. To study projected growth in this rate of alarms, simulations were run from a rate of two per hour to ten per hour. (Of analytical interest, but not practical interest, simulations were also run up to 50 alarms per hour.)

In each simulation, an identical sequence of times for the three functions (alarm, card-pull, dispatch) was used. In this way, variations in the delay characteristics from one simulation to another are not due to different draws from the table of random numbers. Rather, differences in delay characteristics must be due to the aspect of the simulation that was being changed, or the difference in the average number of alarms per hour for a particular simulation. This procedure, which is fairly common in simulation, has the advantage that changes in system characteristics depend upon changes instituted by the analyst. It has the disadvantage that a particular simulation characteristic (say, the absolute length of delay) would differ from simulation to simulation with different sequences of random numbers. If this variation is not investigated, the analyst may be dealing with unusual output without knowing so.

The raw data from the simulation output are shown in Figure A7–1. From this figure it is obvious that delays increase as the alarm rate increases, but the research team did not feel that this table would be of any value to the superintendent of fire alarms. Hence, several other measures were developed. Figure A7–2 shows one such display, in which the alarm rate, the percentage of alarms with no delays, and the percentage of alarms with no delay or with a delay of 40 seconds or less are shown. The choice of 40 seconds was arbitrary. The research team felt that this relatively small amount of information would be a useful way of describing the way the alarm system would operate under higher

FIGURE A7-1

Effect of Alarm Rate on Frequency and Duration of Delay (based on a simulation of 3,000 alarms)

Number of Alarms with Delay Less than:

Alarm Rate (per hour)	None	10 Sec.	20 Sec.	30 Sec.	40 Sec.	50 Sec.	60 Sec.	70 Sec.	80 Sec.
2	2,947	2,960	2,973	2,984	2,987	2,991	2,992	2,995	2,998
4	2,897	2,924	2,945	2,961	2,971	2,981	2,987	2,990	2,994
6	2,844	2,882	2,921	2,947	2,961	2,975	2,980	2,985	2,991
8	2,793	2,851	2,894	2,929	2,950	2,970	2,976	2,983	2,986
10	2,750	2,813	2,865	2,910	2,939	2,960	2,975	2,981	2,984
15	2,606	2,718	2,798	2,867	2,906	2,941	2,964	2,974	2,981
20	2,472	2,613	2,720	2,814	2,871	2,916	2,944	2,967	2,976
25	2,335	2,493	2,634	2,744	2,824	2,880	2,927	2,951	2,967
30	2,206	2,378	2,541	2,665	2,782	2,836	2,892	2,934	2,953
35	2,060	2,264	2,445	2,592	2,707	2,786	2,859	2,906	2,936
40	1,949	2,139	2,352	2,510	2,639	2,742	2,810	2,875	2,913
45	1,827	2,031	2,252	2,424	2,569	2,682	2,756	2,822	2,874
50	1,712	1,929	2,144	2,345	2,504	2,607	2,713	2,779	2,838

FIGURE A7–2

Delays in Dispatching

Alarm Rate *(per hour)*	*Percentage of Alarms* *with No Delay*	*Percentage of Alarms* *with a Delay of* *40 Seconds or Less*
2	98.2	99.6
4	96.6	99.0
6	94.8	98.7
8	93.1	98.3
10	91.7	98.0

alarm rates. Figure A7–3 shows similar data for a wider range of alarm rates in graphical form.

In reviewing these findings with the Denver Superintendent of Fire Alarm, it was suggested that a possibility might be to install repeating tape recorders in each fire house. This recorder would repeat the alarm

FIGURE A7–3

Delay vs. Alarm Rate (based on a simulation of 3,000 alarms)

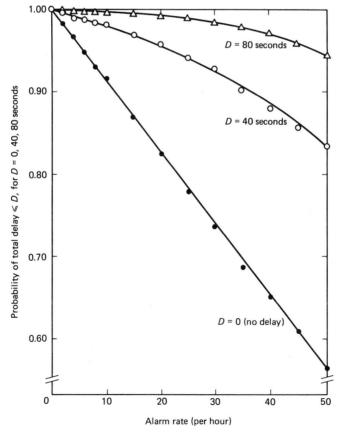

FIGURE A7–4

Delays in Dispatching (effect of 15-second reduction in dispatch time)

Alarm Rate (per hour)	Percentage of Alarms with No Delay		Percentage of Alarms with a Delay of 40 Seconds or Less	
	Existing Procedure	*Shortened Procedure*	*Existing Procedure*	*Shortened Procedure*
1	98.2	98.8	99.6	99.7
4	96.6	97.4	99.0	99.6
6	94.8	96.2	98.7	99.2
8	93.1	95.0	98.3	99.1
10	91.7	94.0	98.0	98.9

instructions several times after the dispatcher had stated the information one time; this might reduce the dispatch time by 15 seconds. Simulations were executed with a 15-second reduction in the time for the dispatch function (but never less than ten seconds for the dispatch function), with the results shown in Figure A7–4. The overall effect was about a 30 percent reduction in the number of alarms that experienced a delay, an improvement that could be achieved at a relatively small cost.

The conclusions from this simulation are that delays in dispatch will increase as the alarm rate increases, and predictions were made for this increase. It was also learned that a relatively inexpensive system of repeating tape recorders could effect a worthwhile reduction in dispatch delays at a fraction of the cost of a computer system.

Appendixes

Appendix A

Some Concepts of Probability

THE CONCEPTS OF PROBABILITY are described in Chapter 2. Whether the probabilities under consideration are *objective* or *subjective*, certain rules for the manipulation of probabilities hold true. Letting $P(A)$ represent the probability that event A will occur, it must be true that:

$$P(A) \geq 0$$
$$P(A) \leq 1$$

for any event.

In some instances it is useful to describe combinations of events. For example:

$P(A \text{ and } B)$ is the probability that both events A and B will occur;

$P(A \text{ or } B)$ is the probability that *either* A *or* B, or both, will occur.

Pictorially, $P(A \text{ and } B)$ is represented in Exhibit 1.

EXHIBIT 1

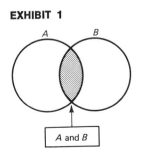

A and B

$P(A \text{ or } B)$ is represented in Exhibit 2.

EXHIBIT 2

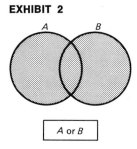

A or B

Another concept is *conditional probability*. A condition attached to a probability changes the information upon which a probability is based. For example, consider rolling a fair six-faced die. The probability that a "five" will show is $\frac{1}{6}$:

$$P(\text{five}) = \frac{1}{6}$$

If, however, one is given the added information that an *odd* number of spots (1, 3, or 5) is showing, this information changes the probability. The probability of a five, given that an odd number is showing, is $\frac{1}{3}$. This is stated as:

$$P(\text{five}|\text{odd}) = \frac{1}{3}$$

The vertical line is read "given."

Two rules of probability tie these concepts together:

$$\begin{aligned} P(A \text{ and } B) &= P(A)P(B|A) \\ &= P(B)P(A|B) \\ P(A \text{ or } B) &= P(A) + P(B) - P(A \text{ and } B). \end{aligned}$$

If two events, C and D, cannot simultaneously occur, they are said to be *mutually exclusive* or *disjoint*. For two mutually exclusive events, C and D:

$$P(C \text{ or } D) = P(C) + P(D),$$

since $P(C \text{ and } D) = 0$, by definition of mutual exclusivity.

If the occurrence of one event, E, does not affect the probability of another event, F, then the two events are said to be independent. Symbolically, if

$$P(E|F) = P(E),$$

then E, F are independent. For independent events, E and F:

$$P(E \text{ and } F) = P(E)P(F).$$

A *random variable* may be thought of as a *chance quantity*. Although this is not a technically precise definition, it conveys the idea of something that will take on a numerical value, and that value is described by a probability distribution. As an example of a random variable, consider flipping a penny and a nickel and counting the number of heads. Call this number of heads X. The random variable X will assume a value of either 0, 1, or 2. The probability of each value of X is summarized in this *probability distribution* for the random variable X.

X	P(X)	Calculation
0	¼	P(T, penny) P(T, nickel) = (½)(½) = ¼
1	½	P(T, penny) P(H, nickel) + P(H, penny) P(T, nickel) = (½)(½) + (½)(½) = ½
2	¼	P(H, penny) P(H, nickel) = (½)(½) = ¼

In many situations, it is convenient to express a probability distribution as a formula.

The random variable (number of heads) can take on only certain discrete values; hence, it is called a *discrete probability distribution*. Discrete distributions often arise when something (such as coin heads) is being counted. In other cases, a random variable will be *continuous*, meaning that within some interval along the real number line *any* value may occur; for example, the weight of cereal in boxes can conceivably be *any* weight between, say, 0 and 19 oz. Weights such as 13.07 oz., 14.2378 oz., and 12.876432197 oz. are all possible (the number of decimals is limited in reality by the precision of the measuring device). A continuous random variable often arises when something (such as weight, time, distance) is measured.

Probability distributions for continuous random variables are conveniently represented by smooth curves. The equation for the curve is called the *probability density function*, usually shortened to *density function*. It is given the notation $f(X)$, where X is the random variable. Any density function must be constructed so that the area between the curve and the X-axis is equal to one. A density function is shown in Exhibit 3.

A probability for a continuous random variable always refers to some interval. The probability that the value of the random variable X will fall between X_1 and X_2 is noted:

$$P(X_1 \leq X \leq X_2).$$

This probability is the area enclosed between the X axis, the curve of the density function, and the vertical lines at the boundaries of the interval, X_1 and X_2.

A particularly useful probability distribution is the *normal* distribu-

EXHIBIT 3

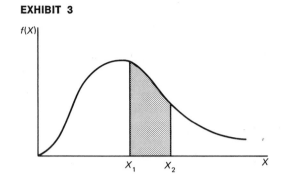

tion. The density function for a normal distribution has a symmetrical, bell-shaped appearance, as shown in Exhibit 4. There are many normal distributions: tall ones, flat ones, those moved far to the right, far to the left, and so on. To specify a particular normal distribution, a *mean* (μ) and a *standard deviation* (σ) must be specified. The mean of a probability distribution is a measure of the "center" of the distribution. Changing the mean changes the position of the distribution. Increasing the mean, μ, moves the curve to the right; decreasing the mean, μ, moves the curve to the left. The standard deviation, σ, describes the dispersion, or spread, of the distribution. Increasing σ causes a more "spread out" or flatter curve; reducing σ increases the height of the curve.

To find probabilities for a random variable described by the normal distribution, one uses a table of the *standard* normal distribution. This table shows the probability that Z, a *standard* normal random variable, will exceed the tabulated values. This table is given in Table 1. The left-

EXHIBIT 4

A Normal Distribution

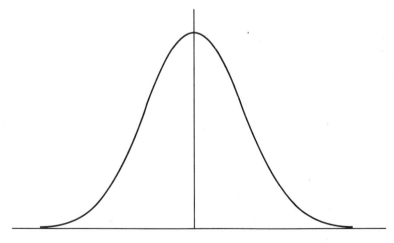

TABLE 1

Right-Tail Areas under the Unit Normal Density Function (Z is a standardized normal random variable [$\mu = 0$, $\sigma = 1$])

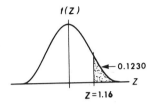

Z	.00	.01	.02	.03	.04	.05	.06	.07	.08	.09
0.0	.5000	.4960	.4920	.4880	.4840	.4801	.4761	.4721	.4681	.4641
.1	.4602	.4562	.4522	.4483	.4443	.4404	.4364	.4325	.4286	.4247
.2	.4207	.4168	.4129	.4090	.4052	.4013	.3974	.3936	.3897	.3859
.3	.3821	.3783	.3745	.3707	.3669	.3632	.3594	.3557	.3520	.3483
.4	.3446	.3409	.3372	.3336	.3300	.3264	.3228	.3192	.3156	.3121
.5	.3085	.3050	.3015	.2981	.2946	.2912	.2877	.2843	.2810	.2776
.6	.2743	.2709	.2676	.2643	.2611	.2578	.2546	.2514	.2483	.2451
.7	.2420	.2389	.2358	.2327	.2296	.2266	.2236	.2206	.2177	.2148
.8	.2119	.2090	.2061	.2033	.2005	.1977	.1949	.1922	.1894	.1867
.9	.1841	.1814	.1788	.1762	.1736	.1711	.1685	.1660	.1635	.1611
1.0	.1587	.1562	.1539	.1515	.1492	.1469	.1446	.1423	.1401	.1379
1.1	.1357	.1335	.1314	.1292	.1271	.1251	.1230	.1210	.1190	.1170
1.2	.1151	.1131	.1112	.1093	.1075	.1056	.1038	.1020	.1003	.0985
1.3	.0968	.0951	.0934	.0918	.0901	.0885	.0869	.0853	.0838	.0823
1.4	.0808	.0793	.0778	.0764	.0749	.0735	.0721	.0708	.0694	.0681
1.5	.0668	.0655	.0643	.0630	.0618	.0606	.0594	.0582	.0571	.0559
1.6	.0548	.0537	.0526	.0516	.0505	.0495	.0485	.0475	.0465	.0455
1.7	.0446	.0436	.0427	.0418	.0409	.0401	.0392	.0384	.0375	.0367
1.8	.0359	.0351	.0344	.0336	.0329	.0322	.0314	.0307	.0301	.0294
1.9	.0287	.0281	.0274	.0268	.0262	.0256	.0250	.0244	.0239	.0233
2.0	.0228	.0222	.0217	.0212	.0207	.0202	.0197	.0192	.0188	.0183
2.1	.0179	.0174	.0170	.0166	.0162	.0158	.0154	.0150	.0146	.0143
2.2	.0139	.0136	.0132	.0129	.0125	.0122	.0119	.0116	.0113	.0110
2.3	.0107	.0104	.0102	.0099	.0096	.0094	.0091	.0089	.0087	.0084
2.4	.0082	.0080	.0078	.0075	.0073	.0071	.0069	.0068	.0066	.0064
2.5	.0062	.0060	.0059	.0057	.0055	.0054	.0052	.0051	.0049	.0048
2.6	.0047	.0045	.0044	.0043	.0041	.0040	.0039	.0038	.0037	.0036
2.7	.0035	.0034	.0033	.0032	.0031	.0030	.0029	.0028	.0027	.0026
2.8	.0026	.0025	.0024	.0023	.0023	.0022	.0021	.0021	.0020	.0019
2.9	.0019	.0018	.0018	.0017	.0016	.0016	.0015	.0015	.0014	.0014
3.0	.0013	.0013	.0013	.0012	.0012	.0011	.0011	.0011	.0010	.0010
3.1	.0010	.0009	.0009	.0009	.0008	.0008	.0008	.0008	.0007	.0007
3.2	.0007	.0007	.0006	.0006	.0006	.0006	.0006	.0005	.0005	.0005
3.3	.0005	.0005	.0005	.0004	.0004	.0004	.0004	.0004	.0004	.0003
3.4	.0003	.0003	.0003	.0003	.0003	.0003	.0003	.0003	.0003	.0002
3.5	.0002	.0002	.0002	.0002	.0002	.0002	.0002	.0002	.0002	.0002
3.6	.0002	.0002	.0001	.0001	.0001	.0001	.0001	.0001	.0001	.0001
3.7	.0001	.0001	.0001	.0001	.0001	.0001	.0001	.0001	.0001	.0001
3.8	.0001	.0001	.0001	.0001	.0001	.0001	.0001	.0001	.0001	.0001
3.9	.0000	.0000	.0000	.0000	.0000	.0000	.0000	.0000	.0000	.0000

most column in this table shows values of Z; the body of the table shows the probability that the value of Z will be exceeded. For example, using the left two columns of the table, $P(Z > 1.1) = 0.1357$. When Z has more than one digit past the decimal, the column heading (.01, .02, .03, . . . , .09) is added to the value of Z at the left of each row. For example, $P(Z > 1.16) = 0.1230$ is found in the 1.10 row, .06 column (1.10 + .06 = 1.16).

To convert any normal random variable, X_1, to a standard normal variable, Z, the following relationship applies:

$$Z = \frac{X - \mu}{\sigma}$$

For example, when $X_1 = 10$, $\mu = 5$, $\sigma = 2$, $Z_1 = \frac{X_1 - \mu}{\sigma} = \frac{10 - 5}{2} = 2.5$, then:

$$P(X > 10) = P(Z > 2.5) = 0.0062.$$

The normal distribution is symmetrical, so that the table shows only positive values of Z. The symmetry permits statements such as:

$$P(Z > 2.1) = P(Z < -2.1)$$
$$P(-1.7 < Z < -0.2) = P(0.2 < Z < 1.7)$$

and so on.

Appendix B

Random Number Table

54941	72711	39406	94620	27963	96478	21559	19246	88097	44026
02349	71389	45608	60947	60775	73181	43264	56895	04232	59604
98210	44546	27174	27499	53523	63110	57106	20865	91683	80688
11826	91326	29664	01603	23156	89223	43429	95353	44662	59433
96810	17100	35066	00815	01552	06392	31437	70385	45863	75971
81060	33449	68055	83844	90942	74857	52419	68723	47830	63010
56135	80647	51404	06626	10042	93629	37609	57215	08409	81906
57361	65304	93258	56760	63348	24949	11839	29793	37457	59377
24548	56415	61927	64416	29934	00755	09418	14230	62887	92683
66504	02036	02922	63569	17906	38076	32135	19096	96970	75917
45068	05520	56321	22693	35089	07694	04252	23791	60249	83010
99717	01542	72990	43413	59744	44595	71326	91382	45114	20245
05394	61840	83089	09224	78530	33996	49965	04851	18280	14039
38155	42661	02363	67625	34683	95372	74733	63558	09665	22610
74319	04318	99387	86874	12549	38369	54952	91579	26023	81076
18134	90062	10761	54548	49505	52685	63903	13193	33905	66936
92012	42710	34650	73236	66167	21788	03581	40699	10396	81827
78101	44392	53767	15220	66319	72953	14071	59148	95154	72852
23469	42846	94810	16151	08029	50554	03891	38313	34016	18671
35342	56119	97190	43635	84249	61254	80993	55431	90793	62603
55846	18076	12415	30193	42777	85611	57635	51362	79907	77364
22184	33998	87436	37430	45246	11400	20986	43996	73112	88474
83668	66236	79665	88312	93047	12088	86937	70794	01041	74867
50083	70696	13558	98995	58159	04700	90443	13168	31553	67891
97765	27552	49617	51734	20849	70198	67906	00880	82899	66065
49988	13176	94219	88698	41755	56216	66832	17748	04963	54859
78257	86249	46134	51865	09836	73966	65711	41699	11732	17173
30946	22210	79302	40300	08852	27528	84648	79589	95295	72895
19468	76358	69203	02760	28625	70476	76410	32988	10194	94917
30806	80857	84383	78450	26245	91763	73117	33047	03577	62599
42163	69332	98851	50252	56911	62693	73817	98693	18728	94741
39249	51463	95963	07929	66728	47761	81472	44806	15592	71357
88717	29289	77360	09030	39605	87507	85446	51257	89555	75520
16767	57345	42285	56670	88445	85799	76200	21795	38894	58070
77516	98648	51868	48140	13583	94911	13318	64741	64336	95103
87192	66483	55649	36764	86132	12463	28385	94242	32063	45233
74078	64120	04643	14351	71381	28133	68269	65145	28152	39087
94119	20108	78101	81276	00835	63835	87174	42446	08882	27067
62180	27453	18567	55524	86088	00069	59254	24654	77371	26409
56199	05993	71201	78852	65889	32719	13758	23937	90740	16866
04994	09879	70337	11861	69032	51915	23510	32050	52052	24004
21725	43827	78862	67699	01009	07050	73324	06732	27510	33761
24305	37661	18956	50064	39500	17450	18030	63124	48061	59412
14762	69734	89150	93126	17700	94400	76075	08317	27324	72723
28387	99781	52977	01657	92602	41043	05686	15650	29970	95877

Source: Extracted from "Table of 105,000 Random Decimal Digits," Statement No. 4914, File No. 261–A–1 (Washington, D.C.: Interstate Commerce Commission, 1949).

Appendix C

Matrix Operations

THE PURPOSE of this appendix is to provide a brief review of some of the notation and topics of matrices and their operations. This is not a comprehensive review but merely covers those topics used in the text. The references given at the end of the appendix provide more detailed coverage of these topics.

SUMMATION NOTATION

It is convenient to represent a sum of terms using the $\sum$ summation symbol. This notation can eliminate a good deal of writing when using lengthy expressions. The following examples illustrate the use of the notation.

The sum

$$x_1 + x_2 + x_3 + \cdots + x_n$$

can be expressed as

$$\sum_{i=1}^{n} x_i$$

where i is called the index of summation. Any other index would have the same meaning; for example

$$\sum_{j=1}^{n} x_j$$

would be the same. Typically the index of summation is chosen as i or j.

Some other examples are:

$$c_1 x_1 + c_2 x_2 + \cdots + c_n x_n = \sum_{i=1}^{n} c_i x_i$$

$$c x_1 + c x_2 + \cdots + c x_n = c \sum_{i=1}^{n} x_i$$

When two indices are involved (as in the transportation model) we use a double summation. That is the sum

$$x_{11} + x_{12} + x_{13} + x_{21} + x_{22} + x_{23}$$

can be written

$$\sum_{i=1}^{2} \sum_{j=1}^{3} x_{ij}$$

In general when i takes on values $1, 2, \ldots, m$ and j takes on values $1, 2, \ldots, n$ the notation is:

$$\sum_{i=1}^{m} \sum_{j=1}^{n} x_{ij} = \sum_{j=1}^{n} \sum_{i=1}^{m} x_{ij}$$

which also indicates that the order of summation is unimportant.

MATRICES

A matrix is a rectangular array of real numbers usually denoted by a capital letter with elements given by a doubly subscripted lower case letter. The size (dimension) of a matrix is given by the number of rows (m) and the number of columns (n).

An example of a 2×3 matrix is

$$A = \begin{pmatrix} a_{11} & a_{12} & a_{13} \\ a_{21} & a_{22} & a_{23} \end{pmatrix}$$

A 3×2 matrix is

$$Z = \begin{pmatrix} 6 & 1.7 \\ 4 & 2 \\ -2 & 5 \end{pmatrix}$$

Any element in a matrix can be referenced by specifying the element's row and column index. For some matrix A, a_{ij} represents the element in the ith row and jth column of A.

There are some matrices with special structures that deserve special mention:

A *square matrix* is a matrix for which $n = m$; that is, an $n \times n$ matrix.

An *identity matrix*, denoted by I, is a square matrix with ones on the diagonal and zeroes elsewhere. For example, the 3×3 identity matrix is:

$$I = \begin{pmatrix} 1 & 0 & 0 \\ 0 & 1 & 0 \\ 0 & 0 & 1 \end{pmatrix}$$

A *row vector* is a matrix with one row and n columns; that is

$$X = (x_1, x_2, \ldots, x_n) \text{ is an } 1 \times n \text{ matrix.}$$

A *column vector* is a matrix with m rows and one column; that is

$$b = \begin{pmatrix} b_1 \\ b_2 \\ \cdot \\ \cdot \\ \cdot \\ b_m \end{pmatrix}$$

is an $m \times 1$ matrix.

MATRIX OPERATIONS

The usual algebraic operations, addition, subtraction, and multiplication, when applied to matrices and vectors must satisfy certain rules. The summation notation is useful in defining these operations.

Matrix Addition

Two matrices of the same size can be added to yield a resultant matrix (of the same size) whose components are the sums of the corresponding components of the original matrices. If B and C are matrices of size $m \times n$, then $A = B + C$ is a $m \times n$ matrix where the elements of A are given by

$$a_{ij} = b_{ij} + c_{ij}$$

For example, if

$$B = \begin{pmatrix} 4 & -3 \\ 2 & 7 \end{pmatrix}, \quad C = \begin{pmatrix} 1 & 4 \\ 2 & 1 \end{pmatrix}$$

then

$$A = B + C = \begin{pmatrix} (4+1) & (-3+4) \\ (2+2) & (7+1) \end{pmatrix} = \begin{pmatrix} 5 & 1 \\ 4 & 8 \end{pmatrix}$$

Matrix Multiplication by a Scalar

A $m \times n$ matrix can be multiplied by a scalar to yield a $m \times n$ matrix whose components are the original components multiplied by the scalar. For the matrix

$$A = \begin{pmatrix} a_{11} & a_{12} \\ a_{21} & a_{22} \\ a_{31} & a_{32} \end{pmatrix}$$

Then kA, where k is a scalar, is

$$kA = \begin{pmatrix} ka_{11} & ka_{12} \\ ka_{21} & ka_{22} \\ ka_{31} & ka_{32} \end{pmatrix}$$

Matrix Multiplication

The product, AB, of two matrices, A and B, is defined only if the number of columns of A is the same as the number of rows of B. Otherwise, the product is not defined. Specifically, let A be a $m \times n$ matrix and B a n by k matrix. Then $C = AB$ is a $m \times k$ matrix where the elements of C are given by

$$c_{ij} = \sum_{p=1}^{n} a_{ip} b_{pj}$$

That is, element c_{ij} is the sum of the products of the elements in the ith row of A and the jth column of B. The following examples illustrate the concept of matrix multiplication.

(a)
$$A = \begin{pmatrix} 3 & 2 \\ 2 & 1 \\ -1 & 4 \end{pmatrix} \qquad B = \begin{pmatrix} 1 & 3 & 1 \\ 2 & 0 & 3 \end{pmatrix}$$

$$C = AB = \begin{pmatrix} (3 \cdot 1 + 2 \cdot 2) & (3 \cdot 3 + 2 \cdot 0) & (3 \cdot 1 + 2 \cdot 3) \\ (2 \cdot 1 + 1 \cdot 2) & (2 \cdot 3 + 1 \cdot 0) & (2 \cdot 1 + 1 \cdot 3) \\ (-1 \cdot 1 + 4 \cdot 2) & (-1 \cdot 3 + 4 \cdot 0) & (-1 \cdot 1 + 4 \cdot 3) \end{pmatrix} = \begin{pmatrix} 7 & 9 & 9 \\ 4 & 6 & 5 \\ 7 & -3 & 11 \end{pmatrix}$$

Since A is a 3×2 matrix and B is a 2×3 matrix, the product exists and is a 3×3 matrix. Note, however, that the product BA is a 2×2 matrix, and is obviously different from the product AB.

(b)
$$A = \begin{pmatrix} a_{11} & a_{12} & a_{13} \\ a_{21} & a_{22} & a_{23} \end{pmatrix} \qquad B = \begin{pmatrix} b_1 \\ b_2 \\ b_3 \end{pmatrix}$$

$$C = AB = \begin{pmatrix} (a_{11}b_1 + a_{12}b_2 + a_{13}b_3) \\ (a_{21}b_1 + a_{22}b_2 + a_{23}b_3) \end{pmatrix}$$

Matrix C has size 2×1.

Matrix Inverse

Suppose B is a square matrix (i.e., $m = n$). Then the square matrix, B^{-1}, is the inverse of B if the following conditions hold.

$$B^{-1}B = BB^{-1} = I = \text{identity matrix}$$

Not all square matrices have inverses. For a discussion of when an inverse exists and how to compute it for the general case, the reader is referred to the references. We present here a simple procedure inverting a 2×2 matrix, when that inverse exists. Consider any 2×2 matrix B:

$$B = \begin{pmatrix} b_{11} & b_{12} \\ b_{21} & b_{22} \end{pmatrix}$$

The determinant, d, of B is a real number given by

$$d = b_{11}\, b_{22} - b_{21}\, b_{12}$$

If $d = 0$, then the inverse of B does *not* exist. For $d \neq 0$, the inverse exists and is given by

$$B^{-1} = \begin{pmatrix} \dfrac{b_{22}}{d} & \dfrac{-b_{12}}{d} \\ \dfrac{-b_{21}}{d} & \dfrac{b_{11}}{d} \end{pmatrix}$$

As an example, consider

$$B = \begin{pmatrix} 2 & 2 \\ 1 & 3 \end{pmatrix}$$

The determinant, d, is

$$d = (2)(3) - (1)(2) = 4$$

and thus B inverse exists and is given by

$$B^{-1} = \begin{pmatrix} \dfrac{3}{4} & -\dfrac{2}{4} \\ -\dfrac{1}{4} & \dfrac{2}{4} \end{pmatrix}$$

As a check we compute

$$BB^{-1} = \begin{pmatrix} 2 & 2 \\ 1 & 3 \end{pmatrix} \begin{pmatrix} \dfrac{3}{4} & -\dfrac{2}{4} \\ -\dfrac{1}{4} & \dfrac{2}{4} \end{pmatrix} = \begin{pmatrix} 1 & 0 \\ 0 & 1 \end{pmatrix} = I$$

The reader should show that $B^{-1}B = I$ also. It is more computationally cumbersome to invert larger matrices.

Linear Equations

Matrix notation and matrix algebra is very useful when dealing with systems of linear equations. For example, consider a system of two equations and three unknowns.

$$a_{11} x_1 + a_{12} x_2 + a_{12} x_3 = b_1$$
$$a_{21} x_1 + a_{22} x_2 + a_{23} x_3 = b_2$$

By defining the matrix A to be

$$A = \begin{pmatrix} a_{11} & a_{12} & a_{13} \\ a_{21} & a_{22} & a_{23} \end{pmatrix}$$

and vectors x and b to be

$$\mathbf{x} = \begin{pmatrix} x_1 \\ x_2 \\ x_3 \end{pmatrix} \qquad \mathbf{b} = \begin{pmatrix} b_1 \\ b_2 \end{pmatrix}$$

the linear system can be written in matrix form:

$$\begin{pmatrix} a_{11} & a_{12} & a_{13} \\ a_{21} & a_{22} & a_{23} \end{pmatrix} \begin{pmatrix} x_1 \\ x_2 \\ x_3 \end{pmatrix} = \begin{pmatrix} b_1 \\ b_2 \end{pmatrix}$$

which can be written simply as $A\mathbf{x} = \mathbf{b}$.

Any system of linear equations can be written in the form $A\mathbf{x} = \mathbf{b}$ as long as A, x, and b are of the appropriate dimensions. An important special case of linear equations is the system

$$B\mathbf{x} = \mathbf{b}$$

where B is a square matrix whose inverse, B^{-1}, exists. Pre-multiplying both sides of the equation by B^{-1} gives

$$B^{-1} B\mathbf{x} = I\mathbf{x} = \mathbf{x} = B^{-1}\mathbf{b}.$$

That is, the solution to the system of equations is given by

$$\mathbf{x} = B^{-1}\mathbf{b}.$$

REFERENCES

Campbell, H. G. *Matrices with Applications.* New York: Appleton-Century-Crofts, 1968.

Searle, S. R., and W. H. Hausman. *Matrix Algebra for Business and Economics.* New York: Wiley Interscience, 1970.

Painter, R. J., and Yantis, R. P. *Elementary Matrix Algebra with Applications.* 2d ed. Boston: Prindle, Weber & Schmidt, 1977.

INDEX

Index

This book has been set in 10 point and 9 point Caledonia, leaded 2 points. Part and chapter numbers are 48 point Helvetica Bold. Part titles are 24 point (Large) Helvetica Bold, and chapter titles are 18 point Helvetica. The size of the type page is 27 x 45½ picas.